The F

The Cosmic Principle of Christ

The Fleeing Youth:
The Cosmic Principle of Christ

Richard Distasi

ISBN 978-0-557-08609-2

Contents

The Raising of Lazarus 1

The Young Man in the Tomb 19

The Nativities..34

The Cosmic Christ and the Tree of Life...................45

The Evolution of Christ 57

The Son of Man and the Event of Golgotha 78

The Gospel of Mark..82

From Jesus to Christ...116

The Fifth Gospel 129

The Sun Initiation of John the Baptist 146

The Gospel of John...154

Baptism and Initiation...169

The Gospel of Matthew 189

The Gospel of Luke 210

The Voice of Mary 234

The Cosmic Significance of the Mystery of Golgotha 254

The Revelation of the Cosmic Christ.......................271

A New Genesis..292

Plate 1..328

Bibliography 329

"Wisdom is the prerequisite for Love; Love is the result of Wisdom that has been reborn in the I."
Rudolf Steiner

I

The Raising of Lazarus

"When we look back into olden times, we see rise up before us within the traditions of Judaism the prophetic figure of Elijah. We know what significance the prophet Elijah had for the people of the Old Testament, and therewith for all mankind; we know how he set before them the goal and destiny of their existence. And we have shown how in the course of time the Being who was present in Elijah appeared again at the very most important moment of human evolution, appeared again so that Christ Jesus Himself could give him the Initiation he was to receive for the evolution of mankind. For the Being of Elijah appeared again in Lazarus-John – who are in truth one and the same figure, as you will have understood from my book, `Christianity as Mystical Fact'. "

- Translation by George Adams – source: www.elib.com.

These words are from Rudolf Steiner's, The Last Address, given in Dornach on September 28, 1924 during the season of Michaelmas. In Rudolf Steiner's, The Last Address, he delves into the successive incarnations of Elijah-John the Baptist. What is significant in the above words from Rudolf Steiner and which is a major point of focus in this present work is his disclosure of the Initiation of John the Baptist. The Initiation that will be addressed in this work is the simultaneous Initiation of John the Baptist at the time of the Raising/Initiation of Lazarus while at the same time becoming one with Lazarus within the consciousness soul of Lazarus. A crucial premise of this work rests on the assertion that after his execution and the loss of his mineral body John the Baptist remained within the earthly realm while continuing his presence among the Apostles as their group-soul spirit. This work adopts the term Rudolf Steiner used to describe the unseen human physical body which he designated as the phantom body. In esotericism, the phantom body is deemed to be the true non-visible physical body that is devoid of the earthly substances of mineral, water and air. This work proposes that during the time of Christ's ministry on earth John the Baptist, after his execution, remained present in his phantom body and continued to accompany the Christ in a non-visible fashion. A more comprehensive discussion pertaining to the phantom body is addressed in chapter seven.

Moreover, in this work the author's references to the Risen Christ contend that the Christ was present in His resurrected phantom body throughout the centuries since the time of the Event of Golgotha. Though Steiner does assert that it was the etheric body of Christ that is seen after His resurrection this work accepts this assertion. However, allowance is made which holds that Steiner applies a more encompassing usage of the term 'etheric body' which includes the phantom body. In centuries past, for those who experienced the Risen Christ from the time of the Event of Golgotha to the time of 1933 this work contends that many were primarily experiencing Christ in His resurrected phantom body within the realm of the earth's own phantom/physical sphere as well as within the earth's etheric sphere. The Event of Golgotha established the redemption of the human phantom body through Christ Jesus: "This was the mission of Christ upon earth; by His deed to substitute the true form for the false form of death." (GA112; lecture XIII). The Event of Golgotha also induced the germinal stages of the eventual and complete redemption of the earth's phantom, etheric and astral spheres. This work postulates the thesis that until 1933 the phantom body of Christ was the body of prominence to many of those who experienced an appearance of Christ. However, during the time period of 1933-1945 Christ's work within the earth's etheric sphere had reached its zenith which resulted in the culmination of the earth's etheric sphere becoming sun-like; the creation of which had been in progress since Christ's Ascension. Prior to this time, the earth's astral sphere alone was sun-like due to the blood that flowed from the wounds of Christ Jesus on Golgotha. The First Dispensation of Christ had come to an end in 1933. Following the time period of 1933-1945 Christ has been active in an etheric body within the etheric/astral sun-sphere of the earth. This marked the beginning stages of the Second Dispensation of Christ which is more conventionally referenced as the Second Coming of Christ. This time period inaugurated the second phase of Christ's exalted and enduring work regarding the eventual transfiguration of the earth, the solar system and the zodiacal cosmos. It has proceeded from the epoch of the Dispensation of Christ's phantom body prominence in the earth's etheric element in centuries past to the present epoch of the Dispensation of Christ's etheric body prominence within the earth's astral element which will continue for centuries to come. Future Dispensations will include Christ in an astral body within the realm of Lower Devachan. While further in the future Christ will appear in an Ego Form within the realm of Upper Devachan.

The fundamental questions presented in this work are: Did the raising of Lazarus salvage the Event of Golgotha. Was the mission of Christ in jeopardy of failing due to the incomprehension of the Apostles. Was this incomprehension of the mission and nature of the Christ Being by the Apostles a significant component to the agony that Christ experienced in the garden of Gethsemane. In answer to these questions the Mystery of Golgotha can be viewed as comprising of two aspects. In one aspect Christ imbued the earth with life forces which gave life to what would have become a dying and lifeless planet over the successive centuries. This afforded humanity the possibility of continuing to evolve on earth. This was a gift from Christ to humanity and the earth. This gift needed no corresponding deed from humanity. The other aspect of the Event of Golgotha did require a corresponding human deed. Christ held within Him the macrocosmic Ego which was to unite with the human microcosmic Ego to the extent that would allow Christ to endow a human with a temporary mantle of an Atma body along with the Buddhi and Manas bodies. This mission was to be achieved through the twelve Apostles in conjunction with what they were to internalize from both the Christ and from the hierarchical Beings who occupy the regions of the twelve zodiacal constellations. However, due to the Apostles' incomprehension of the Christ Being and their eventual incapacity to consciously follow Christ through His Passion, Death and Resurrection John the Baptist, the group soul and unitary consciousness of the Apostles, acted as their surrogate. John the Baptist was able to do so because of the high initiation he simultaneously received from Christ at the time of the raising of Lazarus. This initiation provided John the Baptist the internalization of both his Ego forces and the Ego forces of Christ within his phantom body. This enabled him as a singular human Being to receive from Christ a temporary Atma body condition as well as the other higher bodies. These bodies came to full expression as the young man in the tomb on Easter morning as narrated in Mark's Gospel. This accomplishment of both Christ and John the Baptist together became the new seed force for the further evolution of all of humanity.

There are two accounts of the raising of Lazarus that are paramount in this study: one is the account narrated in the Gospel of John and the other is a lesser known account given in, "The Secret Gospel of Mark." The primary objectives in this work are to formulate a detailed study of the relationship of Christ to John the Baptist and the Apostles and to understand the meaning of the relationship between the fleeing youth and the young man in the tomb as narrated in Mark's Gospel. Though the Initiation of Lazarus is portentous in the Gospel of John, Steiner conveys to us the additional account and revelation that John the Baptist is also significantly engaged in this Initiation. This is an Initiation of Lazarus but it is also an Initiation of John the Baptist at a higher level. John is brought into the consciousness soul of Lazarus to which Lazarus' name is then changed to John. This Initiation of both Lazarus and John the Baptist which is presented to us in the Secret Gospel of Mark as transpiring six days before the Passover and Crucifixion was also a protracted Initiation of John the Baptist that extended beyond the initiation of Lazarus. For John the Baptist it extended further than the elapsed time of the Initiation of Lazarus being raised from the dead as recounted in John's Gospel. It extended beyond the foot of the Cross on Golgotha when the mantle of the astral body of Christ was passed over to Lazarus as well as to John the Baptist. Moreover, this Initiation of John the Baptist was then only completed on Easter morning at the time of the Resurrection of the Christ Being. The completion of this Initiation of John the Baptist was finalized when John the Baptist, appearing as the young man in the tomb, announced to Mary Magdalene and the other women that Christ had Risen as narrated in the Gospel of Mark. Why was it necessary for John to interpenetrate the soul of Lazarus. Why did this even need to come about. What was its purpose. Steiner answers this with the following from his Last Address: "Elijah appeared again at the very most important moment of human evolution, appeared again so that Christ Jesus Himself could give him the Initiation he was to receive for the evolution of mankind."

The following is what Steiner disclosed in regard to the raising of Lazarus in his lecture cycle on the Gospel of St. John given in Hamburg in 1908. From Lecture IV we read: "Through Christ Jesus a new Initiation had to arise to replace the old, an Initiation produced by means of forces of which we have yet to speak. The old form of Initiation must end, but a transition had to be made from the old to the new age and to make this transition, someone had once more to be initiated in the old way, but initiated into Christian esotericism. This only Christ-Jesus Himself could perform and the neophyte was the one who is called Lazarus. `This sickness is not unto death,' means here that it is the three and a half day death-like sleep. This is clearly indicated. You will see that the presentation is of a very veiled character, but for one who is able to decipher a presentation of this kind it represents Initiation. The individuality, Lazarus, had to be initiated in such a way that he could be a witness of the spiritual worlds. An expression is used, a very significant expression in the language of the Mysteries, `that the Lord loved Lazarus.' What does `to love' mean in the language of the Mysteries? It expresses the relationship of the pupil to the teacher. `He whom the Lord loved' is the most intimate, the most deeply initiated pupil. The Lord Himself had initiated Lazarus and as an Initiate Lazarus arose from the grave, which means from his place of Initiation. This same expression, `Whom the Lord loved', is always used later in connection with John, or perhaps we should say in connection with the writer of the Gospel of St. John, for the name `John' is not used. He is the `Beloved Disciple' to whom the Gospel refers. He is the risen Lazarus himself and the writer of the Gospel wished to say - `What I have to offer, I say by virtue of the Initiation which has been conferred upon me by the Lord Himself.' Therefore the writer of the Gospel distinguishes between what occurred before and what occurred after the raising of Lazarus. Before the raising, an Initiate of the old order is quoted, one who has attained a knowledge of the Spirit, one whose testimony is repeatedly announced to be true: `However, what is to be said concerning the most profound of matters, concerning the Mystery of

Golgotha, I myself say, I the Risen One; but only after I have been raised, can I speak concerning it!' And so we have in the first part of the Gospel, the testimony of the old John – in the second half, the testimony of the new John whom the Lord Himself had initiated, for this is the risen Lazarus. Only thus do we grasp the real meaning of this chapter. These words are written there because John wished to say: `I call upon the testimony of my supersensible organs, my spiritual powers of perception. What I have related I have not seen in the ordinary physical world, but in the spiritual world in which I have dwelt by virtue of the Initiation which the Lord has conferred upon me.' Thus we must attribute the characterization of Christ-Jesus, which we find in the first chapters of the Gospel of St. John as far as the end of the 10th Chapter, to the knowledge which might be possessed by anyone who had not yet, in the deepest sense of the word, been initiated through Christ-Jesus Himself."

This final paragraph at first seems to suggest that John the Baptist was not actually initiated at all at the time of the raising of Lazarus though we have read previously from Steiner that Elijah appeared again to receive an Initiation for the benefit of the evolution of humanity. This is resolved if we read the following paragraph below in which Steiner speaks of the old prophets; the prophets of the Old Testament who were never initiated by the Christ. Here John the Baptist serves a dual purpose. He bridges the Old Testament to the New Testament. He inspires Lazarus to write the first half of the Gospel as an Old Testament prophet would understand it. However, since John the Baptist was initiated by Christ at the raising of Lazarus he then inspires Lazarus to write the second half of the Gospel with the new knowledge of one initiated by Christ Jesus.

From Lecture IV of the 1908 Hamburg lectures: "Now, you will say: `Yes, but we have already in these lectures listened to profound words about Christ-Jesus as the incarnated Logos, the Light of the World, etc.' It is no longer surprising that these profound words concerning Christ-Jesus were spoken even in the very first Chapters, for in the ancient Mysteries, Christ-Jesus, who was to appear in the world at a future time, in other words, the Christ, was not perhaps an unknown Being. And all the Mysteries point to One who was to come. For this reason the ancient Initiates were called `prophets' because they prophesied concerning something that was to take place. Thus the purpose of Initiation was to let it be clearly understood that in the future of mankind the Christ would be revealed, and in what he had already learned at that time, the Baptist found the truth which made it possible to state that He, who had been spoken of in the Mysteries, stood before him in the person of Christ-Jesus."

The raising of Lazarus, of which we read in the Gospel of John, may have been a precautionary deed enacted by Christ in order to eventually pass on the forces that were contained in His cosmic aura to both Lazarus and John the Baptist. These new cosmic evolutionary forces could then be seeded into the souls of human Beings as the first seeds of the new forces of human and earthly evolution. Originally, these forces were to be internalized by the Apostles whom He had chosen. However, after John the Baptist's execution, he was gradually being prepared for a very special mission. His immediate purpose and mission, after the raising of Lazarus, was to internalize the Cosmic Principle, the Cosmic Aura of Christ through the entire Passion from the time of the arrest of Christ to Easter morning if the Apostles were to fail to do so. The Cosmic Principle of Christ, 'with its cosmic laws and its cosmic forces' which were to enter earthly life, was there 'as long as' Christ was 'united' with His chosen Apostles as Steiner explicitly stated in Lecture IX of his cycle on the Gospel of Mark. The three chosen Apostles, Peter and the two brothers James and John ben Zebedee, were bestowed a final opportunity in the Garden of Gethsemane to establish that they were capable of comprehending the Event of Golgotha. Instead, they were unable to remain united in consciousness with Christ through His Passion. The Cosmic Aura of Christ which was to enter earthly life was in jeopardy of possibly dissipating if it did not retain its micro-zodiacal configuration in the souls of the Twelve chosen human Beings; that is, if it couldn't be carried within the micro-zodiacal configuration that the Apostles afforded Christ. It seems that Christ anticipated this. He saw this potential catastrophe when the Apostles were "heavy with sleep" (Luke 9:32) during part of the Transfiguration. This is why John the Baptist was initiated by Christ at the same time Lazarus was initiated which is referred in the bible as Lazarus being raised from the dead. This gave John the Baptist the greater capacity to carry this aura through the entire Passion and on through to the Resurrection. It can be argued that Christ could not be taken and could not pass through death as long as this aura was enveloping His Being. It was to be sacrificially given over to the Apostles and seeded within their souls but they in turn were not capable of holding such a powerful cosmic force. However, at the time of the arrest and at the moment of the separation of the fleeing youth from the Christ Being, the Cosmic Aura of Christ was passed on to John the Baptist who stood as the surrogate for the Twelve Apostles for the very reason that he had become their group soul/spirit and their unitary consciousness. At this point in time it was only John the Baptist who was capable of carrying this cosmic auric Principle through to the Resurrection. The incomprehension of the Apostles, to which Steiner pointed as the source of the agony of Christ in Gethsemane, was also surmounted in part by the awakened, initiated consciousness of Lazarus. It was Lazarus who was able to stay with Christ through the Crucifixion and His Death. However, it was John the Baptist who, in spirit, also remained with Christ through His Death. He then followed Christ into hell; that is, into the sub-realms according to the Gospel of Nicodemus. While on Easter morning he took part in the Resurrection as the young man sitting in the tomb who announces to the women that Christ has Risen.

6

Thereby, the Event of Golgotha was no longer in jeopardy of failing. It was salvaged by the Initiation of both Lazarus and John the Baptist. It was Lazarus who comprehended the Crucifixion and Death of Christ, John the Baptist who comprehended the Resurrection of Christ and later it was Paul who comprehended the Ascension of Christ thereby completing the Trichotomy of human understanding of the Crucifixion and Death, the Resurrection and the Ascension of Christ. If we examine both Judas Iscariot and Lazarus/John the Baptist we see two opposing archetypal individuals. Judas was the archetypal figure in which the Apostles' incomprehension was most typified. Their incomprehension was analogous to an indirect and unknowing betrayal of Christ while their fears and failures were like a death between them and Christ. It was the weight of this extreme incomprehension by Judas which later culminated in his suicide. Lazarus/John as one individual stands as the polarity to Judas. Lazarus offered the Christ the necessary human comprehension and awakened consciousness to internalize the Death of the Christ Being as he stood at the foot of the Cross. Whereas, John the Baptist had the strength of soul and spirit to carry the Aura of Christ through to the morning of Easter where it was now to become the focal Impulse of human evolution. Lazarus and John the Baptist, together as one, acted as a singular archetypal figure of that which the Apostles were to accomplish as a body of Twelve. A key principle in this study is the principle of understanding. It was the incomprehension of the Apostles which caused 'the sweat to drop as blood' and which became the force that gradually severed the bond between Christ and themselves. In the Luke Gospel their incomprehension and its eventual calamitous consequence is intimated in the following passage: "But Jesus taking to Himself the Twelve said to them, `Behold, we are going up to Jerusalem, and all things that have been written by the prophets concerning the Son of Man will be accomplished. For He will be delivered to the Gentiles, and will be mocked and scourged and spit upon; and after they have scourged Him, they will put Him to death; and on the third day He will rise again.' And they understood none of these things and this saying was hidden from them, neither did they get to know the things that were being said." (Luke 18: 31-34).

It is noteworthy that immediately prior to this in Luke 18 we read about the rich ruler. He is told to give up all that he possesses and to follow Christ. This rich ruler is Lazarus. Lazarus came into this life with the riches and abundance of ancient wisdom gained over many fruitful lifetimes while passing through the Mysteries lifetime after lifetime. However, in this particular lifetime while Christ was now on Earth Lazarus was admonished to take leave of his earthly wealth and power. This ultimately led to his exile to Patmos Island. Moreover, in spiritual matters he was to sacrifice all that he possessed that is of the past and that a new form of Mystery wisdom is to enter the course of human evolution. He is to cross over from an Old

7

Testament wisdom that was ascertained from past wisdom to a new Apocalyptic wisdom that draws one to the future with its life renewing, soul transfiguring forces. Instead of the ancient Mystery wisdom that looks to the past for its knowing and understanding, Lazarus was now given the Apocalyptic wisdom that comes to us from the future. Again, this ultimately led to his Patmos Island experience. These two accounts in chapter 18 from the Luke Gospel telling of the change in understanding that Lazarus is to develop and the Apostles' lack of understanding of the words of Christ about His Death and Resurrection are purposefully juxtaposed to indicate the critical element that understanding is to have in the success of human participation in the mission of Christ. The success of the Mystery of Golgotha was a twofold equation. It involved both the forces that Christ brought to the Earth and the ability of Christ-initiated individuals to understand the mission of Christ. This understanding was not to be simply an intellectual understanding which is not. It was an understanding in which one was expected to be able to take into oneself the living forces that Christ had to offer as well as comprehending the meaning and purpose of the Mystery of Golgotha.

Before proceeding any further, the following should be noted from Steiner's lecture cycle, "The Fifth Gospel," Lecture VI: "Now we may ask ourselves how the Mystery of Golgotha was understood at the time when it happened. It is important for us to grasp the reality of this Mystery, understanding what it really was about. Was it a matter of what people were taught at the time? If that were the crux of it, people who maintain that most of the things Christ Jesus taught had also existed in earlier times would be partly right, though we know that this is not completely true. But that is not primarily what it was all about, but something entirely different. What happened on Golgotha and in connection with that event is what matters, and this would have happened even if not a single soul on the whole Earth had understood it. It was not a question of a fact being realized at the time, but merely of the event taking place. The significance of the Golgotha event lies not in what people have understood, but in what happened for the sake of humanity, and happened in such a way that the stream of this event has come to expression in the world's spiritual realities. The Mystery of Golgotha truly came at a strange time."

When Steiner said - "What happened on Golgotha and in connection with that event is what matters, and this would have happened even if not a single soul on the whole Earth had understood it." - he is referring to an intellectual understanding of the Event of Golgotha. An intellectual understanding of the Event of Golgotha at that time was not necessary. What was needed from humanity in the way of understanding was a fully conscious and comprehensive experience of the Event of Golgotha that paralleled that which Christ experienced from the Crucifixion to the

8

Resurrection. If not, then we have to question why Steiner asserts that Christ agonized over the lack of incomprehension from His Apostles in the Garden of Gethsemane. All that Christ experienced in transforming and redeeming the human physical/phantom body was also to be achieved by the Apostles. When the Apostles failed in their mission John the Baptist, the group-soul of the Apostles, acted as their surrogate. In the above quote Steiner mentions that the Mystery of Golgotha, " . . . came at a strange time." It came at a strange time in that it happened at a time when people had lost the capacity to spiritually experience the meaning and significance of this Event. As Steiner indicates in this same lecture, the time of the Indian epoch was a time when this would have been experienced most deeply in the soul; the Persian epoch in a lesser sense and the Egypto-Chaldean epoch even less so. By the time of the Graeco-Latin epoch very few individuals were capable of understanding and spiritually experiencing the Event of Golgotha. From what Steiner said in the above quote, it could be asserted that the Event of Golgotha was an event that was independent of any human involvement. If that had been so, then it raises the question of Christ's Agony in the Garden due to the Apostles' incomprehension of the Mystery of Golgotha. Why did Christ agonize over their incomprehension? It was because Peter, James and John were not going to be able to spiritually follow Christ through His Passion, Death and Resurrection. The Event itself would have taken place and the Christ Principle would have become part of the Earth. However, it was also critical that the forces of the Event of Golgotha seed itself at the time of its immediate occurrence in at least one, single human soul for the sake of future human evolution.

From Lecture V of, "The Karma of Materialism," Steiner addressed these critical points on the Mystery of Golgotha; Berlin, August 28, 1917: "One comes to realize that one must bring to the Mystery of Golgotha all the depths of one's thoughts and feelings; for example when one attempts to relate the Mystery of Golgotha to the secrets of human death and man's subsequent awakening in the astral body and 'I.' It is through thoughts, through contemplation that one draws near to this Mystery. It is of no use to express through empty words a general wish to reach union with Christ; what is needed is a concrete understanding of what the actual appearance of Christ in earth evolution means for one's own life. It is not without meaning that the same time span elapsed between the death and the resurrection of Christ Jesus as the one that elapses between our leaving the physical body and our leaving the ether body in death. There is an intimate bond between Christ's life on earth and the man of today living after the Mystery of Golgotha. It is now possible to say with greatest conviction: Christ came in order that man should not be lost to the earth. Had the Mystery of Golgotha not taken place man's body would have become larva-like, directed from above by his soul. Death would gradually have removed man from the earth altogether. Through the Mystery of Golgotha man's connection with the earth was restored.

Through the Mystery of Golgotha the possibility of consciousness arising from death was created."

"The Christ Being, that lived for three years in and through the body of Jesus of Nazareth, spoke the secrets connected with human consciousness to this body. This could be done, only at the moment of death, for it is only then that the entire secret connected with human consciousness is drawn together. Did not the Christ have to lead Jesus through death in order that this whole impulse of consciousness could stream into mankind? Indeed, it did! And death is also that moment when we too may hope to attain an intensified comprehension of Christ. This is because at that moment all the forces are present which have sustained our consciousness throughout life. We are adapted at the moment of death to absorb what is in fact the secret of our consciousness and to absorb with it the Christ Impulse. We are preparing ourselves to receive it when we seek not only to understand but to experience the reality of the Christ Impulse. However what meets us at death we can understand only when our organ for understanding is set free. That means that while the moment of death does indeed provide the condition for union with Christ, it is only when we are free of the etheric body that the astral body and 'I'-the organization for understanding-can actually perceive this union. Something else had to take place at the Mystery of Golgotha to bring about these conditions: After Christ had-in dying on Golgotha-entrusted to Jesus as it were the secrets of man's future consciousness, a momentous event had to occur: Jesus, in whom the Christ dwelt, rose to new life through the force of death. In other words, the Resurrection had to occur in order that we could understand that Resurrection when, a few days after death, we experience our ether body separating from us as explained by anthroposophical science. In this more inward death- i.e., the separation from the ether body a few days after death-we relive in a certain sense the Mystery of Golgotha. For it was life, that is, consciousness, which rose out of death: a living consciousness. At no time before the Mystery of Golgotha had this ever happened; life had always risen from life. Never before had there been a necessity to understand how life can come from death, only how life comes from life. This is one of many approaches to the Mystery of Golgotha."

Also in the same lecture: "Let us for a moment imagine what would have happened had the Mystery of Golgotha not taken place: Evolution would have continued the way it was before, which means that more and more human beings on the earth would lose all direct connection with the spiritual world. Eventually humanity would no longer be able to incorporate the spirit; man's body would become larva-like consisting only of organic and etheric members. A long time ago men's souls would have been incapable of living in the bodies available; they would have hovered above them in the spiritual world. Only those souls who, in an earlier epoch had reached higher development, would be able to inspire their bodies from above. Consciousness of the spiritual world would have been possible only in the case of individuals receiving inspiration in the Mysteries. The human spirit itself would not inhabit the earth. In the mystery centers it would be possible to receive inspiration but Ahriman would battle against this. He would distort the inspirations thus preventing the larva-like human bodies from carrying out what was intended."

Comprehension of the Mystery of Golgotha is essential to the future evolutionary path for all humanity. As Steiner had stated in the above: "It is through thoughts, through contemplation that one draws near to this Mystery." This vital element of understanding began to shift from the Apostles to Lazarus and John the Baptist at the time of the raising of Lazarus. In Emil Bock's, "The Three Years," he addresses the question of the raising of Lazarus in terms of its meaning and relation to Initiation. Bock writes: "Lazarus is said to have been a rich man, endowed with possessions on a princely scale. Then his destiny led him to a meeting with Jesus. He followed Him, and took His words and deeds deeply to heart. So he was present when Jesus raised the son of the widow. This event affected him so profoundly that he broke with his former life and gave all he had to the poor. The legend leaves it open whether the shock of the experience might even help to explain his death. But through these legendary pictures shines an indubitable truth. The riches offered up by Lazarus under the influence of Christ were not purely material. They were the rich fruits brought from former earthly lives, in which he had been repeatedly ranked among the highest Initiates. In the Christ there appeared to him something entirely new, in comparison with which the old dispensation seemed faded and worthless. In Christ he saw the fulfillment; all the rest had only been preparation and prophesy. Clearly, the hierophantic approach of Jesus to the bier of the young man of Nain must have had a specially disturbing influence on Lazarus' inner life. There are significant parallels between his destiny and that of the young man. With the young man a former Initiation repeats itself, and having formerly brought about a tragic crisis, it is now directed to a good purpose through the Christ. With Lazarus too, potent forces from former Initiations are liberated, and he is no longer able to keep his soul, awakened to such overwhelming riches, bound to its bodily vehicle. In him, too, the Temple Sleep and Mystic Death of many former lives comes to expression once more." It should be noted that Bock asserts that Lazarus witnessed the raising of the widow's son of Nain. This scene is not included in the Gospel of John. Thereby, Bock's assertion differs from that which Karl Koenig suggests in regard to Lazarus which is addressed in chapter 2.

Bock also adds: "What takes place in Bethany while Jesus and His disciples are absent, is like an enormous heightening of the mysterious shocks and crises in the destinies of the Old Testament prophets. With them, only echoes and memories of an earlier Initiation broke through into the present.

With Lazarus, the dynamic power of fate is something greater. It drives him actually into death. But now there appears One who has prepared Himself to be the master of fate, and so acts that not only an echo but a real Initiation is attained, the first Christian Initiation in human history." Bock speaks of the raising of Lazarus as an actual death as well as an Initiation. Steiner does say the following in his book, "Christianity as Mystical Fact": "The earthly body has actually been dead for three days." However, he also said in, "Christianity as Mystical Fact": "The earthly part had to die a pictorially real death. The fact that his body was then put in a somnambulistic sleep for three days can only be regarded, in contrast to the immensity of the transformation of life which preceded it, as an external event to which a far more significant spiritual one corresponds." From the same work Steiner addressed the raising of Lazarus as an Initiation when he said, "A mystery in the true sense of the word stands before us. In the language of the Mysteries, he became an Initiate. Thus the event related to us must be an act of Initiation." If it had been an actual death we would have to ask why Steiner would express it as a condition of somnambulistic sleep. Certainly there are those who would agree with Bock while others say that the raising of Lazarus was purely an Initiation; the Temple Sleep or the Mystic Death. Christ says twice that Lazarus is sleeping. He later says that, "Lazarus is dead." (John 11:14). Thomas also says before they go to the tomb, "Let us also go, that we may die with him." (John 11:16). The writer of the Gospel seems to be saying that there is to be a different understanding of the term 'death'. Certainly Thomas does not suggest that they pass through death as we commonly understand it. Rather, the terms Temple Sleep and Mystic Death are being referenced here. Again, Christ uses both terms: sleep and death. One could ask: if Lazarus did not die then why did Christ say, "Lazarus is dead." Lazarus is in a condition somewhat similar to death in that the etheric body from the upper portion of the physical body is now separated from the physical body. A reference to the 3 ½ day Temple Sleep is also veiled in the words of Martha, ". . .for he is dead four (3 ½) days." (John.11:39). Other passages in Chapter 11 of John's Gospel also lift the veil showing that this was an Initiation, such as, "And Jesus wept. The Jews therefore said, 'See how He loved him'." (John 11: 35-36). The disciple whom Jesus loved is understood to be a reference to the Initiation of Lazarus by Christ as Lazarus is Christ's most advanced pupil. At the end of an Initiation the Initiate would say the words, "My God, my God you have glorified me." Immediately after Martha makes her reference to Lazarus being dead for four days Christ then speaks in words that mirror what would be spoken by a Hierophant to His Pupil-Initiate at the conclusion of his Initiation when Christ Jesus says, ". . . if thou believe thou shalt behold the Glory of God." (John 11:40). It was the raising of Lazarus which sealed the fate of Christ. The chief priests had wished to do away with Christ Jesus prior to this. Now they were even more determined to do so. Christ breached a major tenet of the

Mysteries in that one does not reveal the act of the Temple Sleep in public. One is not even to talk about it to anyone outside the inner circle. This is punishable by death and the Gospel does mention that the chief priests and Pharisees planned to put Christ Jesus to death because He had Initiated Lazarus in public: "So from that day forth their plan was to put Him to death." (John 11:53). Also, the Gospel alludes to the same when in it reads: "But the chief priests planned to put Lazarus to death also." (John 12:10).

The chronology of the Gospels intimates to us that though Lazarus, as the rich ruler, may have been a watchful follower of Christ he did not interact with Christ as the beloved disciple until the final days of Christ's ministry prior to His entry into Jerusalem. This would indicate that though Lazarus' name was changed to John after his Initiation he was not one of the three disciples who, for instance, witnessed the Transfiguration of Christ. The raising of Lazarus was achieved after the Transfiguration. Moreover, he was not one of the three Apostles who was overcome with sleep at the time of the Agony in the Garden. The Gospel of Matthew addresses this in the following passage: "And He took with Him Peter and the two sons of Zebedee, and he began to be saddened and exceedingly troubled." (Matthew 26:37). His Initiation would have precluded the same lack in consciousness that hindered Peter, James and his brother John ben Zebedee. When we read in the Luke Gospel about the rich ruler we are presented with the turning point in the spiritual life of Lazarus when he is admonished by Christ to give up his wealth in order to gain Eternal Life. There are much deeper elements to this account than what we may at first apprehend from the words in the Gospel. Lazarus is told to give up what he has relied upon from his past incarnations; that is, all the wisdom that he has gained from the Old Testament Wisdom that looks back to the past for its understanding. Lazarus was rich in this regard. When Christ spoke to Lazarus He did not simply speak at Lazarus. Rather, He spoke into him. All that Lazarus held within himself from the past was now being shattered by the words of Christ which shook the very foundation of Lazarus' soul. The passage reads: "When he heard these things, he was much grieved, for he was very rich." (Lk. 18:23). The soul-shattering ramifications of this admonition from Christ were already being felt within the soul of Lazarus at its very most depths once the Christ spoke to the inner Self of Lazarus. Over the intervening time between the moment when Christ spoke these words to Lazarus to the time of the Initiation and raising of Lazarus this force then built to a critical and climactic point to where he then may have passed into a coma from the overwhelming shock to his soul or possibly a protracted near-death experience while in the condition of a somnambulistic sleep. Either way, it affords Christ the opportunity to effect the Initiation of Lazarus which gives Lazarus the needed soul forces to stand at the foot of the Cross and receive the mantle of the unfallen astral body of the Nathan Soul from Christ Jesus. This, in turn, gives Lazarus the soul

13

forces to write the Gospel of John and the Apocalypse. The power of the voice of Christ, The Word, comes full circle from the time that Christ tells Lazarus, the rich ruler, to sacrifice his riches which begins the overwhelming shock to his soul to the time when Christ, ". . . cried out with a loud voice, 'Lazarus come forth!'." It's reasonable to surmise that the Initiation of Lazarus actually covered this entire time span and that it reached its climax in the four (3 ½) days at Bethany. In some of the older forms of Initiation the candidate would be required to drink an entheogen that would render him unconscious and place him in a coma-like state while his physical body was in a condition of deep paralysis. This condition would thereby simulate rigor mortis. Steiner referred to this drink as the 'drink of oblivion'. The candidate would appear as if he were dead and in a sense he would be in a condition that was like death. He would be in a suspended death-like condition once the upper portion of the candidate's etheric body had separated from his physical body. This death-like paralysis seemed to have been a necessary condition in the old forms of Initiation; a condition which Christ was to change once and for all. In regard to Lazarus, the gradually building, soul-shattering shock to his Being possibly brought on the same effect which culminated in a paralytic, coma-like rigor mortis condition to which his astral body and Ego then took leave of his physical body just as they do when one is asleep. Christ first said of Lazarus that, "This sickness is not unto death, but for the glory of God, that through it the Son of God may be glorified." (John 11:4). The Son of God in this passage refers to the Ego of Lazarus. And before He said, "Lazarus is dead" He said, "Lazarus, our friend, sleeps. But I go that I may wake him from sleep." (John 11:11). When Christ finally announced that Lazarus is dead He was intimating that the etheric body is now lifted from the physical body which is similar to the condition of death so that the Ego and astral body may imprint their experiences upon the etheric body. Christ knew that Lazarus was in this paralytic condition and that this now afforded Christ the opportunity to bring to its culmination the Initiation of Lazarus which began at the time of the admonition to the rich ruler to sacrifice and surrender all that he had. Those who were around Lazarus at the time did not truly understand what was actually transpiring. This is why Martha had said, "Lord, by this time he is already decayed, for he is dead four days." (John 11:39). It is highly probable that no one had actually entered the tomb since the time that Lazarus had been placed there because we know that he was not decayed. The life forces of the 'far reaching, mighty aura' of Christ which worked from a distance preserved the body of Lazarus; that is, Christ preserved it with the unfallen Tree of Life forces that He had brought to Earth for all of humanity.

In Steiner's book, "Christianity as Mystical Fact," he gives us some key points of insight into understanding the mystery of the raising of Lazarus: "It must be admitted that the whole account in John's Gospel is wrapped in a veil of mystery. To gain insight into this we need only demonstrate one point. If the report is to be taken in a literal, physical sense, how are we to understand these words of Jesus: `This sickness is not unto death, but for the glory of God, that the Son of God might be glorified thereby.' (John 11: 4). This is the customary translation of the words, but the situation would be better realized if we were to translate them thus – as would be correct according to the Greek also: `for the manifestation (revelation) of God, that the Son of God might be revealed thereby.' And what do these other words mean: Jesus says, `I AM the Resurrection and the Life: he who believes in Me, though he die, yet shall he live' (John 11: 25). It would be trivial to believe that Jesus wished to say that Lazarus had become ill only in order that Jesus might demonstrate his skill through him. And it would be a further triviality to think that Jesus meant to assert that belief in him restores life to someone who is dead in the ordinary sense of the word. For what would be remarkable about a person raised from the dead, if after his resurrection he was the same as before death? Indeed, what would be the sense of describing the life of such a person in the words: `I AM the Resurrection and the Life' The words of Jesus at once come to life and make sense when we understand them as the expression of a spiritual occurrence, and then even take them in a certain way literally as they stand in the text. Jesus actually says that He is the resurrection that has happened to Lazarus, and that He is the life that Lazarus is living. Let us take literally what Jesus is according to the Gospel of John. He is the `Word that became flesh'. He is the Eternal that existed in the beginning. If He is really the resurrection, then the `eternal, primordial' has risen again in Lazarus. We are dealing therefore with the resurrection of the eternal `Word'. And this `Word' is the life to which Lazarus has been awakened. We have to do with the case of `illness'. But it is not an illness leading to death, but to the `glory of God,' that is, to the revelation of God. If the `eternal Word' has risen again in Lazarus then in truth the whole process serves to make God manifest in Lazarus. For through the whole process Lazarus has become another man. The `Word,' the Spirit, did not live in him before; now this Spirit lives in him. This Spirit has been born in him. It is true that every birth is accompanied by an illness, the illness of the mother. But this illness does not lead to death, but to new life. That part of Lazarus becomes `ill' from which the `new man,' permeated by the `Word', is born. Where is the tomb from which the `Word' is born? To answer this question we need only remember Plato, who calls man's body the tomb of the soul. And we need only recall that Plato also speaks of a kind of resurrection when he refers to the coming to life of the spiritual world in the body. What Plato calls the spiritual soul, John calls the `Word'. And for him Christ is the `Word'. Plato might have said, Whoever becomes spiritual has caused the divine to rise from the tomb of his body. And for John this resurrection is what happened through the `Life of Jesus'. It is no wonder then that he

15

causes Jesus to say, `I AM the Resurrection.' There can be no doubt that the event at Bethany was an awakening in a spiritual sense. Lazarus became a different person. He was raised to a life of which the `eternal Word' proclaims: `I Am this life.' What, then, took place in Lazarus? The Spirit came to life within him. He partook of the life which is eternal."

"A mystery in the true sense of the word stands before us. Into Lazarus the `eternal Word' has entered. In the language of the Mysteries, he became an Initiate. Thus the event related to us must be an act of Initiation. Let us now place the whole event before ourselves as an Initiation. Jesus loved Lazarus (John 11: 36). This indicates no ordinary affection. The latter would be contrary to the spirit of John's Gospel, in which Jesus is the 'Word'. Jesus loved Lazarus because He found him ready for the awakening of the `Word' within him. Jesus was connected with the family at Bethany. This simply means that Jesus had prepared everything in that family for the great final act of the drama: the raising of Lazarus. Lazarus was the pupil of Jesus. He was a pupil of such caliber that Jesus could be quite certain that the awakening would be accomplished in him. The final act of the drama of awakening was a pictorial action revealing the Spirit. The person involved in it not only had to understand the words, `Die and come to life,' he had to fulfill them himself by a spiritually real action. His earthly part, of which his higher Being in the sense of the Mysteries must be ashamed, had to be laid aside. The earthly part had to die a pictorially real death. The fact that his body was then put into a somnambulistic sleep for three days can only be regarded, in contrast to the immensity of the transformation of life which preceded it, as an external event to which a far more significant spiritual one corresponds. This act, however, was indeed also the experience which divided the life of the mystic into two parts. One who does not know from experience the deeper content of such acts cannot understand them. He can only appreciate them by means of a comparison. - The substance of Shakespeare's Hamlet may be condensed into a few words. Anyone who learns these words can say in a certain sense that he knows the content of Hamlet. And intellectually he does. But someone who allows all the wealth of Shakespeare's drama to stream in upon him perceives Hamlet quite differently. The content of a life, which cannot be replaced by a mere description, has passed through his soul. The idea of Hamlet has become an artistic, personal experience within him. - On a higher level a similar process is accomplished in man through the magic, significant process of Initiation. What he attains spiritually he lives through pictorially. The word `pictorially' is used here in the sense that while an outer event is really accomplished materially, at the same time it is nevertheless a picture. We are not dealing with an unreal, but with a real picture. The earthly body has actually been dead for three days.

From death comes forth the new life. This life has outlasted death. Man has acquired faith in the new life. - This is what happened with Lazarus. Jesus had prepared him for the awakening. He experienced a pictorially real illness. The latter is an Initiation, which after three days leads to a really new life. Lazarus was ready to accomplish this act. He wrapped himself in the robe of the mystic. He enclosed himself in a condition of lifelessness which was at the same time a pictorial death. And when Jesus came there, the three days had been fulfilled. 'Then they took away the stone from the place where the dead was laid. And Jesus lifted up His eyes, and said, Father, I thank thee that thou hast heard me.' (John 11: 41). The Father had heard Jesus, for Lazarus had come to the final act of the great drama of cognition. He had perceived how resurrection is attained. An Initiation into the Mysteries had been fulfilled. It was an Initiation such as had been understood throughout the ages. It had been demonstrated by Jesus as the Initiator. Union with the divine had always been represented in this manner. In Lazarus, Jesus accomplished the great miracle of the transformation of life in the sense of ancient traditions. Through this event Christianity is linked with the Mysteries. Lazarus had become an Initiate through Christ Jesus Himself. Thereby Lazarus had become able to rise into the higher worlds. He was at the same time both the first Christian Initiate and the first to be initiated by Christ Jesus Himself. Through his Initiation he had become capable of perceiving that the 'Word' which had come to life within him had become a person in Christ Jesus, and thus there stood before him in the personality of his 'awakener' the same which had been revealed within him spiritually. From this point of view the following words of Jesus are significant: 'And I knew that thou hearest Me always: but because of the people which stand by I said it, that they may believe that thou hast sent Me.' (John 11: 42). That is to say, it is a question of revealing that in Jesus the 'Son of the Father' lives in such a way that when He awakens his own Being in man, man becomes a mystic. In this way Jesus made it plain that the meaning of life lay hidden in the Mysteries, and that they paved the way to this meaning. He is the living Word; in Him was personified what had become ancient tradition. And the Evangelist is justified in expressing this in the sentence: In Him the Word became flesh. He rightly sees in Jesus Himself an incarnated mystery. And because of this, John's Gospel is a mystery. In order to read it rightly we must bear in mind that the facts are spiritual facts. If a priest of an ancient order had written it, he would have described traditional rites. For John, these rites took the form of a person. They became the 'Life of Jesus.' . . . If we examine the Gospel of John and behold in the sphere of pictorially physical reality the drama, of cognition enacted by the ancients, we are looking upon the Mystery itself.

In the words 'Lazarus, come forth,' we can recognize the call by which the Egyptian priest-initiators summoned back to everyday life those who had subjected themselves to the processes of 'Initiation,' which withdrew them from the world that they might die to earthly things and gain a conviction of the reality of the eternal. But with these words Jesus had revealed the secret of the Mysteries . . . For Jesus the main point in the Initiation of Lazarus was to represent before all 'the people which stand by,' an event which, according to ancient priestly wisdom, might be accomplished only in the secrecy of the Mysteries. The Initiation of Lazarus was to prepare the way for the understanding of the 'Mystery of Golgotha'. Previously only those who 'saw', - that is to say, who were initiated – were able to know something of what was achieved by Initiation; but now a conviction of the secrets of higher worlds could also be gained by those who 'have not seen and yet have believed'."

II

The Young Man in the Tomb

In Karl Koenig's, "The Mystery of John and the Cycle of the Year," he defines the expressions such as the 'rich youth', the 'young ruler' and a 'certain young man' that are found in the Gospel of John as well as the other Gospels as terms that define Lazarus. This pattern that weaves throughout the Gospels is expressive of the description of Lazarus as well as the term, 'the Beloved Disciple' - or - 'the disciple whom Jesus loved'. As Steiner had expressed in his, "Christianity as Mystical Fact," this term has a deeper esoteric meaning in that it is used to express the truth that this is someone who has been Initiated by Christ Himself. A similar expression is also used to describe Martha and Mary Magdalene, the sisters of Lazarus, to which we can surmise that they too were Initiates of Christ. (John 11:5). The phrase, young ruler, also indicates a key insight into Lazarus' background. Koenig notes that the term - ruler - is used to describe one who is of the caste of the high priesthood. Koenig describes how the separation of Lazarus/John and John ben Zebedee is made clear throughout the Gospel of John if we recognize that in the Gospel of John it is mostly a written eyewitness account of the Mystery of Golgotha. The scene of the Resurrection in John's Gospel in which Mary Magdalene sees and speaks to the Resurrected Christ and He speaks to her is explained by Koenig as possibly an account of Lazarus being present also but at the same time being silent about his presence at the tomb during their encounter with the Resurrected Christ. This, however, is difficult to substantiate. It is difficult to confirm this without any actual Imaginative research into this particular scene of the Gospel. Though it does appear that most of the Gospel of John was an eyewitness account, it would seem that such a scene as Mary Magdalene's first encounter with the Risen Christ was strictly between Mary Magdalene and Christ as Peter and the other disciple, Lazarus, left and "went away again to their home." (John 20:10). Koenig makes it clear that Lazarus/John and John, the brother of James ben Zebedee, are not one and the same individual. The Gospel of Matthew also alludes to the same with the following: "Now after six days Jesus took Peter, James and his brother John, and led them up a high mountain by themselves and was transfigured before them." (17:1). Lazarus was the brother of Martha and Mary Magdalene to which there is never any mentioning of Lazarus having a brother. The scenes in the Synoptic Gospels where John ben Zebedee is present are missing in the Gospel of John. For instance, the raising of the daughter of Jairus, the Transfiguration and the Agony in the Garden are not mentioned in the Gospel of John as well as the Sermon on the Mount, the feeding of the four thousand and the healing of the woman with an issue of blood. The disciple John in these instances was John ben Zebedee and not Lazarus/John. Koenig writes: "There is silence (in John's Gospel) regarding these events which, when described by the Synoptists, place particular emphasis on calling Peter, James and John (ben Zebedee) by name." In addition to Koenig's assertion, when Christ Jesus was brought before Annas to be judged both Peter and 'another disciple' followed Him. This other disciple was Lazarus, the rich ruler, who was "known to the high priest." The maid at the portal recognizes Peter as a follower of Christ Jesus. However, she does not implicate Lazarus. (John 18: 15-17). If Lazarus had been John of 'Peter, James and John', then it is almost certain that she would have implicated Lazarus as well as they were the most recognized Apostles of Christ Jesus. Whether the Gospel of John is a complete eyewitness account by Lazarus of the Mystery of Golgotha is debatable since there is no mentioning of John during Mary Magdalene's witnessing of the Resurrected Christ. Since, however, she was his sister her personal account was what he added to his Gospel. Koenig goes on to say: "Many sayings, miracles and deeds of Christ remain untold in this Gospel (of John)." Also, he adds that, "Lazarus tells his own story; not that of the other chosen disciples."

However, if Lazarus had been present with Mary Magdalene when Christ appeared to her why then would he not report it himself as being there along with her? Since Mary Magdalene encounters Christ while alone at the tomb, this then raises an interesting question. It seems to circle back to the Wedding at Cana when Christ speaks to his Mother and says, in Steiner's interpretation, "Something passes from me to you." As it was at the Wedding at Cana, the scene of the first sign Christ effected, there was at the tomb on Easter morning a repetition of the marriage feast at Cana as a feminine personage and Christ were interacting with one another in His first act as the Risen Christ. In a higher repetition of the scene at Cana, the Resurrection portrays a picture of what it is that weaves and flows between the Christ forces and the Sophian forces such that these forces are to become One from that time onward in our continuing evolution. It was the beginning of the resurrection of the Sophian Principle in human consciousness. In this scene, Christ appears as a tiller of the Earth and is in communion with the 'redeemed' Sophian forces which Mary Magdalene represents. Together, the Christ Principle and the Sophian Impulse become forces that over time transfigure and create a new Earth. In reading the Gospels, Mary Magdalene's encounter with the two men/angels in the Luke and John Gospels and the young man in Mark's Gospel needs to be closely examined in order to distinguish between the two men/angels and the young man. We read that in Mark's Gospel the young man in the tomb is 'sitting' while in

Luke's Gospel the two men, "stood by them in dazzling raiment." These are three separate individual apparitions. One, however, could possibly assert that in John's Gospel it reads that the two angels are sitting and thereby conclude that the young man in Mark's Gospel is one of the two angels of which the Gospel of John mentions. At closer examination we read that in John's Gospel, Mary Magdalene observes the two angels, ". . . sitting, one at the head and one at the feet. . . ." However, this encounter with the two angels in John's Gospel was during her second visit to the tomb and not during the first visit. On the first visit the two men were `standing' as narrated in Luke's Gospel. In Mark's Gospel she also encounters the young man `sitting' during her first visit to the tomb with the other women and not during the second visit. In other words, during the first visit the young man, "clothed in a white robe," was sitting while at the same time the two men were standing beside the women. The young man sitting in the tomb wearing a white robe, which is told to us only in the Gospel of Mark, was not one of the two men/angels that we read about in the Gospels of Luke and John respectively. Also, the words of the two angels in John's Gospel are not the same as in Mark and Luke because the Mark and Luke Gospels give the account of Mary Magdalene and the other women on the first visit to the tomb. Mary Magdalene went back the second time without the other women. She returns with Peter and Lazarus who then leave her to herself at the tomb when they see that the tomb is empty. It is then that the two angels of John's Gospel now ask her, "Woman, why are you weeping?" (John 20: 13). This question resonates again when Christ asks the very same question of her. (John 20: 15). The two angels are the etheric and astral sheaths of Jesus of Nazareth through which the Spirit of Christ speaks into her soul.

Again, if we put Mark's Gospel and Luke's Gospel together as an account of the first trip to the tomb by Mary Magdalene with the other women we could say that the two men in Luke's Gospel were standing while the young man of Mark's Gospel was sitting. All three made their appearance to Mary Magdalene during her first visit to the tomb. However, the young man sitting in the tomb only made one appearance to her and that was during her first visit. Luke's Gospel gives us the account of the etheric and astral sheaths of Jesus of Nazareth on the first visit to the tomb. Mark's Gospel gives us the account of the presence of the entelechy of John the Baptist enveloped by the Cosmic Aura, the Youth forces of the Christ Principle during the women's first visit to the tomb. Whereas John's Gospel also gives us the account of the presence of the etheric and astral sheaths of Jesus of Nazareth as well as the presence of the Risen Christ during Mary Magdalene's second visit. When Mary Magdalene came back the second time with Peter and Lazarus which is narrated to us in the Gospel of John the `young man' was no longer there but the two angels (the two men of the first visit in Luke's Gospel) did reappear to Mary Magdalene after Peter and

Lazarus had left and this time they were now sitting. The young man sitting in the tomb was not Christ because the two men in Luke's Gospel and the young man in Mark's Gospel confirm that He, the Christ, is not here but has Risen. All three spoke very similar words to the women at the tomb. These words were spoken spiritually to the women within the depths of their souls. All three, the two men/angels and the young man, speak similarly because their message was in concordance with one another. It should be noted that Steiner mentioned that the two men/angels were the etheric and astral replicas of Jesus of Nazareth and that the `young man' is the Cosmic Christ; that is, it is the Cosmic Aura of Christ which envelopes the entelechy of John the Baptist.

Previously it was mentioned that there is a two-sided equation to the Mystery of Golgotha. Christ was one side of the equation while humanity was the other side. Though the Mystery of Golgotha was designed to succeed as this was a window into the workings of the Gods there was no certainty that it would succeed. This was cause for great concern to the spiritual world when Christ left the heights of the spiritual realms. Never before had a God fully descended into an earthly incarnation. Yet a God of the Highest Order came to Earth and became flesh. Without the success of the human half of the equation the Mystery of Golgotha, the mission of Christ, would have been greatly diminished if not a failure all together. Christ did not initially know that the Apostles would fail since He did take them through various degrees of Initiation over the three years. Rather, He gave them the Freedom and opportunity to succeed or fail. It gradually became obvious to Christ that the Apostles could not carry the necessary comprehension through the Passion and Resurrection. This is why Christ was reticent to Thomas' remark in regard to the Initiation of Lazarus six days prior to the Passover and His anticipated death when Thomas said, ". . .Let us go, that we may die (be Initiated) with him." (John 11:16). Christ must have begun His decision to initiate only Lazarus and John the Baptist into the highest Mysteries from this point on.

From Steiner's lecture, "The Event of the Appearance of Christ in the Etheric World": In the past, " . . . human Beings were able to experience the Kingdom of Heaven outside of their own It's, in those spiritual distances they reached when they emerged from their lower selves. The human Being had to experience the Kingdom of Heaven, the spiritual world, at a distance from the I. Now this Kingdom of Heaven can not be so experienced; now the human Being has changed so much that the I must experience this kingdom within itself. The Kingdom of Heaven has approached man to such an extent that it now works into the I. John the Baptist proclaimed this to humanity, saying, 'The Kingdom of Heaven is at hand,' that is, (it) approaches the I. Previously, it was to be found outside of man, but now man must embrace in the very core of his Being, in the I, a Kingdom of Heaven (that has) now come near at hand."

Steiner then makes the following startling statement: "If there had been no human Beings at that time capable of understanding this, capable of establishing an active soul connection with the Christ, all human connection with the spiritual world would gradually have been lost and human Beings would not have accepted into their I's the connection with the Kingdom of Heaven. If all the human Beings living at such a crucial time had persisted in remaining in darkness, it might have happened that this significant event would have passed by them unnoticed. Then human souls would have become withered, desolate and depraved. To be sure, they would have continued to incarnate for a time without the Christ, but they would not have been able to implant in their I's what was necessary for them to regain their connection with the Kingdom of Heaven."

From the above excerpt it can be inferred that there were individuals who did understand the Christ and became deeply connected with Him for the sake of all humanity. It was such that their understanding benefitted us all and the whole course of human and earthly evolution. However, not everyone fully internalized the Event of Golgotha on through to the final act of the Resurrection. It was John the Baptist who had attained the most profound and comprehensive understanding of the Cosmic Christ and who carried this all-embracing connection to the Christ completely through to the Resurrection. It was an event of macrocosmic significance that will continue to have macrocosmic implications for our planetary system and the zodiacal constellations. The coalescence of Spirit wrought between Christ and John the Baptist during the Event of Golgotha has implications for the redemption of the human physical/mineral body. The human phantom body will be able to house the I to its full benefit while the mineral body will, over time, no longer stand as an eclipse to the Ego. It will become translucent in form as did Christian Rosenkreutz's body as the result of his Initiation in the Thirteenth century. This is signified by the 'young man' in the tomb in Mark's Gospel; the new human in John the Baptist. The resurrected body of Christ is reflected in the new human Form that will become a reality for all of us in the future.

In Koenig's, "The Mystery of John," he cites the following from Steiner's lecture on December 14, 1911: "All great historic events occur first of all within the human soul. They come about in such a way that one particular human being reaches within himself a new step in his existence, and this works outward and brings about the progress of all mankind." Compare this with what Steiner said in, "The Last Address": "Elijah appeared again at the very most important moment of human evolution, appeared again so that Christ Jesus Himself could give him the Initiation he was to receive for the evolution of mankind."

23

These two quotes from Steiner present emphatic indications that John the Baptist was being prepared for an especially significant role in furthering the evolution of the human race. The individuality who was once the progenitor of the human race as Adam was to become again the first human to take within himself the forces of the Christ-imbued, archetypal Resurrected Phantom of Jesus of Nazareth such that these forces pour over into the first human Being to receive them. This theme will be particularly developed later when we examine Steiner's, "The Fifth Gospel," and, "From Jesus to Christ," lecture cycles. However, the following from Steiner's, "From Jesus to Christ," expresses the vital importance of the bond between Christ and the Apostles and what it truly meant for the whole future of humanity. In Lecture VIII, Steiner said the following: "The human Phantom . . . should not have been attracted to the ashy constituents but only to the dissolving salt constituents, so that it would have taken the path of volatilization insofar as the salt constituents dissolved. In an occult sense one can say that it would have dissolved and passed over, not into the Earth but into the volatile constituents. The remarkable fact is that with the Baptism in the Jordan and the entry of the Christ Individuality into the body of the Nathan Jesus, all connection of the Phantom with the ashy constituents was wiped out; only the connection with the salt constituents remained. This is alluded to in the passage where Christ Jesus wishes to explain to His first-chosen disciples: `Through the way in which you feel yourselves united with the Christ Being, a certain possibility for the future evolution of humanity will come about. It will be possible for the one body risen from the grave - the spiritual body- to pass over into men.' That is what Christ wished to say when He used the phrase, `You are the salt of the Earth'." (Matthew 5: 13).

Steiner is referring to the redemption of the Phantom body which is to become possible for all of humanity through the fact that the Apostles were united with Christ at first. They were to be the seed element through which this act of Christ in His Resurrection of the redeemed Phantom body would begin to take hold of their Phantom bodies as well. They did not, however, stay united with Christ throughout the Crucifixion and Resurrection. Only one individual remained so. Only one individual had attained the level of a Father Initiate that could reach the Macrocosmic level of Initiation in order to remain with Christ all the way through to the Resurrection and that he understood and inwardly experienced, through being united with Christ, the dynamics of such a Macrocosmic Initiation. When the Apostles' bond with Christ was severed, John the Baptist acted as the surrogate for all Twelve once they had fled at the time of the arrest in the garden. He was then seen in the tomb on Easter morning as the "young man. . .clothed in a white robe" (Mark 16: 5). The white robe was his own purified astral body that enshrouded the redeemed Phantom of John the Baptist. John the Baptist was the first human to follow in the footsteps of Christ in this evolutionary leap.

The beginning processes of redeeming the Phantom body of John the Baptist possibly began at the moment of the arrest in the Garden of Gethsemane though John the Baptist was drawing closer to the youth forces of Christ prior to this as we will see later. There is a distinction that can be made between the `linen' that was wrapped around the `fleeing youth' in the garden and the `white robe' of the `young man in the tomb' if we compare them in meaning to the burial linen cloth of Christ when He was taken down from the Cross in Mark 15: 46 to that of the `white robes' of the saints/martyrs in Revelation 6: 11. The linen of the `fleeing youth' that was left behind was a portent of the coming death of Christ on the Cross while the `white robe' of the `young man in the tomb' gives us a picture of future humanity.

The passing of these Cosmic youth forces over onto John the Baptist is similar to the passing over of the mantle/soul forces from Elijah to Elisa. Other examples would be: Isaac passes his mantle onto Jacob; Zarathustra passes his etheric mantle onto Moses and his astral mantle onto Hermes. In Chapter 2 verses 1-18 from the Fourth Book of Kings a wonderful bridge is placed before us that connects the Old Testament to the New Testament. This also draws our attention to a purposeful similarity in the passing of the mantle of Elijah to Elisa at the Jordan River as Elijah then ascends into the spiritual world carried by, "a fiery chariot and fiery horses," to the Baptism in the Jordan of Jesus of Nazareth by John the Baptist when Christ descends with the Mantle of the spiritual world and that of the Sun forces of the Elohim and incarnates into the body of Jesus of Nazareth.

In his essay, "The Son of Man and the Cosmic Christ," (Easter 1971) Oskar Kurten likens the descent of the Holy Spirit to the Cosmic Aura of Christ at the time of the Baptism of Jesus of Nazareth in the Jordan. It is the passing of the Mantle of the spiritual world's life giving forces onto the body of Jesus of Nazareth. It is the descent of both the Spirit of Christ and His Cosmic Aura, the Holy Spirit, onto and enveloping the body of Jesus of Nazareth. Isaac passes his mantle onto Jacob his "son" which prefigures the passing of the Macrocosmic Spiritual Mantle of Christ onto Jesus. Christ is the "only-begotten Son" (John 3: 16) of the spiritual world in the sense that He is an individuated Ego Being; a Macrocosmic Ego Being. He is `begotten' in the sense that He is from the spiritual world. He has descended from it and has left the heights of the spiritual world. The spiritual worlds of the hierarchies and the World-Word, the Twelve Beings of the Zodiac which Steiner names as the Twelve World Initiators Who had Initiated Christ during the Sun Period, have passed their Mantle onto Him and He is to pass it onto us. Steiner addresses this in Lecture X of "Man in the Light of Occultism, Theosophy and Philosophy." [GA 137].

To whom was He to pass on this Mantle initially? They were His Twelve Apostles that He had first chosen. Eventually, however, it became increasingly and alarmingly evident that the Twelve could not take it up in

25

full consciousness. Finally, in the Garden of Gethsemane, the three chosen Apostles also failed to take it up in full consciousness. Even at the tomb of Christ on Easter morning His most gifted prodigy, Lazarus, could not wholly understand in full consciousness the Resurrection. (John 20: 8-9). Only the one individual whose Feast we celebrate at the time of the year when the Earth's Spirit, the Christ, has ascended to the far reaches of the cosmos out into the constellations while we take in these Cosmic Ego forces into us. It was John the Baptist who was there to carry the Mantle in full consciousness. It was he who sat in the tomb in spiritual form in a white robe which can also be understood as the robe of the Cosmic Aura of Christ that permeated his entelechy while he said to the women at the tomb, ". . .He has Risen. . . ." It was he whose incarnations on Earth extend back to Adam.

According to Wilhelm Kelber in his booklet, "The Son of Man," the Mantle of Christ was an aura that protected Christ and vivified the body of Jesus to the point that if He did not willingly sacrifice the aura, Christ would not have been able to pass through death. Also, the timing of His death on the cross was predetermined. The following passages from the Gospels support these suppositions: "For this reason the Father loves me, because I lay down my life that I may take it up again. No one takes it from me, but I lay it down of myself. I have the power to lay it down, and I have the power to take it up again. Such is the command I have received from my Father." (John 10: 17-18). "They sought to seize Him; and He went forth out of their hands." (John 10: 39). To His captors in the Garden of Gethsemane: "I was daily with you in the Temple teaching, and you did not lay hands on me. But it is so that the Scriptures may be fulfilled." (Mark 14: 49). And after confronting the Pharisees at one point: "Jesus spoke these words in the treasury, while teaching in the temple. And no one seized Him, because His hour had not yet come." (John 8: 20).

Koenig makes an intriguing observation by bringing to the reader's attention that in the construction of each of the Gospels there is mention of John the Baptist immediately prior to the `Feeding of the Five Thousand'. The Synoptic Gospels underscore his death while the Gospel of John quotes Christ speaking of John the Baptist as His Witness. However, only in the Gospel of John is there any mention of the presence of a 'young boy', a youth, at the time of this particular Initiation of the Apostles. (John 6: 9). We then read in John 6: 3: "Jesus therefore went up the mountain, and sat there with His disciples." Also in John 6:10: "Jesus then said, `Make the people recline'." In these passages there are strong allusions to an Initiation of Imagination to which the Apostles see many individuals who were fed in part a seed force of the aura of Christ. The whole construction of the Gospels placing the mentioning of John the Baptist, and specifically his death, immediately prior to the feeding of the five thousand leads us to unveil the youth that is mentioned. Steiner had noted that at the time of the death of

John the Baptist he then became the group-soul of the Apostles. The youth with the five loaves and two fishes is a window into the activity of the aura of Christ for a future humanity of the fifth cultural epoch, beginning in the fifteenth century; a future humanity that will later carry the Christ Principle to fruition in their successive incarnations.

Koenig writes: "In the Gospel of Matthew the feeding of the five thousand follows the scene of the beheading. (Matthew 14: 14-21). This is no earthly event but a miracle enacted in the etheric realm. Hungering mankind is nourished as from the spiritual world. The miracle which was performed then reaches right into our own time. The Gospel describes how before the feeding began a youth appeared (John's Gospel) carrying five loaves and two fishes in his hands and offers them to Christ. This youth is the Adam-John Being who was raised, reawakened by Christ. This purified Adam-Being is the helper in the feeding of the five thousand. It is the Adam-John Being who is led by Christ into the body of the resurrected Lazarus."

In the Gospels we are already seeing, by means of their purposeful construction, that John the Baptist is to be the bearer of the Cosmic Aura of Christ and that this Impulse would gradually work into the souls of the Twelve Apostles. This is presented to us even prior to the raising of Lazarus. A new Adam is being prepared in the soul and spirit of John the Baptist. The 'youthful' aura of Christ and John the Baptist are already beginning to be united. Koenig also brings the following passage to our attention which proves to be another proclamation to the youthful forces of the Aura of Christ: "And they came to Capernaum. When He was at home, He asked them, `What were you arguing about on the way?' But they kept silence, for on the way they had discussed with one another which of them was the greatest. And sitting down, He called the Twelve and said to them, `If any man wishes to be first, he shall be last of all, and servant of all.' And He took a little child, and sat him in their midst, and taking him into His arms, He said to them, `Whoever receives one such little child for My sake, receives Me; and whoever receives Me, receives not Me but Him Who sent Me'." (Mark 9: 32-36). This passage is a reference to the Cosmic Aura of Christ that is being taken up by John the Baptist as he becomes the group-soul of the Twelve and through him the Impulse of the Christ Principle is to seed itself into the souls of the Apostles also. They are admonished to take up the new Christ forces into their souls as did John the Baptist at the `feeding of the five thousand'. It seems plausible to say that there appeared before them John the Baptist in spirit who is referred to as the youth in this instance and that he appears again as the young man in the tomb.

In Andrew Welburn's, "The Beginnings of Christianity," we are supplied with additional indications that equate John the Baptist to the young man in the tomb and his being One with the Cosmic Aura of Christ (pp. 102-103): "So Jesus goes to his death, but the curious youthful figure slips away unharmed leaving his linen garment behind. Are we here on the place of outer, physical events - or is the apparition of the Youth a mystical element, a truth of the scene on a higher level? Steiner suggested the latter. He pointed out that we meet the same Youth again later in the Gospel, when the women go to the tomb: ' And entering the sepulcher they saw a young man clothed in a white garment, sitting on the right-hand side . . . ' (Mark 16:5). The Youth announces to them the Resurrection of Christ and his future work. Steiner described the youth as an `Imagination': not a symbol but an imaginative formwhich was a real experience for those who went through the ordeals and processes of Initiation, or for those who through other circumstances had become open to spiritual events. The Youth is an Imagination of the `Cosmic Impulse' of the Christ. The youthful Cosmic Impulse appears alongside the Son of Man who goes to his death on the Cross. But it cannot be grasped by his earthly persecutors, it slips away. This vision is unique to Mark. `No other Gospel tells us that in the moment when men, through their failure to comprehend, lay human hands on the Son of Man, the cosmic element eludes them, the youthful cosmic element which from that decisive point onwards is united with earthly evolution.' It reappears, now clothed in shining white, in the glory of the resurrection, at the end of the Gospel, when the Youth announces the onward working of the Christ. `He goes before you into Galilee!' "

In addition to Welburn's description of the youth as an Imagination and his citing of Steiner's lecture cycle on Mark's Gospel (Lecture IX) in the above, Galilee can be understood as an expression of the continual working of the Christ in the etheric element. Welburn then goes on to write (pg.105): "In the original, esoteric version of Mark we thus find the primary appearance of the Youth in the linen cloth. He is the young man who is being baptized into the cosmic mysteries by Jesus, wearing only his baptismal robe. He reappears later before the visionary eye of the evangelist, as the representative of that cosmic Mystery revealed by the Christ. First we see him again in the half-light of the Garden of Gethsemane, then clad in white in the splendor of the resurrection. And he appears again in early Christian mysticism as the Angel of Baptism, the Young Man who unfolds to Hermas the meaning of his cosmic visions."

In the above, Welburn is addressing the, "Secret Gospel of Mark." He is referring to the Initiation of Lazarus as it is described in the Secret Gospel of Mark; the Initiation in which John the Baptist, the 'Angel of Baptism', was also present and became One with Lazarus. From another ancient document which Welburn cites, the Young Man is identified as the Angel of Metanoia; that is; "the transformation of mind." (pp.103-104): "First, however, we may observe that the figure of the Youth appearing in a mystical and cosmic connection is not unique to Mark and his tradition. Nor does it belong solely to the Gnostic end of the spiritual spectrum of early Christianity. There is something similar in a work that has come down to us, and that seems to have its roots in the Essene-Ebionite wing of Christianity . . . Its title however is `The Shepherd of Hermas' - which, in conjunction with a number of scenes in the book that recall episodes in the Gnostic-Hermetic writings, has prompted some to suppose that the author is also in touch with such pagan traditions of gnosis and is bringing them into Christian form. Anyone who had read in the Hermetic scriptures the opening revelation of Poimandres ("Man-Shepherd") to the Egyptian sage would certainly have found much to approve in the `Shepherd of Saint Hermas.' In the course of a series of Visions, Hermas is shown tremendous scenes of cosmic creation: but he cannot understand the stupendous works of the angelic hierarchies, and is left bewildered by his vision. It is then that a Young Man appears to him, and begins to guide him toward cosmic understanding. It is only gradually that Hermas also learns to recognize this Young Man. He is the 'Angel of metanoia' (repentance; 'transformation of mind'). In the Shepherd of Hermas, then, a Youth also appears as a cosmic guide and instructor to the seer. And he turns out to be the Angel of initiatory transformation, metanoia, which here as in early Christianity generally, means: baptism. It is through baptismal regeneration that the seer finds his way into cosmic reality, guided by the visionary Youth."

The very fact that this Being was often referred to as a Young Man and became known as the Angel of Metanoia in the early centuries of Christianity and to which he became the Angel of Baptism or Initiatory transformation leads us straight to the ongoing work of John the Baptist. His acts of Initiation had now been elevated from his baptizing others in the Jordan to acts of Initiation from out of the spiritual world. So far we have come to see that the coalescence of the Cosmic Principle of Christ with John the Baptist can be identified with what is called the `youth'. Another individual who was also identifiable as a youth and was also united with the cosmic youth forces was Lazarus. In Edward R. Smith's book, "The Disciple Whom Jesus Loved," he gives a cogent dissertation in identifying Lazarus as the disciple whom Jesus loved as well as identifying him as the rich, young ruler. At first, Smith reminds us that the term, `loved', refers to one Initiated by Christ as Lazarus is Christ's closest and most advanced pupil in the Mysteries. He writes: "When one was said to have been `loved' by the teacher and initiator, it meant that this one was the one most highly initiated by him. So when John's Gospel speaks of "the disciple whom Jesus loved," it was speaking of Lazarus. This phrase was never used before John 11, but commenced to be used immediately thereafter. This is the first and most important thing we have to remember in unveiling Evangelist John--- it refers to Lazarus, whose name was changed when he had gone through this experience, just as others in the Bible had their names changed under similar circumstances, not the least of whom were Simon who became Peter, and Saul who became Paul--- but there were many others."

Previously, it was mentioned that Koenig identified John the Baptist as the youth at the feeding of the five thousand when he began to take on the cosmic forces of Christ and to which he also began his activity in the souls of the Apostles as their group-soul spirit. Smith adds to this in the following: "At that feeding, there were five loaves and two fishes. John calls this a 'sign' (John 6: 14). The two fishes are the symbol of Pisces, the five loaves for the five thousand represent the fifth Cultural Age, the Age of the Fishes. Christ, the Lamb of God, came in the Age of the Lamb. But in this passage he 'lifts up his eyes' (John 6: 5) and looks out at the future multitudes in the Age of Pisces. The significance of the sign of the fish is that it points to our Cultural Age as the time when humanity would begin to comprehend the Christ. John's Gospel was written for that Age, as was his Apocalypse." However, throughout the Gospels we see the progressive failings of the Apostles as potential hosts for the Cosmic Aura of Christ. Smith writes the following while referring to the three special occasions in the Ministry of Christ when He selected Peter, James and John from the others: "The important thing about these three instances is that they portray an increasing sequence of Jesus' attempt to bring the three disciples to a higher level of spiritual consciousness. The first of these is the raising of Jairus' daughter, the second is the Transfiguration, and the third occurs in the Garden of Gethsemane. Surprisingly, all three are found in all three synoptic Gospels while none is found in John's Gospel---the reason being that while Zebedee John was present for all three, the Evangelist John was not present for any. Something very special is being told to us by the sequence of these three events. We shall see in them a progressive failure on the part of Peter, James and John to reach the level of spiritual insight required for going all the way to the Cross with Jesus in their spiritual consciousness. And we shall see at what point Jesus recognizes this and initiates Lazarus for that purpose. Peter, James and John represented humanity in the Cultural Age of the Lamb, while John was prepared to represent it in the Cultural Age of the Fishes (Pisces), our present age."

E.R. Smith also has this interesting footnote in his work: "Finally, as a basis for their understanding that it was the Christ who ate with them, note that immediately before they communed with him, Peter brought them one hundred fifty-three fish (John 20: 11). The esoteric significance of the otherwise puzzling number must be deciphered by adding the digits. When the one, five and three are added they total nine, the full ninefold nature of the 'one like a son of man' reflected by the nine characteristics (three times three; e.g., 1. long robe, golden girdle and snow-white hair; 2. flaming eyes, burnished bronze-like feet and voice like many waters; 3. seven stars, two-edged sword and sun shining in full strength) in Evangelist John's Apocalypse (Rev. 1: 13-16; see 'The Burning Bush', pp. 16, 151, 187, 214, 433 and 646). This is the basis for their communion and knowledge that "it was the Lord" (John 21: 12)."

As an added note to the number `nine', the same can be said for humanity's number; that is, the number 144,000 which we also find in the Apocalypse. In this number we find the reflection of the ninefold nature of the Son of Man in the ninefold nature of humanity. The ninefold nature of humanity would be: physical body, etheric body, astral body, sentient soul, intellectual-mind soul, consciousness-spiritual soul, Spirit Self (Manas), Life Spirit (Buddhi) and Spirit Man (Atma).

Continuing with Smith in regard to Peter, James and John: "Then we come to the Transfiguration itself and we are told that Jesus spoke with Moses and Elijah. Luke tells us that all three, Peter, James and John, slept through this discussion and only woke to see their presence (Luke 9: 30-32), meaning, of course, that they were not conscious of a significant part of the main event. Later we know that Christ perceived Peter's shortcomings and told him that he would deny the Christ three times, as he in fact did. But Christ was aware of Peter's shortcomings long before that. We must now go to Mark's Gospel because in the light of modern developments it is the most illustrative (though Matthew and Luke contain most all of it too). Mark demonstrates step by step the successive inadequacies of these three, particularly of Zebedee John.

First, shortly after the Transfiguration, Zebedee John tells Jesus that they saw a man casting out demons in Jesus' name and forbade him (Mark 9: 38-39). Jesus had to explain to him how the action was the wrong thing to do. So by now all three have slept through part of the Transfiguration, and Zebedee John has then demonstrated his misunderstanding. We move into Chapter 10 and the next thing in sequence is Mark's account of what we know as the `rich, young ruler' incident (Mark 10: 17-27). . . . The next thing in the Gospel of Mark as it is in the canon is the request by the Zebedee brothers, James and John, to have a special place on both sides of Jesus when he comes in his glory (Mark 10: 35-37). Jesus tells them they don't know what they are asking (vs. 38). Imagine the effrontery---impossible in one with a high spiritual consciousness.

Now let us return to the 'rich, young ruler.' This account is found at Mark 10: 17-27, sandwiched between the deficiencies of all three at the Transfiguration as well as the correction of Zebedee John's improper action, on the one hand, and the bald request for privilege on the other. And what is said about the youth? It says, `And Jesus looking upon him loved him.' (vs. 21). Nowhere in any Gospel is Jesus said to have `loved' an individual save in the case of Lazarus and his sisters, Mary Magdalene and Martha."

At this point it is critical to examine what many believe is the most significant fragment from the, "Secret Gospel of Mark," which Smith quotes in his book from Morton Smith's, "Clement of Alexandria and a Secret Gospel of Mark.": "And they come into Bethany and a certain woman, whose brother had died, was there. And, coming, she prostrated herself before Jesus

31

and says to him, 'Son of David, have mercy on me.' But the disciples rebuked her. And Jesus being angered, went off with her into the garden where the tomb was. And straightway a great cry was heard from the tomb. And going near, Jesus rolled away the stone from the door of the tomb. And straightway, going in where the youth was, he stretched forth his hand and raised him, seizing his hand. But the youth, looking upon him, loved him, and began to beseech him that he might be with him. And going out of the tomb, they came into the house of the youth, for he was rich. And after six days Jesus told him what to do, and in the evening the youth comes to him, wearing a linen cloth over his naked body. And he remained with him that night, for Jesus taught him the mystery of the kingdom of God."

Smith continues: "One is `Naked' when only the Ego, soul, or `I Am,' is considered. One thus stands `naked' in judgment. Since this sentence seems to relate to the more esoteric passage of the Secret Gospel, it is probably better to see in it the reality that the soul of Lazarus/John at that moment stood spiritually before Christ and the capturing band."Smith then writes a refutation to the belief that Lazarus, as the youth, fled on the night of the arrest of Christ Jesus: "On the contrary, that Lazarus/John did not flee is suggested by the statement in the Secret Gospel, `And he remained with him that night, for Jesus taught him the mystery of the Kingdom of God.' `That night' was the night of the trial. Moreover, we shall see that Lazarus/John had a status among the authorities that the other disciples did not have, and thus had no reason to flee them."

In Steiner's lectures on the Gospel of Mark he tells us that the `fleeing youth' is the Cosmic Christ. It is the narrative account of a suprasensible event in which the Cosmic Aura of Christ was loosening itself from the Being of Christ. Later we will look at this cycle of lectures in depth; particularly the ninth lecture. When we begin to see Lazarus, in the excerpt that was quoted above, in a 'linen cloth', it should be noted as well that John the Baptist is now interpenetrated within the consciousness soul of Lazarus. In regard to the `linen cloth', it unveils the mystery in which all that Christ was to give to Lazarus was thereby given to John the Baptist and more, as the linen cloth is converted to the `white robe' at the Resurrection. Smith notes that Steiner expressed to his physician, Ita Wegman, this understanding that John the Baptist interpenetrated the consciousness-soul of Lazarus. Smith writes: "The doctor recorded and notarized it. It reads: `At the awakening of Lazarus, the spiritual Being, John the Baptist, who since his death had been the overshadowing Spirit of the disciples, penetrated from above into Lazarus as far as the Consciousness Soul; the Being of Lazarus himself, from below, intermingled with the spiritual Being of John the Baptist from above. After the awakening of Lazarus, this Being is Lazarus-John, the disciple whom Jesus loved'." Smith also gives us a descriptive analysis of the name John in the following: "The name `John' came from the Hebrew, Johanan, which combined Yahweh or Yah with `Anna'. And the `Anna' meant `grace'. The Christ event was an event of grace, as we find in the Prologue of John's Gospel. The name `John' was unique in New Testament times because then it could be connected only with the source of grace, the Christ. In the New Testament, the name `John' had to describe one who was a forerunner or announcer of the Christ. This is why so much emphasis is laid on the fact that the Baptist had to be called `John' in the birth story in Luke's Gospel."

As noted previously, the Trichotomy of the understanding of the Mystery of Golgotha is completed in the three individuals that were Initiated by Christ Himself. Lazarus comprehended the Crucifixion, John the Baptist comprehended the Resurrection and Paul comprehended the Ascension. Smith cites an excerpt of Lecture XII from Steiner's, "The Gospel of St. John," cycle which underscores Lazarus' special connection with the Crucifixion: "The Mother of Jesus - the Virgin Sophia in the esoteric meaning of Christianity – stands at the foot of the Cross, and from the Cross the Christ says to the Disciple whom He loved: `Henceforth, this is thy Mother' and from this hour the Disciple took her unto himself. This means: `That force which was in My astral body and made it capable of becoming bearer of the Holy Spirit, I now give over to thee; thou shalt write down what this astral body has been able to acquire through its development.' `And the Disciple took her unto himself,' that means he wrote the Gospel of St. John. And this Gospel of St. John is the Gospel in which the writer has concealed powers which develop the Virgin Sophia. At the Cross, the mission was entrusted to him of receiving that force as his mother and of being the true, genuine interpreter of the Messiah."

III

The Nativities

Up to this point, in this study, a variety of works by several writers have been presented. These writers have written works, in one form or another, that have been useful in establishing a basis from which to build the theme of understanding John the Baptist as one who is deeply connected with the Cosmic Principle of Christ. This, thereby, deepens our awareness of what this means for the future evolution of humanity and the Earth. However, it is the spiritual research of Rudolf Steiner which is the cornerstone of all that is in this work. In Sergei Prokofieff's, "The Eternal Individuality: Towards a Karmic Biography of Novalis," he opens by explaining that Elijah was, according to Steiner, a `Boddhisattva-like' Being because of his partial incarnation. Centuries later, John the Baptist was similar in nature. Steiner also spoke of an Angel that worked through John the Baptist and according to Prokofieff the Nirmanakaya of Buddha and the Angel that appeared before the shepherds in the fields both influenced the development of John the Baptist at the time of his birth. He writes: "The Ego of John is, therefore, from the time of his birth, under this twofold influencewhich proceeds from two Beings: an Angel and the Nirmanakaya of Buddha. One could also say, the Nirmanakaya of Buddha `awakens' the Ego of John the Baptist in his earthly incarnation, in the sixth month of Elizabeth's pregnancy. . . ."

Prokofieff ties the Luke Gospel and the Mark Gospel together by highlighting two similar themes of both Gospels. In the Luke Gospel there is the Angel who announces the birth of Jesus and in the opening of the Mark Gospel we are presented with the words of Isaiah which are directed to the identification of John the Baptist as the `messenger'. Prokofieff states: "In each case we have one and the same proclamation issuing from one and the same Angelic Being. In each case the proclamation has to do with the birth or the coming of the `Ego, the ruler of the soul-forces': this is how Rudolf Steiner translates into today's language the word `Kyrios', Lord, that we find in both Gospels. Of John he adds the following: `Hence John the Baptist declared to his disciples: Through the Waterman Initiation, I can place at the disposal of my Angel only those powers which enable him to proclaim the coming of Kyrios, the Lord'."

Who is this Angel of John the Baptist? The circumstances surrounding the birth of John the Baptist would suggest that it is the former Angel of Buddha who had been released from the care of Buddha as Buddha's guardian Angel. Once the Gautama-Boddhisattva had become a Buddha his Angel was thereby released. This Angel was known in Teutonic Mythology as Vidar. In the Luke Gospel we are presented with the enigmatic figure of Mary, the Mother of the Nathan Jesus; that is, the Jesus that descended from the David and Nathan ancestry. Regardless of her mysterious nature, she has always been venerated through the centuries. Rudolf Steiner's spiritual research into the Akashic record has established that her incarnation 2,000 years ago was her first and only incarnation. In contrast, we find that the Mother Mary of the Matthew Gospel has had many incarnations. This difference in terms of reincarnation raises the questions: who was Mary of the Luke Gospel and why was her incarnation a one-time event? Sergei Prokofieff may have provided an answer in addressing the Vidar Mystery, though he does not make any claim that Mary of the Luke Gospel is connected with Vidar. In, "The Cycle of the Year as a Path of Initiation," Prokofieff addresses two lectures of Steiner. In the chapter entitled - "The Vidar Mystery" - Prokofieff refers to Steiner who had spoken of a Being from Teutonic mythology in his lectures of June 17, 1910 in Kristiania and December 21,1913 in Bochum. This Being is named Vidar. Prokofieff proposes that this Being was the guardian Angel of the Gautama-Boddhisattva. This Angel was freed to ascend to the ranks of the Archangels when the Gautama-Boddhisattva became a Buddha in the 6th. century B.C. According to Prokofieff, Vidar renounced its ascent for 2,500 years as a sacrifice, but retained the form of an Archangel. During this time, Vidar was a Being among the Hierarchy of Angels but having the inner nature of an Archangel with the Spirit-Self (Manas) and Life-Spirit (Buddhi) spiritual sheaths. This Being later became a part of the Hierarchy of Archangels in 1879 and took the place of the Archangel Michael among the ranks of the Archangels as the leader of the Archangels and as the, "guardian of the Nathan Jesus," in the spiritual world. The Luke Gospel mentions an Angel and the Host of Angels that appeared before the shepherds in the fields tending their flocks who 'announce' to them the tidings of the birth of Jesus in Bethlehem. The term 'shepherds' is a Mystery reference to those who are the Initiates of the inner path of 'Inspiration'; that is, spiritual hearing. According to Steiner's studies of the Luke Gospel it was the Nirmanakaya (Spirit-Self) of Buddha that appears to the shepherds as the Host of Angels. Prokofieff adds that the Angel which announced the birth of Jesus of Nazareth and appeared before the shepherds was the Angel-Archangel Vidar. He then goes on to write that Vidar was also the Angel that appeared to Christ-Jesus and rejuvenated the body of Christ-Jesus in the Garden of Gethsemane. This appearance of the Angel in the Garden is only mentioned in the Luke Gospel (Luke 22: 43). Prokofieff identifies the Angel at the beginning of the Luke Gospel and the Angel in the Garden of Gethsemane as one and the same Angel.

35

Prokofieff asserts that Vidar is the former Angel of Buddha. He also postulates that there was an 'inseparable connection' between the Nathan Jesus and Vidar. Steiner mentions that the maternal astral-soul sheath of the Nathan Jesus separates from him at the age of twelve as this discarded astral sheath then unites with the Nirmanakaya of Buddha. Later, the Nirmanakaya of Buddha now overshadows and inspires John the Baptist in his later ministry. Another point of interest is Steiner's account of how the Nirmanakaya of Buddha, working through the Nathan Jesus, activates the embryo of John the Baptist and advances and develops the Ego of John the Baptist during Elizabeth's pregnancy. Mary was present at the enlivening of the Baptist's Ego and it was the maternal astral-soul sheath of Jesus which descended from Mary onto the Nathan Jesus that was later taken up by the Buddha. Prokofieff adds that the maternal formative life-body, the etheric sheath, of the Nathan Jesus is taken up by Vidar at approximately seven years of age and as Vidar was the Angel in the Garden of Gethsemane as Prokofieff claims, it is these youthful, etheric life forces which rejuvenate Christ Jesus. He continues by saying that this maternal etheric sheath contains, to a 'high degree', the unfallen, youthful, human etheric forces of the Adam soul; that is, the Tree of Life forces. If the Angel-Archangel Vidar gave life sustaining forces to the body of the Nathan Jesus at the end of its mission in the Garden of Gethsemane did he also give life to this body at its beginning at the time of the birth of the Nathan Jesus? Since Vidar can be considered the guardian of the Nathan Jesus in the spiritual world, can this same Being be considered the guardian of the Nathan Jesus in the physical realm? Prokofieff writes that the Nathan Jesus was directed and guided by the Archangel Michael in three pre-Golgotha sacrifices which transpired in the spiritual world before Christ's incarnation into Jesus of Nazareth at the Baptism in the Jordan and that Vidar will guide and direct the Nathan Jesus in three post-Golgotha stages. Further, he states that the Nathan Jesus soul was completely on its own in the physical realm; that is, no guidance from Michael or Vidar on Earth. However, Prokofieff says that the mission of Vidar is to fashion the etheric form of the Etheric Christ now in our age and in the future. If this is the mission of Vidar, did Vidar also possibly have the mission of fashioning the physical, etheric, and astral-soul bodies of the Cosmic Human, the soul of the Nathan Jesus, into its microcosmic form in Jesus of Nazareth? Could Vidar perhaps have been the guardian and original possessor of the maternal astral and etheric sheaths which later would have directly descended from him to Mary then to Jesus of Nazareth if he, as the guardian of the Nathan Jesus, had been profoundly connected with Mary of the Luke Gospel? It should also be noted that although Zarathustra, who according to Rudolf Steiner's research of the Akashic record incarnated as Jesus of the Matthew Gospel, that is, he descended from the David and Solomon ancestry, at that time was a very advanced human individuality, he was not able to incarnate into the bodies of

36

the Nathan Jesus until after the maternal sheaths had separated from the Nathan Jesus. Zarathustra incarnated into the Nathan Jesus soul during the time of the Feast of the Passover when the Nathan Jesus was twelve years of age. What had lived within the Nathan Jesus as an Ego until his twelfth year is described by Steiner in Lecture VIII in his, "From Jesus to Christ," lecture cycle in the following manner: " . . . it was indeed something we can think of, in contrast to other human Egos, as an empty sphere still completely virginal with regard to all earth experiences - a nothing, a negative, in this respect. Hence it seemed a though the Nathan-child, described in the Luke Gospel, really had no Ego; as though he consisted only of physical, etheric and astral body. And it is quite adequate if at first we say that an Ego, developed as Egos had developed in Atlantean and post-Atlantean times, was not there at all in the Luke Jesus child." In the 'three days' at the Temple, Zarathustra's Ego incarnates into the soul and body of the Nathan Jesus. (Luke 2: 41-52).Steiner addresses the question of Zarathustra and the Nathan soul in Lecture IV from his cycle on the Gospel of St. Luke: "Zarathustra was a great and unique Individuality, an altogether exceptional case. Yet not even Zarathustra himself could have ensouled the body of Jesus up to the time of puberty in such a way as to enable the discarded astral sheath to unite with the Nirmanakaya of Buddha. Whence, then, came the great vivifying, vitalizing power of the Nathan Jesus-child?

It came from the Mother-Lodge of humanity directed by the sublime Sun-Initiate, the Manu. A great individualized power had been nurtured and fostered there. This individualized power, this `Individuality', was then sent down into the child born of the parents called `Joseph' and `Mary' in the Gospel of St. Luke. Who was this Being? To answer this question we must go back to the time before the Luciferic influence had penetrated into the astral body of man. This influence approached humanity at the time when the ancestral human couple were living on the Earth. This ancestral couple had been strong enough to master human substance and to incarnate, but had not been strong enough to resist the Luciferic influence. The effects of the influence extended into the astral bodies of this couple too, with the consequence that it was impossible to allow all the forces that were in `Adam and Eve' to be transmitted to their descendants. The physical body had necessarily to be transmitted through the generations, but the leadership of humanity held back a portion of the etheric body. This was expressed by saying: `Men have eaten of the Tree of Knowledge of Good and Evil' - that is to say, they have partaken of the Luciferic influence; but it was also said: `The possibility of eating also of the Tree of Life must now be taken from them.' This means that certain of the forces of the etheric body were kept back and did not pass on to the descendants. Thus after the Fall, certain forces were no longer in `Adam', and the still guiltless part of his Being was nurtured and fostered in the great Mother-Lodge of humanity. This was, so to speak, the

37

Adam-soul as yet untouched by human guilt, not yet entangled in what had actually caused the 'Fall' of man. These pristine forces of the Adam-Individuality were preserved; they were there and were then led as a virginal 'Ego' to the child born to Joseph and Mary. Thus in his early years this Jesus-child bore within him the power of the original progenitor of earthly humanity.

This soul had remained young in the true sense. It had not been led through incarnations but had been kept at a very early stage . . . . Who, then, was the Being in the child born to Joseph and Mary of the Nathan line? The progenitor of humanity, the 'old Adam' as a 'new Adam!' This secret was known to St. Paul and lies behind his words. And St. Luke, the writer of the Gospel - who was a pupil of St. Paul - knew it too. For this reason he speaks of it in a special way. He knew that a very definite process was necessary in order that this spiritual substance might be led down to humanity; he knew that a blood relationship reaching back to 'Adam' was necessary. Hence for Joseph he shows a lineage reaching back to Adam who issued directly from the spiritual world and in the words of the Gospel was a 'son of God'. The sequence of generations is traced back to Godhood.

A mystery of great significance is contained in the genealogical chapter of St. Luke's Gospel, namely that homogeneous blood had to flow through the generations and unbroken sequence be maintained until the last descendant, in order that the spirit too might be led down to the descendants when the time was fulfilled. And so this infinitely youthful Being was united with the body born of Joseph and Mary of the Nathan line - a Being untouched by earthly destinies, a young soul whose powers, if we wanted to discover their origin, would have to be traced back to ancient Lemuria. This Being alone was strong enough to penetrate into the astral sheath and, when this sheath was detached, to pass over to it the forces it needed in order to establish a living union with the Nirmanakaya of Buddha.

We may therefore ask: What is actually described to us in the Gospel of St. Luke when it speaks of Jesus of Nazareth? In the first place it describes a human Being whose physical body, in respect of blood-kinship, is to be traced back to Adam - to the times when, in the period of devastation on the Earth, humanity was saved through an ancestral pair. It further describes the incarnation of a soul who had waited the longest before incarnating. In the Nathan Jesus-child there was present the Adam-soul as it was before the Fall - the soul which had waited the longest. We may therefore say, fantastic as it will seem to modern humanity, that the Individuality who had been led into the Jesus-child by the great Mother-Lodge had not only descended from the physically oldest generations of mankind but was also, in a sense, the incarnation of the very first member of humanity. We know now who was presented in the temple and shown to Simeon, and who, according to St. Luke, was the 'Son of God'. St. Luke was not speaking of the present human Being but was testifying that this was the reincarnation of a Being who was the earliest blood-ancestor of all the generations."

In the above lecture, Steiner had made reference to the, "pristine forces of the Adam-Individuality." These particular forces are of the etheric body and are known esoterically as the Tree of Life. They were restored to the reincarnated Adam, John the Baptist, who became the first human to receive them at the time of the Resurrection as the, "young man in the tomb sitting on the right side clothed in a white robe". John the Baptist became the seed force for all humanity when he received the newly restored forces of the Tree of Life into his soul and his Phantom. This made it possible for all humans to receive this same Impulse from the Christ which redeems and transfigures the human Phantom; the human physical body. Steiner also mentions, in the above excerpt, the expression: Son of God. In his lecture cycle, "The Bhagavad Gita and the Epistles of St. Paul," he speaks about the Manu Individualities that have appeared throughout the course of human evolution as Sons of God. From the following, we can begin to understand the Christ Being as the Macrocosmic Manu; the Macrocosmic 'Son of God.' From Lecture III: "Let us suppose that in olden times there was a man who, in the truest sense of the words, had brought Manas to expression within him, who had certainly in himself experienced Ahamkara, but had allowed this as an individual element to retire more into the background and on account of his external activity had cultivated Manas; then according to the laws of the older, smaller, human cycles - and only quite exceptional men could have experienced this - such a man would have had to be a great law-giver, a leader of great masses of people. And one would not have been satisfied to designate him in the same way as other men, but would have called him after his prominent characteristic, a Manas-bearer; whereas another might only be called a senses-bearer. One would have said: That is a Manas-bearer, he is a Manu. When we come across designations pertaining to those olden times, we must take them as descriptive of the most prominent principle of a man's human organization, that which most strongly expressed itself in him in that particular incarnation. Suppose that in a particular man what was most specially expressed was that he felt divine inspiration within him, that he had put aside all question of ruling his actions and studies by what the external world teaches through the senses and by what reason teaches through the brain, but listened instead in all things to the Divine Word which spoke to him, and made himself a messenger for the Divine Substance that spoke out of him! Such a man would have been called a Son of God. In the Gospel of St. John, such men were still called Sons of God, even at the very beginning of the first chapter.

The essential thing was that everything else was left out of consideration when this significant part was expressed. Everything else was unimportant. Suppose we were to meet two men; one of whom had been just an ordinary man, who allowed the world to act upon him through his senses and reflected upon it afterwards with the intellect attached to his brain; the other one into whom the word of divine wisdom had radiated. According to the old ideas we should have said: This first one is a man, he is born of a father and

39

mother, was begotten according to the flesh. In the case of the other, who was a messenger of the Divine Substance, no consideration would be given to that which makes up an ordinary biography, as would be the case with the first who contemplated the world through his senses and by means of the reason belonging to his brain. To write such a biography of the second man would have been folly. For the fact of his bearing a fleshly body was only accidental, and not the essential thing; that was, so to speak, only the means through which he expressed himself to other men. Therefore we say: The Son of God is not born of flesh but of a Virgin, he is born straight from the Spirit; that is to say, what is essential in him, through which he is of value to humanity, descends from the Spirit, and in the olden times it was that alone which was honored. In certain schools of initiation it would have been considered a great sin to write an ordinary biography, which only alluded to everyday occurrences, of a person of whom it had been recognized that he was remarkable because of the higher principles of his human nature. Anyone who has preserved even a little of the sentiments of those old times cannot but consider biographies such as those written of Goethe as in the highest degree absurd. Now let us remember that in those olden times mankind lived with ideas and feelings such as these, and then we can understand how this old humanity was permeated with the conviction that such a Manu, in whom Manas was the prevailing principle, appears but seldom, that he must wait long epochs before he can appear." [December 30, 1912; GA142; source: www.elib.com].

It is the Christ who leads the way for our own development of Manas in the next condition of consciousness: the Jupiter Planetary condition of consciousness. In this present Planetary condition of consciousness, the Earth Manvantara, He is the Macrocosmic Ego and Universal Archetype for the evolution of our Egohood.

Steiner then gave the following in regard to the Ego of John the Baptist in Lecture V from his cycle on the Gospel of St. Luke: "A forerunner of Jesus of Nazareth was to arise in John the Baptist. To say more about the Individuality of the Baptist will only be possible as time goes on. But to begin with we will consider the picture presented to us - John as the herald of the Being who was to come in Jesus. John proclaimed this by gathering together and summarizing with infinite power everything contained in the Old Law. What the Baptist wished to bring home to men was that there must be observance of what was written in the Old Law but had grown old in civilization and had been forgotten; it was mature, but was no longer heeded. Therefore what John required above all was the power possessed by a soul born as a mature - even over-mature - soul into the world. He was born of old parents; from the very beginning his astral body was pure and cleansed of all the forces which degrade man, because the aged parents were unaffected by passion and desire. There again, profound wisdom is expressed in the Gospel of St. Luke. For such an Individuality, too, provision is made in the

40

Mother-Lodge of humanity. Where the great Manu guides and directs the processes of evolution in the spiritual realm, from thence the streams are sent whithersoever they are needed. An Ego such as that of John the Baptist was born into a body under the immediate guidance and direction of the great Mother-Lodge of humanity in the central sanctuary of earthly spiritual life. The John-Ego descended from the same holy region as that from which the soul-Being of the Jesus-child of the Gospel of St. Luke descended, save that upon Jesus there were chiefly bestowed qualities not yet permeated by an Ego in which egoistic traits had developed: that is to say, a young soul was guided to the place where the reborn Adam was to incarnate. It will seem strange to you that a soul without a really developed Ego could be guided from the great Mother-Lodge to a certain place. But the same Ego that was withheld from the Jesus of the Gospel of St. Luke was bestowed upon the body of John the Baptist; thus the soul-Being in Jesus of the Gospel of St. Luke and the Ego-Being in John the Baptist were inwardly related from the beginning."

Drawing from Steiner's, "From Jesus to Christ," in Lecture VIII he says: "We have seen that when this Luke Jesus-child was born, he was provided with everything that had not been influenced by the Luciferic-Ahrimanic forces. He did not possess an Ego that had been through a series of incarnations; therefore nothing had to be discarded when, in his twelfth year, the individuality of Zarathustra passed over from the Solomon Jesus-child into the Nathan Jesus-child. I have already said that the human element which had remained behind, and up to this time had developed in the Mysteries by the side of the rest of humanity, was born for the first time in the Palestine period as the Nathan Jesus-child. There was a transference from a Mystery center in Western Asia, where this human kernel had been preserved, into the body of the Nathan Jesus-child. This child grew on, and in his twelfth year the individuality of Zarathustra passed into him. We know also that this passing over is intimated in the scene of the twelve-year-old Jesus in the Temple. It was quite natural that the parents of the Nathan Jesus-child, who were accustomed to regard him in the light we have described, should find a remarkable change when they discovered him in the Temple after he had been lost. For that was the moment when Zarathustra passed over into this twelve-year-old child. From the twelfth to the thirtieth year, therefore, we have to do with the individuality of Zarathustra in the Luke Jesus-child.

Now in the Luke Gospel we have a remarkable expression which indicates something that can be made clear only by occult investigation. You know that in the Luke Gospel, after the description of the scene with the twelve-year-old Jesus in the Temple, there is a passage: `And Jesus increased in wisdom and stature, and in favor with God and man'. (Luke 2: 52). In truth this passage stands as follows when we restore the text of the Gospels from the Akashic record: The twelve-year-old child increased in everything wherein an astral body can increase, i.e., in wisdom; in everything wherein

41

an etheric body can increase, i.e., in all the qualities of kindliness, goodness, etc.; and in everything wherein a physical body can increase, i.e., in all that pours itself into external beauty of form. In this passage, therefore, a special indication is given that the Jesus-child, not having gone from incarnation to incarnation, had up to his twelfth year remained untouched, and could not be touched in his individuality, by the Luciferic and Ahrimanic forces. The Luke Gospel intimates this again by tracing the sequence of generations back through Adam to God, thus indicating that the substance in question was uninfluenced by all that had taken place in human evolution.

So this Jesus-child lived on, increasing in all that was possible for a three-fold organism not touched by the contamination which has affected the three-fold bodies of other men. And this enabled the individuality of Zarathustra, from the twelfth to the thirtieth year of life, to pour into this three-fold human Being all that could come from the heights to which he himself had previously attained. Hence we form a correct idea of Jesus of Nazareth, up to the thirtieth year of his life, when we think of him as a lofty human individuality, for whose coming into existence the greatest possible preparations had been made."

Though Zarathustra was a 'lofty human individuality', Steiner also added: "Yet not even Zarathustra himself could have ensouled the body of Jesus up to the time of puberty in such a way as to enable the discarded astral sheath to unite with the Nirmanakaya of Buddha." The question could be asked: Before the twelfth year in the life of the Nathan Jesus-child, were these maternal sheaths, the etheric and astral sheaths, too powerful even for Zarathustra to incarnate into them. They were endowed for the first twelve years with the virginal Ego that proceeded from the great Mother-Lodge of humanity which was directed and guided, "by the sublime Sun-Initiate, the Manu." If these maternal sheaths were so spiritually potent, did they possibly belong to Vidar? If so, then was there a sacred avatar connection between Vidar, the Angel-Archangel, and Mary of the Luke Gospel, the Mother of the Nathan Jesus, while she was living? Could there have been an avatar connection between Mary and Vidar comparable to that of Vidar and John the Baptist? Many indications seem to suggest that there was. It is noteworthy that at the Baptism in the Jordan the Cosmic Aura of Christ enveloped Him like a spiritual Sun which then gradually entered ever more deeply into the Form of Jesus of Nazareth until the time of the arrest when it began to separate itself from Christ Jesus. At the Crucifixion it hovered again near the Christ as it did at the beginning of His ministry. It had come full-circle. It should also be noted that at the Crucifixion Lazarus was present and within his consciousness-soul was the presence of individuality of John the Baptist/Elijah/Adam. Also present at the foot of the Cross was Mary, Mother of Jesus, of the Gospel of Matthew who was Eve in the time of the Lemurian Age. The lost, primal etheric forces of the Tree of Life were present in the

42

soul of the Nathan Jesus which were imbued by the Macrocosmic Ego of the Christ. The Divine Sophia shone upon the soul of the entelechy of the Luke Mary whose forces then lit up in the soul of the Matthew Mary. The opposing powers of the Adversarial Trinity were there as well. They are more specifically represented in the Luke Gospel rather than the other Gospels. Luke's narration of the two thieves is the supersensible account of the presence of Lucifer, represented as the repentant thief and Ahriman, represented as the unrepentant thief. The Gospels of Matthew and Mark clearly state that the two thieves were not repentant at all. Thereby, Luke's Crucifixion account is strictly the supersensible account of the presence of Lucifer and Ahriman. The Gospel of Luke is also the only one that mentions - the darkening of the Sun - at the time of the Crucifixion as opposed to saying that a darkness came over the land as in Matthew and Mark. This reference to the darkened Sun in the Luke Gospel is a veiled reference to the third force of opposing powers: the forces of the Sun demon, Sorat.

If we picture this scene of the Crucifixion in this way, we may see it as the presence of Christ, the Son of God, the Son of Man, the Logos, the Alpha and the Omega, who was upon the Cross. The Nathan soul was also present as well as John the Baptist/Elijah/Adam, who was the complimentary soul/spirit of the Nathan soul. He was present through Lazarus. Mary/Eve of the Matthew Gospel was present. The Divine Sophia through Mary of the Luke Gospel, the sister soul of Eve was present as she shone upon the Matthew Mary. Lucifer, Ahriman and Sorat were also present at the Crucifixion. All of these most significant individualities who were there at the beginning of human and earthly evolution to some degree or another as well as the adversarial Beings were now grouped together at the Crucifixion on Golgotha. The words of Christ - It Is Finished - brought the Original forces of the Fall to their redemption while, pictorially speaking, the Cross on Golgotha became the seed for a new Cosmos. In regard to John the Baptist, the Luke Mary and the Matthew Mary as well as Lazarus, Sergei Prokofieff in, "Eternal Individuality," writes: "On the Earth, in the physical world, we behold the figure of the crucified Son of Man and, standing beneath the Cross, the `Mother of Jesus' and the `disciple whom the Lord loved' (John 19: 25-26). From above, from the Cross, sound the words: `Behold, your Mother - behold, your soul!,' signifying the forging of a new spiritual union, the creation of a higher archetype for all subsequent mystical unions between rose and lily. The mystical marriage of the two spiritual principles - whose representatives are the `Mother of Jesus' and the `beloved disciple' - is being accomplished. From the heights of the Cross, like a higher priestly blessing, this union between the Sophia-impulse living in the soul of the `Mother of Jesus' and the impulse of the `I Am', which John (Lazarus) has borne in his spirit since his Initiation as Lazarus, shines forth for the entire future evolution of the Earth.

That is the picture of what took place in the earthly sphere. In the spiritual sphere that immediately adjoins it, however, the following picture

43

opens up before our inner eye. Before us there appears the spiritual Being of the Luke Mary, who overshines the `other Mary' from above, from the higher worlds, and is thereby supersensibly present at this moment on the Hill of Golgotha. Then we see the entelechy of John the Baptist, who overshines the `beloved disciple' beneath the Cross from above, from the spiritual surroundings. Both these spiritual Beings, the Being of the Luke Mary and the entelechy of John the Baptist, are enshrouded by and immersed in the mighty aura of the Cosmic Christ which, like a radiant, supersensible cloud surrounding the crucified Son of Man, unites them in a higher mystical union. And from this radiant cosmic aura there sounds at this moment - no longer in human language but in the language of spiritual archetypes - what in its echo in the lower world becomes earthly words on the lips of the Son of Man: `Behold, your Son - behold, your Mother!"

In the non-canonical Gospel of Nicodemus, it asserts that Christ descended into the sub-realms while John the Baptist accompanied the Christ through these sub-realms. Previously, it had been indicated that John the Baptist became One with Lazarus at the time of the raising of Lazarus. This being so, then how is it that John the Baptist could be One with Lazarus while the Gospel of Nicodemus exclaims that he was with Christ in the sub-realms up to the time of the Resurrection? It's reasonable to surmise that John the Baptist separated himself from the soul of Lazarus at the time of the Death of Christ on the Cross. This may explain why Lazarus, on the morning of the Resurrection 'saw and believed' yet he was still incapable of fully comprehending the Mystery of the Resurrection. (John 20: 9). In Spirit, John the Baptist, followed the Christ through the sub-realms until the morning of the Resurrection when he became capable of revealing himself to Mary Magdalene and the other women as the young man in the tomb. While in the tomb he was able to reveal himself to their physical senses of perception due to the 'special circumstances' of that morning. The other question is: When did he conjoin himself to the soul of Lazarus once more? This question is more difficult to solve. A possibility would be that John the Baptist became One with the soul of Lazarus once more during Pentecost at which time the Impulse of the Holy Spirit descended upon the Apostles, Mary, the Mother of Jesus and all else who had been there gathered in the upper room.

IV

The Cosmic Christ and the Tree of Life

In Hans-Werner Schroeder's, "The Cosmic Christ," he offers the following intriguing observations of the nature of Christ. In Chapter III he writes: "The four Gospels describe for us the earthly work of Christ. In the main, they concentrate on the three years during which the Christ walked on Earth. The interesting question now arises whether anything shines through in the Gospel accounts themselves of the cosmic element which, if our considerations are correct, there must be about this man who wanders through the Holy Land. Does the cosmic dimension disappear completely on the earthly paths of Christ, or are there moments in the Gospels when something of it comes to the fore?

Already in the childhood stories passed down to us by Matthew and Luke we find some indications. In both accounts, cosmic elements shine out. In Matthew it is the star which appears over the child and leads the kings of the East on their journey to worship the child. This star shows in a picture that with the birth of the Jesus-child on Earth a worldwide Being has appeared, that a cosmic dimension lights up over the earthly Being of the little child.

And another special motif is contained in this account by Matthew: the kings come from the Orient and worship the child, so that the significance of Jesus for mankind is emphasized from the moment of his birth. The one who is being born there is of importance not only for the Jews but also for the foreign, non-Jewish peoples. The most high-ranking representatives of mankind show this through their adoration of him. In this child lives something comprehensive and all-embracing. In the Gospel of Luke it is the host of Angels who tell the shepherds in the fields of a heavenly element which is to bring peace to the Earth: `Revelation of God in the heights, Peace on Earth to human Beings who are of good will' (Luke 2:14). Here again we are shown the cosmic background to the appearance of Jesus on Earth. And here, too, the Angel proclaims expressly that the joy of this event is to become the portion of all peoples on Earth: `See, I proclaim to you a great joy which is to be for all peoples!' - again, an all-embracing element for all mankind. A further event which brings to the fore the cosmic background of the appearance on Earth of the Christ-Jesus is the Baptism of Jesus (Matthew 3, Mark 1, Luke 3). The heavens open, the Spirit descends upon Jesus as he steps out of the river Jordan, and a voice is heard from the higher world:

`You are my beloved Son. In you I have revealed myself.' We see that the Gospel itself shows the cosmic background quite plainly. The same happens a little later at the Transfiguration on the mountain (Matthew 17, Mark 9, Luke 9). Jesus leads his three most intimate disciples, Peter, John and James, up the mountain, and they experience how his appearance changes: `His face and his garment became shining white, as if radiating lightning.' In Matthew it even says: `His face shone like the Sun.' And, as at the Baptism, a voice sounds from the spiritual world: `This is my chosen Son, hear his word!' (Luke 9: 35).

Star and Sun are two different images for the cosmic Christ. The star in Matthew's account of the birth expresses the relationship to the universe which extends past the planets to the widths of the realm of the fixed stars. Yet at the same time, in the star approaching the Earth we also have the reality before us that the cosmic Being of Christ becomes knowable for human Beings, that, in approaching Man, it does not overwhelm him, as the Sun would do with its overpowering strength. In contrast to this, the image of the Sun radiating from the countenance of Christ shows how the almighty cosmic power which is present in him, controlled, contracted and concealed, can nevertheless burst through his human appearance for a few moments - although it then overwhelms those human Beings who are present: Peter and the two others fall to the ground unconscious.

These are, then, three moments in the Gospel accounts which confirm the cosmic dimension of the event:

Birth: The cosmic element lights up over the child as a star and as the angelic host.

Baptism: The cosmic spheres (the Heavens) open, and the world-Spirit descends into the thirty-year old Jesus.

Transfiguration: The cosmic powers of light and Sun ray forth from the form of the Christ-Jesus.

Here we can see quite clearly the three stages of the increasingly profound union of the cosmic element with the human, earthly appearance. Until the thirtieth year, the divine forces of the Christ weave around the growing boy. With the Baptism, Christ enters into Jesus of Nazareth. At the Transfiguration, the human Being is permeated to the degree that something of the cosmic power of Christ can radiate out from the human form. And finally, at Christ's death images of the cosmic background also arise; this time not in the human appearance but in Sun and Earth: `And the Earth shook, and the rocks were torn apart, and the graves opened.' (Matthew 27: 52). `And after the sixth hour [noon] there was darkness over the whole Earth until the ninth hour.' (Mark 15: 33). `And it was about the sixth hour, and there was darkness over the whole Earth until about the ninth hour, and the Sun lost its light.' (Luke 23: 44). The Sun and the Earth react to the Jesus' death on the Cross; this illustrates that the significance of the events of this

46

death reaches beyond the human level. Similarly for the Resurrection: 'There was a great earthquake.' (Matthew 28: 2). The stone which closed the burial chamber in the rock was rolled aside by this earthquake; because of that, the grave is open, as all four Gospels report. In addition, Mark notes that the Sun is rising just as the women arrive at the grave on Easter morning and find the stone rolled away: once again we have the Sun motif - this time not in a human Being but in the cosmos. This is hardly likely to be a mere external 'stage direction' in the Gospel of Mark, in view of the special relationship that this Gospel has with the cosmic background. Lastly, with our subject in mind, let us look at the endings of the three Gospels, which point to a transition to a new level of the working of Christ, the re-establishment of his cosmic power; they do this in quite different ways: 'To me has been given all power in heaven and on earth . . .See, I am with you all the days until the end of earthly time.' (Matthew 28: 18). 'Go out into all the world and proclaim the Gospel to all created Beings [or: all creation].' (Mark 16: 15).

A particular cosmic feature stands out, again with Mark: the emphasis is on the significance of Christ for all creation, whereas Matthew speaks in more general terms of the power in heaven and on Earth which has been given to Christ. In Luke it is again different:'He led them out towards Bethany [on the Mount of Olives] and raised his hands in blessing over them. And as he blessed them he vanished [(from) their awareness] and ascended into the heavenly spheres.' (Luke 24: 50). At this point, then, there is already reference to the Ascension. Remarkably, it takes place precisely in immediate association with the blessing which Christ bestows on mankind and the Earth. This is surely no coincidence, either."

Concluding with Schroeder: "The cosmic background of the working of Christ can be characterized, as we said earlier, through the images of star and Sun: Christ is the spiritual Sun of the cosmos, or, as John records, 'the light of the world'; but this Sun has a relationship to the forces of the starry universe from whence it actually originates."

So far the cosmic aura of Christ has not been clearly defined and it is also not explicitly defined in Steiner's ninth lecture of his lecture cycle on the Gospel of Mark. In other places he speaks of the 'Pleroma' or fullness of Christ. In his lectures on the Gospel of John he makes it clear that Christ brought to Earth the 'fullness' of the spiritual forces of the six Elohim Beings of the Sun. In doing so, the spiritual forces of the Sun are now also present upon the Earth due to the advent of the Christ here on Earth. This gives the Earth the capacity to eventually transfigure itself into the likeness of the Sun to which it and the other planets will unite once more with the Sun. Something other than the Pleroma of the six Elohim Beings has also been brought to the Earth and is part of this cosmic element that enveloped the Christ while He was physically present on Earth. It was the 'Tree of Life' that Christ brought back to Earth and to humanity. Prokofieff, too, mentions this

47

in his book, "The Eternal Individuality": ". . .for only through the mediation of the Christ Being, or to be more precise, through uniting with the impulse proceeding from the Mystery of Golgotha, was the individuality of Adam-Elijah-John the Baptist able to enter upon the path leading to his gradually being united with the lost forces of the Tree of Life, with the primordial etheric forces that had been preserved by the Nathan Soul. Only after he had - as a result of his spiritual union with Lazarus/John – been supersensibly present on the Hill of Golgotha was this individuality able in the spiritual world to enter upon this path of becoming once again like his archetype, the 'heavenly Adam', the Nathan Soul."

The Tree of Life would be the pre-fallen, untainted etheric forces that were preserved in the 'Mother Lodge of humanity' of the spiritual sun. They were taken from humanity when humanity was passing through its Fall due to the infection of luciferic impulses into the souls of humanity during the Age of Lemuria. More specifically they were the unfallen sound and life etheric forces which are brought back to the region of the Earth by Christ such that evolving humans can gradually have greater control and power again over these forces to which humanity can thereby, through consciously willed effort and understanding, actually transfigure the Earth; raising the Earth to become more Sun-like and eventually reuniting the Earth with the Sun. The Tree of Life gives humans the power to effect the transubstantiation of matter.

Sylvia Francke and Thomas Cawthorne address this in their book, "The Tree of Life and the Holy Grail": "When the blood flowed from the cross two events of immense evolutionary importance occurred. First of all the influence of Lucifer and Ahriman was cast out from the human sheaths so that the full Tree of Life forces could be safely returned to the human blood. Secondly, the power of these four ethers was returned to the earth. At the Last Supper the Christ had already directed the attention of His followers to the new condition of the earth when he taught them to view the wine and the bread as his body and blood. At the climax of the Crucifixion the Logos passed into the earth."

And they add: "In finding a relationship between the transformation of Jesus Christ's physical body and the body of the earth much of what one hears described as the raising of the earth's energy and the transformation of negative energies begins to be clarified. Steiner's interpretation of these events led to a practical understanding of the Mystery of the Last Supper and also began to shed light on the Rosicrucian ideal - the transformation of the earth into a sun. At the so-called Last Supper, Christ had taken bread and wine and stated that these were now His body. If the words of Christ are taken literally they seem not to lead to a new form of ritual . . . but to a realization that the earth is now, in a totally real sense, the body of Christ.

For the earth itself is a Grail, and if we are called to be guardians of the Grail then it is to her that we must direct our efforts."

They cite this from, "Rudolf Steiner to Countess Keyserlingk after the Koberwitz lectures": "We know that in the moment when the blood flowed from the cross upon Golgotha that, there in the interior of the earth, a new sun globe was born." Continuing with Francke & Cawthorne: "During the three days following the event on Golgotha, Christ descended to the center of the earth. Since the Fall this has been the bastion of the centric forces, the region of the fallen ethers , the habitation of their corresponding `backward' Beings. There the Christ, now as 'Spirit of the Earth', together with the human physical body in which the laws of matter are in the process of being reversed, confronts these fallen forces of light ether (electricity) where Lucifer is working, chemical ether (magnetism), which is Ahriman's realm, and the life ether (the Third Force), relating to the Asuras or Rakshasas."

They then write: "In, `The Fifth Gospel,' Rudolf Steiner describes how an earthquake followed the darkening of the sun when Jesus' body had been laid in the grave: `It shook the grave in which the body of Jesus had been laid and the stone covering it was wrenched away; a fissure was rent in the earth and the corpse was received into it. Another tremor caused the fissure to close again over the corpse. And when the people came in the morning the grave was empty, for the dead body of Jesus had been received into the earth.' The physical body of Jesus descended into the earth and the transformation of the physical substance took place in those regions where the centric forces predominate, laying the foundation for the future transformation of all `physical' earthly conditions. The power of those Beings particularly concerned with fallen matter was thus held in check and an impulse was then given to the whole of fallen creation by the body of Jesus Christ as it was transformed within the earth. After this the way lay open towards the metamorphosis of the Earth into the next planetary condition: Jupiter evolution - the New Jerusalem."

Francke & Cawthorne then mention the transfiguring possibilities of 'living' thinking: "In the chapters on the new etheric science we considered the need for a new type of thinking, a living thinking that is holistic and fully self-conscious right down into the depths of its soul-filled activity. The capacity for this thinking came through the Mystery of Golgotha. It is the working of Christ within the sphere of the heart that creates the possibility for thinking to become a spiritual force within human evolution. . . the Fall created an inner chasm in humanity, an almost unbridgeable abyss between the human soul and its higher self. The new freedom-filled thinking is the Christ-capacity that will heal the chasm introduced into human consciousness by the Fall."

In examining human thinking and the Divine Will, what we think is the activity of thinking and thought is actually a mere silhouette of the real spirit

49

forces that make up thinking. When we have a conscious thought, those spiritual forces of the Ego immediately become dead in our consciousness. The activity of living thinking is the activity of the Ego in the spirit realms and our thoughts are mere shadows of the impulses that we perceive in our consciousness. When one creates an image in one's mind one has to go past that image and begin to perceive the forces that actually created the image. It is the Ego which creates that image in one's consciousness. In going deeper into this level of Ego-awareness one comes into closer contact with one's own I AM. When one becomes conscious of one's Ego then one also becomes conscious of the world Ego. In other terms, one has the experience that Moses had when he 'ascended the mountain; that is, the elevation and extension of his consciousness, and had the `burning bush' experience. Edward R. Smith indicates in his book, "The Burning Bush," that the `burning bush' is a symbol of one's Ego. As Moses ascended in consciousness to the awareness of his own Ego, he then came into contact with the World I AM. He experienced the revelation of Christ in the words, "I AM the I AM." This is the creative activity of cosmic, living, spiritual thought that truly pervades everything in the cosmos. The Cosmic I AM element came into Moses' consciousness because he was now in a symbiotic relationship of consciousness with the Christ I AM due to experiencing and being fully conscious of his own I AM. For Moses, all of nature was now alive with the activity of the Cosmic I AM element.

During such an experience, one no longer sees, for example, in nature a rose `only' which is, in a manner of speaking, merely a shell of its true reality. One sees the living rose with its etheric form and universal astral element while also experiencing in one's own spiritualized thinking the living, spiritual Thought that is in the creation of the rose. One then comes into contact with Beings in Devachan who create the living, spiritual archetype for the rose. This level of thinking activity is the work that recreates the world and eventually raises the Earth and ourselves into the etheric, astral and devachanic realms. Our thoughts literally do create the world around us. Spiritualized thinking, a devachanic consciousness, will dissolve the dead, mineral matter into cosmic dust and will raise the Earth and this planetary system to higher realms. We then become co-workers with Christ in the entire Resurrection and Ascension processes that eventually bring us to the next condition of form: the astral condition. This astral condition of form will be the germinal seed for the far distant Jupiter planetary condition; the, " . . . New Jerusalem, coming down out of heaven from God . . ." (Rev. 21: 2).

In the opening pages of Dennis Klocek's, "Seeking Spirit Vision," he addresses the polarity of human selfhood and Divine Will as follow: "In prehistoric times the human capacity for thought was embedded in the universal currents of Will. Human Will and Divine Will flowed in the same stream of consciousness, in a state which can be called Intuitive thinking.

Human consciousness was at one with the Divine consciousness. After the Temptation in Paradise and the subsequent fall into matter and Individuality, however, human consciousness felt the separation of its forces from the forces of the Godhead. In order for individual selfhood to arise, it became necessary for human currents of Will to flow counter to the original Will currents of the Creator and to focus upon itself. Thus, during Vedic, Persian, and Egyptian times, there was a gradual transformation in the human soul from a God-centered consciousness to an Earth-centered consciousness. The present human consciousness is now like a swirling vortex of selfhood in a great stream. The vortex sustains itself through resistance to the prevailing motion of the whole, and the flow of Divine Will is reversed within it. In a vortex two currents meet again, having arisen by being separated by an obstruction or a resistance. In the vortex of selfhood the resistance to the flow of Will from the future separates out the field of activity of the separate intellect with its resistant forces of antipathy."

"The vortex of selfhood arises through antipathy, which is the foundation of thinking in the intellect."

The 'vortex of selfhood' that Dennis Klocek addresses can also be thought of as the fallen human form of the physical, etheric and astral bodies, which, through resistance to the Divine Will, allows the Ego to gain its individual consciousness. It was the death forces of sense-bound thinking that brought about the loss of Sophian revelation, of Intuitive thinking in human consciousness. Over great eons of time, the human form and its sphere of activity, the Earth, gradually came to reflect the hardening forces of the human brain and head. Rudolf Steiner remarks in the lecture cycle, "The Temple Legend," that our thoughts, when they have condensed into the physical, manifest as electricity, and that the atom is 'frozen electricity'. Jesaiah Ben-Aharon in his book, "The New Experience of the Supersensible," writes: "Objects are maya, illusion, when compared with their appearance to the higher, enlivened, ensouled and spiritual perception. They are our (unconsciously, livingly killed) dead creations. An object must, therefore, be readily redeemable and dissolvable. In the moment we cease its unconscious consolidation, it etherizes, becomes transparent and rent in twain, revealing the real living and ensouled world-man behind it. . . . An 'object' is, in the purely sense world, an etheric-elemental flowing reality, fixated, cemented and sedimented, made dense and heavy through - and only through - our bodily, willed touch, from which we abstract, conceptually, all our metaphysical material notions. . . . At this point we may begin the living deconstruction process of the opaque, external object."

This 'living deconstruction process of the opaque, external object,' the redemption and resurrection of our brain-bound intellect and perception and all of their consequences, is also intimated in the following scenes from the Gospels: the Agony in the Garden, the Crucifixion, and the Risen Christ as

51

a gardener. In the scene of the Agony in the Garden there is the passage, "Father, if you are willing, remove this cup from me; yet not my Will but yours be done." (Luke 22:42). This passage has often been poorly interpreted as a plea from Christ to the Father to circumvent His impending Passion and Death. Steiner, however, interprets it as the anguish that Christ felt due to the realization that none of the Apostles is able to comprehend the Mystery of Golgotha in full consciousness. Steiner had also stated that 'truth' can be understood from twelve sides. A truth can have multiple aspects and the same is true for the archetypal scenes and images in the Gospels. Thereby, the Cup of Agony may also be interpreted as the human Form; that is, 'the vortex' of the astral, etheric and physical bodies. This human Form is referred to in Genesis as pain (astral body), toil (etheric body) and death (physical body). The human Form, the vortex, flows counter to the Divine Will of the heavenly Hierarchies which in this specific moment may also be referred to as the Father. Christ's plea to the Father is, therefore, a proclamation that He is now ready to reverse the countering individual Will forces in the human Form and again unite it with the Divine Will. Moreover, as Christ begins the process of transfiguring the vortex of the human Form He makes it possible that in the distant future this Cup consisting of the astral, etheric and physical bodies are converted into their respective higher spiritual forms: Manas (Divine Wisdom), Buddhi (Divine Love) and Atma (Divine Will).

In view of the Crucifixion we are given the word `Golgotha' which translated means: "the place of the Skull." (Mark 15: 22). This leads us to consider the human head and its forces in relation to the archetypal scene of the Crucifixion on Golgotha. The Crucifixion is a scene that depicts a dark, solid, sense-bound image. Its image of death is an image of the nadir of brain-bound thinking with its crucifying, hardening forces. It is a picture that projects the reality of solid, dark mineral matter created by 'fixated, cemented and sedimented' thoughts. We see in this image the crucifixion and death of living Imagination and Intuitive thinking; the sense-bound thinking that now must be spiritualized and resurrected.

The Gospel of John then progresses from the scene of Golgotha to the image of Christ on Easter morning as a gardener; a tiller of the Earth. From an image of the dark, solid mineral we move to an ethereal image of Christ as the human representative who dissolves the mineral into the love imbued etheric-astral ring which now envelopes the Earth. This ring is formed through a consciously Willed spiritualization of thinking. The Risen Christ as a gardener was a living Imagination experience of the phantom body presence of Christ. It was Mary Magdalene who was the first human to have this experience while alive in a mineral body. However, it was John the Baptist as the young man in the tomb who was the first human overall to experience the Risen Christ and was the first human who began to internalize the Aura, the Pleroma of the Christ. Mary Magdalene may be pictured as bearing the archetypal, redeemed human astral-soul body which has attained the achievement of the new Sophian impulses, thereby giving her the capacity to recognize the Risen Christ. The image of Christ as a gardener of the Earth reflects back to us that through the experience of Imagination and Intuitive thinking we can participate in the transfiguration of the earth, eventually bringing it to a future astral condition of form.

The above mentioned work of Jesaiah Ben-Aharon is again cited: "...the modern Christ experience, achieved through the knowledge drama of the Second Coming, is this: that man can begin today consciously to create the new vital and sentient sheaths of the Earth through his actively awakened sensible-supersensible cognition...."

"...the spiritualized process of sense perception . . . is the beginning of the conscious macrocosmic construction process of the planetary Heaven of the earthly-human Sun, in a form that will become part of the universal, spiritual and social life of awakened humanity in the coming millennium."

Francke & Cawthorne also address this theme with the following intriguing comments in their book in regard to the role of anti-matter: "This realm of `anti-matter' is the etheric realm. It is a type of space that is devoid of all material substance, an emptiness that is formative in its activity. The etheric realm has been described as both the source of life and the region into which the dead first pass after leaving their earthly bodies and from which the newly incarnating spirit descends at the time of birth."

It is in this realm that living thinking begins to transfigure matter. That which lives in the soul, the moral element of individuals, is reflected in the configuration of matter. Francke & Cawthorne carry this theme over into the mysteries of the blood and nervous system: "The Knights Templar lived at a time when the power of the sword - in its intermediate phase - was still at work. They inherited the Mysteries of the Grail, which are the `Mysteries of the purified blood of Christ.' In a lecture given in Dornach, 2 October 1916, Rudolf Steiner speaks with great emphasis of how: `Inwardly considered, the order of the Knights Templar express a specially deep approach to the Mystery of Golgotha on the part of modern humanity. [They] knew how to stand in real inward livingness in that life which, ever since Golgotha, the innermost forces of men are living through the fact that Christ has united himself with earthly existence . . . The blood of the Templars belonged to Christ Jesus . . . Every moment of their life was to be filled with the perpetual consciousness of how in their soul there dwelt, `Not I, but Christ in Me!' "

Francke & Cawthorne continue: "In his lecture cycle, "Manifestations of Karma," Rudolf Steiner describes how an intense contemplative preoccupation with the life of Christ, inwardly maintained as a free act of the spirit, causes the nerves to withdraw from the blood: `In ordinary life the process that takes is such that each influence transmitted by means of the nerves inscribes itself in the blood as on a tablet, and in doing so records

53

itself in the instrument of the Ego. (This connection can be artificially interrupted so that nerves and blood no longer interact upon each other.) But let us suppose that in spite of the interrupting of the connection between the nerves and the blood a certain impression is made upon the nerve. This can be brought to pass through an external experiment by stimulating the nerve through an electric current. (Through certain spiritual scientific practices this can be brought about also.) When man practices a rigorous inner concentration of the soul on such imaginative concepts, forming these into symbols . . . It then happens, if he does them in fully awake consciousness, that he takes complete control of the nerve and, as a result of this concentration, draws it back to a certain extent from the course of the blood. (When this experiment takes place, one no longer lives in his ordinary Ego.)' [Lecture X]."

Francke & Cawthorne then add: "If the `external impression' made upon the nerves was brought about by the Templars in their constant contemplation and devotion to the example of Jesus Christ, then it may have eventually come about that the Templar `no longer lived in his ordinary consciousness', but that his Ego was replaced by the Christ. When this came about a further effect may have become possible: of spreading this penetration of the Christ in the human individual to the body of the Earth itself. This may have been a direct effect of the Templar's spiritual work, whether effected consciously or unconsciously by them. The nervous system as the vehicle for consciousness and intellectual thought has attained its present deathly and hardened state through the incorporation of ahrimanic forces. The blood and tissues remain alive, an organic part of the wider world process. However, the blood is inscribed by the nerves with which it interacts in the normal state. In this way the ahrimanic forces within the human structure can inscribe themselves upon the inner nature of man. When the blood and the nerves are withdrawn from each other, access to the inner nature is denied; the death forces and the blood become available to the spirit.

Taking this into account it becomes easier to understand Rudolf Steiner's statement that the blood of the Templars belonged fully to Christ. The Templars were not occult Initiates in the usual sense of belonging to a guarded Mystery school, but through their very life style they attained to a naturally won Initiation. The power of the Tree of Life that had been returned to Earth by the Christ and brought to perfection within the body of Jesus became available to the Templars. With this personal Initiation came the possibility of extending this permeation of the individual human blood-stream to the Earth itself. In his lecture, `The Face of the Earth and the Destiny of Mankind', Guenther Wachsmuth gives us an insight into how such a process could occur:"

Francke & Cawthorne then cite G. Wachsmuth: "We have seen that certain forces mould the body of the Earth and of man in accordance with uniform, harmonious laws. In conclusion, we will consider yet another deeply illuminating phenomenon that can tell us how and why the destiny of man is bound up with the Earth; why, in effect, the face of the Earth becomes part of the destiny of man. Let us now pass from the horizontal to the vertical plane of the body of the Earth. We will start, for the sake of simplicity, from the classification of substances given by Empedocles, and apply this to the Earth. The Earth has a solid body over which we move. This solid body is surrounded by the so-called hydrosphere, the watery sphere, this again by an air sheath, and as Dr. Steiner has taught us, this air sheath is enclosed with a `mantle' of warmth. This is a picture of the realm outside the Earth, but passing from thence to the Earth's interior we find something very remarkable. The outer is reflected in the inner! The most recent geological investigations confirm what has already been taught by spiritual science, namely, that below the solid body over which we move there is a watery sphere, the magma; further inwards the substance assumes a gaseous form, finally passing over into a condition of warmth, of fire. This is a remarkable phenomenon. Enumerating these spheres, we have: 1) mantle of warmth; 2) air sheath; 3) hydrosphere; 4) solid earth surface; 5) interior fluidic earth; 6) interior gaseous earth; 7) interior Earth warmth. Thus these seven spheres of the body of the Earth, governed by the formative forces, are of such a nature that the seventh corresponds to the first, the sixth to the second, the fifth to the third, but the fourth represents something entirely new and unique. There is a most wonderful correspondence between the interior and exterior of the Earth, and furthermore, there is a correspondence in another sphere, that of the consciousness of humanity.

When we study this interior nature of the Earth we find yet another profound and far-reaching connection with the inner Being of man. If the modern investigator will turn his gaze for a moment away from outer nature and direct it to man himself, to the most significant element living within the human Being, namely, the blood, he will find when he thus penetrates into a blood corpuscle that it has a body of a peculiar kind, again divided into four spheres. Outside there is a highly transparent sphere, then a more opaque sphere peculiarly saturated and, as it were, inflated with the watery element, then again a somewhat more transparent sphere and, fourthly, again a less transparent [sphere]. This is the form revealed by a section of a blood corpuscle. A study of the etheric formative forces which on the one hand are responsible for the formation of the interior body of the Earth, and on the other for the structure of the human blood corpuscle, will reveal the fact that the solid Earth is ruled by the life ether, the fluid elements by the chemical ether, the airy elements by the light ether, and the warmth process by the warmth ether. We find exactly the same thing in the corpuscle of human blood! Thus, we can study the configuration of the etheric body of the Earth which is a reflection of our own inner Being and we must realize that the etheric forces moulding the body of the Earth are the same as those in our blood corpuscles. Today, it is not possible to say anything more of this phenomenon. It can only live within us as a deeply significant cosmic mystery, of which we may perhaps become fully conscious in the course of time. The etheric world, with the same forces, moulds and governs the interior of the Earth in a wonderful harmony. Furthermore, it now also becomes clear that if new etheric forces arise within the Earth in the course of cosmic 'becoming' this reflects itself right into the corpuscles of the human blood; on the other hand, when a change takes place in the etheric structure of human blood, this will be reflected into the etheric sphere of the Earth, because, in effect, the Earth and the blood corpuscles are formed according to the same laws.

When we are able to perceive this unity between the body of the Earth, the configuration of the Earth, and the forces of consciousness, we shall live with quite different feelings. As we walk about, we shall set our feet with greater reverence on the body of the Earth; we shall feel the body of the Earth to be 'holy ground' . . . We are thus led into a quite different relationship with Earth, a truly Christian knowledge of the spirituality of the Earth, to a Gaia-Sophia. More and more we shall realize the connection between the body of the Earth and the destiny of mankind."

It seems to follow from reading the above from Wachsmuth that we are slowly awakening to the realization that human consciousness is gradually becoming aware of its potential in transfiguring the whole structure of the Earth. Our conscious and Willed connection with the Impulse of the Christ gives us the potential to slowly evolve our own bodies thereby also evolving the Earth itself. Could we then say that Christ is slowly handing over to us the capacities to consciously work with the chemical/sound and life ethers, the Tree of Life forces, along with an increasing understanding of our capacities so that we, over time, bring about the evolution of this planet and reunite it with the Sun?

V

The Evolution of Christ

Up to this point we have examined the lectures of Rudolf Steiner and the writings of others that have significance in regard to the topic of the fleeing youth. The presentation of excerpts from several lectures of Rudolf Steiner will continue to be the remaining focus in this work. In doing so, the intention will be to further establish a synthesis of the copious material that he has conveyed to us in relation to what is postulated in this work that, overall, the fleeing youth was the Cosmic Principle of Christ as Steiner had claimed. The primary endeavor of this work attempts to construct a foundation of material which supports the thesis that the entelechy of John the Baptist, who appeared to Mary Magdalene and the other women, was the entity of the young man in the tomb enshrouded by the forces of the fleeing youth; the forces of the Cosmic Aura of Christ. Thereby, we can begin to apprehend the meaning and significance of the relationship between John the Baptist and the Cosmic Principle of Christ and what that relationship means to the future evolution of humanity and the Earth.

Before continuing the study of the fleeing youth and John the Baptist, however, it is essential to examine Steiner's research into the evolution of the Christ Being. Along with this, there are added comments in regard to the Holy Trinity at the end of this chapter.

On June 3, 1909 [GA109] Steiner expressed the following comments pertaining to the evolution of the Christ Being: "We must realize that Christ has not always been the same and in His distinctive ways of working we must recognize how He, too, advances from one evolutionary stage to another. It gives rise to an overwhelming feeling of exultation when a man is made aware that just as in the case of his own soul and its incarnations and progress, the spiritual Beings also reach higher and higher stages and become more and more powerful. This realization gives one a living feeling of evolution. It is an essential part of Rosicrucian esotericism to show how a Being such as Christ has worked both in the past and at the present time, in Moses and Paul, and to see from this how even a Being of such sublime eminence makes progress. This gives a rise to an intimate concept of evolution."

In other lectures Steiner asserts that the Christ Being was once a microcosmic hierarchical Being who ascended from the hierarchy of the Archangels. Steiner also stated that all three Beings of the Holy Trinity were once microcosmic hierarchical Beings. In each successive Manvantara a particular hierarchy attains Egohood. During the Saturn Period the Archai Beings assumes Egohood. At the time of the Sun Period the Archangels did so and throughout the Moon Period the Angels attained their Egohood as well. Each successive hierarchy of Beings which were evolving their Egohood had one Being who was the most highly evolved. From the 1907 cycle, "Theosophy of the Rosicrucian," [GA 99] in Lecture IX, Steiner claims that the Being we now recognize as the Christ was once a Fire-Spirit. He was the most highly evolved of the Archangels during the Sun Period. Steiner refers to the Archangels during the Sun Period as Sun Spirits or Fire Spirits. Christ, Who was an Archangel at that time, was the Regent of the Archangels: "And the highest evolved Spirit Who was on the Sun as Fire Spirit, Who today is still active upon the Earth, with very highly evolved consciousness, this Sun or Fire Spirit is the Christ. In the same way the most evolved Saturn Spirit is the Father God." . . . "As the highest Regent of Saturn, the Ego Spirit appears to us as the Father God, the highest God of the Sun, the Sun-God, as Christ, so will the Regent of the Moon-stage of the Earth appear to us as the Holy Spirit with His Hosts, which in Christian esotericism are called the Messengers of the Godhead, the Angels."

Steiner returns to this theme in Lecture X from the aforementioned cycle: "The Spirits of Egohood on Saturn had as their Leader a Being whom man calls the Father-God. The Spirits of Fire on the Sun had as their Leader the Christ, or in the sense of St. John's Gospel, the Logos. On the Moon the Leader was the same Spirit as is known in Christianity as the Holy Ghost." Again from the same cycle, Lecture XI: "We have designated the outstanding Leader of these Spirits (the Spirits of Twilight; Angels) as the 'Holy Spirit' or the 'Holy Ghost,' the Regent of the Fire Spirits as the 'Christ,' that of Saturn as the 'Father God.' And lastly, from "Theosophy of the Rosicrucian," Lecture XII: " The pupil must at least find it possible to believe that the most lofty Being, the Leader of the Fire-Spirits of the Sun evolution, was physically incorporated as Jesus of Nazareth . . ."

In the 1909 Gospel of St. Luke cycle Steiner conveys the following from Lecture VII: "The Christ Being cannot be understood if we think of Earth evolution alone. The Christ is the Leader of those spiritual Beings who left with the Sun when it separated from the Earth and established for themselves this higher sphere of action in order to work upon the Earth from outside. . . . The Leader of all the Beings who send their beneficent influences from the Sun to the Earth is He Who was later called Christ."

It could be surmised that Steiner, in this excerpt from the Luke cycle, may be referring more specifically to the Spirits of Form, the Exusiai, who reside within the spiritual sphere of the sun. Christ is particularly interrelated with the Spirits of Form due to his past evolution during the Sun Manvantara. He was an Archangel who ascended to the same condition of Being as the Spirits of Form during the Sun Period. At the time of the Sun Period the Spirits of Form were planetary Beings similar to that of the Archangels today. For this reason the Christ is deeply related to both the Archangels and the Spirits of Form. From the lecture cycle, "Man in the Light of Occultism, Theosophy and Philosophy," Rudolf Steiner gives us the following in Lecture X:

"We learn how Christ already on the old Moon overcame Lucifer, and in the scene that is given us in the Gospels we have to see, as it were, a recurrence of the fact that Christ attained to victory over Lucifer. On Earth Christ repels Lucifer from the outset. This is because on the Moon, when He was Himself less highly evolved, for Christ also undergoes evolution, He had repelled, through the uttermost devotion of His Being to Highest Powers, all the attacks of Lucifer which at that time still meant something to Him. Already on old Moon Lucifer approached Christ. On Earth he was no longer dangerous to Him: on Earth Christ repels Lucifer at once. On the Moon, however, Christ had to exert all the forces at His disposal in order to repel Lucifer. This is then the added experience that comes to us when we cast back the gaze of higher consciousness into the remote time of Moon. If we go still further and attain to the second consciousness of a higher kind, then as well as learning about facts that have meaning for Earth, such as the history of Buddha, we learn also what has again been described in outline in my Occult Science, we learn of the still earlier incarnation of our Earth, - the Sun. In that far-off time the conditions were quite essentially different, and the difficulty you have in understanding this particular section in Occult Science can itself be an indication of how difficult it was to describe the state of old Sun. I took pains to describe more especially scenes that are less remote from man and can even remind us of the scenery of Nature. One would have found little understanding, in the time when Occult Science was written, for the things of a more moral nature which are experienced in a study of the Sun incarnation. When we go back to the time of the old Sun, we do not find there any story of the Temptation! We find the Sun still as a planet among the seven planets, we find Venus with Lucifer as her ruler; and these two, the Sun Spirit and the Venus Spirit - in other words, Christ and Lucifer - appear at first sight like brothers. Only by straining to the utmost our powers of perception are we able to remark the difference between them. For the difference between Lucifer and Christ, in the time of old Sun is not apparent to an observation of their external being, it requires a more inward observation and study. It is indeed extraordinarily difficult to find outward means of demonstrating wherein the difference lies. Please, therefore, take what I am now going to say as no more than an attempt to characterize, as well as may be, the difference that clairvoyant consciousness can perceive between Christ and Lucifer in the time of the ancient Sun.

When we direct our gaze now to Christ, now again to Lucifer, a new perception begins to dawn upon us. Lucifer, the ruler of Venus, appears in a form that is extraordinarily full of light, - I mean, of course, spiritual light.

We have the feeling that all the glow and brilliance we can ever experience on Earth in looking upon a manifestation of light is weak and dim in comparison with the majesty of Lucifer in the old Sun time. But then we notice, when we begin to perceive his intentions - and we are able to see through these-, that Lucifer is a Spirit endowed in his very nature with infinite pride, so great a pride that it can prove a temptation to man. For, as is well-known, there are things which up to a point are not temptations for man but become so when they grow majestic in their proportions, and pride is one of them. When pride is majestically great it tempts man. Lucifer's proud greatness, Lucifer's pride in his majestic figure of light - these contain a seductive element. 'Unmanifest light', light that does not shine outwardly but has immense, strong power in itself - that Lucifer has in full measure. And how does the Christ figure look beside Lucifer? The Christ figure in the time of old Sun - the Lord and Ruler of the Sun planet - is a picture of utmost devotion, entire devotion to all that is around Him in the world. Whereas Lucifer looks like one who thinks only of himself - we are obliged to clothe it all in human words, notwithstanding the fact that these are quite inadequate - Christ appears as wholly given up, in devotion, to all that is around Him in the great wide world.

The great wide world was not then as it is now. If we were to transport ourselves in these days to the present Sun, then, looking outwards in all directions as from the center of a circle, we should perceive in the first place the twelve Signs of the Zodiac. These were not then externally visible; but instead, twelve great Forms, twelve Beings were present who let their words ring forth from the depths of the darkness, - outer space being of course not then filled with light. What kind of words were these? They were words - the word 'word' is again only a makeshift, to indicate what is here meant - they were words that told of primeval times, of times that even then were in a remote and ancient past. The twelve were twelve World-Initiators.

Today we behold standing in the directions of these twelve World-Initiators the twelve Signs of the Zodiac, but from them resounds, for the soul that is open to the whole world, the original being of the Unspoken Word of the Worlds, that could take form in the twelve Voices. And whilst Lucifer alone - I must now begin to speak more in pictures; human words do not in the least suffice - whilst Lucifer had the impulse to let stream out upon all things the light that was present in him and therewith come to a knowledge of all things, the Christ on the other hand, gave Himself up to the Impression of this Word of the Worlds, received It in its fullness and entirety into Himself, so that this Christ Soul was now the Being that united in Himself all the great Secrets of the World that sounded into Him through the inexpressible Word. Such is the contrast that presents itself, - the Christ Who receives the Word of the Worlds, and the proud Lucifer, the Spirit of Venus, who rejects the Word of the Worlds and wants to found and establish everything with his own light.

60

All subsequent evolution is a direct outcome of what Lucifer and Christ were at that time. The Christ Being, as we saw, received into Himself the great and all-embracing secrets of the Worlds. The Lucifer Being, having what I can only describe as a 'proud figure of Light,' lost thereby his kingdom, lost his Venus kingdom. On other grounds, to enter into which would take us too far afield, the other Spirits of the Planets lost also their kingdoms, or rather changed their natures. But they need not concern us here. What is important for us here is the contrast between Christ and Lucifer. It came about that Lucifer lost more and more of his rulership; the kingdom of Venus gradually fell away from him. Lucifer with his light became a dethroned ruler, and the planet Venus had thenceforward to do without a proper ruler and was consequently obliged to undergo a backward evolution. The Christ, however, had during the old Sun time received the Word of the Worlds, and this Word of the Worlds has the quality of kindling itself to new light in the soul by which It is received; so that from that time forward the Word of the Worlds became in the Christ Light, and the planet of which the Christ was ruler, the Sun, became the center of the whole planetary system, the other planets being brought into subjection to It. The same is true also of their spiritual Rulers."[Christiana, June 12, 1912; (GA137)/source: www.elib.com].

Though Christ originated from the hierarchy of the Archangels it must be remembered that during the Sun Period they were assuming their human stage; or better said, they were acquiring their Egohood. The Spirits of Form were at that time two stages above the Archangels. Today, during the present Earth Period, the Archangels are two stages above humanity. It becomes conceivable that a Being such as the Christ Being would have had a spiritual nature similar to those Beings who stood two stages higher if we take into account the spiritual composition of the Nathan soul in its descent to earth. Though this soul was human, it stood two stages higher than humanity as Christ 'ensouled Himself' within the Nathan soul in order to accomplish His three pre-earthly sacrifices. In the lecture, "The Four Sacrifices of Christ," Steiner says the following: "Then came the fourth, the earthly mystery, that of Golgotha. The same Christ Being Who had ensouled Himself three times in archangelic form incarnated through what we call the Baptism by John in the Jordan in the body of Jesus of Nazareth." The Nathan soul provided the archangelic form that the Christ had assumed in His three pre-Golgotha sacrifices. In similar fashion, it then becomes comprehensible that Christ, though He was of the Archangels who were proceeding through their Egohood during the Sun Period, was able to ascend at that time to the level of the Spirits of Form because He, ". . . gave Himself up to the Impression of this Word of the Worlds, received It in its fullness and entirety into Himself, so that this Christ Soul was now the Being that united in Himself all the great Secrets of the World that sounded into Him through the inexpressible Word."

It was the fullness of the Word of the Worlds that the Christ received within Himself that enabled Him to become the Regent of the Archangels during the Sun Period. Though Christ was of the Archangelic hierarchy He was in essence a planetary Being during the Sun Period. He was similar in composition to that of the Spirits of Form during the Sun Period.

Steiner made it clear in his June 12, 1912 lecture when he said that Christ ascended and evolved as a microcosmic Being. A salient comment from that lecture is the following: ". . . This is because on the Moon, when He was Himself less highly evolved - for Christ also undergoes evolution . . ." This comment from Steiner and his other comments previously cited in this chapter allow us to surmise that Christ was once a Being of the Hierarchies. According to Steiner, Christ is now, during the Earth Manvantara, above all of the Hierarchies due to His Macrocosmic Initiation during the Sun Manvantara. He then descended through the various Hierarchies over the ages during the Earth Manvantara until He appeared in the flesh in Jesus of Nazareth at the time of the Baptism in the Jordan.

From Colossians.1:15-17 we read: "He (Christ) is the image of the invisible God, the firstborn of every creature. For in Him were created all things in the heavens and on the earth, things visible and things invisible, whether Thrones, or Dominions, or Principalities, or Powers. All things have been created through and unto Him, and He is before all creatures, and in Him all things hold together."

This passage avows that Christ is, "the firstborn of every creature." This may be understood to express that at the beginning of the Earth Period, when Christ ascended as a Being Who stood above all the Hierarchies, He was the `First' to emerge from the Pralaya interval; the Cosmic Night which extended from the ending of the Moon Period to the beginning of the Earth Period. The Hierarchies awakened after Him in a sequential order with the higher Beings emerging first. Steiner mentions in his Genesis lectures that the Elohim awakened from their slumber when the earth and the sun were separating from one another during the Earth Period. All things in our planetary system were created through Him. His Macrocosmic Ego poured forth through all of the Hierarchies that brought forth the creation of the earth as well as our entire planetary system during the Earth Period. "He is before all creatures, and in Him all things hold together," affirms that the Cosmic Principle, the Cosmic Element of His Macrocosmic Self which now lords over this planetary system lives in all things. It is during the Earth Period that Christ is evolving His Macrocosmic Ego to its fullest development (See Rudolf Steiner's lecture: "Cosmic Ego and Human Ego"/GA 130).

How may we address the nature of the Godhead if they too are Beings that evolved over Great Ages of time? This assertion contradicts that which has come to be accepted as traditional doctrine. The true nature of God is not one singular Being. Nor is It a Trinity as we commonly believe. Rather, the actuality of God presents Itself as a vast multiplicity of Beings who have ascended beyond the Seraphim. They are Beings who have attained a level of spiritual stature in which they seemingly merge as One. We are unable to differentiate one from the other when we, in spirit vision, perceive them in the spiritual world. The Holy Trinity is comprised of three very advanced Beings which we address as the Father, Son and Holy Spirit. They have dominion over this planetary system. However, from what can be surmised from Steiner's lectures it seems that they do not have dominion over all in the universe and spiritual world as is widely accepted in Christian doctrines. Nevertheless, they are of a spiritual nature that is beyond the Seraphim. All Beings above and beyond the Seraphim appear to merge as One when spiritually perceived by the human soul. Whenever the doctrine of monotheism, of One God, is proclaimed it may very well be proclaiming a higher truth in that when we enter the spiritual world and we perceive Beings beyond the Seraphim we perceive them as only One Entity. This is so because at this level of Godhood beyond that of the Seraphim these Beings can no longer be seen spiritually as separate Beings. Therefore, to one's spirit vision they coalesce as One. This is analogous to a galaxy which is comprised of a great multiplicity of stars. However, when we view a galaxy from a far distance we see it as One whole. We view it as one singular celestial body. Moreover, there may be other Beings that have evolved beyond the level of Beings that we recognize as the Father, Son and Holy Spirit of this planetary system. Therefore, it may be that Beings of such stature who have ascended far beyond the Holy Trinity are not discernible to any degree by any human Being.

Where would such Beings primarily reside in relation to cosmic space. To begin the search for an answer to this question we could possibly begin by probing the most mysterious features of the universe. Science has determined that our galaxy holds a massive black hole within its center as do other galaxies. Could it be that Beings above the stature of this solar system's Holy Trinity reside within the 'negative space' element of our galaxy's central black hole. It is possible to surmise this because we understand that the Spirits of Form of this solar system reside within the inner negative space element of our sun. In regard to higher Beings residing within our galaxy's black hole the principle is the same as that of the Spirits of Form residing within the sun's negative space but on a higher gradation. These galactic black holes radiate tremendous amounts of energy outwardly; even beyond their very own galaxies. The principle of energy dispersion from the periphery of the inner negative space of our galaxy's black hole is the same as the dispersion of energy from our sun's inner negative space but on a much greater scale. The sun spots that are observed by science act as windows into this negative space. This negative space element is ubiquitous within all cosmic bodies and it is the primary cause for gravity. The earth

63

holds a sphere of negative space within its core. Negative space is the residual aspect of the Saturn Period phase through which all planets, suns, solar systems and galaxies pass. The counter force of balance to a planet's inner negative space centripetal gravity element is the centrifugal force exerted by the rotation of a planet. A planet's perpetual rotation preserves it from collapsing within itself. While its inner negative space holds it from flying apart. The same holds for the centrifugal element of the planets revolving around the sun and the solar systems revolving around the center of the galaxy; all of which is orchestrated by hierarchical Beings. Negative space and gravity are residuary to Cosmic Will.

The following is from the lecture cycle, "The Book of Revelation and the Work of the Priest." They were lectures addressed to the priests of the Christian Community Church Movement in 1924.

"The apocalyptist sees the grand picture of the heavens opening (Rev.19: 11). On a white horse there rides towards him a power about whom the apocalyptist speaks, and by the way he speaks he shows that he bears the Trichotomy of the Godhead not only in his understanding, in his intellect, but also in his whole human Being. The way he speaks shows how he knows with his whole soul that the three Persons are three forms of the One God and that if you go beyond the physical world you cannot speak of the one or the other, for they merge into each other. Placed into the physical world, however, the picture shows three Persons, so that we have to distinguish between the Father God, who is at the foundation of all natural facts including those that work into human nature, the Son God, who has to do with all that leads into freedom of soul experience, and the Spirit God, who lives in a spiritual, cosmic order that is far away from nature, entirely foreign to nature. Here on the physical plane these three Persons appear thus sharply differentiated.

On stepping across the threshold to the spiritual world, the human Being enters a condition I have described in my book, "Knowledge of the Higher Worlds," a condition in which he becomes structured into three Beings, so that Thinking, Feeling and Will each attain a degree autonomy. In contrast to this, when we leave the physical plane and arrive in the higher worlds we see the Threefold God coming towards us more and more as One God. It is with this especially in mind that we must read the Book of Revelation. We must not follow the pattern of the physical world and distinguish between Father God, Son God and Spirit God." [Lecture X: Dornach, 14 September, 1924].

Beings evolve, ascend and become ever greater Creator Beings, such as the Twelve World Initiators from whom resounded the Word of the Worlds. Beings of this stature are individually indiscernible to humans once these Beings ascend beyond the ranks of the Seraphim. To human spiritual perception, they appear to us as One God in the spiritual world as they seemingly merge as One.

Over the centuries it has been an orthodox canon of Christianity that Christ was and is a Being that was present as a God of the Trinity from all time and that He was the Creator of all other Beings from the beginning. It has been the accepted doctrine that the Christ Being is a Being who was uncreated. When ascertaining what Rudolf Steiner had stated in regard to the evolution of the Christ Being along with the many statements he offered in addressing the ascension of Michael the Archangel to the stature of the Archai hierarchy, a foundation is established for understanding that in the normal course of evolution, Beings progress to ever higher stages of existence. This raises the question: What becomes of the Seraphim in the course of their evolution? According to orthodox dogma the Trinity is the supreme level of Godhood and that no other Beings could ever ascend to that level of spiritual expression. Steiner, however, overturns this dogma when he said that the Christ originated from the Archangel hierarchy. In accepting this truth from Steiner it then becomes reasonable to suggest that all other Beings have the innate potential capacity to progress and evolve into Beings similar to that of the present stature of the Christ Being. Other Beings from within our cosmos will eventually become Firstborn, Creator Beings as Christ is now while Christ Himself will continue to evolve to an ever greater stature.

These Beings who are presently above the Seraphim intermingle and live within one another as Steiner did say. These Beings live within and intermingle with one another yet are still individuated. All Beings of the Hierarchies are capable of this. However, this seems to be more pronounced when we speak of Beings beyond the Seraphim. At this level of spiritual expression, Steiner's research suggests that there is a multiplicity of Lofty Beings throughout the universe equal to that or greater than the Holy Trinity Who are both One and many at the same time. Steiner's research also indicates that the Holy Trinity has Regency over this solar system of ours while other Beings at levels beyond the Seraphim have Regencies over other planetary systems and galaxies. It should be noted that it is not so much the physicality of planetary systems and galaxies that are of the essence. Rather, the planetary systems and galaxies are the physical manifestations of spiritual activity.

If Christ had always been what He is now and that He, the Father and Holy Spirit were the absolute 'First Cause' then that would be tantamount to saying that there is a limit to evolution; the Seraphim would evolve no higher. Though some Beings may have regressed in their evolution, most Beings of the Hierarchies are in the process of continuously evolving and ascending. This has been intimated in the above lecture excerpts in which Steiner said that Christ also has evolved and will continue to do so in the future. It seems possible to say then that the Beings of the Hierarchies have the potential to evolve to a condition of Being in their evolution where they too become Beings similar in nature to the present condition of Being which

65

the Holy Spirit, the Christ and the Father now possess. The Holy Trinity will also continue to evolve beyond what they are now. It should be noted that the Father Being was the Regent over this planetary system throughout the Saturn, Sun and Moon Periods. While during the Sun and Moon periods Christ, who originated from the hierarchy of the Archangels, progressed beyond the normal course of evolution. During the Sun Period Christ was Initiated by the Twelve World Initiators, the World-Word, and rapidly evolved beyond the Hierarchies. He then ascended to a condition of Being in which He became the subsequent Regent of this planetary system at the beginning of the Earth Manvantara.

In pursuing the study of the Gospel of St. John, the question arises as to whether Steiner references any time period to the opening words of this Gospel in terms of world evolution. When examining the question of human and world evolution, the Gospel of St. John offers us significant insights. In the first two lectures of Steiner's 1908 Gospel of St. John cycle and more specifically in the initial sentences of the third lecture he alludes to the indication that the opening words of the Gospel of St. John pertain to the evolution of "pre- humanity" prior to the Earth Period; that is, the prologue of the Gospel of St. John references the beginning of the Saturn Period and takes us through to the present Earth Period. In the Book of Genesis the opening words, "In the beginning God created the heavens and the Earth . . . ," marks the period in this Earth Manvantara, this Earth Condition of Consciousness, when the Elohim awoke from their pralaya, their cosmic sleep, and began their works of creation during this Earth Period. The opening words of John's Gospel, however, refer to the very beginning of the creation of humanity which dawned during the Saturn Period.

What is noteworthy is that Steiner speaks of the Logos as a divine creative Principle. It is something that lives in all creative spiritual Beings who can express the awareness of their own I AM. It is this creative divine Principle which is the First Cause of all things. It is the I AM forces from a multiplicity of Beings which are behind the creation of all things that were created. The Logos is not any one singular Being. It is a universal Principle. Christ can be viewed as the First Cause during the Earth Manvantara in that in this cosmos He, proceeding from the Father, was the First to emerge from the previous Cosmic Night of our planetary cosmos which extended from the ending of the Moon Period to the beginning stages of the Earth Period. All other Beings in this sphere of activity later emerged sequentially from their cosmic slumber and that His Being flowed through these creative hierarchies. As mentioned previously, Genesis begins with the awakening of the Elohim at the time of the separation of the sun from the earth during the Earth Manvantara; "In the beginning the Elohim created the heavens [sun and planets] and the earth." The Universal Creative Principle which emanates from any I AM Being was also present in germinal form in the human Being during Saturn when the earliest stages of the creation of the human larynx was formulated, in its most nascent stage, during Saturn. Steiner had said that the creative activity of the Hierarchies is spiritual speech. That which flows from out of the soul and spirit is the Word of creation. This is the Logos. That which is created by an I AM Being is spiritual speech and the forces which flow from any I AM Being during their activity of creating is the Logos. Christ said, "the heavens and earth may pass away but my 'words' will never pass away," which may be understood to convey that His activity as a Macrocosmic Creator Being among other creator Beings will never cease. In Lecture IV from, "Occult Signs and Symbols," Steiner offered this remark: "In the literal sense of the word, all of you are words uttered by divine Beings." This Universal Cosmic/Creative Principle of being able to create was always there in the beginning. The creative principle that emanates from all I AM Beings is the Word that was there in the beginning. Eventually throughout the course of His evolution Christ ascended to a level where He could, at the beginning of the Earth Period, become Regent of this solar system. It wasn't until the Earth Manvantara that He became a Macrocosmic Being.

In Lecture I from, "The Gospel of St. John in Relation to the Other Gospels," notice how Steiner reads the opening words to the Gospel of St. John: "In the beginning was the Word, and the Word was with God, and a God was the Word. The same was in the beginning with God. All things were made by It; and without It was not anything made that was made. In It was life; and the life was the light of men. And the light shineth in the darkness; and the darkness comprehended it not." (John 1: 1-5).

It should be noted that Steiner interchanges the pronoun 'It' for the standard interpretation which uses the pronoun Him. When employing the word, It, this directs us to the Divine and Universal Creative Principle of all I AM Beings. This Creative Principle lives in the Being of Christ as it does in all other I AM Beings. "In the beginning" the Word, the Divine Creative Principle, existed during the Saturn Period and extended beyond to unfathomable ages which manifested before the Saturn Period. During the Earth Period, the Creative Word expresses Itself through the Macrocosmic Christ throughout our solar system. The Word, the Logos, was with Christ who is a God. It lives in Him as It lives in all I AM Beings. The Word is the inner capacity to both create and recognize oneself as an individuated Self. In accordance with the Universal Creative Principle, Christ brought a Redeeming Principle to the Earth by bringing cosmic 'youth' forces ("an aura through which cosmic forces and cosmic laws descended to Earth"; Lecture IX on Mark's Gospel) that would reverse the direction of the course of human and earthly evolution. When Christ said - It Is Finished - the Fall was now being halted while the Ascension of the earth and humanity was underway.

In Lecture I from his 1908 John cycle Steiner says this in regard to the creative principle: "The followers of St. John said further: What appears last in the human Being existed in the world in the very earliest times. We fancy that the human Being in his present form did not exist in the earlier conditions of the earth. But in an imperfect, mute form he was there and little by little he evolved into a Being endowed with the Logos or the Word. This became possible through the fact that what appears within him later as the creative principle was there from the very beginning, in a higher reality. What struggled forth out of the soul was in the beginning the divine creative principle. The Word, which sounds forth from the soul, the Logos, was there in the beginning and so guided evolution that at last a Being came into existence, in whom it also could manifest. What finally appears in time and space was already there in spirit from the beginning."

"When we go back in human evolution we meet an imperfect human Being and the significance of evolution is, that finally the Logos or Word which discloses the depths of the human soul may appear as its flower. In the beginning this mute human Being appears as seed of the Logos-endowed human Being, but, on the other hand, has sprung from the Logos-endowed God. The human Being has sprung from a mute human creature, not gifted with speech, but: In the beginning was the Logos, the Word.

Thus those who understand the Logos-doctrine in its earlier significance press forward to the divine creative Word which is the beginning of existence and to which the writer of the Gospel of St. John refers. Let us hear what he says in the very first words: 'In the beginning was the Word and the Word was with God and the Word was a God.'

They will ask where is the 'Word' today? The Word is also here today and the Word is with men and the Word has become man! Thus the writer of the Gospel of St. John forges a link between man and God and indeed we find sounding forth in the beginning of this Gospel a doctrine easy for every human heart to understand."

Working from this premise it becomes conceivable to postulate another rendering to the opening of John's prologue:

"In the beginning was the Word . . .":

These first three words, "In the beginning," direct us to the Saturn Period. The, 'Word', is the ubiquitous Creative Principle which pervades the universe. In these words John is already alluding to the Word of the Twelve World Initiators as well as to the future status of the Christ as the Logos. Though the Thrones acted as key components of human and world evolution during the Saturn Manvantara it is suggested in this study that the opening sentences of John's prologue are primarily focused on the key components of the evolution of the Christ Being. John does combine the evolution of humanity with the evolution of the Christ in his prologue. However, in John's prologue, it is the evolution of the Christ which is predominant.

68

"... and the Word was with God ...":

These words direct us to the Sun Period; the Manvantara in which Christ was Initiated by the Twelve World Initiators. This was when Christ received the living wisdom and creative forces of the World-Word from the Twelve World Initiators. They were Beings who were beyond the Seraphim and who surrounded our cosmos from the beginning. These words also extend to the Moon Period as Christ continued to unite Himself with the World Word. The terms, 'Word' and 'God', become interchangeable as they may refer to the Christ as the Word-filled One who later became a Logos God while they also indicate the single coalescence of the Twelve World Initiators within the realm of Godhood. Christ and the World-Word of the Twelve World Initiators became intermingled during the Sun and Moon Periods.

"... and the Word was (a) God":

These words lead us to the Earth Period. The creative principle of the Twelve World Initiators, the World-Word, now lived in Christ. He embodied, during the present Earth Period, the fullness of the World-Word. At the beginning of the Earth Period, He became a Logos God Who stood above the Hierarchies and was no longer a microcosmic hierarchical Being but had become a Macrocosmic Being.

Lecture X from the previously cited cycle, "Man in the Light of Occultism, Theosophy and Philosophy," (MLOTP) gives us solid ground on which to consider that Christ is also an evolving Being. Steiner also mentioned in, "Cosmic Ego and Human Ego," (CEHE) that Christ evolves His Macrocosmic Ego during the Earth Period and will later evolve His Macrocosmic Manas and Buddhi in the subsequent Jupiter and Venus Periods respectively. We can assume from this pattern that He will also develop His Macrocosmic Atma during the Vulcan Period. If Christ had always been, from the beginning of the Saturn Period, a part of an All-Universal Creator Trinity He would have had these aspects within His Being from the beginning. However, this is not so. Christ has always been an evolving Being and continues to evolve.

The following is a portion of what Steiner said in his lecture, "Cosmic Ego and Human Ego": "The Christ is quite radically different from other Beings who share in the Earth evolution. He is a Being of quite another order; He is a Being who remained behind, not only during the Moon evolution, as the Luciferic spirits did, but who, foreseeing the Moon evolution, actually remained behind still earlier, namely, during the old Sun evolution; and it was from a certain assured wisdom far above the human that He remained behind during the old Sun evolution. We cannot regard this Being as microcosmic in the sense which applies to the other Beings we have been considering; for we have to regard as microcosmic Beings those who were connected with this Earth evolution from its beginning. The Christ was not directly connected with the Earth evolution, but with the Sun evolution.

69

He was a macrocosmic Being from the beginning of the Earth evolution on, a Being who was exposed to entirely different conditions of evolution from those of the microcosmic beings. And His evolutionary conditions were of a special sort; they were such that this macrocosmic Christ Being evolved the macrocosmic Ego outside earthly conditions. For this Christ evolution it was normal to bring to Ego-perfection, outside the earth, an Ego of a macrocosmic sort, and then to descend to earth. And so for the evolution of the Christ Being it was normal, when He descended from the macrocosm to our earth, to bring into it the great impulse of the macrocosmic Ego, in order that the microcosmic Ego, the human Ego, might take up this impulse, and be able to go forward in its evolution. It was normal for the Christ to have the macrocosmic Ego-impulse - not the microcosmic Ego-impulse - just as much evolved as man upon the earth had developed the microcosmic. Thus the Christ Being is a Being Who in a certain sense is like the human being, only that man is microcosmic and has brought his four principles to expression microcosmically, and hence has his Ego also microcosmically as earth-Ego - but the Christ as Cosmic Ego. His evolution was such that He was great and significant because of the perfect development of this Ego, which He brought down to earth. And He had not the fifth macrocosmic principle, and not the sixth, for He will evolve these on Jupiter and on Venus, in order that He may give them to man."[source: www.elib.com]

One point of significance from the above is the following: "He was a macrocosmic Being from the beginning of the Earth evolution on." This suggests that Christ was in the process of passing through an evolution during the Sun and Moon Manvantaras in which He was in the initial stages of `developing' a Macrocosmic Ego which He then brought to Earth. He was the First Cause and "created all Beings" in that He was the first to come forth from the slumber of the Cosmic Pralaya which preceded the Earth Manvantara. He was the Being that brought the microcosmic Beings, the Hierarchical Beings, from out of their slumber and into activity, stage by stage, hierarchy after hierarchy. As mentioned previously, the Elohim awakened at the time when the sun and earth were separating from one another during the Earth Manvantara.

To further elaborate the indication that Christ evolved to the stature of a Macrocosmic Being some quotes from Lecture X of MLOTP should be noted, such as: "On Earth Christ repels Lucifer from the outset. This is because on the Moon, when He was Himself less highly evolved - for Christ also undergoes evolution . . ."

". . . we have to show how Christ through His own special character and nature has, during the course of the evolution that has taken place between old Sun and the present time, passed through an upward evolution, and from having been a Spirit who was of like nature with the planetary Spirits has become the Ruler or Regent of the whole solar system."

70

Notice that when Steiner says, ". . . of the whole solar system . . . ," he does not mention that Christ has Regency beyond this solar system. In this lecture Steiner specifically describes how it was the Twelve World Initiators that Initiated and elevated Christ to the status that He has attained. The above quotes from Steiner have been cited to support the position that Christ was not always a Macrocosmic Being. That is, He was not always a Being that was beyond the Hierarchies. He was a planetary Being during the Sun Period as was Lucifer. Steiner compares them as being like 'brothers'; brothers who evolved in opposing directions. Christ became a Being whose evolution was then outside the normal progression of evolution as He began to surpass all the other hierarchical, microcosmic Beings during the Sun and Moon Periods. It was during the Sun Period that He began to receive the necessary spiritual impulses of attaining the stature of a Macrocosmic Being. This is why Steiner states in CEHE that, "We cannot regard this Being as microcosmic in the sense which applies to the other Beings we have been considering." Though Christ received from the Twelve World Initiators the World-Word, He sacrificially remained behind in His evolution during the Sun and Moon Periods until the beginning of the Earth Period. It was not until the beginning of the Earth Period that Christ fully achieved the stature of a Macrocosmic Being as stated by Steiner. Afterwards, during the Earth Manvantara, He once again sacrifices His position in the spiritual worlds and descended to Earth. Christ's descent to Earth did not take place until after the 'Fall'. Christ will continue His Macrocosmic evolution throughout the Jupiter, Venus and Vulcan Periods after which the Holy Spirit will become the leading Spirit in more distant Manvantaras while the Father was the leading Macrocosmic Spirit during the Saturn, Sun and Moon Periods.

Returning to the earlier question whether the Seraphim eventually become Macrocosmic Beings; evolution would suggest that this is so. A more definitive answer to this question may be found in the previously cited, "Man in the Light of Occultism, Theosophy and Philosophy" - Lecture X. Steiner clearly stated in this lecture that, during the Sun Period, Christ was a planetary Being. And from, "Cosmic Ego and Human Ego," he said the following: "Christ was a Macrocosmic Being from the beginning of the Earth evolution on." It should also be noted that during the Sun period He did not descend from higher spheres of the spiritual world to this position as a planetary Being . Rather, He was originally a microcosmic hierarchical Being among other microcosmic hierarchical Beings at that time; though He eventually ascended beyond the normal course of evolution of other microcosmic Beings due to His cosmic Initiation during the Sun Period. He was the Regent of what was then to become our present sun while Lucifer was the Regent of a planetary sphere which has become the present planet Venus. Eventually, during the Sun Manvantara and throughout the Moon Manvantara He was removed from the normal course of evolution and began

71

His ascent to the condition of a Macrocosmic Being which He did not attain until the beginning of the Earth Manvantara.

It was the Twelve World Initiators, the Twelve Lofty Beings, Who were above that of the planetary Being, the Christ, and Who were from the regions of what are now the Twelve zodiacal constellations. It was they who elevated Christ to His eventual status as a Macrocosmic Being. All of this was during the Sun and Moon Periods. The above material from Steiner gives support to the assertion that Christ did go through an evolutionary progression. The biblical quotations of Christ as the First Cause are references to Christ as the first to reawaken the evolution of this planetary system from out of the depths of its Cosmic Night, its Pralaya, which extended from the last of the Moon Period to the beginning of the Earth Period. The Impulse of His Macrocosmic Ego permeates all things which have been created during this Earth Period in our planetary system. He stands behind the whole of this present manifestation of our planetary cosmos. He is the Alpha and the Omega of this Earth Period in that He was the First Cause, the first to emerge from the last Cosmic Night, and He will be the last to pass into the next Cosmic Night.

After reading the previously cited lectures, it seems appropriate to assert that Christ never made any previous descent from higher spheres until the Earth Manvantara. It is interesting to note that in Steiner's, "Occult Science: An Outline," in the chapter - The Evolution of the Cosmos and Man - Steiner never mentions the Christ Being throughout all of his discourse on the evolution of the Saturn, Sun and Moon Periods. In fact, he doesn't mention Christ until he begins to speak of the Fall during the Earth Period. This is when he speaks of the Mystery of Golgotha as a, "window into the affairs of the Gods." It was only then that the Gods decided to send the Christ Being to Earth and reverse its course of evolution from a descending path to one that is on a path of ascension. Secondly, who were these Gods that had sent Christ? Were they the Twelve World Initiators that Steiner speaks of that initiated Christ during the Sun Period?

In MLOTP, Steiner had said: ". . .the Christ on the other hand, gave Himself up to the Impression of this Word of the Worlds, received It in its fullness and entirety into Himself, so that this Christ Soul was now the Being that united in Himself all the great Secrets of the World that sounded into Him through the inexpressible Word."

The Word of the Worlds is the cumulative Impulse from the Twelve World Initiators that flowed into Christ who completely dedicated Himself to Them. Gathering all that Steiner had said from MLOTP and CEHE Christ could not have been a Macrocosmic Being nor a part of the present Holy Trinity any time before the Earth Manvantara. It seems clear that He did not descend from greater spheres beyond the Hierarchies to the level of a planetary Being during the Sun Period. Nor did He manifest from higher spheres through any planetary Being of lower rank at this time as He did

72

through Jehovah during the Earth Period until He eventually incarnated on earth.. This was so because the Being we have come to recognize as the Christ was a planetary Being Himself from the ranks of the Archangels during the Sun Manvantara and was not a Macrocosmic Being at that time.

Steiner said the following from CEHE: ". . . He was a Macrocosmic Being from the beginning of the Earth evolution on, a Being who was exposed to entirely different conditions of evolution from those of the microcosmic Beings. And His evolutionary conditions were of a special sort; they were such that this Macrocosmic Christ Being evolved the Macrocosmic Ego outside earthly conditions."

Once Christ had been initiated by the Twelve World Initiators, Christ's evolution was such that, ". . . His evolutionary conditions were of a special sort; they were such that this Macrocosmic Christ Being evolved the Macrocosmic Ego outside earthly conditions." Christ moved beyond and stepped out of the normal course of evolution. From the Twelve World Initiators He received the possibility and potentiality to spiritually evolve and ascend beyond the various levels of Hierarchies but He chose not to do so at that time. Instead, He dedicated His Self to the World Word and sacrificed His ascent while staying behind as a planetary Being. He then overcame Lucifer during the subsequent Moon Period which during the Sun Period He anticipated would be necessary. [It should be noted that the term, 'Christ', is used only as a means to identify Him as He was not the Christ as we presently understand Him to be until the Earth Period]. This sacrificing of His own ascent during the Sun and Moon Periods gave Him even greater potential to ascend beyond the Hierarchies. It was only after His Initiation, His sacrifice and the overcoming of Lucifer during the Sun and Moon Manvantaras that this planetary Being had reached the degree of a Macrocosmic Being; " He was a Macrocosmic Being from the beginning of the Earth evolution on."

The above excerpts from Steiner's lectures give us an entirely different understanding of the Holy Trinity. From that which Steiner has stated in the above excerpts the doctrines pertaining to the Holy Trinity of universal omnipotence and omnipresence are overturned. The Holy Trinity, which we regard as the Father, Son and Holy Spirit, has a limited regency over this solar system alone. There is, from our very limited perspective, One Trinity to which we are connected. However, we can project the possibilities that there are a multiplicity of Gods throughout this galaxy and throughout the whole universe. Beings who evolve to a certain level will break away and create new planetary systems and galaxies thereby becoming the Gods of those solar systems and galaxies. Is it then possible to conceive of a Being reaching a high level of evolutionary achievement and subsequently becoming a Supreme God for an entire galaxy; a God whose condition of Spirit is far above that of the Holy Trinity of our planetary system?

Through the study of Anthroposophy it is possible to discern patterns that are applicable to various realities. In other words, patterns that apply to macrocosmic realities are often applicable to microcosmic realities as well. For instance, through Anthroposophy we have come to know that advanced Beings departed from the earth and assumed an existence on the sun. This reality is applicable on a much larger scale as well. For instance, when highly evolved Beings come to such an advanced stage in their evolution they separate themselves from one solar system or galaxy and create a new solar system or new galaxy. Before creating a new galaxy, that portion of the older galaxy where these advanced Beings have Regency becomes like an embryo for a new galaxy within the older galaxy until it reaches the stage where it can then separate and sever itself from the older galaxy. When this portion of the older galaxy, which serves as the embryo of a new galaxy, finally severs itself from the older galaxy it creates the birth of a new galaxy while the older galaxy acts as a mother galaxy giving birth to the newer. In the Hermetic axiom -As above; So below, - we see the birthing process at many levels. The birthing of a new galaxy is another manifestation of the Cosmic and Spiritual Principle which is expressed in the Hermetic axiom.

* * * * * * * * * * *

Throughout these discussions the term, Father, has been observed several times. Throughout the copious volumes of Steiner's lectures he often distinguishes different renderings of the term, Father. He has utilized it in the following contexts:

THE FATHER:

1) The Father Being of the Holy Trinity.
2) The Ground and Foundation of the realm of Matter.
3) The Father can also be a reference to one's own Ego. During Christ's healing miracles and raising of the dead Christ indicated that they were performed for the Glory of the Father; or, in other words, theses miracles were enacted for the Initiation of the human Ego. "I and the Father are One," is a reference to the interconnection between Christ and the human Ego.
4) Jehovah is referred to as the Father of our physical body. When we pass through the spiritual realm of the Moon's elliptical sphere during the processes of incarnation we pass through the sphere of Jehovah to receive the forces for our new born physical body.
5) The Father is also a reference to Cosmic Space. Steiner also refers to all of the spiritual Hierarchies as the Father. The previously mentioned, "I and the Father are One," as said by Christ also makes use of the multiplicity of various meanings to the term, Father. When the term Father is used to denote 'cosmic space' it thereby makes

reference to the truth that Christ is the Macrocosmic Ego-Being and Regent of this planetary system and the zodiacal constellations.

6) The term Father is applied to those who have achieved the attainment of the seventh level of Initiation. The sixth level is referred to as a Sun Initiate or Sun-Hero. The fifth level is referred to as an Initiate who is one with the people; i.e. Israelite, Persian and so forth.

7) The Father is a term that is applied to the aspect of Death. Later, this will be presented and explained more fully from Steiner's lectures.

8) The Atma, or Spirit Human, is referred to as the Father aspect of the individual. Whereas, the Life Spirit, the Buddhi, is the Son aspect and the Spirit Self, the Manas, is the Holy Spirit aspect of an individual.

9) Higher Beings have eighth, ninth and tenth aspects beyond Manas, Buddhi and Atma to which are referred as Holy Spirit, Son or Word, and Father respectively.

10) The term Father can refer to the first hierarchy consisting of the Seraphim, Cherubim and Thrones. These Beings are most closely connected with the Father. The second hierarchy of the Dominions, Mights and Spirits of Form is associated with the Son. While the third hierarchy of the Archai, Archangels and Angels is affiliated with the Holy Spirit.

THE HOLY SPIRIT:

Below is an excerpt from Rudolf Steiner's, "The Deed of Christ and the Opposing Spiritual Powers: Lucifer, Ahriman, Asuras," claiming that the redeemed Lucifer is the Holy Spirit. According to Rudolf Steiner, Lucifer is ,". . . the light over the Lodge of the Twelve;" and he is also referred to as, ". . . the Thirteenth (who) is the Leader of the Lodge of the Twelve." The Twelve is a reference to the Twelve Bodhisattvas. It should be noted that the essence and identity of the redeemed Lucifer is better understood as similar to that of Jehovah through whom Christ manifested Himself to the Hebrew people prior to His incarnation into the body of Jesus of Nazareth. Christ, a Logos Being, reflected his Self downwardly through a Spirit of Form, an Exusia Being known as Jehovah. In like manner the Logos Holy Spirit reflects itself downwardly through the redeemed Lucifer.

Steiner:

"In the spiritual sense, Whitsuntide belongs inseparably to Easter. This 'Holy Spirit' is none other than the Lucifer-Spirit, resurrected now in higher, purer glory - the Spirit of independent understanding, wisdom-inwoven. Christ Himself foretold that this Spirit would come to men after Him, and in the light of this Spirit their labors must proceed. What is it that works onward in the light of this Spirit? The world-stream of spiritual science, if rightly

75

conceived! What is this spiritual science? It is the wisdom of the Spirit, the wisdom that lifts into the full light of consciousness that in Christianity which would otherwise remain in the unconscious. The torch of the resurrected Lucifer, of the Lucifer now transformed into the good, blazons the way for Christ. Lucifer is the bearer of the Light - Christ is the Light! As the word itself denotes, Lucifer is the 'Bearer of the Light.' That is what the spiritual scientific movement should be, that is implicit in it. Those who know that the progress of mankind depends upon living apprehension of the mighty Event of Golgotha are they who as the 'Masters of Wisdom and of the Harmony of Feelings' are united in the great Guiding Lodge of mankind. And as once the "tongues of fire" hovered down as a living symbol upon the company of the Apostles, so does the 'Holy Spirit announced by Christ Himself reign as the Light over the Lodge of the Twelve. The Thirteenth is the Leader of the Lodge of the Twelve. The 'Holy Spirit' is the mighty Teacher of those we name the 'Masters of Wisdom and of the Harmony of Feelings.' It is through them that his voice and his wisdom flow down to mankind in this or that stream upon the earth. The treasures of wisdom gathered together by the spiritual scientific movement in order to understand the universe and the Spirits therein, flow through the 'Holy Spirit' into the Lodge of the Twelve; and that is what will ultimately lead mankind step by step to free, self-conscious understanding of Christ and of the Event of Golgotha. Thus to `cultivate' spiritual science means to understand that the Spirit has been sent into the world by Christ; the pursuit of spiritual science is implicit in true Christianity. This will become more and more evident to men; and then they will realize that in spiritual science they have a potent asset in their lives. Men owe to spiritual science the consciousness which dawns in them by degrees, that Christ is the Spirit Who fills the world with light. And the consequence will be that here on this earthly globe, in the physical world itself, men will make progress in their moral life, in their life of will, in their intellectual life. Through physical life itself the world will be spiritualized in ever-increasing measure. Men will grow in goodness, strength and wisdom and will gaze with ever deepening vision into the foundations and origins of existence. They will bear with them into the supersensible life the fruits acquired in this physical life, and ever and again bring these fruits back from the supersensible life into a new incarnation."

It should be noted that in Steiner's lectures on the Gospel of St. Luke, Lecture VII, he also refers to Christ as the Thirteenth among the Twelve Bodhisattvas. Steiner said the following: "Whence do these Bodhisattvas receive what they have to proclaim from epoch to epoch? - If you were able to look into the great Spirit-Lodge of the Twelve Bodhisattvas you would find that in the midst of the Twelve there is a Thirteenth - one who cannot be called a `Teacher' in the same sense as the Bodhisattvas, but of whom we must say: He is that Being from whom wisdom itself streams as very substance. It is therefore quite correct to speak of the Twelve Bodhisattvas in the great Spirit-Lodge grouped around One who is their Center; they are wrapt in contemplation of the sublime Being from whom there streams what they have then to inculcate into earth evolution in fulfillment of their missions. Thus there streams from the Thirteenth what the others have to teach. They are the `Teachers', the `Inspirers'; the Thirteenth is Himself the Being of whom the others teach, whom they proclaim from epoch to epoch. This Thirteenth is He whom the ancient Rishis called Vishva Karman, whom Zarathustra called Ahura Mazdao, whom we call the Christ. He is the Leader and Guide of the great Lodge of the Bodhisattvas."

We may be able to resolve this question of the `Thirteenth' which Steiner mentions, be it Christ or Lucifer, if we consider that the redeemed Lucifer now acts as the intermediary Holy Spirit to the Bodhisattvas. Steiner had also stated that Lucifer is the Holy Spirit among humanity. He is the intermediary, the intercessor between our inner Self and the Christ Being. The Holy Spirit works as a reflection of the Christ Impulse which then enters our soul and Ego. At this stage in our development, without the Holy Spirit one's soul and Ego would be overwhelmed by the Christ Impulse. Without the intercession of the Holy Spirit our individuated consciousness would be subjugated by the Christ Impulse. That which streams to us from Christ comes to us through the Holy Spirit; thereby we retain our self-consciousness. For the Bodhisattvas, there too, Lucifer acts as an intermediary. The future evolutionary Impulses for humanity and the earth flow from Christ and then pass through Lucifer as the Holy Spirit to the Bodhisattvas who are the `Teachers' of humanity. In this manner both Christ and Lucifer act in conjunction with one another and thereby are conjoined as One.

VI

The Son of Man and the Event of Golgotha

In Wilhelm Kelber's, "Christ and the Son of Man," he makes note of certain points from the lectures of Steiner that help tie the connection of the Adam/Nathan soul and the soul of John the Baptist together. In regard to the untarnished Adam soul, Kelber writes: "Three times he was mediator of the deeds of the pre-existing Christ in epochs called Lemurian and Atlantic periods. As sensitive organ, feeling for the suffering of earthly humanity, he became aware of the dangers humanity was exposed to through the Luciferic influence. `He sought in His inner Being fully to feel this tragic aspect of humanity's development.' . . . we saw how Christ describes the Son of Man as a soul-Being who extends His perception into all human souls, who perceives when `one of the least of my brothers' is given food or drink, is clothed or, conversely, is ignored (Matthew 25: 35). That is a characteristic of the Son of Man which he evidently keeps for all time. He already has proved it when he assisted in the three deeds of the pre-existent Christ. From His parting from the earthly path of fallen humanity to the Last Judgment, this quality characterizes His role in the development of humanity.

This quality should not be thought of as limitless dedication only. Rather, the case is that the soul-processes of all human Beings are reflected in the collective Adam soul-Being, as if they were its own. This relates the Adam soul (or, as we said, the Son of Man) to Christ, Who has the same relationship to the `I' of human Beings as this soul has to the soul-nature of all human individualities. Thereby it was enabled `to be penetrated in the spiritual world by the Christ Being.' Christ entered into the Adam soul, `ensouled' Himself in it, as later He `embodied' Himself in Jesus, and through this union He was able to heal the soul-forces of earthly humanity. The Christ Being evidently needed a mediator between human Beings, a `transformer,' in order to impart His forces to humanity. The Adam soul is neither divine nor human, but an intermediary Being, suitable for this function."

Since Christ had entered a physical incarnation on Earth circa 2000 years ago both the Adam soul and the soul of John the Baptist became intermediaries for the Christ Impulse. They were once again united in purpose such that the Adam-soul served the Christ in His incarnation and that the Christ Aura was taken up by John the Baptist thereby initiating the First Cause in transforming the Phantom of a human Being in John the Baptist.

Kelber then cites the following from the Gospel of Matthew: "Among all who were born of earthly mothers, none is greater than John the Baptist. And yet the least of the Beings in the heavenly world is greater than he." (Matthew 11: 11). He then adds: "In other words: since the creation of the world no greater spirit has arisen from the succession of generations than John, but now a new humanity is beginning to emerge in the Kingdom of God come to Earth. The first example of a human bodily nature of this kind, that of Jesus, is imbued with the Adam soul and the Christ Spirit. Founded by the second Adam, the beginning of a new humanity has been established, no longer by physical procreation but through the indwelling of the Son of Man and Christ in human souls."

Here again the archetypal Phantom was established by the Christ through the intermediary, the Adam-soul, and that the first human who truly began to receive this newly creative Impulse for the transformation of the human Phantom was the kindred soul to the Adam-soul: John the Baptist. In Chapter IV, "The Son of Man in Anthroposophy," Kelber then writes the following: "Rudolf Steiner gave the term Son of Man a second meaning when he spoke about the `Sons of Man of past generations.' He says: `Although in the fourth epoch normally only the mind soul was developed, there must, among the leaders of humanity, have been some who had already developed the inner potential of the consciousness soul, into which shines the Spirit Self. Outwardly, however, they would have looked like other people.' (The Gospel of St. Matthew, lecture 11)."

Kelber: "Here the term Son of Man is used in the sense which we already know, and for persons we have also met before. Ezekiel and Daniel lived in the sixth century B.C., Ezra in the fifth. The writer of the "Book of Enoch" must also be placed in the fourth post-Atlantean epoch, as must the `Sons of Man of past generations' of whom Paul writes in his letter to the Ephesians. We can now understand better how they came by their special mission. From the indication of time, that is, the fourth epoch (and no earlier) we can conclude, in addition, that one result of this investigation is correct, namely that Zaratas did indeed inaugurate the Son of Man stream. The term Son of Man can describe three things: in a microcosmic sense, a stage of development in human consciousness; in a historical sense, leaders of humanity who have reached this level in advance of others, and in a macrocosmic sense that superhuman heavenly Being whom we have come to know as the pure Adam soul. The first two meanings we have now also found in Anthroposophy. Concerning the third meaning, Rudolf Steiner makes the most tremendous statements about the Adam soul, surpassing everything we have heard so far.

In his lectures on the Gospel of St. Mark, Steiner draws a distinction between two cosmic Beings in the Christ Jesus, namely, the Cosmic Christ and the Son of Man. . . . In Jesus the pure Adam soul was incarnated. It had become the Jesus soul. When the Zarathustra `I' left this soul again at the Jordan Baptism, the Cosmic Christ `I' entered it. Let us, for the moment, ask purely

79

theoretically: what must remain, when Christ left this Jesus of Nazareth? Only the Adam soul, the Son of Man, would remain as a Being separate from him. And that is how it is described: 'The chosen people had shown no understanding: whereupon the aura gradually withdrew from the man Jesus of Nazareth, and Christ and the Son of Man, Jesus of Nazareth, became ever more estranged from one another.' [The Gospel of St. Mark, Lecture 9]."

In contrast to Kelber, it has been a motif of this work which states that the Christ Ego did not abandon the body of Jesus of Nazareth. Rather, it was strictly the aura of Christ, the Cosmic Element of Christ, which loosely separated itself from the body of Jesus of Nazareth at the time of the arrest in the Garden of Gethsemane. The complete union of the Christ Ego with the physical body of Jesus of Nazareth did not reach its finality and culmination until the concluding moments of the Crucifixion when Christ then fully incarnated into the marrow of the bones of Jesus of Nazareth. It was only then that the full ingression of the Christ Spirit into the human Phantom/Form of Jesus of Nazareth was completed. After all that Steiner had said in regard to the common misunderstandings and misinterpretations of the Agony in the Garden it would be a complete reversal of his position to say that Christ abandoned the body of Jesus of Nazareth even if a vicarious connection between the Christ Spirit and Jesus of Nazareth still existed at the Crucifixion. It was the Cosmic Element, the Cosmic Auric Principle of Christ, the fleeing youth, that had actually separated from the body of Jesus of Nazareth and not the Christ Spirit.

Kelber then continues: "From these indications we learn that Christ's cosmic aura could only maintain itself in the Son of Man, with Jesus of Nazareth as its center, so long as a number of human souls on Earth were available to serve as a substantial basis. Perhaps we may understand the 'dozen,' the 'twelvehood,' of disciples in this sense. Could it be that twelve representatives of the forces working out of the zodiac were required to keep the Christ aura secured in the soul of Jesus - a soul which itself was not actually an ordinary individual soul? And might this aura only remain effective on Earth so long as it had the 'houses' of the disciples' souls at its disposal, just as the Sun sends its power to Earth from the twelve heavenly 'houses'? Evidently, the conditions needed for the effective working of the Christ aura through the incarnated Son of Man were no longer met when the lack of understanding in the disciples came to the fore: in the betrayal of Judas, perhaps already in Peter's misunderstanding at Caesarea Philippi and later in the disciples' flight in the Garden of Gethsemane and from Golgotha. It was not the Son of Man who was the cause of the estrangement between himself and Christ. Rather, he was the victim of this estrangement. This is how it might be understood:

Steiner on Mark's Gospel; Lecture IX: 'Everywhere, Christ is connected with a far-reaching effective aura. This effective aura existed because he was linked in soul with the people he had chosen; and it existed as long as He was at One with them. . .'

'The people chosen had shown no understanding, and so the aura gradually withdrew from the man Jesus of Nazareth . . .'

'And whereas previously the cosmic Christ could act within the Temple and drive out the merchants, and could proclaim the most mighty teachings yet nothing adverse happened - now that there was only a much looser connection between Jesus of Nazareth and Christ, his enemies could prevail against Him'."

Kelber then writes: "Christ was protected by the power of His divine aura. On occasion this shows, for instance when He is about to be captured. Then he slipped away 'through the midst of their ranks' (Luke 4: 30, compare John 8: 59). Human hands could not hold Him. The Son of Man could only be caught and held when the Christ aura no longer worked in Him in the way it had before. The Gospel accounts of the Son of Man can be taken as literally as that. Earlier, we wondered why there is such striking emphasis in the foretellings of the Passion on phrases like: the Son of Man will fall into the hands of sinners, and similar formulations. We now have the complete explanation and confirmation; the naked youth who, according to Mark's Gospel (14: 52), fled when Jesus was captured in the Garden of Gethsemane was, according to Rudolf Steiner's investigations, Christ who, at this moment, freed Himself a degree more from the Son of Man. This separation had to come if the capture - and the subsequent death of the Son of Man on the Cross - was to become possible."

Here again, in contradistinction to Kelber, it was the Cosmic Element of Christ and not the Christ Ego that separated from Jesus of Nazareth. Steiner had at times loosely referred to the Cosmic Element as simply Christ but simultaneously not referring to the actual Ego of Christ. Often times he did not use the strictest and most literal description of the Cosmic Element of Christ. To say that the Christ Spirit, the Christ Ego had separated itself from Jesus of Nazareth at the time of the arrest and identifying this Cosmic Aura of Christ as the Christ Ego would be comparable to saying that one's astral body is the Spirit of the individual when in fact the true Spirit of any individual is one's Ego and not one's astral body. It was the Cosmic Aura that separated from Christ Jesus while the Ego of Christ remained with the body of Jesus of Nazareth through the final moments of the Crucifixion.

Kelber then adds this in Chapter IV: "The Mystery of Golgotha, death on the Cross and the Resurrection, was accomplished for the benefit of the human body. Not only for a resurrection body at the Last Judgment, but already for the bodies of human Beings living on Earth. The emphasis moves to this truth when we have found insight into the mission of the Son of Man in the Mystery of Golgotha. Death had to be overcome where the power-base of death is: in the human body."

VII

The Gospel of Mark

In the previous chapters we have covered material that has been important in establishing a foundation for examining the question of the fleeing youth narrated in the Gospel of Mark. Later, we'll further study John the Baptist's connection with this Mystery along with examining the Cosmic Principle of Christ. The design of this chapter is to establish the groundwork for indicating clearly that the Cosmic Aura of Christ is a body of cosmic forces that Christ brought with Him to Earth. From this point on, the lectures of Rudolf Steiner become paramount and are virtually the exclusive and primary remaining focus of this work. We will begin with his lectures on the Gospel of Mark given in 1912 and establish lecture IX of this lecture cycle as the focal point of this entire study.

Steiner begins in Lecture II by asking: "What are we told at the beginning of the Gospel? We are particularly told to turn our attention to the figure of the Baptist. You can understand him only when you take into account the Jewish prophets, whose voice has become alive in him. The whole Jewish nation went up to be baptized by him. This means that there were many among them who recognized that the old prophets spoke through John the Baptist. That is stated at the beginning of the Gospel."

"After the Baptist is introduced to us, and we are shown how the people regard him and his mission, Christ Jesus is Himself introduced. But in what manner? At first we are told only that He is there, that He is recognized not only by men, but He is also recognized by Beings other than man. That is the point to be borne in mind. Around Him are those who wish to be healed from their demonic possession, those in whom demons are active. Around Him stand men in whom not merely human souls are living, but who are possessed by supersensible spirits who work through them. And in a significant passage we are told that these spirits recognize Christ Jesus. Of the Baptist we are told that men recognized him and went out to be baptized by him. But Christ is recognized by the supersensible spirits, so that He has to command them not to speak of Him. Beings from the supersensible world recognize Him, so it is said; that Being is entering who is not only recognized by men, but His appearance is recognized and considered dangerous by supersensible Beings. That is the glorious climax confronting us directly in the beginning of the Gospel of Mark. On the one side is John the Baptist, recognized and honored by men; and on the other He who is recognized and feared by supersensible Beings - who nevertheless have something to do with the Earth - so that they realize that now they must leave. Nowhere else is such an upward dramatic progression presented with such simplicity."

Steiner then moves to describing the karmic backgrounds of the Twelve Apostles saying: "The Twelve were deeply rooted in a nationality which had constituted itself in the grandest form. They stood there as if they were naked souls, simple souls, when Christ found them again. There had been a quite abnormal interval between their incarnations. The gaze of Christ Jesus could rest upon the Twelve, the reincarnated souls of those who had been the seven sons of the Maccabean (mother) and the five sons of Mattathias, Judas and his brothers; it was of these that the Apostolate was formed. They were thrown into the element of fishermen and simple folk."

Steiner then explains the background of Judas Iscariot and why he was prone to the act of betrayal: "Now perhaps your attention may be called to something else. Among the five sons of Mattathias is one who is already called Judas in the Old Testament. He was the one who at the time fought more bravely than all the others for his own people. In his soul he was dedicated to his people, and it was he who was successful in forming an alliance with the Romans against King Antiochus of Syria (I Macc: 8). This Judas is the same who later had to undergo the test of the betrayal, because he who was most intimately bound up with the old specifically Hebrew element, could not at once find the transition into the Christian element, needing the severe testing of the betrayal."

Previously it has been mentioned in this work that comprehension is vital in one's own particular bond with the Christ. It was essential in the bond between Christ and the Apostles. Steiner next speaks about how the baptism of others by John was an act that could transform the consciousness and awareness of the individual. He says in Lecture III: "A new impulse, new capacities, must come to humanity. The Baptism of John was therefore a question of knowledge. `Transform your minds, but don't merely turn your gaze backwards as would still be possible. Turn your gaze now to something else, to the God who manifests in the human `I'. The kingdoms of the divine have approached you.' The Baptist did not only preach that; he made it manifest to them by bestowing the baptism on them in the Jordan. Those who had been baptized knew then as a result of their own clairvoyant observation, even though it lasted but a short time, that the words of the Baptist expressed a world-historical fact."

In Lecture III Steiner begins to establish the very close connection that Christ and John the Baptist had between each other in that Christ now begins to work in the spiritual atmosphere that has been created by John the Baptist, especially at the Baptism in the Jordan and after his beheading: "This was the great fact now proclaimed by Elijah-John himself when he said, as he baptized the people, something like the following, `What until now was in the supersensible worlds and worked from these worlds you must now take into your souls as impulses that have come from the Kingdom of Heaven right into the hearts of men.' The spirit of Elijah itself shows how in multiplied form it must enter human hearts, so that in the further course of world history they may gradually take up ever more and more of the Christ Impulse. The meaning of the Baptism by John was that Elijah was ready to prepare the way for the Christ. This was contained in the deed of the baptism by John in the Jordan, 'I will make a place for Him; I will prepare the way for Him into the hearts of men. I will no longer merely hover over men, but will enter into human hearts, so that He also can enter in.'"

"John the Baptist has gone away but what he is as the Elijah-spirit remains, and in this Christ can work best. Here He can best pour forth His words, and in that atmosphere that has remained behind, the Elijah-atmosphere, He can best perform His deeds. That we can expect."

"But then something strange happens. We are shown how, after John the Baptist had met his physical death, Christ Jesus came to the very neighborhood where John had worked . . . Jesus Christ appears among the throng of followers and disciples of John the Baptist, and this fact is expressed in a sentence to which we must give careful attention: `And as Jesus came out He saw a great crowd,' by which could be meant only the disciples of John, `and He had compassion on them . . .' (Mark 6: 34). Why compassion? Because they had lost their master, they were there without John, whose headless corpse we are told had been carried to the grave. But even more precisely it is said, `for they were like sheep who had lost their shepherd. And He began to teach them many things.' It cannot be indicated any more clearly how He teaches John's disciples. He teaches them because the spirit of Elijah, which is at the same time the spirit of John the Baptist, is still active among them. Thus it is again indicated with dramatic power in these significant passages of the Mark Gospel how the spirit of Christ Jesus entered into what had been prepared by the spirit of Elijah-John. Even so this is only one of the main points, around which many other significant things are grouped."

"On two occasions it is indicated to us that Christ Jesus really entered the aura of the Baptist just when the physical personage was withdrawing more and more into the background, finally leaving the physical plane altogether. But it is shown in very clear words precisely through the very simplicity of the Mark Gospel how through the entry of Christ Jesus into the element of Elijah-John a wholly new impulse enters the world."

In Lecture VI Steiner now speaks of John the Baptist as the group soul of the Twelve Apostles: "This Elijah-soul is at the same time the soul of the Old Testament people, as it enters the Baptist and lives in him. When he is imprisoned and then beheaded by Herod, what happened then to his soul? This we have already indicated. His soul left the body and worked on as an aura; and into the domain of this aura Christ Jesus entered. Where then is the soul of Elijah, the soul of John the Baptist? The Mark Gospel indicates this clearly enough. The soul of John the Baptist, of Elijah, becomes the group soul of the Twelve; it lives, and continues to live in the Twelve."

However, now that the soul of John the Baptist lives in the souls of the Twelve Apostles, which became a reality at the `feeding of the five thousand', Christ Jesus makes higher demands from them for the understanding of spiritual truths. Steiner continues in Lecture VI: "However, a change takes place when the soul of Elijah is freed from John the Baptist and works on further in the Twelve as a group soul. And this is indicated, for from this time onward - this is quite clear if we read the passage and reread it - Christ makes greater demands on His disciples than before. He calls upon them to understand higher things. . . . But now Christ Jesus demands of His disciples that they should understand in particular the meaning of this increase of bread. Before that time He had not spoken to them in such terms. Now they ought to understand what was the destiny of John the Baptist after he had been beheaded through Herod, what happened in the case of the feeding of the five thousand when the fragments of bread were collected in twelve baskets, and what happened when the four thousand were fed from the seven loaves and the fragments were collected in seven baskets. . . .He reproaches them severely because they cannot understand the meaning of these revelations."

Immediately preceding the `feeding of the five thousand' Christ tells the Apostles to, "Come apart into a desert place and rest a while." (Mark 6: 31). The Apostles are led by Christ into a higher condition of consciousness. Steiner then continues: "But because Elijah's spirit as a group soul came near to the Twelve and permeated them like a common aura, they could, or at least it was possible for them to become in a higher sense clairvoyant."

"What now do they see? In this different condition what do they see? They are led into a new kind of clairvoyance, which they are able to enter because the spirit of Elijah-John now overshadows them. And what do they see? They see in comprehensive pictures the development of humanity, they see how the peoples of the future gradually come near to the Christ Impulse. The disciples see in the spirit what is described here as the multiple increase of bread. It is an act of clairvoyance."

"They see Him actively working from His own epoch onward through countless millennia, casting His Impulse forward spiritually into all perspectives of the future. They perceive how all human Beings of the future come near. In this process they are indeed in very special measure united with the Christ."

We should note that in the Gospels people had often thought that Christ Jesus was enveloped by the spirit of John the Baptist just as Herod had thought that the spirit of the Baptist lived on in Christ Jesus after he had John

85

beheaded. Steiner indicates this in the following: "Christ asks the disciples, 'Who do the people say I am?' And they answer, 'Some say you are John the Baptist!' But John the Baptist had been beheaded a short time before, and in any event Christ was already teaching while John was still alive! Could the people have been talking such obvious nonsense when they took Christ for John the Baptist while the Baptist was still living? It might have been acceptable when they said He was Elijah or another prophet."

This is a further affirmation that the Christ worked in the spiritual atmosphere which John the Baptist had prepared for Him. Steiner concludes this lecture with the following words on the Mystery of Golgotha: "Yet the whole meaning of the further evolution of humanity is that with the Mystery of Golgotha something that otherwise took place only in the depths of the mysteries had now been manifested on the plane of world history. Through what happened on Golgotha, the lying in the grave for three days, the Resurrection, through this what otherwise had taken place only in the depths and darkness of the mysteries was placed historically on the Earth plane. In other words, the moment in time had now come when what had hitherto been regarded as a sacred law: that silence must be preserved about the mysteries, must be broken. The law that one has to be silent about the mysteries had been established by men. But now, through the Mystery of Golgotha, the mysteries must become manifest! Within the soul of the Christ a decision was taken, the greatest world-historical decision, when He resolved that what until now had always, according to human law, been kept secret must now be made manifest before the sight of all, before world history."

Steiner speaks of Christ rebuking Peter after Peter had chided Christ for speaking of His Death and Resurrection. "Get behind me Satan." (Mark 8:33) was what Christ said in response to Peter. Immediately following this Christ gives a soliloquy. Steiner calls this, "the soliloquy of the God," in which Christ refuses to accept the common practice of confining the Mysteries among a select few. They should no longer be hidden from common knowing. It is the resolution of Christ to reveal the Mysteries to the world. Obviously, we are not given the whole monologue of what Christ had to say in this regard in the Bible but Steiner says the following about this soliloquy: "In this passage we have to do with the greatest monologue in world history, the greatest that has ever taken place in the whole of Earth evolution, the monologue of a God about making manifest the mysteries."

Steiner develops this further at the beginning of lecture VII: "We must recognize that the whole episode was especially concerned with the relationship between Christ Jesus and His closest disciples. And we must include in such a study most particularly what was said yesterday, that the spirit of Elijah, after it had been freed from the physical body of John the Baptist, was actually active as a kind of group soul of the disciples. What happened then cannot just be related in a simple external way since it took

86

place in a much more complicated manner. To a certain extent there was a deep and inner connection between the soul of the Christ and the souls of the Twelve. Everything that took place within the soul of Christ was made up of processes of significance for that time, rich and manifold processes. But all that took place in the soul of Christ took place again in a kind of reflected image, a reflection in the souls of the disciples, but divided into twelve parts. In this way each of the Twelve experienced, as in a reflected image, a part of what happened in the soul of Christ Jesus; but each of the Twelve experienced it somewhat differently. What took place within the soul of Christ Jesus was like a harmony, a great symphony, reflected in the souls of each of the Twelve, in much the same way as twelve instruments can give forth a harmony. So any event that concerns one or more of the disciples in particular may be described from two sides. It is possible to describe how the event in question appeared within the soul of Christ, as, for example, in the case of the great world-historical monologue of Christ Jesus. It is possible to describe how it was experienced within His soul, and then it appears as it was described yesterday. But it also takes place in a certain reflected image in the soul of Peter. Peter has the same soul experience. But, whereas in the case of Christ Jesus it encompasses the whole of mankind, Peter's identical experience encompasses only a twelfth part of all mankind, a twelfth, a single zodiacal sign of the entire Christ spirit. For this reason it must be pictured differently when it concerns Christ Jesus Himself."

From the above we begin to see the deep bond between Christ and the Apostles. This bond is interconnected with the macrocosmic spiritual forces of the zodiac. Christ and the Apostles are united and this bond is paramount in bringing to humanity the evolutionary Impulse needed to advance humanity. This bond is absolutely critical between Christ and the Apostles so that the Cosmic Principle of Christ, the Pleroma/Fullness of Christ is passed onto the Apostles who are to be the seeds for the rest of humanity in regaining what was once lost: the Tree of Life. This bond between Christ and the Twelve Apostles was greatly facilitated by the presence of John the Baptist; the group soul of the Twelve: ". . .after the spirit of John the Baptist had passed over into them He could lead them more deeply than He could earlier into the comprehension of spiritual secrets."

In this same lecture Steiner briefly draws attention to the 'concentrated etheric body' of Christ Jesus after the Resurrection in the following: "The events that occurred during the period when the Christ dwelt in the body of Jesus of Nazareth had actually resulted in the genuine physical death of the physical body of Jesus of Nazareth. The Spirit of Christ remained for three days outside the physical body but it then returned. And now it was not in the physical body but in the concentrated etheric body, concentrated in such a way that it was possible for the disciples to perceive it, as described in the

Gospels - with the consequence that Christ could walk and become visible also after the event of Golgotha."

He had also mentioned that though it was an etheric body it was able to move about as any other physical/material body would be able to do so. In E.R. Smith's, "David's Question: What is Man?", he outlines the fission processes of the forces of etheric warmth, light, sound and life and their consequential physical manifestations as heat, gas, water and solid matter during the Elohim's seven days of creation of the Earth period. At the beginning of Earth's evolution these etheric forces were fused into a concentrated element of warmth ether. Without any detailed or explicit description from Steiner in regard to the composition of the Phantom one can surmise that the Phantom, the pure physical body, may possibly be a body that recapitulates this stage of human development on Earth. There's reason to presume that the Phantom may be a body comprised of concentrated etheric warmth forces with the remaining etheric forces fused into it. The true physical body, less its earthly components, is what Steiner had called the Phantom body. It may be permissible to surmise that the Phantom is comprised of Will forces along with the etheric warmth element.

In Lecture VII on the Luke Gospel Steiner expresses the following: "As physical man is constituted today, everything that is of the nature of soul expresses itself in his physical and etheric constitution, but is also connected with certain etheric substances. What we call, 'will', expresses itself etherically in what we call 'fire'."

Thereby, a concentrated etheric body consisting of the etheric element of warmth with the other etheric elements, or portions of them, concentrated or fused within it along with Will forces are what would seem to comprise the composition of the Phantom. This also leads us back to the Saturn Period when the human physical body was a body of concentrated etheric warmth forces created by the Will forces of the Thrones - the Spirits of Will. However, the full completion of the human Phantom did not come about until the Earth Period. It is the Spirits of Form who have created the Phantom as we have it now. They live in our Phantom bodies. Knowing this we see again the deep interconnectedness between Christ and the Spirits of Form. The Resurrected Phantom body of Christ Jesus echoes back to us the beginnings of our own physical origins.

Steiner, in Lecture VI from his lectures, "From Jesus to Christ," speaks of the Phantom which originates as a `thought': "As the sculptor must have the `thought' which he impresses on the substance, so is a `thought' related to the human body: not in the same way as the thought of the artist, for the material of the human body is not marble or plaster, but as a real thought, the Phantom, in the external world. Just as the thought of the plastic artist is stamped upon his material, so the Phantom of the physical body is stamped upon the substances of the Earth which we see given over after death to the grave or the fire. The Phantom belongs to the physical body as its enduring part, a more important part than the external substances. The external substances are merely loaded into the network of the human Form, as one might load apples into a cart. You can see how important the Phantom is. The substances which fall asunder after death are essentially those we meet externally in nature. They are merely caught up by the human Form."

"We know that the foundation, the germ, of this Phantom of the physical body was laid down by the Thrones during the Saturn Period; during the Sun Period the Spirits of Wisdom worked further upon it, the Spirits of Movement during the Moon Period, and the Spirits of Form during the Earth Period. And it is only in this period that the physical body received the Phantom. We call these Spirits the Spirits of Form, because they really live in the Phantom of the physical body. So in order to understand the physical body, we must go back to the Phantom."

Though the composition of the phantom body has been addressed as a body in which etheric forces and will forces are concentrated this does not yet describe the fundamental and innate essence of the phantom body. Its core essence consists of a bodily form of devachanic forces brought to earth during one's incarnation. The form of the phantom body is spiritually accessed in the Continental region of devachan. In Lecture III from, "Theosophy of the Rosicrucian," Steiner says the following: "Firstly, there is a region which may be compared with solid, physical regions: it is the Continental region of Devachan. What is physical here on the earth is, in this region of Devachan, found to be a multitude of spiritual Beings. Think, for example, of a physical human Being. To devachanic vision he appears like this: what the physical senses perceive, vanishes, and light flashes up in the sphere immediately around the physical man, where otherwise there is a void; in the middle, where the physical body is, there is an empty, shadowy space - like a kind of negative."

It may be possible to surmise that in devachan this 'empty, shadowy space' is present here on earth as the phantom body due to one's physical incarnation but is imperceptible to the physical senses. In other words, the devachanic forces that make up the 'form' of the phantom body have descended to earth thereby creating a corresponding image of negative space in devachan as a silhouette-like form. Its counter-image on earth is the earthly mineral body that we do perceive with our senses which fills out the space of which it occupies. By descending to earth these earthbound devachanic forces of the phantom body simultaneously result in the creation of a negative shadowy void in devachan. In a manner of speaking, the negative space remaining in devachan is a space that has been hollowed out. Moreover, because the phantom body is comprised of devachanic forces which have descended to earth during one's incarnation, it is consequently present in a tainted form. It is the long-term goal of humanity to integrate our increasingly Christ-imbued Egos into the devachanic forces which comprise our present and future phantom bodies. Throughout the Earth Manvantara and future Manvantaras the affected cumulative residual elements of the redeemed devachanic forces of our phantom bodies will create the eventual spiritual forms of our Atma bodies.

Returning to the Mark Gospel, Steiner continues in Lecture VII: "The events that occurred during the period when the Christ dwelt in the body of Jesus of Nazareth had actually resulted in the genuine physical death of the physical body of Jesus of Nazareth. The spirit of Christ remained for three days outside the physical body but it then returned. And now it was not in the physical body but in the concentrated etheric body, concentrated in such a way that it was possible for the disciples to perceive it, as described in the Gospels - with the consequence that Christ could walk and become visible also after the event of Golgotha."

The Apostles belonged to the Old Testament people as Steiner tells us and this presents for them difficulties in comprehending His Death and Resurrection as an Initiation. He says: "But one consequence of this was that the Apostles, who belonged to the Old Testament people, had at first no understanding of the words that characterize Initiation. Christ Jesus spoke about Initiation when He expressed himself in such terms as hastening toward death, remaining in the grave for three days and being raised from the dead. This is a description of Initiation. If he had described it in a different way they would have understood Him. But because such a way of speaking of Initiation was foreign to the Old Testament people the Twelve could not at first understand His description. So it is quite correctly pointed out to us that the disciples were astonished and did not know to what He was referring when He spoke of the suffering and death and raising of the Son of Man."

What did John the Baptist bring to the people in preparing a spiritual atmosphere for the souls of those he baptized prior to the incarnation of Christ? Steiner: "Before the Mystery of Golgotha man could not unite himself with the spiritual worlds even by making use of all the forces pertaining to his Ego. The secret that was to be revealed to the people through the Baptism of John was that the time had come near when the Kingdoms of Heaven were to shine right into the Ego; they were to approach the Ego, the earthly Ego."

Steiner then gradually begins to lay the foundation that the force of the Ego greatly impacts the physical body. Later we shall see that the physical body must be transformed into ever higher forms so that the Ego may increasingly be able to fully express itself and that the mineral/physical body no longer acts as an eclipse to the Sun forces of the Ego. Steiner: "The passage (Zechariah 12: 10) is so formulated that it runs approximately as follows, `A man who unites in himself the full force of Egohood and is confronted with the human body, sees it wounded, pierced through with holes. For the higher Ego force which in ancient times could not yet live within the inner self, pierces through, penetrates and makes holes in the body.' This is an impulse that runs through the evolution and development of mankind for the reason that as the result of the influence of Lucifer and Ahriman in pre-Christian times only a portion of the Ego could be bestowed on man. And because the body is adapted only to the smaller portion and not the whole force of the Ego, it is worn down. It was not because this took place in the pre-Christian era but because in the case of Christ Jesus the full power of the Ego entered all at once, and entered with the utmost strength into His bodily Being, that this body had to appear not only with a single wound, as was the case with so many human individualities who carried a superego, but with five wounds. These were necessary because the Christ-Being, that is, the full Ego of man, projected far beyond the bodily form appropriate for those times. It was for this reason that the Cross had to be erected on the physical plane of world history, that Cross that bore the body of Christ, a human body such as that of man would be if for a moment the whole of man's nature, a large part of which has been lost through the influence of Lucifer and Ahriman, were to live within one single human Being."

Steiner goes on to say that understanding the Mystery of Golgotha is vital if the Mystery of Golgotha is to work properly in the world. He states: "In a certain way the disciples had to be led toward this understanding; and all of those who had to be led gradually to a new understanding of the evolution of mankind, Peter, James and John proved to be the most suitable."

He then adds this about our own understanding: "We need everything that human understanding can contribute if we are to grasp the significance of what entered human evolution at that time, something that had been maturing during the preceding centuries and took place about the time of the Mystery of Golgotha, thereafter slowly preparing and conditioning the further evolution of humanity."

In Lecture VIII Steiner begins with some intriguing comments about how the old clairvoyance was more disposed to Imaginations when one was near water, as by a lake and that one was more disposed to Inspirations when on a mountain. Steiner: "By the lake, by the water, and in masses of mist, the clairvoyant consciousness is especially disposed to perceive Imaginations, all kinds of things through Imagination, and to make use of what has already been acquired. On the mountain, in the rarefied air where the proportion of nitrogen and oxygen is differently distributed, clairvoyant consciousness is more attuned to receiving Inspirations, allowing something new to arise through clairvoyance. Hence the expression, 'to ascend the mountain', is not meant only symbolically but is used because the conditions obtaining on the mountain favor the possibility of developing new occult powers in oneself. Likewise the expression, 'to go to the lake', is not meant symbolically, but

91

was chosen because coming in contact with the lake favors Imaginative vision and the use of occult powers."

"When it is said that something took place by the lake, when being by the lake is referred to, definite forces are being applied and healing powers or powers of vision are unfolded. Thus Christ Jesus appears to His disciples by the lake in Imagination only since He Himself is involved in the entire episode because of His capacity to exteriorize Himself. Although they do not have Him there in the physical body, the disciples see Him. In such an experience separation in space has no importance. He was together `with them' by the lake. For the same reason when reference is made to the soul forces of the Apostles, the `mountain' is spoken of, as it was when the Twelve were appointed and their souls were enjoined to take into themselves the group soul of Elijah. And when the Christ wished to appear in the whole grandeur of His world-historical and cosmic manifestation, again the mountain is spoken of. The Transfiguration therefore takes place on the mountain.

It is indeed from this point of view that we must picture the scene of the Transfiguration. The three disciples Peter, James and John prove themselves to be capable of being initiated into the deeper secrets of the Mystery of Golgotha."

The three Apostles, however, did not completely pass through this Initiation in a fully awakened consciousness. When fully awake they were able to see Christ in His 'cosmic manifestation' along with seeing Elijah and Moses in spirit and hearing them speak of the impending death of Christ. The Gospel of Luke describes this in the following passage: "Now it came to pass about eight days after these words, that He took Peter, James and John and went up the mountain to pray. And as He prayed, the appearance of His countenance was changed, and His raiment became a radiant white. And behold, two men were talking with Him. And these were Moses and Elijah, who, appearing in glory, spoke of His death, which He was about to fulfill in Jerusalem. Now Peter and his companions were heavy with sleep. But when they were fully awake, they saw His glory and the two men who were standing with Him." (Luke 9: 28-32).

It is here that it begins to become apparent that Christ is able to take only three of His chosen Apostles to this level of Initiation and yet even these three could not experience this Initiation in a fully awakened condition. They could not make the transition from their Old Testament consciousness to the new understanding that would be required to comprehend the Death and Resurrection of the Christ. When we understand that Steiner had mentioned that one is able to receive Inspirations while on a mountain we get an insight into the level of Initiation that these three Apostles had received. However, they still had not received the capacity to attain the level of Intuition. In fact, they were only able to achieve the level of Inspiration partially. In the ascending levels of Initiation, Inspiration would be the third level of seven levels of Initiation. The first level is that of the student before attaining supersensible consciousness. The level of the student is followed by the level of attaining Imagination and then attaining Inspiration. The next level would be that of attaining Intuition. It was in the garden of Gethsemane that Christ Jesus tried to take His chosen three Apostles, Peter, James and John, to the next level of Initiation; that is, the Initiation of Intuition. It was here that Peter, James and John had failed. They could not ascend to that level of consciousness in any capacity of wakefulness. Not only were they were unable to stay with Christ and remain with Him to the final moments of the Crucifixion, they were unable to stay with Him in their souls and inwardly experience the Passion of Christ with Him. They were unable to remain as One with Him in their souls while He, as a God of the Highest Order, passed through physical death.

Steiner advances to Lecture IX which is the focal point of this entire work. In this lecture he emphasizes the imperative necessity to gain an understanding and comprehension of the Mystery of Golgotha. The understanding of which Steiner speaks is not merely the understanding of the intellect. Rather, he speaks of the necessity for the Apostles to develop an inward, Intuitive bond with Christ such that through them they would be the first to receive what Christ brought to the Earth and to humanity. This would then seed itself into all human souls. The Fullness of Christ was to seed itself into the souls of Twelve individuals whose souls were to be the chosen vessels for the newly Christ-imbued cosmic, spiritual impulses of the Twelve zodiacal constellations which now flow, since the Event of Golgotha, into all of us. Also, as mentioned earlier, what Christ brought to the Earth were the forces of the Tree of Life which were to begin to be taken up again by humanity and the first to receive these forces of the Tree of Life were to have been the Twelve Apostles. The spiritual forces of the Sun were also included within the Cosmic Aura of Christ. So that now, we have the forces of attraction between the Sun and the Earth which will gradually and eventually transfigure the Earth into the likeness of the Sun and will reunite the Earth and all the planets of this planetary system with the Sun again.

All of this was to have been internalized by the Chosen Twelve who were to be the human seeds for the Principle of Christ and that this would then pour over into the souls of all of humanity. What they were to take up from the Aura of Christ would eventually become the possession of everyone and, through one's free will and conscious understanding, both cognitive and Intuitive, would become a new cosmic evolutionary Impulse for all of humanity, the Earth and this planetary system as well as eventually advancing this cosmos to its future astral condition of form.

Steiner begins his ninth lecture addressing the issue of understanding: "It is particularly shown in the Mark Gospel, not so much in the wording but in the general tone of the presentation, that Christ is to be seen as a cosmic Being, an earthly and supra-earthly manifestation, while the Mystery of Golgotha is shown as an earthly and supra-earthly fact. But something else is also emphasized, and here we are faced with the fine artistic element, especially toward the end of the Gospel. It is emphasized that a cosmic element is shining into the concerns of the Earth. It truly shines in; and it was the task of earth Beings, of earthly human Beings to bring their understanding to this Impulse. Perhaps nowhere else is it indicated so well as in the Mark Gospel how fundamentally the whole of Earth evolution will be necessary to enable us to understand what shone here out of the cosmos into Earth existence, and how at the time of the Mystery of Golgotha such understanding was altogether impossible. And even today this understanding is still absent. The truth that at that time there was only an initial impetus toward an understanding that can come into being only with the further development of mankind is shown in a quite wonderful way in the artistic composition of the Gospel. We can discern something of this artistic composition if we enquire into the form of understanding that could have been possible and brought to bear on the Mystery of Golgotha at the time it took place."

Steiner implies here that very little understanding of the Mystery of Golgotha existed at that time and even today there is no full understanding of it among humanity. It should be emphasized that what he says here is that there was no common understanding of the Mystery of Golgotha by humanity nor even among His Apostles at that time and that humanity's full and complete understanding of the Mystery of Golgotha will be an ever on-going process; " . . . the whole of Earth evolution will be necessary to enable us to understand." However, there was an Intuitive, inner understanding of the Mystery of Golgotha but only by His most chosen Initiates. There was the understanding of the Crucifixion, Resurrection and Ascension by His Chosen Initiates: Lazarus, John the Baptist and Paul. They came to intuitively understand and inwardly experience the Crucifixion, Resurrection and Ascension respectively.

Steiner: "Essentially three kinds of understanding were possible, and they could arise at three different levels. Firstly, understanding could have been found in those who were nearest to Christ Jesus, His chosen disciples."

"The chosen disciples of Christ Jesus could have understood the Mystery of Golgotha in such a way that they could have interpreted the supra-earthly, cosmic aspect of this world-historical fact. This might have been expected from those disciples whom He had chosen."

"A second kind of understanding could have been expected to be found among the leaders of the ancient Hebrew people, from the high priests, the chief justices, from those who knew the Scriptures and knew the historical evolution of the Old Testament people. What could have been asked of them?

The Gospel shows clearly that they were not called upon to understand the realities of Christ Jesus, but they were expected to understand the fact that Christ Jesus came to the ancient Hebrew people, that with His individuality He was born into the blood of the people, that He was a Son of the House of David, inwardly linked to the essence of what came through David into the Jewish people. This is the second and lesser kind of understanding. That Christ Jesus had a mission that marked the high point of the mission of the whole Jewish people is indicated in a wonderful way toward the end of the Mark Gospel when it is shown ever more clearly - see in what a delicately artistic way this is indicated - that here we have to do with the Son of David. Thus, while the disciples were called upon to have an understanding of the mission of the cosmic hero, those who considered themselves as belonging to the Jewish people were called upon to understand the truth that the time had come for the completion of the mission of David. That is the second kind of understanding. The Jewish people should have known that the end of their old mission had come and that there could come a new flaming up of their own particular mission.

And the third kind of comprehension - where should this have been found? Again something lesser is demanded, and it is remarkable with what delicacy the artistic composition of the Mark Gospel indicates it. Something lesser is demanded and this lesser element was required of the Romans. . . The Romans were expected to understand that He signified something in the development of the Jewish people - not a climax of this development but something that was to play a leading part in it. If the Romans had understood this what would have been the result? Nothing much different from what came about in any case; only they failed to understand it. We know that Judaism spread indirectly over the whole Western world by way of Alexandria. The Romans could have had some understanding for the fact that the moment in world history had arrived for the spread of Jewish culture. Such an understanding was again less than what the scribes ought to have understood. The Romans were called upon to understand simply the significance of the Jews as a part of the world. That they did not understand this, which would have been a task of that age, is shown through the fact that Pilate did not understand why Christ Jesus was looked upon as the king of the Jews, and regarded it, indeed, as a harmless matter that He should have been presented as a king of the Jews.

Thus a threefold understanding of the mission of Christ Jesus might have been expected: first, that the chosen disciples could have had an understanding of Christ as a cosmic Being, secondly, the understanding that the Jews were supposed to have for what was burgeoning in the Jewish people itself, and thirdly, the understanding that the Romans ought to have had of the Jewish people, how they were ceasing to expand only over Palestine, but were beginning to spread over the greater part of the Earth."

From this point on, in Lecture IX, Steiner focuses on the task of the Apostles to understand the cosmic nature of the Christ and their eventual failure to be able to do so. He says: "The first question must be: Are the Apostles, the chosen disciples equal to the task of comprehension imposed on them? Did they recognize Christ as a cosmic spirit? Did they recognize that there in their midst was one who was not only what He signified to them as man, but who was enveloped in an aura through which cosmic forces and cosmic laws were transmitted to the Earth? Did they understand this?

That Christ Jesus demanded such an understanding from them is clearly indicated in the Gospel. For when the two disciples, the sons of Zebedee, came to Him and asked that one of them might sit on His right hand and the other on His left, He said to them, `You do not know what you ask. Can you drink from the cup that I drink, or be baptized with the baptism with which I am baptized? (Mark 10: 38). It is clearly indicated here that Christ Jesus required this of them, and at first they solemnly pledge themselves to it. What might then have happened? There were two possibilities. One would have been that the chosen disciples would really have passed in company with Christ through all that is known as the Mystery of Golgotha, and that the bond between Christ and the disciples would have been preserved until the Mystery of Golgotha. That was one of the two things that could have happened. But it is made very clear, especially in the Mark Gospel, that exactly the opposite occurred. When Christ Jesus was taken prisoner, everyone fled, and Peter who had promised solemnly that he would take offense at nothing, denied Him three times before the cock crowed twice. This is the picture presented from the point of view of the Apostles. But how is it shown that, from the point of view of the Christ, it was not at all like this?

Let us place ourselves with all humility - as we must - within the soul of Christ Jesus, who to the end tries to maintain the woven bond linking Him with the souls of the disciples. Let us place ourselves as far as we may within the soul of Christ Jesus during the events that followed. This soul might well put to itself the world-historical question, `Is it possible for me to cause the souls of at least the most select of the disciples to rise to the height of experiencing with me everything that is to happen until the Mystery of Golgotha?' The soul of Christ itself is faced with this question at the crucial moment when Peter, James and John are led out to the Mount of Olives, and Christ Jesus wants to find out from within Himself whether He will be able to keep those whom He had chosen. On the way He becomes anguished. Yes, my friends, does anyone believe, can anyone believe that Christ became anguished in the face of death, of the Mystery of Golgotha, and that He sweated blood because of the approaching event of Golgotha? Anyone who could believe that would show he had little understanding for the Mystery of Golgotha; it may be in accord with theology, but it shows no insight. Why does the Christ become distressed? He does not tremble before the cross.

96

That goes without saying. He is distressed above all in face of this question, 'Will those whom I have with me here stand the test of this moment when it will be decided whether they want to accompany me in their souls, whether they want to experience everything with me until the cross?' It had to be decided if their consciousness could remain sufficiently awake so that they could experience everything with Him until the cross. This was the 'cup' that was coming near to Him. So He leaves them alone to see if they can stay 'awake,' that is in a state of consciousness in which they can experience with Him what He is to experience. Then He goes aside and prays, 'Father, let this cup pass from me, but let it be done according to your Will, not mine.' In other words, 'Let it not be my experience to stand quite alone as the Son of Man, but may the others be permitted to go with me.'

He comes back, and they are asleep; they could not maintain their state of wakeful consciousness. Again, He makes the attempt, and again they could not maintain it. So it becomes clear to Him that He is to stand alone, and that they will not participate in the path to the cross. The cup had not passed away from Him. He was destined to accomplish the deed in loneliness, a loneliness that was also of the soul. Certainly the world had the Mystery of Golgotha, but at the time it happened it had as yet no understanding of this event:; and the most select and chosen disciples could not stay awake to that point."

What the Apostles were unable to achieve before the Death and Resurrection of Christ began to become possible for them after the Resurrection due to the presence and manifestation of the Risen Christ among them. The bond that had united the Cosmic Principle, the Cosmic Aura of Christ to His Apostles was now beginning to be restored once more. The prayer that Christ prayed to the Father in the Garden of Gethsemane that the cup of agony may pass and that His three chosen Apostles would be able to follow Him through the Crucifixion comes full-circle after Christ had Risen. The beginning stages for the restoration of the bond between Christ and the Apostles begins immediately prior to the Ascension of Christ. In the Garden of Gethsemane, before His capture, He prayed to the Father that His Apostles may be able to follow Him. It is parabolic in that, before the arrest, the prayer in the garden came immediately prior to the final point of disintegration of the bond between Christ and His chosen Apostles. This was followed by the Crucifixion, Death and descent into the sub-realms. The Resurrection marked the turning point in the bond between Christ and His Apostles. Christ's prayer to the Father prior to His Death, while in the Garden of Gethsemane, is now reversed in Christ's address to His Apostles prior to His Ascension. In a reversal to the prayer of Agony, Christ does not directly address the Father in regard to the Apostles. Instead, He now addresses His Apostles in regard to the authority of the Father as well as the descent of the Holy Spirit which will come upon them. This began the process of fully

97

restoring their cosmic bond with Christ. Later, this process reaches its culmination at Pentecost with the descent of the Holy Spirit onto Mary and the Apostles. The prayer to the Father in the Garden of Gethsemane and the subsequent disintegration of the bond between Christ and the Apostles were now reversed in Christ's address to His Apostles prior to His Ascension which began to reintegrate this bond.

We see the intimation of the beginning stage of this process in the book of the Bible, "The Acts of the Apostles": "But He said to them, "It is not for you to know the times or dates which the Father has fixed by His own authority; but you shall receive power when the Holy Spirit comes upon you, and you shall be witnesses for Me in Jerusalem and in all Judea and Samaria and even to the very ends of the Earth." (Acts 1: 7-8). Steiner had said that Lazarus remained with Christ through to the Death on the Cross. It was Lazarus who was Initiated to the level commensurate with understanding the Mystery of Golgotha such that the experience of Christ on the Cross was also the experience of Lazarus. It was then that Lazarus received the Mantle of the astral body of Christ which gave to him the ability to write the Gospel of John and the Apocalypse. It seems reasonable to say that at the time of the `raising' of Lazarus he was Initiated to the level of a Sun Initiate; that would be an Initiate of the sixth level, an Initiate of the Mysteries of the Sun and the enveloping Planets. One is then a world Initiate who is differentiated from an Initiate of the fifth degree. An Initiate of the fifth degree would be an Initiate of a people. Nathaniel, who is mentioned in the Gospel of John as 'a true Israelite' (John 1: 45-51), was an Initiate of a people. It is possible to surmise that Lazarus had attained such a level of Initiation from his own writing in the Book of Revelation. After being `raised from the dead' by the Christ, the name Lazarus was changed to John to reflect the fact that the spirit of John the Baptist now interpenetrated the consciousness soul of Lazarus. Lazarus is a Sun-World Initiate in that he is an Initiate of all the peoples of the world whereas an Initiate of the fifth degree is One with the group soul/spirit of a particular people only.

Lazarus had a style of writing in which he had ways of identifying himself as the writer. In the Book of Revelation we see the pattern of seven passing into twelve: the seven letters to the seven churches, the seven seals etc., pass into the theme of twelve such as: the 144,000 of those who were sealed, the twelve gates with the twelve angels and the names of the twelve tribes inscribed on them. These are examples of this pattern of writing utilized by Lazarus/John. In the Gospel of John, Lazarus/John writes of the seven I AM sayings of Christ along with mentioning the Son of Man twelve times. These patterns act as veiled signatures to those books that were written by the same writer and that the writer of both books was Lazarus/John. In the same manner, Lazarus/John gives the account of his own Initiation in chapter 11 or approximately within the middle of the Gospel of John. In his Book of

Revelation Lazarus/John does something similar in chapter 10; again approximately within the middle of the book. He gives us a clue to which degree of Initiation he had attained. As mentioned above, he tells us that he is an Initiate of the sixth degree; an Initiate of all of the peoples of the world. In chapter 10 in the Book of Revelation we can read this intimation that he is an Initiate of the sixth degree; a Sun Hero; a World Initiate. Similar to the Gospel of John in regard to the raising/Initiation of Lazarus, this sign is approximately within the middle of the Book of Revelation. He writes: "And I took the scroll from the angel's hand, and ate it up, and it was in my mouth sweet as honey, and when I had eaten it my stomach was made bitter. And they said to me, 'Thou must prophesy again to many nations and peoples and tongues and kings.'" (Rev.10: 10-11).

In a lecture given in Munich on May 1, 1907 Steiner said the following which is also applicable to understanding the Initiation of Lazarus: "We see how, at first, the mysteries of the physical plane are described and then, out of the sealed book, the astral Imaginations. They approach us in pictures. After the seer has perceived the spiritual Beings in the astral light for a while, they begin to sound forth. This is described in the resounding of the trumpets when the sixth seal is opened. That is the condition of Devachan. The seer becomes `clairaudient,' able to hear spiritual sounds - the spiritual ear is opened. The stage then follows when the seer expands his consciousness over the entire Earth. This is indicated in the swallowing of the book. It expresses the ascent into the higher regions of the spiritual worlds."

The devouring of the book is further elaborated in Lecture VIII from Steiner's cycle, "The Apocalypse of St. John": "We see the two forces which the Earth has received as heritage from the Cosmos of Wisdom and the Cosmos of Strength, and we see all that appears as the fulfillment of the Earth's mission, as the force of love which man develops. The whole appears to us as the personification of the man of the future. The man of the future here confronts us symbolically, supported by these forces, permcated by this power. The message of love, the book before him, is a book which not only influences him from without but which he has to devour. Here we behold before us the mighty picture which appears at this stage: And I saw another mighty Angel (that is a Being who is presented thus, because he is already above the present man) descend from the spiritual spheres (that is how it is seen by the seer) clothed with a cloud, and his countenance was as it were the sun and his feet as pillars of fire (these are the two forces of which we have spoken, which the Earth has received as a heritage). And he had in his hand a little book open; and his right foot was set upon the sea and his left upon the Earth . . . And I said unto him, Give me the little book. And he said unto me, Take it, and eat it up; and it shall make thy belly bitter, but in thy mouth it shall be sweet as honey. And I took the little book from the hand of the Angel and ate it up; and it was in my mouth sweet as honey.

Here we have the feeling arising in the seer when he directs his gaze to the point when the Earth passes from the physically material into the astrally spiritual, when the Earth mission is attained. And when the seer sees this he learns what is really connected with this message of love, which entered in as an Impulse in the fourth age, he learns even in his present life, as the Apocalyptist learnt, what bliss is and the bliss that may lie before mankind. But he learns it in his present body; for if a Being wished to live with man, however high he might be, he would be obliged to incarnate in the flesh. And in many respects the present body, just because it offers the spirit the possibility of rising high, gives also the possibility of suffering. While, therefore, the soul is able to ascend - the soul of the seer described by the Apocalyptist - into spiritual regions, in order to receive the Gospel of Love, and in spirit is able to feel the bliss sweet as honey, yet the seer lives in a present-day body, and in accordance with this he must say that the ascent produces in the present body the antithesis of that bliss in many respects. He expresses this by saying that although the little book is at first sweet as honey, it gives him severe pains in the belly when he has swallowed it. But this is only a small reflection of `being crucified in the body'. The higher the spirit rises, the more difficult it is for it to dwell in the body, and this is the symbolical expression for these pains: `being crucified in the body'."

Continuing further through Lecture IX on Mark's Gospel Steiner now begins to draw our attention to the power and extended activity of the aura of Christ. When Steiner speaks of the Cosmic Christ he is relating to us the cosmic element of the aura of Christ that envelops the Christ Being. It not only envelops the Christ Being but it also works through others as well; such as His Apostles in that many of the adversaries of Christ could not tell who was the Christ. Those who wished to arrest Him needed the assistance of a traitor to point the Christ out to His captors. Steiner shows us that in many circumstances those who wished to harm and capture the Christ before the arrest in the garden never were actually able to do so. Why was that? One reason was that at many times Christ was outside His physical body. Another reason was the aura of Christ was a powerful element that shielded Him from harm. In the Gospel of John there is a passage which alludes to the power of the aura of Christ which He demonstrates to us in His voice immediately prior to Christ being taken captive. This particular passage makes it clear that Christ willingly gave Himself over to His captors and that, as Steiner says later, His aura then separates from the Christ Spirit as He takes leave of His own cosmic element when His captors seize Him. This passage reads as follows: "Jesus therefore knowing all that was to come upon Him, went forth and said to them, `Whom do you seek?' They answered Him, `Jesus of Nazareth.' Jesus said to them, `I AM'. Now Judas, who betrayed Him, was also standing with them. When, therefore, He said to them, `I AM', they drew back and fell to the ground. So He asked them again, `Whom do you seek?'

And they said, `Jesus of Nazareth.' Jesus answered, `I have told you that I AM. If, therefore, you seek me let these go their way.' That the word that He said might be fulfilled, `Of those whom thou hast given me, I have not lost one.'" (John 18: 4-9). Christ willingly relinquishes His cosmic element so that the Mystery of Golgotha and the physical death of the body of Christ Jesus would be fulfilled for the benefit of all of humanity.

Continuing in Lecture IX, Steiner addresses the mystery of the fleeing youth; the Cosmic Principle of Christ: "The Christ is everywhere connected with a widely extended, actively working aura. This aura was present and active because He was linked with the souls of those whom He had chosen, and it remained present as long as He was linked to them. The cup had not passed away from Him; the chosen human Beings had shown no comprehension. So this aura gradually withdrew from the man Jesus of Nazareth; Christ became ever more estranged from the Son of Man, Jesus of Nazareth. Toward the end of His life Jesus of Nazareth was more and more alone, and the Christ became ever more loosely connected with Him."

Before continuing, it should again be emphasized that it is not the Christ Spirit that withdraws from Jesus of Nazareth. Steiner does not necessarily speak here in the strictest Anthroposophical sense. Notice that he says, ". . . this aura gradually withdrew from the man Jesus of Nazareth." It was not the Christ Spirit who withdrew from the physical body of Jesus. The Christ Spirit remained united with the body of Jesus of Nazareth through to His last breath while on the Cross. Both the Gospel of John and Steiner acknowledge this. The account of the Death on the Cross in the Gospel of John reads: "And bowing His head He gave up the Spirit." (John 19:30). The Gospel of Matthew reads similarly. It should also be noted that the entire incarnation and death of Christ was in reverse to that of a human Being's birth and death. As one begins to descend from the spiritual worlds to incarnate on earth humans bring with them their higher bodies to their physical/mineral bodies. With Christ's descent to earth it was different in that He would discard higher bodies one after another throughout the eons until he finally brought His Macrocosmic Ego to the body of Jesus of Nazareth at the Baptism in the Jordan. This descent from the higher worlds and the sacrificing of His higher bodies were, in a sense, a long and protracted spiritual crucifixion of the Christ Being of indescribable suffering. This pain and suffering did not reach its culmination until the time of His Death on the Cross. The Event of Golgotha was the last phase of a process of pain and suffering that had been taking place for ages. While here on earth, the sacrifice of His Cosmic Aura and the sacrificial death and submersion of the ashes of the mineral body of Jesus of Nazareth into the earth itself were the last bodies to be sacrificed by the Christ in this long succession of sacrifices. It was not until the moment of Death on the Cross that Christ became truly born into the earth's aura.

This indescribable suffering experienced by the Christ throughout the ages and while here on earth made it possible for Christ to fully integrate His Ego into the body of Jesus of Nazareth. This was not completed until the final moments on the Cross. At the time of the Baptism in the Jordan the Christ had descended mostly no further upon Jesus of Nazareth than the etheric body of Jesus. Steiner intimates this in Lecture VII of his Luke cycle when he asks the following question: "Who is this Being who united at that time with the etheric body of the Nathan Jesus?" The full integration of Christ into the physical-mineral body of the Nathan Jesus was gradually achieved over the three years. In Steiner's lecture cycle, "The Fifth Gospel," he specifically mentions that the Christ Being does not become completely One with the body of Jesus until the very last moments on the Cross. He says: "It is a strange and mysterious fact that during the first period (after the Baptism) the connection of Christ with the body of Jesus of Nazareth was not a firm connection. As time went on the connection became closer and closer; it was only towards the end of the three years that the Christ Being and the body of Jesus of Nazareth were one---not completely one until the time of the Death on the Cross. The process of union entailed suffering of greater and greater intensity in the course of these three years. Only by indescribable suffering could the Christ Being unite with the body of Jesus of Nazareth---in telling these things, no vestige of sentimentality is present." ["On the Fifth Gospel", Lecture III, Berlin: November 18, 1913].

We can now see that Steiner did not necessarily speak with the strictest description of the aura of Christ and often uses the term, `Christ', when actually referring to the aura of Christ. It was only the aura of Christ, the cosmic element of Christ, that became loosely connected with the body of Jesus of Nazareth. Returning to Lecture IX, Steiner then says: "Although the cosmic element was there until the moment pictured as that of the sweating of blood in Gethsemane, and Christ up to this moment was fully united with Jesus of Nazareth, now through the failure of human Beings to understand this connection the link was loosened. And whereas earlier the cosmic Christ was active in the temple and drove out the money-changers, expounding mighty teachings, and nothing happened to Him, now, when Jesus of Nazareth was only loosely connected with the Christ the posse could come near Him. However, we can still see the cosmic element present, but less and less connected with the Son of Man. This is what makes the whole episode so soul-shattering! Because the threefold understanding could not be forthcoming, what did the men finally have in their hands? What could they seize, what could they condemn, what could they nail to the cross? The Son of Man! And the more they did all this, the more did the cosmic element withdraw that had entered the life of Earth as a youthful impulse. It escaped them. For those who sentenced Him and carried out the judgment there remained only the Son of Man, around whom only hovered what was to come down to Earth as a youthful cosmic element."

When Steiner refers to the Son of Man he is referring here to the Christ within the physical body of Jesus of Nazareth. Continuing he says: "No Gospel other than that of St. Mark tells how only the Son of Man remained, and that the cosmic element only hovered around Him. Thus in no other Gospel do we perceive the cosmic fact in relation to the Christ event expressed with such clarity, the fact that at the very moment when men who failed to understand laid their violent human hands upon the Son of Man, the cosmic element escaped them. The youthful cosmic element which from that turning point of time entered Earth evolution as an impulse, escaped. All that was left was the Son of Man; and this is clearly emphasized in the Mark Gospel. Let us read the passage and find out if the Mark Gospel does indeed emphasize how, just at this moment in the unfolding of events, the cosmic acts in relation to the human. `And Jesus spoke to them, `You have set out with swords and sticks to take me prisoner, as if I were a murderer. I was daily with you in the temple teaching, and you did not seize me. But the scriptures must be fulfilled.' And they all forsook Him and fled.' (Mark 14: 48-50). He stands alone. But what has become of the youthful, cosmic element? Think of the loneliness of this man, permeated as He was by the Cosmic Christ, who now confronts the posse like a murderer. And those who should have understood Him flee! `And they all forsook Him and fled,' it says in the 50th. verse. Then in verses 51 and 52: `And there was a youth who was following Him closely who wore a fine linen garment over His bare body, and they seized Him. But He let go of the linen garment and fled naked.'

Who is this youth? Who was it who escaped here? Who is it who appears here, next to Christ Jesus, nearly unclothed, and then slips away unclothed? This is the youthful cosmic impulse, it is the Christ (my note: it is the Cosmic Christ meaning: the cosmic element of Christ) who slips away, who now has only a loose connection with the Son of Man (my note: the Christ Being within Jesus of Nazareth). Much is contained in these 51st and 52nd verses. The new impulse retains nothing of what former times were able to wrap around man. It is the entirely naked, new cosmic impulse of Earth evolution. It remains with Jesus of Nazareth, and we find it again at the beginning of the sixteenth chapter. `And when the Sabbath was over Mary Magdalene and Mary the mother of James and Salome brought spices and went there to anoint Him. And early in the morning on the first day of the week they came to the tomb as the Sun was rising. And they said among themselves, `Who will roll away the stone from the door of the tomb for us?' And when they looked up they saw that the stone was rolled away, for it was very large. And as they entered the tomb they saw a youth sitting on the right side, clothed in a long white robe; and they were startled. But he said to them, `Do not be frightened. You seek Jesus of Nazareth, the crucified one. He has Risen!' (Mark 16: 1-6).

This is the same youth. In the whole artistic composition of the Gospels nowhere else does this youth confront us, the youth who slips away from the people at the moment when they condemn the Son of Man, who is there again when the three days are over, and who from now onward is active as the cosmic principle of the Earth. Nowhere else in the Gospels - you should compare the others - except in these two passages does this youth confront us, and in such a grandiose manner. Here we have all we need in order to understand the profound meaning of just this Gospel of St. Mark, which is telling us that we have to do with a cosmic event, with a cosmic Christ. Only now do we understand why the remainder of the Mark Gospel had to be artistically composed as it was. It is indeed remarkable that, after this significant appearance of the youth has come twice before us, the Gospel quickly comes to an end, and all that remains are a few striking sentences. For it is scarcely possible to imagine that anything that came later could have still yielded any further enhancement. Perhaps the sublime and marvelous element could have been enhanced, but not what is soul-shattering and of significance for the Earth evolution. Consider again this composition of the Mark Gospel: the monologue of God; the cosmic conversation on the mountain above the Earth to which the three disciples were called but did not understand; then Gethsemane; the scene on the Mount of Olives when Christ had to acknowledge that those who had been chosen could not attain to an understanding of what was about to happen; how He had to tread this path alone, how the Son of Man would suffer and be crucified. Then the world-historical loneliness of the Son of Man who is abandoned, abandoned by those He had chosen and then abandoned gradually by the Cosmic Principle. Thus, after we have understood the mission and significance of the youth who slips away from the eyes and hands of men, we come to understand in an especially profound manner the words, `My God, my God, why hast Thou forsaken me?' (Mark 15: 34). Then the reappearance of the youth, whereupon it is briefly shown how the youth is a spiritual, supersensible Being, who becomes sense-perceptible only through special circumstances, when He first shows himself to Mary Magdalene. Then afterward, `He revealed Himself in another form to two of them as they went for a walk into the countryside.' (Mark 16:12). The physical could not have shown itself `in another form.'"

As mentioned earlier, Christ became increasingly aware that His Apostles were not going to remain consciously connected with Him throughout the entire Event of Golgotha. This was becoming apparent at the Transfiguration when Peter, and the brothers James and John of Zebedee were 'heavy with sleep' (Luke 9:32). They also did not comprehend many of the deeds (miracles) of Christ whereas Lazarus had a much deeper grasp of the Mysteries. Christ then had to seek and rely on others who would be

104

capable of retaining the Cosmic zodiacal connection between themselves and the Christ. Initially, Christ was united with His Twelve Apostles because each separate Apostle was a human microcosmic portal for each separate constellation of the zodiac. Chris Bamford cites the following lecture in his book, "Isis Mary Sophia": "You will find the twelve parts of the human Being reproduced and concealed in the names of the Apostles. The twelve Apostles are to the collective Body of Christ as the twelve parts are to the ordinary body. The part representing the 'I' dominated by egotism, which eventually causes the death of the Christ, is Judas Iscariot." (November 5, 1906; Munich; GA 94).

The zodiac became the outward expression of the Twelve World Initiators/Beings Who initiated Christ during the Sun Period (see Lecture X: June 12, 1912/GA 137). Because the connection between the Christ and His Twelve Apostles was disintegrating, the Initiation of Lazarus became exceptionally significant for this very reason. The Cosmic connection between what lives in the constellations and thereby lives in each human Being had to be maintained throughout the entire Mystery of Golgotha. It was maintained due to the Initiation of Lazarus. The Initiation of Lazarus allowed the spirit of John the Baptist, the group soul and unitary consciousness of the Twelve Apostles, to live within the consciousness soul of Lazarus to which Lazarus then became known as John the Evangelist; the writer of the Gospel of John and the Apocalypse. As the evolution of the Earth and humanity progressed, the connection between the Hierarchies, humanity and the Earth became increasingly estranged. Humanity and the Hierarchies were losing their connection with one another. Christ came to Earth to fully re-establish and redeem this connection. He had to reverse this pattern of evolution that, over time, caused an increasing estrangement between humanity and the Hierarchies. The forces that flowed from the Cross on the hill of Golgotha became the point of origin of a new cosmos. These new, youthful forces of creation, which were now centered in and around the Earth, were to begin to expand from Golgotha to the outer reaches of the constellations. This new pattern of creation for a new cosmos now reverses the old pattern of creation when, at the time of the initial stages of the Earth Manvantara, the creative forces came from the constellations inwardly to our Earth and solar system. This region of cosmic space then becomes the region for the next condition of form for the Earth and humanity: the astral condition of form. In the Book of Revelation we see this in the pattern of the numbers of 7 transforming into the numbers of 12; that is, our current physical planetary cosmos transfigures to an astral condition of form. Could it be possible that this outer portion of the Milky Way galaxy which harbors our solar system eventually separates from the Milky Way and begins to form a new galaxy while this future astral condition of form becomes its spiritual center. This became possible on Golgotha and could only become possible because the forces of the Cross were able to be taken up by those who were capable of 'understanding' the Event of Golgotha. Therefore, the Initiation of both Lazarus and John the Baptist, which is regarded as the 'raising of Lazarus', was critical for the future evolution of humanity, the Earth and this cosmos. The Event of Golgotha was salvaged through it. Because the raising of Lazarus salvaged the Event of Golgotha due to John the Baptist becoming interpenetrated into the consciousness soul of Lazarus we would then have to ask: What would have become of the Advent of Christ if that bond had been completely aborted and not taken up by Lazarus and John the Baptist? The bond between Christ and the Apostles was crucial, according to Steiner, in seeding the cosmic 'youth' forces into the souls of humans and into the spiritual aura of the Earth. This bond was severed between Christ and the Apostles at the arrest of Christ Jesus, and in the suicide of Judas to which there were no longer Twelve Apostles but Eleven. This spiritual and cosmological bond was thereby salvaged through the higher connection that was created among Christ, Lazarus and the individual who became the group-soul and unitary consciousness of the Apostles: John the Baptist.

Briefly citing what Steiner said from his St. Mark lectures: Christ had, ". . . an aura through which cosmic forces and cosmic laws descended to Earth . . . This aura with its powerful influence was there because He was united with the souls of those He had chosen: and it remained so as long as He was united with them."

"And the stronger their action became (His captors), the more the cosmic element withdrew; which as a youthful impulse was to enter Earth life."

"Whereas the cosmic element was completely united with Jesus of Nazareth up to the moment when the "sweating of blood" takes place on Gethsemane, man's incomprehension now loosens this connection."

"It then hovered over Jesus of Nazareth."

"There remained behind the Son Of Man, around whom now merely hovered what was to come forth as the young cosmic element."

Steiner tells us that when the captors of Christ began to seize Him, it is at this moment that the Cosmic Aura that enveloped Christ now separated from Him and thereby we are given the account of the fleeing youth in the Gospel of Mark. "Then all of His disciples left Him and fled and a certain young man was following Him, having a linen cloth wrapped about his naked body, and they seized him. But leaving the linen cloth behind he fled away from them naked." (Mark 14: 50-52). Who was this "certain young man". It is the same young man sitting in the tomb in a white robe on Easter morning. Steiner remarks, "The reappearance of the youth, sitting in the tomb, is a spiritual, supersensible Being, who becomes sense-perceptible only through special circumstances, when he first shows himself to Mary Magdalene." The same description cannot be applied to the fleeing youth at the time of the arrest in the Garden of Gethsemane. The fleeing youth in the Garden was a supersensible element that was not perceptible to the physical senses. This moment marks the final stages of the passing of the Auric Mantle, the Cosmic Principle, of Christ onto John the Baptist until It became ever more united with the entelechy of John the Baptist and finalized on Eater morning. Steiner says that the youth in the tomb is, "a spiritual, supersensible Being who becomes sense-perceptible only through special circumstances." These special circumstances are the forces of the Resurrection of Christ that permeated the soul of John the Baptist. The fleeing youth forces, the forces of the Cosmic Element of Christ, manifested themselves in the Phantom body of John the Baptist who then becomes momentarily visible to Mary Magdalene and the other women.

In Chris Bamford's, "Isis Mary Sophia," he cites the following from Steiner's lecture of November 20, 1907 in Basel: "With the advent of Jesus Christ, something entirely new appeared in relation to the process of initiation. Imagine that you have transformed your entire astral body into Spirit Self. Your Spirit Self would then imprint itself into your etheric body like a seal into sealing wax, and give it its form. In this way your etheric body is transformed into Life Spirit. When this is done, the Life Spirit penetrates the physical body, and transforms it into the Spirit Human (the Risen Body). Only with the appearance of Christ did it become possible for the Life Spirit to directly influence the physical body.

This means that the experiences attained in the higher worlds could now be incarnated in the human brain without the need for a preliminary separation of the etheric body. The first Being whose etheric body was completely penetrated by the Spirit Self and whose physical body was completely penetrated by the Life Spirit was Jesus Christ. When Jesus Christ came to the Earth, it became possible for those connected with Him to undergo the same initiation, without needing to separate the etheric body from the physical body."

And from the same lecture: "While Lazarus's body lay in the grave, apparently dead, his etheric body was taken out to undergo initiation and receive the very same power that resides in Christ. Thus he became a "Risen One," the person whom the Lord loved and who wrote the Gospel. If we read through the Gospel, we notice that not a single line contradicts this, although the process of initiation itself is described 'under a veil'."

It seems that there are two levels of Initiation mentioned here. One is the Spirit Self impacting the etheric body and the other is the Life Spirit impacting the physical body. It would seem that from what Steiner had said in the above lecture in regard to Lazarus's etheric body being lifted out, Lazarus had undergone the Initiation of the Spirit Self upon the etheric body. During the Initiation/Raising of Lazarus we can surmise that John the Baptist received the same Initiation. However, he was also receiving the beginning

107

stages of the higher Initiation of the Life Spirit upon his physical/phantom body. This Initiation did not reach its culmination until the morning of the Resurrection. It was this final stage which provided the "special circumstances" that made it possible for the women at the tomb to perceive with their senses the momentary "Risen Body" of John the Baptist whom the Gospel of Mark describes as the young man sitting in the tomb. This explains why Lazarus could follow the Christ through the Crucifixion and Death on the Cross but could not follow Him through to the Resurrection. Only John the Baptist received the Life Spirit Initiation necessary to understand the mystery of the resurrected phantom body. What is suggested in the above is that Christ achieved, microcosmically in His human form, all that the human would achieve in the remaining Earth condition and in the Jupiter, Venus and Vulcan conditions. A corresponding achievement in a human was also necessary throughout the Event of Golgotha. For the human Being, however, this was only in its most germinal condition during the Event of Golgotha; a 'seed' force which manifested brightly within John the Baptist and Lazarus due to the immediate intercession of the Christ. The Buddhi and Atma conditions of Lazarus and John the Baptist, respectively, were mantles that were bestowed on them by the Christ; they were not of a permanent nature. However, they were the germinal beginnings of what humanity will achieve in the distant future. They were seed forces that will continue to burgeon throughout the remaining Earth condition and onto the Jupiter, Venus and Vulcan periods. The momentary Buddhi and Atma conditions of Lazarus and John the Baptist, respectively, were issued to them by the Christ which enabled them to vicariously experience the Crucifixion and Resurrection of the Christ with a greater capacity of understanding and assimilation of the Christ Aura.

Rudolf Steiner refers to this in his Last Address: "Lazarus(John) could only develop fully out of the earth-forces at this time as far as the Intellectual or Mind-Soul; the Mystery of Golgotha took place during the fourth post-Atlantean period and at that time the Intellectual or Mind-Soul was being developed. Therefore, another Cosmic Being had to lend him the forces from the Consciousness Soul upwards: Manas, Buddhi and Atma. Through that a human Being confronted Christ who extended from the depths of the earth into the highest heaven and who bore the physical body in perfection throughout all its members into the spiritual bodies of Manas, Buddhi and Atma as they will one day be developed by all humankind in a far distant future."

Though the final stages of John the Baptist receiving the Cosmic Aura of Christ began in the Garden of Gethsemane this does not indicate that the entelechy of John the Baptist became momentarily visible to the senses of all those present at the time of the arrest in the Garden. Since the feeding of the five thousand, John the Baptist, in spirit, had been gradually becoming One

108

with the Aura of Christ. That Oneness began to culminate at the arrest and finally manifested itself fully as the young man in the tomb on Easter morning. At the arrest, the Gospel of Mark is describing the fleeing youth as an account of the separation of the Aura of Christ from the body of Jesus of Nazareth. This is an account of a supersensible phenomenon. However, the account of this event is veiled in what seems to be tangible, physical circumstances. It borders on the supersensible and the physical in that what is described is the loosening of the Aura of Christ from the physical body of the Son of Man; the Being of Christ in Jesus of Nazareth. The Aura flees from Christ Jesus; that is, it almost entirely separates itself from the Son of Man. To whom, then, does it pass onto? The Aura of Christ was now passed onto and assimilated by John the Baptist. This event bordered on the supersensible and the physical at the threshold of the spiritual in that John the Baptist ultimately became visible in a condensed phantom/etheric body as the young man sitting in the tomb wearing a white robe on Easter morning. Steiner, in agreement with Paul, calls the Resurrected Christ the New Adam; also named the Second Adam. However, Christ would be the New Adam in a macrocosmic sense. A new human Adam, however, is now created. John the Baptist is the archetypal human through which the new creative forces of the Resurrection now live in this prototypal human seedling. The Gospel verse, "I must decrease, so that He may increase." (John 3: 30) indicates that the forces of the old Adam must away and so must the forces of the old Earth over time. A new Adam, who was imbued with these new cosmic forces which have been brought to us by Christ, had been born and thereby begins the genesis of a new Earth and cosmos.

Steiner remarks in the lecture cycle, "Cosmic Forces in Man," saying, "When we study the human form, we are led to the spheres of the fixed stars, that is to say, to their representatives, the zodiacal constellations." This Aura of Christ had to retain its connection with the souls of the Apostles who were to be as portals for the Twelve constellations. Or, it at least had to seed itself into one singular human soul that would enable the zodiacal configuration of constellations to be consolidated into one unitary consciousness as in John the Baptist; the group soul of the Apostles. It was, therefore, John the Baptist who was the young man sitting in the tomb that said to the women in referring to Christ, "He has Risen!" Steiner then mentions in Lecture IX that the youth, referring to the cosmic element of Christ, was again present when Christ Himself appeared to the two disciples who were on their way to Emmaus. When the Apostles had fled, the bond had now been totally dissolved to which the cosmic aura of Christ then passed over to John the Baptist. Steiner had said that the aura remained with Jesus of Nazareth but we should remember that it hovered loosely over Him. What was critical throughout the entire Ministry of Christ was that the aura was to remain united between Christ and at least one human soul throughout the entire

Passion of Christ and on through to the Resurrection. What Christ had experienced during His Passion and Death, His descent into the sub-realms and in His Resurrection had to be experienced by a human as well. Along with these events were the spiritual and cosmic forces which had to be assimilated by a human Being. These forces had to become part of the human experience for the sake of human evolution. They had to seed themselves first in human souls who were capable of comprehending and uniting their souls with such forces. Lazarus' comprehension of the Crucifixion was critical for the eventual assimilation of these forces that flowed from the Christ into the human soul and which will eventually live fully in all of those who come to a comprehension of the nature of the Being of Christ and His mission on Earth. The same could be said of John the Baptist in terms of his comprehension of the Resurrection and who brought to bear the unitary consciousness of the Twelve Apostles. This comprehension and the assimilation of the forces of the Resurrection into his soul then became available for all humans.

In a lecture given in Berlin on August 6, 1918 Steiner makes the following remarks in regard to the human Being as the seed of the earth that must be fructified for the salvation of the earth: "If we ask: 'Where is the germ of something which will continue to grow on after the Earth, Jupiter and Venus developments - from the present civilization into the future?' The answer must be: 'In nothing external on earth; only in man.' In the part of his Being accessible only to supersensible knowledge, man is the cradle of the seed for the future. . . . Thus the Christ, descending from worlds becoming more and more inaccessible to human knowledge, had to unite Himself with Mankind - to take up His abode in Jesus of Nazareth and become Christ-Jesus, so that in a human body there might dwell that which bears within it the future of the Earth development. So we have in the Christ the Cosmic Being, that Christ Being whom ancient knowledge alone could grasp directly; and in the Jesus to whom the Christ came, we have what henceforth bears within it, in human Will alone, the seed for the future. . . . And 'Jesus' cannot be understood without taking into account the Christ Who drew into him. Unless we give due weight to this fact of the Christ in Jesus, we cannot grasp that only through the human seed on earth can the cosmic be saved for the future. . . . In man lies the seed of the future; but it must be fructified by Jesus."

It must be understood that Steiner was speaking of the sheaths of Jesus of Nazareth that afforded the Christ the capacity to become the archetypal, universal 'New Adam' for all of humanity. However, the New Adam seed force of the Christ in Jesus had to be initially internalized by at least one single human Being which was John the Baptist. It is also paramount to take note of Steiner's assertion that the seed of the future lies in the, "human Will alone". The human assimilation of the New Adam seed force of the Christ

110

within the sheaths of Jesus of Nazareth, which over time transfigures the human phantom, etheric and astral bodies in order to facilitate the increasingly expedient expression of the human Ego, must be an act of conscious human Will. John the Baptist was the first human to initialize this process for all other human Beings. John the Baptist was the one single human soul who was fully capable of following Christ through to the Resurrection. It was he who was elevated to the seventh degree of Initiation and was initiated into the mysteries of the Life Spirit upon the physical body. He could comprehend the mysteries of the macrocosm; that is, the mysteries of the solar system, the constellations and a complete synthesizing of the mysteries of all of the zodiacal constellations. This is why he was able to be the surrogate-soul for the Twelve Apostles once their bond with Christ had finally dissolved at the time of the arrest. It was essential that one human Being, who was an Initiate of the seventh degree and of the Life Spirit mysteries, accomplish this. Lazarus was not quite capable of achieving this because he was an Initiate of the sixth degree and was initiated into the Spirit Self mysteries but not the Life Spirit mysteries. We are also told in his own words that he could not completely comprehend the whole Mystery of Golgotha at the time of the actual Event. In the Gospel of John we read the account of Peter and Lazarus as they arrived at the tomb. Lazarus believed, but, did not fully understand the Scripture. This can be understood to say that he did not understand the Mystery of the Resurrection at that moment. It reads: "She ran therefore and came to Simon Peter, and to the other disciple whom Jesus loved, and said to them, `They have taken the Lord from the tomb, and we do not know where they have laid Him.'

Peter therefore went out, and the other disciple, and they went to the tomb. The two were running together, and the other disciple ran on before, faster than Peter, and came first to the tomb. And stooping down he saw the linen cloths lying there, yet he did not enter. Simon Peter therefore came following him, and he went into the tomb, and saw the linen cloths lying there, and the handkerchief which had been about His head, not lying with the linen cloths, but folded in a place by itself. Then the other disciple also went in, who had come first to the tomb. And he saw and believed; for as yet they did not understand the Scripture, that He must rise from the dead. The disciples therefore went away again to their home." (John 20: 2-10). What was it that Lazarus and Peter did not understand? The words in the Gospel of John can direct one to truths of the highest matters. What they truly did not understand was that the Death and Resurrection of the Christ was an Initiation of the Christ Being. It was a Macrocosmic Initiation and that the Father was the Hierophant. It was this and all of its implications that Lazarus and Peter did not comprehend.

Steiner addresses this in his lecture cycle, "From Jesus to Christ." In Lecture VI he says: "First, we have to understand the Resurrection as a translation into historic fact of the awakening that took place in the holy Mysteries of all times, only with the difference that he who in the Mysteries raised up the individual pupil was the Hierophant; while the Gospels indicate that He who raised up Christ is the Being whom we designate as the Father - that the Father Himself raised up the Christ. Here we are shown that what had formerly been carried out on a small scale in the depths of the Mysteries was now and once for all enacted for humanity by the Divine Spirits, and that the Being who is designated as the Father acted as Hierophant in the raising to life of Christ Jesus. Thus we have here, enhanced to the highest degree, something which formerly had taken place on a small scale in the Mysteries. That is the first point. The other is that, interwoven with matters which carry us back to the Mysteries, there are descriptions so detailed that even today we can reconstruct from the Gospels the situations even to their minute particulars, as we have just seen in the passage read to you. But this passage includes one detail that calls for particular attention. There must be a meaning in the words, `For they did not as yet know the Scripture, that He must rise from the dead. Then the disciples went back to their homes.' Let us ask: Of what had the disciples been able so far to convince themselves? It is described as clearly as anything can be that the linen wrappings were there, but the body is not there, is no longer in the grave. The disciples had not been able to convince themselves of anything else, and they understood nothing else when they now went home. Otherwise the words have no meaning. The more deeply you enter into the text, the more you must say that the disciples who were standing by the grave were convinced that the linen wrappings were there, but that the body was no longer in the grave. They went home with the thought: `Where has the body gone? Who has taken it out of the grave?' "

If we compare what Peter and Lazarus were not able to comprehend at the tomb to that of the two disciples who had later seen and experienced the Risen Christ on the way to Emmaus it presents a startling contrast to Peter and Lazarus who had as yet not seen nor experienced the Risen Christ. The two disciples who were on their way to Emmaus only recognized Him once they reached the village and sat with Christ while He broke bread, blessed it, and gave it to them to eat. It was then that their eyes were open. The bread and that of the whole Earth are now His body. The eating of the bread, the receiving of the body of Christ, opened their eyes to recognize the Risen Christ. This entire passage allows us to see that comprehension of the Resurrection of the Christ begins to imbue one with the forces of the Resurrection that work into the whole person: body, soul and spirit. Its impact within the entirety of their souls began immediately while on the way to Emmaus even before their eyes were open after breaking bread. However, these forces do not completely take hold of the two disciples until the actual consumption of the bread that is of the new Christ-imbued earth forces. This is intimated in the following passage: "And

112

they said to each other, `Was not our heart burning within us while He was speaking on the road and explaining to us the Scriptures?' " (Luke 24:32).

Compare this to a passage in Mark when the two try to explain this to those who have not as yet experienced the Risen Christ: "After this He was manifested in another form to two of them, as they were walking on their way into the country. And they went and brought word to the rest, and even then they did not believe (comprehend)." (Mark 16:12-13).

From this passage we can see that the soul transfiguring forces of the Risen Christ had not yet taken hold of the other disciples at this time. This explains their inability to comprehend the Resurrection. However, the time had come for the Apostles to be restored to their rightful position in their relationship with Christ; though this was not fully made whole again until Pentecost when they were Initiated in the sixth degree. In the following passage we do see the beginning stages of this Initiation of the Apostles as the Impulse of the Father's Macrocosmic Initiation upon the Christ begins to be passed over to the them: "He therefore said to them again, `Peace be to you!' As the Father has sent me, I also send you.' When He had said this, He breathed upon them, and said to them, `Receive the Holy Spirit; whose sins you shall forgive, they are forgiven them; and whose sins you shall retain, they are retained.'" (John 20: 21-23).

Also, we know the story of Thomas who had doubted the others yet he came to believe; that is, comprehend, when he pressed his hand into the resurrected body of Christ to which the Resurrection Impulse began to work upon his soul as he said, "My Lord and My God!" (John 20: 28). The forces of the Risen Christ began to live within the entirety of Thomas' body, soul and spirit. It is noteworthy though that not all were ready and able to receive the Christ and their doubt becomes a hindrance. The Gospel of Matthew makes this point: "And when they saw Him they worshiped Him; but some doubted." (Matthew 28: 17). The Christ Impulse needs an accepting soul from out of one's free will and understanding in order to fully work within the soul. The understanding of the nature of the Christ is a key step in the eventual evolution of the human soul. We can discern this from the Gospel of John when Christ Jesus spoke to Thomas: "Jesus said to him, `Because thou hast seen me, thou hast believed. Blessed are they who have not seen, and yet have believed.' " (John 20: 29). Steiner has explained this passage to say that those who have not passed through the old form of Initiation but will have come to accept the reality of the nature of the Christ will be blessed. And that we who come to eventually comprehend the Mystery of Golgotha and the mission and nature of Christ will eventually receive spiritual vision.

In the concluding lecture on Mark's Gospel, Steiner has these words to say on the great importance of understanding the Mystery of Golgotha and the nature and mission of the Christ. All that preceded the Advent of Christ proved to be ineffective in bringing an understanding and awareness of the actuality of the Advent of Christ. What we gain in understanding the Mystery of Golgotha from this time forward works in our souls as forces that will bring about the future condition of the Earth. In Lecture X Steiner affirms this truth with the following: "For only then will men truly grasp the reality that the Earth is linked with the spiritual worlds, when they understand how the spiritual reality, the Christ, lived as a cosmic Being in the body of Jesus of Nazareth; and when they understand that all the leaders of humanity that the world has ever known were sent out by the Christ as His forerunners with the task of preparing the way for Him so that He could be recognized and understood. All this preparation turned out to be virtually useless when the Mystery of Golgotha took place, for at the decisive moment everything failed. But ever more and more in the future the time will come when people will understand not only the Mystery of Golgotha itself but all the other events that accompanied it, by means of which the Mystery will be ever more fully understood."

Steiner concludes with the following: "The key to the understanding of this Mystery of Golgotha is the Mystery of Golgotha itself! Christ had first to do all that He had to do up to the time of the Mystery of Golgotha, and only through the effects of what He did could the understanding of Himself come forth. Then through what He was, the Word could be enkindled which is at the same time the expression of His true Being. And so through what Christ was, the primal Word is enkindled which is communicated to us and can be recognized again in clairvoyant vision, this Word which also proclaims the true Being of the Mystery of Golgotha. We may also think of this Word when we speak of Christ's own words, not only those that He spoke Himself but those which He also kindled in the souls of those able to understand Him, so that they could both understand and describe His Being from within their human souls.

As long as the Earth endures men will take up into themselves the impulses from the Mystery of Golgotha. Then there will come an interval between `Earth' and `Jupiter'. Such an interval is always linked to the fact that not only the individual planet, but all its surroundings change, pass into chaos, undergo a `pralaya'. And not only the Earth itself will be different in pralaya, but also the heavens belonging to the Earth. But what has been given to the Earth through the Word that Christ spoke, which He kindled also in those who recognize Him, is the true essence of Earth existence. And a right understanding allows us to recognize the truth of that saying that tells us of the development of the cosmos, how the Earth and Heaven as seen from the Earth will be different after the Earth has reached its goal, and Heaven and Earth pass away. But such a Word as could be spoken by Christ about Heaven and Earth will remain. If one rightly understands the Gospels, and feels their innermost impulse, then one feels not only the truth but also the power of the Word which as power passes over into us, enabling us to gaze out beyond the wide world as we take up into ourselves with full understanding the

Word, 'Heaven and Earth shall pass away, but my words shall not pass away.' (Matthew 24: 35).

The words of Christ will never pass away, even if Heaven and Earth pass away. This may be said in accordance with occult knowledge, for the truths of the Mystery of Golgotha that have been spoken will still remain. The Mark Gospel kindles in our souls the knowledge of the truth that Heaven and Earth pass away, while what we can know about the Mystery of Golgotha will accompany us into the ages that are to come, even if Heaven and Earth will have passed away!"

VIII

From Jesus to Christ

In Steiner's lecture cycle, "From Jesus to Christ," we get a better understanding of what the Mystery of Golgotha meant in terms of bringing about the redemption of the physical body and of matter. In Lecture III, Steiner speaks of the acts of the Gods in relation to the evolution of the Earth and humanity: "This becoming entangled in matter was not a human act, but a deed of the Gods, which is something which the Higher Powers of progressive evolution arranged with the Luciferic powers."

"What happened at that time needed a counterpoise. The pre-human event - the Fall of Man - needed a counterpoise, but this again was a concern not of human Beings, but of the Gods themselves. And we shall see that this action had to take its course as deeply in matter as the first action had taken place above it. The God had to descend as deeply into matter as He had allowed man to sink into matter. Let this fact work upon you with its full weight; then you will understand that this incarnation of the Christ in Jesus of Nazareth was something that concerned Christ Himself. And what part was man called upon to take in it? First of all, as spectator, to see how the God compensates for the Fall, how He provides the compensating act. It would not have been possible to do this within the personality of an Adept, for an Adept is one who by his own efforts had worked his way out of the Fall. It was possible only in a personality who was truly man - who, as man, did not surpass other men. This personality had surpassed them before he was thirty years of age - but no longer [note: Steiner is referring to Zarathustra who had to abandon the body of Jesus of Nazareth prior to the Baptism in the Jordan]. Through that which then took place, a Divine event was accomplished in the evolution of mankind, just as had been done at the beginning of human evolution in the Lemurian time. And men were partakers in a transaction which had taken place among Gods; men could look upon it, because the Gods had to make use of the world of the physical plane in order to let their transaction play itself out to the end. Hence it is much better to say: `Christ offered to the Gods the atonement which He could offer only in a physical human body', than to use any other form of words. Man was a spectator of a Divine occasion."

In Lecture VI, Steiner brings to our attention that Paul identified Christ as the `Second Adam'. Paul was another who was directly Initiated by Christ while he was making his way to Damascus. Paul speaks of the incorruptible body; that is, the redemption of the human Phantom body into a Christ-imbued phantom body. This allows the soul to 'make straight the way for the Lord'; meaning, to evolve the Ego such that it impresses itself ever more deeply within the soul and body.

From Lecture VI: "What, from the event of Damascus onwards, was the Being of Christ for Paul? The Being of Christ was for him the 'second Adam'; and he immediately differentiates between the first Adam and the second Adam, the Christ. He calls the first Adam the progenitor of men on Earth because he sees in him the first man, from whom all other men are descended. For Paul, it is the Adam who has bequeathed to human Beings the body which they carry about them as a physical body. All men have inherited their physical body from Adam. This is the body which meets us in external Maya, and is mortal; it is the body of man that decays in death. With this body men are 'clothed'. The Second Adam, Christ, is regarded by Paul as possessing, in contrast to the first, the incorruptible, the immortal body. Paul then affirms that through Christian evolution men are gradually made ready to put on the second Adam in place of the first Adam; the incorruptible body of the second Adam, Christ, in place of the corruptible body of the first Adam. What Paul seems to require of all who call themselves true Christians is something that violates all the old conceptions of the world. As the first corruptible body is descended from Adam, so must the incorruptible body originate from the second Adam, from Christ. Every Christian could say: 'Because I am descended from Adam, I have a corruptible body as Adam had; but in that I set myself in the right relationship to Christ, I receive from Him, the second Adam, an incorruptible body.' For Paul this view shines out directly from the experience of Damascus."

Steiner continues this theme saying: "Paul, however, demands the following. He says: 'If you desire to be a Christian in the true sense, you must conceive that within you something can arise which can live in you, and from which you can draw spiritual lines to a second Adam, to Christ, to that very Christ who on the third day rose from the grave, just as all men can trace lines back to the physical body of the first Adam.' So Paul demands that all who call themselves Christians should cause something within them to arise; something leading to that entity which on the third day rose out of the grave in which the body of Christ Jesus had been laid. Anyone who does not grant this cannot come into any relationship with Paul; he cannot say he understands Paul. If man, as regards his corruptible body, is descended from the first Adam, then, by receiving the Being of Christ into his own Being, he has the possibility of having a second ancestor. This ancestor, however, is He who, on the third day after His body had been laid in the Earth, rose out of the grave."

Steiner then begins to explain the 'Phantom' or what he also called the 'Form' of the physical body. He poses a question about death in asking what is it of the body that does not pass into decay. He answers in the following manner: "But does he really lay aside his physical body? The question seems absurd, for what could be clearer than the apparent fact that at death man lays aside his physical body? But what is it that he lays aside? It is something no longer imbued with the physical body's most important possession during life: its Form. Directly after death the Form begins to withdraw from the dead body. We are left with the decaying substances, no longer characterized by the Form. The body laid aside is composed of substances and elements which we can trace also in Nature; in the natural order of things they would not produce a human Form. Yet this Form belongs quite essentially to the physical human body."

"This Phantom is the Form-shape which as a spiritual texture works up the physical substances and forces so that they fill out the Form which we encounter as the man on the physical plane."

"Out of that path of evolution in which his physical, etheric and astral bodies were still invisible, man was thrown down into denser matter, and was compelled under the influence of Lucifer to take this denser matter into himself. If the Lucifer force had not been introduced into our astral body and Ego, this dense materiality would not have become as visible as it has become. Hence we have to represent man as an invisible Being, made visible in matter only through forces which entered into him under the influence of Lucifer."

From the above excerpts of Steiner's lectures we can examine the scene of the two robbers who were alongside Christ at the Crucifixion with a more esoteric perspective. As we take into account the redemption of the physical body it is fitting then to say that the Luke Gospel gives us the supersensible account of the words of the two robbers who were crucified with Christ Jesus. In the Luke Gospel this account of the two robbers has to do with the physical body of Jesus of Nazareth; the body of the Nathan Jesus of the Luke Gospel. The Luke Gospel brings this very point, the redemption of the human Phantom, to its culmination at the Crucifixion which was wrought by Christ in the body of the Nathan Jesus; the Jesus individuality who is presented to us in the nativity of the Luke Gospel. Steiner had said that the Luciferic forces are what give the human physical body its dense materiality. It is not that one robber repents while the other reproaches Christ. They both reproach Christ and this is accounted for in both the Matthew Gospel and the Mark Gospel.

We read in Matthew 27: 38-44: "Then two robbers were crucified with Him, one on His right hand and one on His left. Now the passers-by were jeering at Him, shaking their heads, and saying, `Thou who destroyest the temple, and in three days buildest it up again, save thyself ! If thou art the Son of God, come down from the Cross! In like manner, the chief priests with the Scribes and the elders, mocking, said, `He saved others, Himself he cannot save! If He is the King of Israel, let Him come down now from the Cross, and we will believe Him. He trusted in God; let Him deliver Him now, if He wants Him; for He said, `I AM the Son of God.' And the robbers also, who were crucified with Him, reproached Him in the same way." Mark gives a similar account in his Gospel and concludes with the following: "And they who were crucified with Him reproached Him." (Mark 15: 32). Both Gospels never mention or suggest that one of the robbers was repentant. Who, then, does say the following in Luke 23: 42?: "And he said to Jesus, `Lord, remember me when thou comest into thy Kingdom.'" The accounts given to us in the Matthew and Mark Gospels seem to contradict the account expressed to us in the Luke Gospel. However, what appears to be contradictions in these accounts actually give us a greater insight into a deeper mystery. The Matthew and Mark Gospels record the account of the human thieves while the Luke Gospel records the account of the presence of Lucifer and Ahriman at the Crucifixion of Christ Jesus.

It is Lucifer who speaks these words of the repentant thief in the Luke Gospel. It is Lucifer presented by Luke as one of the thieves speaking while Ahriman is presented as speaking through the other. These words that are recorded in the Luke Gospel actually may not have been audibly spoken by either of the two thieves. Also, the two thieves may be described as the two `false cultists' who have deceived and misled humanity. What Luke presents to us would be an account of the suprasensible presence of Lucifer and Ahriman at the Crucifixion of Christ. The words of Lucifer which are given to us as the words of the repentant thief direct us to the actuality that Christ has overcome the Luciferic impulses in the human Phantom of Nathan Jesus; in the physical body of Jesus of Nazareth. These words also mark the redemption of Lucifer while Ahriman is still a world spiritual force that is able to turn stones into bread. The contrast in what we read in both Matthew and Mark and what we read in Luke is resolved if we understand that Luke gives us the account of the powers of Lucifer and Ahriman and their presence at the Crucifixion. Immediately following the words of Lucifer, Christ then speaks to him in a way that was possibly only perceived in the supersensible realms: "And Jesus said to him, `Amen I say to thee, this day thou shalt be with me in paradise.'" (Luke 23: 43).

It seems that this entire passage stands as a veiled proclamation to the very mystery that Steiner expounds in regard to the Luciferic influences in the human Phantom. It marks the beginning of the redemption of the Luciferic forces thereby extricating them from the human Form throughout the eventual future course of human evolution. This in turn brings about the redemption of Lucifer from that day forward. When Christ had said - It Is Finished - the Fall had reached its nadir and from that point on, since 'the Turning Point in Time', Lucifer was redeemed. Moreover, the Luciferic spirits that were active then and are still presently active in human evolution

119

begin to gradually recede as adversarial forces to humanity. This is due to the ever increasing activity of Christ within human souls over the course of time and evolution. It is also due to the activity of the conscious and willed effort of each individual to overcome the Luciferic forces within one's own soul.

From a previously cited quote of Steiner's, he had said, "If the Luciferic influence had not been introduced into our astral body and Ego . . . "; this must not be confused with the Asuras who are presently active in the human consciousness soul in the attempt to usurp the human Ego. The above quote is in reference to the far distant past when the Luciferic impulses were first impacting the astral body and thereby negatively obscuring the nascent human Ego in the soul. Steiner is saying that when the original Luciferic impulses infected the astral body of human Beings it also affected the etheric and physical bodies negatively. It stands to reason then that this influence also impacted the Ego such that the Ego could not properly function in the entirety of the human Form. The Ego was clouded by the Luciferic forces that existed in the astral body and could not manifest in the soul as was originally purposed. The Asuras, on the other hand, will continue to try to consume and annihilate the human Ego, now and well into the future. Their activity is presently at its beginning stages.

In the lecture, "The Deed of Christ and the Opposing Spiritual Powers," Steiner spoke of the Asuras: "Fundamentally speaking, man is still working at this unconscious transformation of the physical body, at the development of the consciousness soul. And in the age now approaching, those spiritual Beings known as the Asuras will creep into the consciousness soul and therewith into the human `I' or Ego - for the `I' lights up in the consciousness soul."

"For these Asuric Spirits will prompt what has been seized hold of by them, namely the very core of man's Being, the consciousness soul together with the `I', to unite with earthly materiality. Fragment after fragment will be torn out of the `I', and in the same manner in which the Asuric Spirits establish themselves in the consciousness soul, man must leave parts of his existence behind on the earth."

Returning to Lecture VI of, "From Jesus to Christ," Steiner says the following: "The physical body is itself entirely transparent, and it is the Luciferic forces in man which have brought him to a non-transparent state and placed him before us so that he is opaque and tangible. Hence you will understand that man has become a Being who takes up external substances and forces of the earth, which are given off again at death, only because Lucifer tempted him, and certain forces were poured into his astral body. It follows that because the Ego entered into connection with the physical, etheric and astral bodies under the influence of Lucifer, man became what he is on Earth and otherwise would not have been - the bearer of a visible, earthly organism."

Steiner then concludes Lecture VI: "What now differentiates this Christ Jesus from all other men on Earth? It is this: that all other men bear within them an Ego that once was overcome by Lucifer's temptation, but Jesus no longer bears an Ego within Him; instead, He bears the Christ-Being. So that from this time, beginning with the Baptism in Jordan, Jesus bears within Him the residual effects that had come from Lucifer, but with no human Ego to allow any further Luciferic influences to enter his body. A physical body, an etheric body, and an astral body - in which the residue of the earlier Luciferic influences was present, but into which no more Luciferic influence could enter - and the Christ-Being: thus was Christ Jesus constituted.

Let us set before us exactly what the Christ is from the Baptism in Jordan until the Mystery of Golgotha: a physical body, an etheric body, and an astral body which makes this physical body together with the etheric body visible because it still contains the residue of the Luciferic influence. Because the Christ-Being had the astral body that Jesus of Nazareth had had from birth to his thirtieth year, the physical body was visible as the bearer of the Christ. Thus, from the time of the Baptism in Jordan, we have before us a physical body which as such would not be visible on the physical plane; an etheric body which as such would not have been perceptible; the astral body which makes the other two bodies visible and so makes the body of Jesus of Nazareth into a visible body; and, within this organism, the Christ-Being."

In Lecture VII Steiner once again returns to the theme and principle of 'understanding': "If no Luciferic influence had come in, the destructive and reconstructive forces in the physical body would have remained in balance. But then everything in earthly human nature would have been different; there would, for example, have been no mind incapable of comprehending the Resurrection. For what kind of understanding is it that cannot grasp the Resurrection? It is the kind that is bound up with the decadence of the physical body, and is what it is because the individual has incurred, through the Luciferic influence, the progressive destruction of the Phantom of the physical body. In consequence the human understanding, the human intellect, has become so thin, so threadbare, that it cannot take in the great processes of cosmic evolution. It looks on them as miracles, or says it cannot comprehend them. If the Luciferic influence had not come, and the upbuilding forces in the human body had held the destructive forces in balance, then the human understanding, equipped with all that was intended for it, would have seen into the upbuilding forces, rather as one follows a laboratory experiment. But our understanding is now such that it remains on the surface of things and has no insight into the cosmic depths."

Another aspect to consider is that John the Baptist, as we know, was not present in a physical body during the Passion of Christ. He was not subject to the same blinding forces of the physical body as were the others. This enabled him to steep himself into the mystery of the Phantom body: the

121

human Form. This was due to the ongoing preparation and Initiation of John the Baptist by Christ since the feeding of the five thousand and during and after the raising of Lazarus. The mystery of the Phantom body was the mystery that John the Baptist was destined to comprehend. With this comprehension he could then become the first human to receive into his self the Life Spirit/Buddhi forces that would bring about the eventual redemption of the human Form; the first human to put on the incorruptible body. We could possibly say that John the Baptist came to understand that which Steiner had said in Lecture VII of, "From Jesus to Christ": "The truth is that man, in the course of the Earth-evolution, lost the Form of the physical body, so that he no longer has what the Divine Beings had intended for him from the beginning of the Earth. This is something he must regain; but it had first to be imparted to him once more. And we cannot comprehend Christianity unless we understand that at the time when the Events of Palestine took place, the human race on Earth had reached a stage where the decadence of the physical body was at its peak, and where, because of this, the whole evolution of humanity was threatened with the danger that the Ego-consciousness - the specific achievement of the Earth-evolution - would be lost. If this process had continued unchanged, the destructive element would have penetrated ever more deeply into the human bodily organism, and men born after the time when the Events of Palestine were due would have had to live with an ever-duller feeling of the Ego. Everything that depends on perfect reflection from the physical body would have become increasingly worn out.

Then came the Mystery of Golgotha; it came as we have characterized it, and through it something happened which is so hard to grasp for an intellect bound up with the physical body only, a body in which the destructive forces predominate. It came to pass that one man, who was the bearer of the Christ, had gone through such a death that after three days the specifically mortal part of the physical body had to disappear, and out of the grave there rose the body which is the Force-Bearer of the physical, material parts. The body that was really intended for man by the Rulers of Saturn, Sun and Moon - the pure Phantom of the physical body with all the attributes of the physical body - this it was that rose out of the grave. So was given the possibility of that spiritual genealogy of which we have spoken."

Steiner continues: "And it is possible to establish a relationship with Christ through which an earthly human Being can bring into his otherwise decaying physical body this Phantom which rose out of the grave of Golgotha. It is possible for man to receive into his organism those forces which then rose from the grave, just as through his physical organism at the beginning of the Earth evolution, as a consequence of the Luciferic forces, he received the organism of Adam."

And it was John the Baptist who was the first to do so.

Steiner further elaborates this theme: "It is this that Paul wishes to say. Just as man, through his place in the stream of physical evolution, inherits the physical body in which the destruction of the Phantom, the Force-Bearer, is gradually taking place, so from the pure Phantom that rose out of the grave he can inherit what he has lost. He can inherit it, he can clothe himself with it, as he clothed himself with the first Adam; he can become one with it. Thereby he can go through a development by means of which he can climb upwards again, even as before the Mystery of Golgotha he had descended in evolution. In other words, that which had been taken from him through the Luciferic influence can be given back to him through its presence as the Risen Body of Christ. That is what Paul wishes to say."

Steiner continues in the same lecture: "If indeed Paul really believed that a spiritual body had risen, what has this spiritual body which had risen out of the grave to do with what every man now bears in himself? This is not hard to understand: we need only consider the analogy offered by the coming into existence of a human individual. As a physical human Being he begins from a single cell; a physical body consists entirely of cells which are all children of the original cell; all cells which compose a human body are traceable to the original cell. Now imagine that, through what we may call a mystical Christological process, man acquires a body quite other than the one he has gradually acquired in his downward evolution. Then think of each of these new bodies as having an intimate connection with the pure Phantom that rose from the grave, somewhat as the human cells of the physical body are connected with the original cell. That is, we must think of the Phantom as multiplying itself, as does the cell which gives rise to the physical body. So, in the evolution which follows the Event of Golgotha, every man can inwardly acquire something which is spiritually descended from the Phantom which rose from the grave, just as - to echo Paul - the ordinary body which falls into dissolution is descended from Adam."

"To someone who contemplates evolution with occult sight it is apparent that the spiritual cell, the body which overcame death, the body of Christ Jesus, has risen from the grave and in the course of time imparts itself to anyone who enters into the corresponding relationship with the Christ. . . . The Phantom which rose from the grave communicates itself to those who make themselves fitted for it. This, then, is a fact that everyone who grants the supersensible can understand. If we can inscribe upon our souls what is in very truth the Pauline teaching, we come to regard the Mystery of Golgotha as a reality that took place and had to take place in the evolution of the Earth; for it signifies literally the rescue of the human Ego. We have seen that if the process of evolution had continued along the path it had followed up to the time of the Events of Palestine, the Ego-consciousness could not have been developed; it would not only have failed to advance, but would have gone down ever further into darkness. But the path turned upwards, and will

123

continue to ascend in proportion as men find their relation to the Christ-Being."

". . .if he clothes himself with this incorruptible body, he will become more and more clearly aware of his Ego-consciousness, and of that part of his nature which journeys on from one incarnation to another."

"The important thing is not what Christ taught, but what He gave: His Body. For the Body that rose from the grave of Golgotha had never before entered into human evolution. Never before had there been present on Earth, through the death of a man, that which came to be present as the Risen Body of Christ Jesus. Previously, after men had passed through the gate of death, and had gone through the period between death and a new birth, they had brought to Earth with them the defective Phantom, given over to deterioration. No one had ever caused a perfect Phantom to arise."

It should be noted, as Steiner does in Lecture VIII, that Zarathustra had been instrumental in preparing the body of Jesus for the incarnation of Christ: "And then into this body nature there entered the individuality who above all others had seen most clearly and deeply into the spirituality of the Macrocosm. By this means the bodily instrument, the entire organism, of the Nathan Jesus was so transformed that it could be the vehicle capable of receiving into itself the Christ-extract of the Macrocosm."

Earlier, the following was quoted from Steiner's, "From Jesus to Christ": "The Phantom. . .Should not have been attracted to the ashy constituents but only to the dissolving salt constituents, so that it would have taken the path of volatilization insofar as the salt constituents dissolved. In an occult sense one can say that it would have dissolved and passed over, not into the Earth but into the volatile constituents. The remarkable fact is that with the Baptism in Jordan and the entry of the Christ Individuality into the body of the Nathan Jesus, all connection of the Phantom with the ashy constituents was wiped out; only the connection with the salt constituents remained."

We can now add from Lecture VIII: "Thus it followed that when Christ Jesus was crucified, when his body was nailed to the Cross - you will notice that here I use the exact words of the Gospel for they are confirmed by occult research- when this body of Jesus of Nazareth was fastened to the Cross, the Phantom was perfectly intact; it existed in a spiritual bodily form, visible only to supersensible sight, and was much more loosely connected with the body's material content of Earth elements than has ever happened with any other human Being. In every other human Being a connection of the Phantom with these elements has occurred, and it is this that holds them together. In the case of Christ Jesus it was quite different. The ordinary law of inertia sees to it that certain material portions of a human body hold together after death in the form man has given them, until after some time they crumble away, so that hardly anything of them is visible. So it was with the material portions of the body of Christ Jesus. When the body was taken down from the Cross, the parts were still coherent, but they had no connection with the Phantom; the Phantom was completely free of them. When the body became permeated with certain substances, which in this case worked quite differently from the way in which they affect any other body that is embalmed, it came to pass that after the burial the material parts quickly volatilised and passed over into the elements. Hence the disciples who looked into the grave found the linen cloths in which the body had been wrapped, but the Phantom, on which the evolution of the Ego depends, had risen from the grave. It is not surprising that Mary Magdala, who had known only the earlier Phantom when it was permeated by earthly elements, did not recognize the same form in the Phantom, now freed from terrestrial gravity, when she saw it clairvoyantly. It seemed to her differently. Moreover, we must clearly understand that it was only through the power of the companionship of the disciples with the Christ that all of the disciples, and all those persons of whom the same is told, could see the Risen One, for He appeared to them in the spiritual body, the body of which Paul says that it increases as a grain of seed and passes over into all people."

This 'grain of seed' had to first implant itself into at least one individual human and that it increases from there to all others. That first seedling was John the Baptist. In Lecture IX Steiner opens with this very point: "With Christ there rose out of the grave a kind of seed-kernel for the reconstruction of our human Phantom. And it is possible for this seed-kernel to incorporate itself in those individuals who find a connection with the Christ-Impulse."

And concluding the study of Steiner's, "From Jesus to Christ," is the following from Lecture X: "If the God who is designated by the name of the Father had not at one time permitted the Luciferic influence to come to man, man would not have developed the free Ego. With the Luciferic influence, the conditions for the free Ego were established. That had to be permitted by the Father-God. But just as the Ego, for the sake of freedom, had to become entangled in matter, so then, in order that the Ego might be freed from this entanglement, the entire love of the Son had to lead to the Act of Golgotha. Through this alone the freedom of man, the complete dignity of man, first became possible. For the fact that we can be free Beings, we have to thank a Divine Act of Love. As men we may feel free Beings, but we may never forget that for this freedom we have to thank this Act of Love. Then, in the midst of our feeling, the thought will arise: 'You can attain to the value, the dignity, of a man; but one thing you may not forget, that for being what you are you have to thank Him who has brought back to you your human prototype through the Redemption on Golgotha.' Men should not be able to lay hold of the thought of freedom without the thought of Redemption through Christ: only then is the thought of freedom justified. If we will to be free, we must bring the offering of thanks to Christ for our freedom. Then only can we really perceive it. And those who consider that their dignity as men is restricted when they thank Christ for it, should recognize that human opinions have no significance in face of cosmic facts, and that one day they will very willingly acknowledge that their freedom was won by Christ."

In a brief study of Steiner's, "An Outline of Occult Science," the following quotes are in concert with the progressing line of thought in this work. In Chapter II we read its opening as follows: "In the observation of man the point of view of a supersensible mode of cognition, the general principles of this method become immediately applicable. This observation rests upon the recognition of the `revealed mystery' within the individual human Being. Only a part of what supersensible cognition apprehends as the human Being is accessible to the senses and to the intellect dependent upon them, namely, the physical body. In order to elucidate the concept of this physical body, our attention must first be turned to that phenomenon which, as the great riddle, lies spread out over all observation of life, that is, to death and, in connection with it, to so-called lifeless nature - the mineral kingdom - which always bears death within it."

Comprehension and understanding are key to the advancement of humanity. Steiner then says in the same chapter: "It has already been indicated that the descriptions of the path on which man attains to a higher perception can be of value to him only after he has become acquainted in simple narrative form with the disclosures of supersensible research. For in regard to the supersensible realm it is possible to comprehend what has not yet been observed. Indeed, the right path toward perception is that which proceeds from comprehension."

Previously, we have read from Steiner the account of the Luciferic influences that had infected the whole of the human Form. In Chapter III of, "An Outline of Occult Science," we also read: "The physical body can retain the form and stature suitable for man only by means of the human ether body, which in turn receives its proper forces from the astral body. The ether body is the builder, the architect, of the physical body, but it can only build in the right way if it receives the impulse for this purpose from the astral body. In the astral body reside the prototypes according to which the ether body gives form to the physical body."

We can see from the above statement that when the Luciferic influences infected the astral bodies of humans the entire human Form became corrupted. Thereby, it was absolutely essential to redeem the human Phantom/Form if humanity is to continue on in its proper course of evolution. This is what Christ gave to humanity at the Turning Point in Time. In this act that proceeded from the Hill of Golgotha the Luciferic influences were overcome in the human Form of humanity through Christ. He also laid the foundation for the eventual overcoming of Ahrimanic forces in the distant future. In the chapter, "The Evolution of the Cosmos and Man," Steiner says this in regard to the Mystery of Golgotha: "At the moment in the life of

Christ Jesus, when His astral body contained everything that the Luciferic impulse can conceal, He assumed His mission as Teacher of mankind. From this moment onward the aptitude was implanted in human Earth evolution for receiving the wisdom through which the physical earthly goal can by degrees be attained. At the moment when the Event of Golgotha was accomplished, the other aptitude was injected into mankind by which it is possible to turn the influence of Ahriman to good. Henceforth the human Being is able to carry with him out of life through the portals of death what releases him from isolation in the spiritual world. The Event of Palestine is not only the center of the physical evolution of mankind, but is also the center of the other worlds to which the human Being belongs. When the 'Mystery of Golgotha' was accomplished, when 'Death on the Cross' was suffered, the Christ appeared in the world in which souls tarry after death, and in that region He set bounds to the power of Ahriman. From this moment the realm that was named by the Greeks the 'kingdom of the shades' was illuminated by that spiritual lightning flash that showed its inhabitants that henceforth light would again appear in it. What was attained through the Mystery of Golgotha for the physical world threw its light into the spiritual world. - Thus the post-Atlantean human evolution was, up to this event, an ascent for the physical world of the senses, but it was at the same time a descent for the spiritual. Everything that flowed into the world of the senses poured forth from what had already existed in the spiritual world from primeval ages. Since the Christ event, human Beings who elevate themselves to the Christ Mystery are able to carry with them into the spiritual world what they have acquired in the sense world. It flows back again from the spiritual world into the earthly-sensory world by human Beings bringing back with them into reincarnation what the Christ Impulse has become for them in the world of spirit between death and rebirth.

What the Christ Event bestowed upon mankind's evolution acted within it like a seed. The seed can ripen only gradually. Only the very smallest part of the new wisdom's profundity has penetrated physical existence up to the present. This existence stands just at the beginning of Christian evolution. During the succeeding centuries that have elapsed since that event, Christian evolution has been able to unveil only as much of its inner nature as human Beings, peoples, were capable of receiving, were capable of absorbing with their mental capacities. The first form into which this knowledge could be poured may be described as an all-encompassing ideal of life. As such it opposed what in the post-Atlantean humanity had fashioned itself as modes of life. . . . Mankind proceeded from a unity, but Earth evolution up to the present has lead to differentiation. In the Christ-concept an Ideal is given that counteracts all differentiation, for in the human Being Who bears the name of Christ live also the forces of the exalted Sun Being in Whom every Ego finds its origin. . . . At the outset the fact that in the Christ Jesus lives the Ideal man

127

Who is not touched by the conditions of separation was only comprehended in thought, and Christianity became the Ideal of an all-encompassing brotherhood. Disregarding all separate interests and separate relationships, the feeling arose that the inmost Ego of every human Being has the same origin. (Alongside all earthly forefathers the common Father of all human Beings appears. `I and the Father are One.')"

IX

The Fifth Gospel

Throughout this work it has been asserted that the bond between the Apostles and the Christ Being had been severed at the time of the arrest and the result was that the Apostles had lost the connection they had with the cosmic principle, the cosmic aura of the Christ Being. The Risen Christ began to restore this bond with His chosen Apostles and brought it to its culmination at the time of Pentecost. In Steiner's, "The Fifth Gospel," he addresses this in the following excerpts beginning with Lecture II: "We will begin today by turning our thoughts to the event known as Pentecost. I said in the first lecture that clairvoyant research may first of all be directed to this event, for as we look back into the past it presents itself as a kind of awakening, experienced on the day commemorated in the Whitsun Festival, by those who are generally known as the Apostles or Disciples of Christ Jesus. It is not easy to form clear and precise pictures of all these undoubtedly strange phenomena. And if we want to think truly about the matter we shall have to call up, from deep down in our souls, many things we have learned from previous studies of Anthroposophy.

It seemed to the Apostles that they were like men who had awakened, after living for a long time in an unusual state of consciousness. In very truth it was a kind of awakening from a deep sleep, a wonderful, dream-filled sleep - remember that I am speaking of how it was experienced by the Apostles themselves - a sleep of such a kind that at the same time a man carries out all the affairs of everyday life and goes about just like a normal person, so that people around him do not notice that he is in a different state of consciousness. The moment came when it seemed to the Apostles as if they had been living for a long time, for many, many days, in a kind of dream from which they woke at this time of Pentecost; and the awakening itself was a strange experience. The Apostles felt as if there had actually descended upon them from the Cosmos something that could only be called the Substance of all-prevailing Love. They felt as if they had been quickened from on high by this all-prevailing Love and awakened from the condition of dream into which they had fallen. It seemed to them as if they had been wakened to life by the primal force of Love pervading and warming the Cosmos, as if this primal force of Love had come down into the soul of each one of them. And to others who could observe them and hear how they were now speaking, they seemed altogether strange. The others knew that they were men who until then had lived in extraordinary simplicity, although a few of them had certainly behaved strangely during recent days, as if lost in dream. This was known. But now it seemed to people as if these men had been transformed, as if their very souls had been made new; they seemed to have lost all narrowness, all selfishness in life, to have acquired largeness of heart, an all-embracing tolerance and a deep understanding for everything that is human on the Earth. Moreover, they were able to express themselves in such a way that everyone present could understand them. It was felt that they could look into every heart, could read the deepest, innermost secrets of the soul and so were able to bring consolation to every single individual, to say to him exactly what he needed. It was naturally amazing that such a transformation could take place in a number of men. But these men themselves, who had experienced the transformation, who had been awakened by the Spirit of Cosmic Love, they now felt within them a new understanding of things they had not previously grasped, although these things had indeed come to pass in the most intimate connection with their own souls. Now, at this moment, there dawned in their souls an understanding of what had actually transpired on Golgotha.

And when we look into the innermost soul of one of these Apostles, into the soul of him who is called Peter in the other Gospels, it is revealed to clairvoyant sight that his normal earthly consciousness was completely absent from the moment referred to in the other Gospels as the Denial. He looked back to this scene of the Denial, how he had been asked whether he knew the Galilean; and now he knew that he had denied any such connection because his normal consciousness was beginning to fade and an abnormal condition setting in - a kind of dream condition indicating a withdrawal into an altogether different world. Peter's experience was like that of a man who when he wakes in the morning remembers the last events of the previous evening. Thus did Peter remember the scene usually known as the Denial, the triple denial before the cock had crowed twice. And then, like outspreading night, the intermediate condition pervaded his consciousness. But this intermediate condition was filled, not with mere dream-pictures but with pictures representing a kind of higher consciousness, an experience of things belonging to the world of pure Spirit. And all that had happened, all that Peter had as it were slept through since that time, rose like a clairvoyant dream before his soul. Above all he was now able to gaze at that event of which it can truly be said that he slept through it, because for a full understanding of this event a quickening by the all-pervading Cosmic Love was needed. Now before the eyes of Peter came pictures of the Mystery of Golgotha - the pictures that we, looking back with clairvoyant consciousness, can again evoke if the necessary conditions are induced."

In the above quote it reads: "The Apostles felt as if there had actually descended upon them from the Cosmos something that could only be called

130

the Substance of all-prevailing Love. They felt as if they had been quickened from on high by this all-prevailing Love and awakened from the condition of dream into which they had fallen. It seemed to them as if they had been wakened to life by the primal force of Love pervading and warming the Cosmos, as if this primal force of Love had come down into the soul of each one of them."

What was this 'all-prevailing Love' that descended upon the Apostles? It was the Manas of the Christ which He brought to earth at the time of the Baptism in the Jordan. The Manas is most closely associated with that which is often referred to as the element of the Holy Spirit. In, "Karmic Relationships; Vol. VIII," Lecture VI, Steiner states the following: " . . . the Christ Who had come down to earth leaving His Spirit-Man (Atma) on the Sun and His Life-Spirit (Buddhi) in the atmosphere around the earth, bringing down His Ego and His Spirit-Self (Manas) to the earth . . ."

The Manas of Christ is the Holy Spirit element that is referred to as the tongues of fire that interpenetrated the soul of each Apostle at the time of Pentecost. The descent of the Manas of Christ may also help explain the passage of the descending dove upon Jesus of Nazareth at the time of the Jordan Baptism. (John 1:32). Continuing with Lecture II from, "The Fifth Gospel": "We can be led to these events only when , as seers, we find the way to them as I have indicated, when we sink in deepest contemplation into the soul of Peter or of one of the other Apostles who at the time of Pentecost felt themselves quickened by the all-prevailing Cosmic Love. Only when we contemplate the souls of those men and discern the nature of their experiences, is it possible in this indirect way to gaze at the Cross raised on Golgotha, to behold the darkening of the Earth at that time and the subsequent earthquake. It is not denied that in the external sense this darkening and earthquake were ordinary happenings in nature, but one who, having induced the requisite conditions in his soul, follows and reads these events with clairvoyant sight, will be emphatic that they were as I have described them. For in the consciousness of Peter, what I have now described was, in very truth, an experience that crystallized out of the long sleep. Among the manifold pictures crossing Peter's consciousness, those of the Cross raised on Golgotha, the darkening and the earthquake, for example, stood out in vivid relief. These experiences were for Peter the first result of the quickening by the Cosmic Love at Pentecost. And he now knew something he had not really known before: that the Event of Golgotha had taken place and that the body on the Cross was the same body he had often accompanied in life. Now he knew that Jesus had died on the Cross, that this dying was in reality a birth: the birth of that Spirit outpoured as the all-prevailing Cosmic Love into the souls of the Disciples assembled at Pentecost. Peter felt it as a ray of the primordial, aeonic Love . . . born when Jesus died on the Cross. And this stupendous truth sank down into Peter's

131

soul: It is only illusion that on the Cross a death took place. This death, preceded as it had been by infinite suffering, was in truth the birth of the ray now penetrating his soul. The all-prevailing Cosmic Love, which had previously been present everywhere outside and around the Earth, had, with the death of Jesus, been born into the Earth. In the abstract, such words seem facile, but one must actually be transported for a moment into the soul of Peter to realize what he experienced then for the first time: When Jesus of Nazareth died on the Cross, at that moment there was born for the Earth something previously to be found only in the Cosmos. The death of Jesus of Nazareth was the birth of the Cosmic Love within the sphere of the Earth. This is the first knowledge we are able to read from the Fifth Gospel. What I have now been describing begins with what is called in the New Testament the coming, or the outpouring, of the Spirit. The Apostles were not fitted by their whole inner constitution at that time to participate in the event of the death of Jesus of Nazareth otherwise than in an abnormal state of consciousness."

"Peter, John and James were constrained to recollect how they had fallen into this condition of sleep, and now, as they looked back, the vision lit up of the mighty events which had transpired around the earthly body of Him with whom they had gone about together. And gradually - as submerged dreams rise up into the consciousness of men - gradually the Apostles became conscious of what had occurred during those past days. During those days they had not experienced these happenings in their normal consciousness. What now came into their ken had lain deep down in their souls, submerged as it were for the whole of the period between the Event of Golgotha and Pentecost. This period seemed to them to have been one of deepest sleep - above all through the days between the event known as the Ascension, and Pentecost. As they looked backwards, the whole period - day by day - between the Mystery of Golgotha and the Ascension of Christ Jesus into heaven, came before their souls. They had lived through it all but only now did they become conscious of it - and in a strange and mysterious way."

In Lecture III, Steiner again addresses the Truth that the death of Jesus of Nazareth on the Cross was the earthly birth of the Christ: "In order to achieve some measure of clarity, we will begin by considering the event usually known as the Baptism by John in the Jordan. In respect of the earthly life of Christ, the Fifth Gospel reveals that this event was something like conception in the case of a human Being. And we understand the life of Christ from then onwards until the Mystery of Golgotha when we compare it with the life of the human embryo within the body of the mother. From the Baptism by John until the Mystery of Golgotha, therefore, the Christ Being passes through a kind of embryonic existence. The Mystery of Golgotha itself is to be understood as the earthly birth - that is to say, the death of Jesus is to be understood as the earthly birth of the Christ. His earthly life in the real sense lies after the Mystery of Golgotha, when He communed with the Apostles while they were in an abnormal state of consciousness. This was what followed the real birth of the Christ Being. And with reference still to the Christ Being, we must conceive the event described as the Ascension and the subsequent outpouring of the Spirit as the passing into the spiritual world which, as we know, takes place after the death of a human Being. The further life of Christ in the Earth-sphere, after the Ascension or after Pentecost, is to be compared with the life passed through by the human soul in Devachan, in the Spirit-Land. . . .Christ is a Being in respect of whom all ideas and concepts otherwise acquired concerning the successive stages and conditions of human life must be completely transformed.

After the brief intermediate period known as Kamaloka, the time of purification, the human Being passes over into the spiritual world proper, in order to prepare for the next earthly life. After his death, therefore, the human Being lives through a spiritual life. From the event of Pentecost onwards, the Christ Being passed through experiences which signified, for Him, what the transition into the Spirit-Land signifies for the human Being; they signified His entry into the sphere of the Earth. For instead of passing, as does a human Being, into Devachan, a realm of Spirit, after death, the sacrifice offered up by the Christ Being was that He made the Earth His heaven, sought His heaven upon the Earth. The human Being leaves the earth in order, as we say in ordinary parlance, to exchange his dwelling-place for heaven. Christ left the heavens in order to exchange them, His dwelling-place, for the Earth. . . . It was the forsaking of the sphere of Spirit in order that by living together with the Earth, and with men on the Earth, He might lead them and earthly evolution on to further stages through the Impulse thus bestowed.

This already indicates that before the Baptism in the Jordan, the Christ Being did not belong to the earthly sphere. From worlds beyond the Earth, from super-earthly spheres, He came down to the Earth. And the experiences between the Baptism in the Jordan and Pentecost were necessary in order that Christ, the heavenly Being, might be transformed into Christ, the earthly Being. Infinite depths have been expressed when it is said of this Mystery: Since the event of Pentecost the Christ Being has been together with human souls on the Earth; before then He was not together with human souls on the Earth. The experiences undergone by the Christ Being between the Baptism in the Jordan and the event of Pentecost took place in order that His abode in the spiritual world might be exchanged for His abode in the Earth-sphere. They were undergone in order that Christ, the Divine-Spiritual Being, might take upon Himself the form in which alone it would be possible for Him to live, henceforward, in communion with the souls of men. To what end, then, did the events of Palestine take place? To the end that Christ, the Divine-Spiritual Being, might assume the Form which enabled Him to live in

133

communion with human souls on Earth. Here we have a direct indication that the event of Palestine is unique and without parallel. . . . A higher, non-earthly Being comes down into the Earth-sphere and will remain there, until under the influence of this Being the Earth-sphere shall have been duly transformed. Since the days of Palestine, therefore, the Christ Being has been a power in the Earth itself."

Earlier it had been established that Lazarus indicates to us in the Book of Revelation that he was an Initiate of the sixth degree; a Sun Initiate. At the time of Pentecost the Apostles also were initiated into the mysteries of the sixth degree. The Apostles were now becoming united once more with the cosmic aura of Christ, with the elements of the Tree of Life, with the forces of the spiritual sun and with the all-prevailing Cosmic Love.

Steiner explains this further in Lecture III: "If we are to form a really clear conception of the event of Pentecost according to the Fifth Gospel, we must call to our aid certain concepts that have been worked out in Spiritual Science. We know that in earlier times there were Mysteries, Initiations, and that the human soul was raised through these Initiations into participation in the spiritual life. The most graphic picture of the pre-Christian Initiation is provided by the so-called Persian or Mithraic Mysteries. In these Mysteries there were seven stages. He who was to be led into the higher levels of spiritual experience attained, first of all, the rank called symbolically a `Raven.' Then he became a `Secret One,' a `Hidden One.' In the third degree he became a `Fighter'; in the fourth, a `Lion'; in the fifth degree the name of the people to which he belonged was conferred upon him. In the sixth degree he became a `Sun-Hero,' in the seventh a `Father.' Of the first four degrees it is sufficient to say, here and now, that in them a man was led by stages to deeper and deeper spiritual experiences. In the fifth degree he was ready for an extension of consciousness, giving him the power to become the spiritual guardian of his people, whose name was therefore conferred upon him. An Initiate of the fifth degree in those times participated in a very special way in the spiritual life.

From a Lecture-Course given here we know that the peoples of the Earth are led and guided by those Beings of the Spiritual Hierarchies known as the Archangeloi, the Archangels. An Initiate of the fifth degree was lifted into the sphere where he participated in the life of the Archangeloi. Such Initiates of the fifth degree were needed in the Cosmos; that is why, on the Earth, there was an Initiation into this fifth degree. When such a personality had been initiated in the Mysteries and had lived through the deep experiences and acquired the enrichment of soul proper to the fifth degree, the gaze of the Archangeloi was directed to this soul, reading in it as we read in a book which tells us certain things we need to know in order to perform some deed. In the soul of one who had been initiated in the fifth degree, the Archangeloi read what was needful for this people. To enable the

Archangeloi to lead the peoples rightly, there must be Initiates of the fifth degree on Earth. They are the intermediaries between the true leaders of a people and the people itself. They bear upwards, as it were, into the sphere of the Archangeloi what is necessary for the right leadership of particular peoples.

How could this fifth degree be attained in ancient, pre-Christian times? It could not be attained if the soul of the human Being remained in the body. The soul had to be raised out of the body. Initiation consisted precisely in this lifting of the soul out of the body. And outside the body the soul underwent experiences which imparted to it the content I have just been describing. The soul had to leave the Earth and rise up into the spiritual world in order to attain the goal set before it. When the sixth degree of the old Initiation had been attained, the degree of the Sun-Hero, there became active in the soul of this Sun-Hero a power required not only for the leadership, the guidance, the directing of a people, but for still higher purposes. Study the evolution of mankind on earth and you will see how peoples and nations arise and then pass away, how they are transformed. Peoples are born and peoples die - like individual human Beings. But what a particular people has accomplished for the Earth must be preserved in the whole onward march of evolution. Not only has a people to be directed and guided, but the results of the earthly labors of this people must be led out beyond it. In order that the achievements of a people might thus be led onwards by the Spirits whose task this is, the Sun-Heroes were needed. For what has been brought to life in the soul of a Sun-Hero can be read by Beings in the higher worlds. This was a means of acquiring those forces by which the results of a people's labors may be integrated into the labors of mankind as a whole. The power living in the Sun-Hero transcended the activity of a single people. And just as one who was to become an Initiate of the fifth degree in the ancient Mysteries had to pass out of his body in order to undergo the necessary experiences, so, too, he who was to become a Sun-Hero had to pass out of his body and actually have the Sun as his dwelling-place during the time of his absence. These things sound almost incredible, perhaps sheer folly, to the modern mind. But here too the saying of Paul holds good: that what may be wisdom in the sight of God is often foolishness in the sight of men.

During his Initiation the Sun-Hero lived in communion with the whole solar system, having as his place of abode the Sun, as the ordinary human Being lives on the Earth as his own planet. As mountains and rivers are around us here, se were the planets of the solar system around the Sun-Hero during the time of his Initiation. During his Initiation the Sun-Hero was transported in consciousness to the Sun. In the ancient Mysteries this could be achieved only outside the body. And when he came back into his body he remembered what he had experienced and was able to use these experiences as a potent force for furthering the evolution and well-being of all humanity.

The Sun-Heroes were transported away from the body during the process of Initiation and came back into the body, having gained the power of incorporating the achievements of a people into the evolution of humanity as a whole. And what was it that these Sun-Heroes experienced during the three and a half days of their Initiation while their dwelling-place - for so we may truly call it - was on the Sun? They experienced communion with Christ, who before the Mystery of Golgotha was not yet on the Earth! All the Sun-Heroes of old had been transported into the higher worlds, for in ancient times it was only in those worlds that communion with Christ could be experienced. From this world, into which the old Initiates had to rise during their Initiation, the Christ came down to the earth. And so we may say: what could be attained by a few single individuals in ancient times through Initiation was attained as the result, so to say, of a natural happening during the days of Pentecost, by those who were the Apostles of Christ Jesus. Whereas before then it was necessary for men to rise up to Christ, Christ had now come down to the Apostles. And the Apostles, in a certain respect, had become men who bore within them the substance and content that had belonged to the souls of the ancient Sun-Heroes. The spiritual power of the Sun had poured into the souls of men, working on henceforward in the evolution of humanity. In order that this might be, the events of Palestine were necessary."

Over the course of other lectures as well as these lectures on the Fifth Gospel we have read how the Christ gradually assumes the body of Jesus and doesn't become completely One with it until the final moments on the Cross. The final stages of Christ becoming One with the body of Jesus is part of the anguish that He experiences in the Garden of Gethsemane. It was here that the death of the body of Jesus almost occurred prematurely and that an angel had come to revitalize the body so that the Mystery of Golgotha could be enacted to the fullest and not aborted beforehand. Throughout much of the Ministry of Christ He had a loose connection with body of Jesus. Steiner speaks of this in his lecture cycle, "The Fifth Gospel": "The Fifth Gospel reveals that at the beginning of Christ's earthly pilgrimage, He – the Christ - was not fully united with body of Jesus of Nazareth, that there was only a loose connection between the Christ Being and the body of Jesus of Nazareth. The connection between the bodily form and the soul was not as it is in an ordinary human Being but of such a kind that at any time, or when it was necessary, the Christ Being could leave the body of Jesus of Nazareth. And while the body of Jesus of Nazareth lay somewhere as if in sleep, the Christ Being went His way in the spirit hither and thither, wherever His presence was needed. The Fifth Gospel reveals to us that the body of Jesus of Nazareth was not always present when the Christ Being appeared to the Apostles, but that often the body of Jesus of Nazareth had remained in some place, while the Spirit, the Christ Spirit, appeared to the Apostles - but this Appearance was such that they might well confuse it with the actual body of

Jesus of Nazareth. True, they were aware of a certain difference, but the difference was too slight for them always to perceive it clearly. The other four Gospels give little indication of this but it is there, in very truth, in the Fifth Gospel. The Apostles were not always able to distinguish quite clearly: Now we have Christ Jesus before us, or, now we have only the Christ Spirit before us. The distinction was not always obvious and they did not invariably know whether the one or the other condition held good. Mostly they took the Appearance to be that of Christ Jesus; that is to say, the Christ Spirit in so far as they knew Him in the body of Jesus of Nazareth. But in the course of that earthly life of three years the Spirit bound itself more and more closely to the body of Jesus of Nazareth; the Christ Being - as an etheric Being - assumed an ever closer likeness to this physical body. Notice once again how different it was with the Christ Being from what it is with the body of an ordinary man. The ordinary man is a Microcosm in relation to the Macrocosm; he is an image of the whole Macrocosm. Such is the body of the individual human Being - that is to say, what comes to manifestation in the physical body of a man. What man becomes on Earth reflects the great universe. With the Christ Being the opposite is the case. The macrocosmic Sun Being shapes Himself into likeness with the form of the human Microcosm, narrows and contracts more and more into the human Microcosm. Exactly the opposite!

At the beginning of Christ's life on Earth, directly after the Baptism in the Jordan, the connection with body of Jesus of Nazareth was only very slight. The Christ Being was still quite outside the body of Jesus of Nazareth. The power operating in the Christ Being as He went about the land was still an entirely super-earthly power. Cures were performed such as no human power could have performed. In His discourse with men the Christ Being spoke with the impressiveness of a god. As though fettering Himself to the body of Jesus of Nazareth only when He so willed, Christ worked as the super-earthly Christ Being. But in increasing measure He took on likeness with the body of Jesus of Nazareth, contracted into earthly conditions of existence and experienced the gradual ebbing of the Divine power. All this was undergone by the Christ Being as He identified Himself more and more closely with the body of Jesus of Nazareth . . . in a certain respect it was a retrogressive process of evolution. It was the lot of the Christ Being to feel how the Divine power steadily waned in this process of self-assimilation to the body of Jesus of Nazareth. Stage by stage the God became a Man. Like someone who is in the throes of unceasing pain becomes aware that the body is steadily declining, so was the Christ Being aware of the waning of His spiritual power while as an etheric Being He was gradually identifying Himself with the earthly body of Jesus of Nazareth . . until the similarity was so complete that He could feel anguish like a man. This is also described in the other Gospels when it is said that Christ Jesus went out with His disciples to the Mount of Olives where He - the Christ Being - had upon His brow the

137

sweat of anguish. Stage by stage the Christ had become Man, had become human, had identified Himself with the body of Jesus of Nazareth. In the same measure in which this etheric Christ Being grew to greater identity with the body of Jesus of Nazareth, in the same measure did the Christ become Man. The miraculous, God-begotten power ebbed away from Him. There before us in the whole Way of the Passion - beginning from days shortly after the Baptism by John in the Jordan, when the people, amazed at His deeds, exclaimed: Such wonders have never yet been wrought on the Earth! This was the time when the Christ Being had as yet assumed but little likeness with the body of Jesus of Nazareth. In the three years the path had led from this astonished gaze of the people where the Christ Being had so identified Himself with the body of Jesus of Nazareth that in this sickly body, with which He had made Himself One, the Christ Being could no longer answer the questions of Pilate, of Herod, of Caiphas. The Christ Being had become so closely bound up with the body of Jesus of Nazareth, with this steadily weakening body, that when the question was put: `Hast thou said that thou will destroy the temple and in three days build it up again?' - the Christ Being no longer spoke from the frail body of Jesus of Nazareth and remained as one dumb before the high priests of the Jews, dumb before Pilate who asked: `Hast thou said thou art the King of the Jews?' That was the Way of the Passion - from the Baptism in the Jordan to the point where all power had departed from Him. And forthwith the multitude who had once gazed in amazement at the manifestations of the super-earthly, wonder-working powers of the Christ Being, no longer stood in astonishment around Him but stood before the Cross, mocking the powerlessness of the God who had become Man, in the words: If thou art a God, come down from the Cross! Thou hast helped others, now help thyself ! This was the Way of the Passion - a Way of infinite suffering, to which was added the sorrowing for a humanity that had come to be as it was at the time of the Mystery of Golgotha.

But this suffering gave birth to the Spirit which was poured upon the Apostles on the day of Pentecost. Out of this suffering was born the all-prevailing Cosmic Love which at the Baptism in the Jordan had come down from the super-earthly, heavenly spheres into the sphere of Earth, had taken on the likeness of man, of a human body, and had endured that moment of utmost, divine powerlessness in order to bring forth the Impulse we know as the Christ Impulse in the further evolution of mankind. These are the things of which we must be mindful if we would understand the full significance of the Christ Impulse, as it must be understood in times to come. Men of the future will need to understand it in this way if they are to make progress along their path of culture and evolution."

The bond between Jesus of Nazareth and John the Baptist was rooted in human evolution. As lay brothers of the Essene Order that bond grew stronger. The progression of the evolution of the John's Ego must have become quite evident to Jesus of Nazareth during a certain conversation between him and John the Baptist. Steiner reveals this in the following from Lecture IV: "Many conversations took place between Jesus of Nazareth and John the Baptist. . . . it happened one day that while Jesus of Nazareth was conversing with John the Baptist, he saw the physical form of John the Baptist disappear and there came to Him a vision of Elias."

This suggests that the physical Form can give way to the Ego. Moreover, this vision of Elijah by Jesus portends to the future reality that the physical Form of the human Being becomes redeemed. Thereby, facilitating the eventual greater manifestation of the human Ego within the soul of every human Individuality. This is the very Truth which John the Baptist heralded. In Lecture V Steiner gives us an insight as to why it took someone who was close to Christ Jesus to betray Him: "Christ Jesus worked upon His disciples in a remarkable way. . . . As Christ Jesus went about, His environment was affected in a distinctive way. He was together with the Apostles and disciples and in communion with them, but - because He was the Christ Being - it was as though He were not present there merely in His body. As He went about the country, many a one felt as if the Being that pertained to Christ Jesus was within his own soul, and he would begin to speak words which, in reality only Christ Jesus could have spoken. This band of disciples went about and came into contact with the people . . . and the one who spoke was by no means always Christ Jesus, but was often one of the disciples, for everything - even His wisdom - was shared with the disciples. . . . It was a frequent phenomenon, too, that sometimes when Christ Jesus left the band of disciples, He was nevertheless still among them. He either went about with them spiritually or He appeared to them in His ether-body while He was actually far away. His ether-body was among them and also went about the land; and often it was not possible to distinguish whether He was present in the physical body or whether it was the ether-body that had become visible. Such was the manner of the intercourse with the disciples and with individuals among the people when Jesus of Nazareth had become Christ Jesus.

. . . Whereas in the first periods the Christ Being had been comparatively independent of the body of Jesus of Nazareth, He had more and more to become One with it. And the longer His life continued, the more closely was He knit with the body of Jesus of Nazareth. In the last years, the union with the body of Jesus of Nazareth - which had itself become increasingly frail - caused Him deep suffering. Nevertheless a great multitude now accompanied Christ Jesus as He went about the country. Here or there one among the band of the disciples would speak, and somewhere else, another, and the people might easily believe that the speaker was Christ Jesus, for He spoke through all of them."

139

In Lecture VII Steiner expounds on this theme further: "The union of the Christ Being with the three bodies was a slow and gradual process, lasting for three years. At the beginning, the connection was loose, and only very gradually did the Christ Being draw into the three bodies. The penetration was not complete until the near approach of death. The suffering endured by Christ during the three years when His Being was gradually penetrating into the three human sheaths was infinitely greater than all the suffering and pain which, as I described to you, Jesus of Nazareth had experienced through the three stages of His development. It was unceasing, perpetual pain, but pain that was transmuted into Love, infinite, ever-deepening Love.

The way in which Christ Jesus lived in the circle of His closest disciples during the first, the second and the third years, differed in each period. As I said, in the first year, Christ was connected only loosely with the body of Jesus of Nazareth. At any moment during that period it might happen that the physical body was in one place or another, and the Christ Being Himself elsewhere. When the Gospels narrate that the Lord appeared to His disciples in this place or in that, the physical body was elsewhere and Christ Himself was moving about the land in the Spirit. Thus it was at the beginning. Then the Christ Being united more and more deeply with the body of Jesus of Nazareth. And then, later on, when Christ went about in the circle of His closest disciples, they were so inwardly united with Him that it was as though He did not live apart from them. The more deeply He penetrated into the body, the more deeply did He penetrate into the innermost Being of His disciples. He went about the land in their midst.

Because of this intimate communion, He spoke now through one, now through another of the disciples. So that as they went about, it was no longer Christ Jesus only, but one or another of the disciples who spoke. Christ spoke through the disciple. And this penetration into His disciples was fraught with such power that the very countenance of the disciple through whom Christ was speaking, changed - changed so greatly that the people who listened from the outside to the one who spoke, felt: he is the Master! The power went out of the one who was really the Christ, so that He looked just like an ordinary man. Thus did Christ go about the land, speaking now through one, now through another of the disciples. This was the secret of His working during the third year."

Returning momentarily to Lecture V, Steiner ties Ahriman's Temptation of Christ Jesus in the desert to Judas' Betrayal: "But because of the question that had remained unsolved, the question that Christ could not solve in the spiritual worlds but only on the Earth, Ahriman had gained sufficient power. As a result of the most terrible of all deeds, Christ had to experience what it means to turn stones into bread. For Ahriman made use of Judas from Karioth. On account of the way Christ worked, there would have been no spiritual means of discovering among the men who revered Him which was, in truth, the Christ. For wherever the Spirit was working, wherever even a trace of convincing power was working, He could not be taken. Only where there was one who employed the means which Christ did not know, which He could learn to know only as the result of the most terrible deed wrought on Earth - only where Judas was working could He be seized. The only means of recognizing Him was through one who placed himself in the service of Ahriman, who in actual fact betrayed Him for the sake of money alone. Christ Jesus was connected with Judas because at the Temptation there remained something which, in a God, is comprehensible - He did not know that only in the heavens is it true that stones are not needed for bread. Because Ahriman had retained this as his sting, the Betrayal took place. And then Christ had perforce to come under the dominion of the Lord of Death - and Ahriman is the Lord of Death. Such is the connection of the story of the Temptation and the Mystery of Golgotha with the Betrayal by Judas."

In Lecture VII Steiner further elaborates the theme of our struggles with Ahriman and Lucifer: "During the rest of Earth-evolution, until the Vulcan period, the operations of the higher Hierarchies cannot drive Ahriman altogether from the field. Through spiritual effort it will never be impossible to vanquish the inner tempting of Lucifer, the desires, cravings, passions, and all that arises as pride, vainglory, arrogance. When Lucifer alone attacks a man, he can be vanquished by spiritual effort. When Lucifer and Ahriman in conjunction attack a man, then, too, spiritual victory can be achieved. But when Ahriman is alone, his activity penetrates right down into the material processes of Earth-evolution. And here he cannot be driven entirely from the field. Ahriman, Mephistopheles, Mammon (these concepts are synonymous) are hidden in gold [money]: in everything, moreover, that brings egoism into play in the material world. Inasmuch as some element of materialism must inevitably be part and parcel of human life, Ahriman has to be reckoned with.

If Christ was truly to help man on Earth, He was compelled to allow Ahriman to work. For Ahriman must work, the material element must persist until the end of Earth-evolution. The activity of Ahriman had to remain unvanquished by Christ. Ahriman was not fully conquered. Until the end of Earth-evolution, Christ must lend Himself to the struggle with Ahriman. For Ahriman had to remain. It is within our power as human Beings to vanquish the inner attacks made upon us by Lucifer, and by Lucifer and Ahriman in conjunction. The struggle with the outer, material world must be fought out until the very end of Earth-evolution. Therefore Christ was compelled to hold Ahriman in check, but yet permit him to exist at His side. Thus Ahriman could remain at work through the three years during which Christ dwelt in the body of Jesus of Nazareth, could be near Christ on the Earth, and then creep into the soul of Judas, inciting this soul to the Betrayal. What came to pass through Judas is connected with the question that remained only partially answered in the Temptation after the event at the Jordan."

141

Immediately prior to the Baptism in the Jordan, Jesus of Nazareth holds a conversation with his step-mother; the mother of the Zarathustra Jesus. It is at this time that the soul-forces of Zarathustra pass over to Mary of the Matthew Gospel. In Lecture VI we begin to take note of a parallel with the age of the body of Jesus of Nazareth and the incarnation of Christ into this body to that of the age of the Earth and Christ's incarnation into the body of the Earth as well as humanity's age: "The words which Jesus spoke to his stepmother were not words in the ordinary sense; they were like living Beings, passing over from him to his stepmother, and the forces of His own soul lent wings to the words. During this conversation, everything he had suffered with such intensity passed over with the words into the soul of the stepmother. His own `I' accompanied every word. It was not a mere exchange of words or thoughts, but his soul passed over into her soul on the wings of the words which told of his infinite love but also of his infinite pain. And so he was able to unfold to her, as in a great panorama, what he had experienced three times over. What passed between them was yet further heightened in that Jesus allowed the conversation to lead over gradually to the realization that had come to him from his threefold suffering in connection with the decline that was perceptible in humankind."

In Lecture VIII Steiner adds: "We might say that his own 'I' seemed to go across, as it were, to his mother on the wings of his words, though it did not in fact go across; it was merely that his mother felt she was given new life by those words." One realization that caused Zarathustra great pain was the knowledge that humanity was, as it were, 'approaching middle age', and thereby was in the stage of rapid decline such that the continuing evolution of humanity on Earth was in jeopardy. Steiner continues with the following: "So in this sense we are already approaching the middle period of life, lying in the thirties when, for the individual human Being, the youth-forces no longer work, when man begins to decline. We, in our own day, are living in the epoch corresponding to the period between the 28th and 35th years in the life of the individual, when the decline sets in. Whereas, however, in the individual, other forces enable life to continue, in humanity as a whole, nothing is left. - The deep suffering experienced by Jesus of Nazareth was due to the realization that humanity had to grow old, had left its youth behind, was approaching the age corresponding to the period between the 28th and 35th years. Whence were new forces to come? The youth-forces were exhausted!

Jesus said this to his stepmother in a way that depicted the whole life of evolving humanity as fraught with unspeakable suffering, confronting a prospect of utter hopelessness. The youth-forces were exhausted; humanity was approaching the period of old age. Jesus knew that the life of the individual is able to continue from the 35th year until death because a vestige of the forces remain in him. But in humanity as a whole it is not so.

Something would have to be inculcated into humanity, something that is necessary in the life of an individual human Being between the 28th and 35th years of life. The Earth would have to be imbued with the macrocosmic power with which the individual human Being must be imbued when he is still passing through the ascending phase of life between the 28th and 34th years."

What was needed to be done in order to further the continuing evolution of humanity? The 'anxiety of the Gods' was increasingly desperate due to the fact that the great religions, teachers, leaders and Initiates were no longer able to advance humanity any further. Steiner adds the following in Lecture VII: "This anxiety of the Gods increased; deeper and deeper was the distress in heaven. And then came the resolve to send down the Sun Spirit, to sacrifice Him. The Gods said, in effect: `From now onwards the Sun Spirit will choose a destiny other than that of being in the Council of the Gods. He will go to the domain where live the souls of men. We sacrifice the Sun Spirit ! Until now He has been living among us, in the spheres of the Hierarchies, but now, through the portal of Jesus, He will enter into the aura of the Earth!' So it was in the Council of the Gods, when the Mystery of Golgotha was at hand. That is how it appears from above.

We therefore have to do with an affair of the Gods who guide earthly evolution, not merely with an affair of men. On one side there was the question: What must come to pass in order that humanity may not go utterly astray along the downward path? - and, on the other side, the question: What must we, the Gods, do in order to balance out what has happened because we were obliged to allow Lucifer and Ahriman access to Earth-evolution? We can realize now that the Mystery of Golgotha is not merely an affair of the Earth but an affair of the Gods, an event in the world of the Gods. In truth it meant even more for the Gods to be obliged to give over the Christ to the Earth than it meant for man to be able to receive Him.

What, in reality, is 'knowledge of the Mystery of Golgotha,' apart from recognizing it as the central, pivotal event of Earth-evolution? Knowledge of the Mystery of Golgotha consists in seeing it as an affair of the Gods, so that we realize: The Gods have opened there a window in heaven, and for a brief season their affairs are conducted before the eyes of men! As we contemplate the Mystery of Golgotha we must learn to feel that it is as if we were passing by the ever-closed mansion of heaven and just at this point pass a window through which we are permitted to gaze into what had always until then been visible, hidden within the walls of the Gods' abode. Thus in all reverence does a man possessed of true occult perception contemplate the Mystery of Golgotha. He feels as though he were creeping round a house closed on every side, with only a dim inkling of what is going on within the walls; but at one place there is a little window through which we he can witness a tiny section of what is taking place within. The Mystery of Golgotha is such

143

a window through which man may see into the spiritual world. This must be our feeling in connection with what came to pass when the Christ Being descended into the body, or, better said, into the three sheaths of Jesus of Nazareth. More and more deeply we must steep ourselves in the thought that in the Mystery of Golgotha we are beholding an affair of the Gods."

It is noteworthy to briefly cite the following statement of Steiner's in this same lecture: "After Jesus of Nazareth had received the Christ Being into Himself, He was constrained to go into the `solitude'. And in this solitude He had those visionary experiences which the writers of the Gospels, as seers, were able to describe with approximate accuracy. What happened there can be retold in a similar way, only it must be remembered that the Christ Being was now actually conjoined with the three bodies of Jesus of Nazareth. The Christ Being, that is, had come down from the heights of the Spirit and was now united with the faculties of the three bodies. It would not be correct to imagine that because Christ belonged to a higher world, He now retained direct vision of the spiritual world whence He had descended. That is not so."

Steiner then says: "Because of the faculties bequeathed to the three bodies of Jesus of Nazareth by the Zarathustra-soul, it was possible for the Christ to make use of the residue of these faculties in the three bodies when confronting a Being who set out to kindle the uttermost pride and arrogance of which a human soul is capable."

The above begins to make one ponder the words of Christ on the Cross at the time when these residue faculties were waning when He said the words, "My God, my God why have you forsaken me?" Does He say this because the spiritual realms have gone completely dark for Him at this time? It should noted that these particular words are recorded in the Matthew Gospel and more notably in the Gospel of Mark 15: 35; the Gospel of the Cosmic Christ. Was it at this point that Christ had His greatest separation from His own aura; His own Cosmic element? Was He crying out that He no longer had the faculties of a God and that He now had completely united with the body of Jesus of Nazareth and became fully human at this time? We read earlier that the Death and Resurrection of Christ was a Macrocosmic Initiation of the Christ Being by the Father. In the Initiation of Christ all is reversed from that of the normal proceedings of an Initiation of a human Being. The human Being ascends into the higher spheres when Initiated and at the 'conclusion' of his Initiation he cries, "My God, my God Thou hast Glorified me!" The words, My God, are a reference to one's Ego. With the Initiation of Christ it is all reversed. He says at the 'beginning' of His Initiation the opposite words of that of a human Initiation: "My God, my God, why hast Thou forsaken me?" The higher spiritual realms are closed to the Christ Being. He does not ascend into them. Alternatively, He descends into the sub-realms.

Also, a possible allusion to the Cosmic Element of Christ and its bond with John the Baptist may have also been presented here since Elijah is also mentioned at this very point in the Passion. We know that John the Baptist was present at the Death of Christ because of his presence within the consciousness soul of Lazarus who stood at the foot of the Cross. The entire passage reads as follows: "And when the sixth hour came, there was darkness over the whole land until the ninth hour. And at the ninth hour Jesus cried out with a loud voice, saying, `Eloi, Eloi, lama sabacthani?' which, translated, is, `My God, my God, why hast Thou forsaken me?' And some of the bystanders on hearing this said, `Behold He is calling Elias.' But someone ran, soaked a sponge in common wine, put it on a reed and offered it to Him to drink, saying, `Wait, let us see whether Elias is coming to take Him down.' But Jesus cried out with a loud voice, and expired." (Mark 15: 33-37).

It should be noted that Steiner does give an alternative rendering to the words: "My God, My God why hast Thou forsaken me?" On December 30, 1904 he relates the following: "At the time of the founding of Christianity it was still necessary for an advanced individuality to sacrifice his own I and send it into the astral realm, in order that the Logos might dwell in the body. This is an act upon which light is shed by the last words on the cross. What other meaning could these words contain: 'My God, My God why hast Thou forsaken me?' These words give expression to the mystical fact then consummated. At the moment of Christ's death, the Divine Being had departed from the body, and it is the body of Jesus of Nazareth that utters these words – a body so highly developed that it could voice the reality. And so these words give expression to an event of untold significance." [GA 60].

Throughout much of this work the message of `understanding' is emphasized. Steiner brings to conclusion his lecture cycle on, "The Fifth Gospel," with this particular message. "The purpose and meaning of human evolution on the Earth is that the souls of men shall become more and more conscious of their tasks. Christ has appeared. His Impulse has worked in very truth. For long ages He worked more in the subconscious; later on He could work through what men had so far apprehended. - He worked through what He was, not through what had been apprehended of Him. But it is more and more necessary that men shall learn to understand Him, to understand the Christ who through the bodies of Jesus of Nazareth drew into the aura of the Earth and therewith into the living flow of human happenings."

X

The Sun Initiation of John the Baptist

In the lecture cycle, "Background to the Gospel of St. Mark," we read from Steiner in Lecture IV: "What is the fundamental significance of the Christ Impulse? We have expressed it as follows. - Through the Christ Impulse the human soul became conscious for the first time that an Ego, an `I', was to find a place within it, a self-conscious `I' through which in the further course of Earth-evolution there must be revealed all the secrets formerly revealed by the astral body through natural clairvoyance."

"But preparation was necessary before this stage could be reached. As the lowest rank of the Hierarchies, man had to be prepared by being sent an example of what he must become. The `Messenger' or `Angel' was to proclaim to man that he was to become an `I' in the full sense of the word. And whereas the mission of earlier Angels had been to reveal the spiritual world, it was now the mission of a particular Angel to carry the revelations to a further stage, to make known to man that he was to enter into full possession of the Ego, the `I'. The earlier revelations were of a different character, not intended for a self-conscious `I'."

" . . . but complete assurance that the greatest secrets and mysteries could flow from the `I' itself was brought by the Christ Impulse."

"The messenger of whom Isaiah spoke - who must not be thought of as a man in the ordinary sense - took possession of the soul of the reincarnated Elias - John the Baptist - lived in him and was destined to proclaim to men that the Christ Impulse was at hand. Where, then, did the voice of this messenger resound? It resounded in what I have just described to you as, `the solitude of the soul'."

Before examining the progression of Initiations of John the Baptist as a Sun-Hero and later as a Father Initiate during the raising of Lazarus, the following in Lecture XI from the cycle, "The Gospel of St. Matthew," is of importance: "What is it that must grow in man's inner nature as its forces increase in strength and he develops a higher form of clairvoyance? His qualities must mature to the stage where he can receive into himself the forces of the Spirit-Self, Life-Spirit and Spirit-Man. But when the power that makes him an Initiate, a participant in the Kingdoms of Heaven, will stream into him from above, depends upon the moment when he can become fully mature; it depends upon the karma of the individual. Who knows when the moment has come? It is known only to the very highest Initiates, not to those at lower stages of Initiation. For any individuality who is ready to reach the spiritual world, the hour comes when he does so. Assuredly the hour comes, but in such a way that he is not aware of it - it comes like a thief in the night!

How does a man reach the spiritual world? In the ancient Mysteries - and in a certain respect it is so in the new - there were three stages of Initiation into the Macrocosm. When the first stage had been attained by the aspirant, the powers of the Spirit-Self became active in him and now he was not only a new man but had become one whose nature was said to be that of an `Angel' - that is to say, a Being of the Hierarchy immediately above man. In the Mysteries of ancient Persia, a man possessing the powers of the Spirit-Self was called a `Persian' because he was no longer a separate individual but belonged to the Angel of the Persian people. At the next stage of Initiation the Life-Spirit awakens. A man who had reached this stage was called a `Sun-Hero' in the Persian Mysteries, because he had developed to the stage where he could receive the spiritual forces of the Sun streaming towards the Earth. But such a man was also called a `Son of the Father'. And one with whom Atma, or Spirit-Man, had made contact was called `Father' in the ancient Mysteries. The three stages of Initiation were: Angel, Son or Sun Hero, Father.

Only the very highest Initiates, they and they alone are able to judge when the moment of Initiation can be reached. Hence Christ speaks to the following effect. - Initiation will be attained if you go forward on the paths along which I have led you. You will rise into the Kingdoms of Heaven, but the hour is known neither to the Angels in whom the Spirit-Self is working, neither to the Son in whom the Life-Spirit has awakened, but only to the very highest Initiates, those in whom the Father-Principle is active."

As was mentioned previously, it was suggested that the Angel that lived within the soul of John the Baptist was the Angel Vidar, the former Angel of Buddha. This Angel then Initiated John the Baptist in a partial Sun Initiation; an Initiation of the sixth degree which was examined earlier. In Lecture IV from the cycle, "Background to the Gospel of St. Mark," Steiner then says: "If a candidate was unable at once to attain the highest Initiation, the Sun Initiation, (the assumption is that when Steiner says, 'highest Initiation', he is referring to the full completion of the twelve stages of Initiation for the entire zodiac) but could achieve a partial Initiation only, his soul was directed to the secrets connected with one particular constellation. But his vision must become independent of everything material. This meant that either in the rites of the Mysteries or, as in the case of John the Baptist, by grace from above, the candidate's gaze was guided to a constellation when the Earth lay between him and the constellation - that is to say, by night. Physical eyes see the physical constellation only. But when vision can penetrate through the material Earth - which means that the constellation is masked by the material Earth - then what is seen is not the physical but the spiritual reality, that is to

147

say, the secrets which the constellation expresses. The vision of John the Baptist was trained in such a way that at night he could look through the material Earth into the constellation of Aquarius. When the Angel took possession of his soul he had attained the Aquarius Initiation. Thus John the Baptist was able to place all his faculties and all he knew and felt at the disposal of the Angel, in order that through the Angel the secrets connected with the Aquarius Initiation might be proclaimed and the announcement made of the coming of the `I', . . . the Lord of the soul-forces."

"In this lecture I have put a twofold conception before you. First: the words at the beginning of St. Mark's Gospel indicate processes in the historical evolution of humanity and speak of a higher Power - an Angel who speaks through the body of John the Baptist. Second: the passages in question relate to happenings in the heavens - the progress of the spiritual Sun from the constellation of Aquarius to the constellation of Pisces. Every line of St. Mark's Gospel contains something that can be read rightly only if in following the words we always have in mind both a human and a cosmic-astronomical meaning, and when we realize that there lives in man something that in its true significance can be found only in the heavens.

We must grasp the connection between the secrets of the Macrocosm and the secrets of human nature more exactly than is usual."

In a series of Letters/Studies, Emil Bock wrote the following in Letter XV - "Peter and John.": "The earthly fate of John the Baptist is full of the mighty, passionate breath of tragedy. And yet this tragedy of John is only a prelude to the destiny and work of the Baptist which proceeds further in the supersensible world. In the study of the feeding of the 5000, we already stood at the banks of this stream, which spread far beneath the surface of the world of sense.

John the Baptist was man, and yet more than man. 'He is the greatest of those that are born of woman, but the least in the kingdom of heaven is greater than he.' He is greater than all men, but the measure of his greatness is bounded at the Beings who form the lowest stage in the hierarchies, at the angels. He stands between man and angel. But his spiritual Being towered so far above all human measure that the Gospel itself applies the saying of Malachi to him: 'Behold, I send my angel before thy face, and he shall prepare the way before thee.'" (Matthew 11: 10).

In a human body is incorporated a Being near to the angels, who towers far above the narrow human body. On Eastern altars John the Baptist is always represented as a winged Being. That which lives in the body is not the whole John. At his head rustle angel's wings, which belong not to a strange Being, but to his own. This angelically sublime Being had already worked as Elijah among the people of Israel in human-superhuman form, as a preparer of the way for that which was to come. Elijah was in the Old Covenant, 'my angel, who should prepare the way for thee.' 'My angel' or 'the angel of the

Ego', 'the angel of Jehovah' is called in Hebrew, 'Malachi'. In the Book of Malachi, the last book of the Old Testament the prophesy is contained, which points from Elijah to John the Baptist: 'Behold, I send my angel before thee and he shall prepare the way before thee.' (Malachi 3: 1). Thus, behind the name Malachi, Elijah himself is concealed; that angelic-human Being, which came again in John the Baptist. Much more is said of this angelic Being in the scriptures than one thinks. The name Elijah as well as the name Malachi solves the riddle of the Being. Elijah means the El Javes, the God of Javeh, the Angel of Jehovah, the "Angel of the Lord". Everywhere when the "Angel of the Lord" is mentioned, that Elias-John Being is indicated."

Continuing the study of, "Background to the Gospel of St. Mark," in Lecture VI Steiner makes this brief comment in regard to the New Adam: "Paul was unshakably convinced after his vision near Damascus that in the Event of Golgotha something occurred that was exactly comparable with the descent of man into the flesh. For therewith the impulse was given gradually to overcome those forms of earthly existence into which man had entered through Adam. Hence Paul calls the Being who appeared in the Christ, the `new Adam', whom every man can draw to himself through union with Christ."

And in Lecture XI Steiner expounds further on the theme of John the Baptist's Sun Initiation: "Why was John the Baptist able to be the bearer of the Angel? It was because he had received a particular form of Initiation. Initiations are not all identical in character and individuals who have a definite mission to fulfill must undergo a special form of Initiation. Now the writing of the stars in the heavens is so ordered as to reveal the nature and facts of happenings in the spiritual world. Thus a man may receive the Sun-Initiation, which means that he is initiated into the mysteries of the spiritual world of Ahura Mazdao - the spiritual world of which the Sun is the outer expression. But there are twelve forms of the Sun-Initiation, each of which differs from the other eleven. A man will receive a particular form of Initiation according to the mission he is to fulfill for humanity. His Initiation, though still a Sun-Initiation, may be of such a kind that the forces stream in as they do when the Sun is standing, for instance, in the constellation of Cancer; and these forces will be very different in the case of an Initiation connected with the Sun in Libra. These are the expressions used to indicate specialized Initiations. Individuals chosen for a mission as lofty as that of John the Baptist must receive Initiation in the form that can give the strength necessary for the fulfillment of their mission.. And so in order that he might become the bearer of the Angel, John the Baptist received the Sun-Initiation originating from the constellation of Aquarius. The Sun in Aquarius is the symbol for the form of Initiation received by John the Baptist in order that he might become the bearer of the Angel. He received the Sun-forces which flow when the Sun is standing in Aquarius - the Waterman. The sign was the

149

symbol indicating that John the Baptist had received this particular Initiation. In actual fact the name Aquarius, or Waterman, was given to the zodiacal sign because those who had received that Initiation acquired the faculty which enabled John the Baptist, for example, to achieve what he did. When men were plunged under water, their etheric bodies were momentarily loosened and in that condition it was possible for them to perceive what action was of the greatest importance at that particular time. Baptism in the Jordan revealed to those who underwent it the momentous significance of that period in history. It was to this end that John had received the baptismal Initiation and because this was connected with the rays of the Sun streaming from its position in a particular constellation, the constellation too was known symbolically as the Waterman. The name of the constellation was derived from the human faculty connected with it, and not vice versa."

"John the Baptist could therefore rightly say: `I baptize you with water.' This was the same as saying to his intimate disciples, as he might well have done, that he had received the Aquarius Initiation. The movement of the Sun through the Zodiac as seen with physical eyes is in the direction from Leo to Virgo; the spiritual movement is from Aquarius to Pisces. Consequently John the Baptist was able to proclaim something that would work as the forces of the Sun in Pisces and not in Aquarius; also that the Being who was to come would give a higher kind of Baptism than he himself was able to give. The spiritual Sun progresses from Aquarius to Pisces and when this happens the Aquarius Baptism becomes a Baptism with spiritual water - Pisces, the Fishes. Hence the ancient symbol of fishes for the Being who was the bearer of the Christ. Just as John, through very special influences, had received the Aquarius Initiation, so all the mysteries enacted around and in Jesus of Nazareth belonged to a Pisces Initiation. The Sun had moved forward, spiritually, from one zodiacal constellation to another, indicating that Jesus of Nazareth had passed through a Pisces Initiation.

All this is hinted at in St. Mark's Gospel but such things have to be presented in pictures. Christ Jesus draws to Himself those who are seeking that of which Pisces is the symbol. Hence His first disciples are all of them fishermen. The indication of the Sun's progression into Pisces is clear when we read the words of John the Baptist: `I have baptized you with water, but He will baptize you with the Holy Spirit.' And as Christ passes along the shore of the Sea of Galilee, that is to say, when the Sun has moved so far that its counterpart could be seen rising in Pisces, the fishermen known as Simon and Simon's brother, James and James's brother, are inspired to follow Him."

In Lecture XII Steiner adds to this: "On the Old Moon the Angels reached the human stage and man has reached the human stage on the Earth. Consequently it devolved upon the Beings who were man's forerunners to make preparation for what man was to become on the Earth. The Angel-nature must penetrate into the astral body before the Ego can become active.

150

Man's mission on Earth was prepared for by his forerunners - the Angels. Hence it is possible at certain times for an Angel to enter into a human personality. When this happens the Earth-man himself may well be maya, for a Being of higher rank is making use of his soul. The man is in truth the figure we see before us, yet he may be the sheath of some other Being. Thus it came about that the same Individuality who had once lived as Elijah and was reincarnated as John the Baptist became the vehicle of an Angel who spoke through him. . . . A deed of the Gods mingles with human life and creates human destiny.

Thus in John the Baptist a deed of the Heavens was united with human destiny. A divine Being, an Angel, worked in and through him. What John achieved was possible only because, while the man John was maya, another Being lived within him, having the mission to proclaim in advance what man's destiny on Earth was to be. Consequently, if we are to translate the passage in a way that helps us to understand what is actually expressed, the rendering would have to be something like this. - `Take heed: the `I' which is to appear in man's Being sends in advance the Angel who prepares its way.' The Angel is the Being who lived in the personality of John the Baptist . . ."

In these lectures Steiner states that: "Everything Christ Jesus did was connected with macrocosmic events." In the following excerpts from Lectures XI And XII Steiner speaks of the Sun Element of the Christ Being.

Lecture XI: "And when this body - the body of Jesus - moved from one place to another it was simply that the Sun-force was being made visible. This Sun-force was able of itself to move from place to place, independently of a physical body. Occasionally, Christ Jesus was said to be `in the house', that is to say, in the flesh; but the Being in the flesh also moved about without a body. In the Gospel of St. John, above all, the Evangelist often writes exactly as if the Sun-force were present in a body of flesh when in reality the Christ is moving from place to place in the spirit.

That is why it is so important for the deeds of Christ Jesus always to be brought into relationship with the physical Sun - which is the outward expression for the spiritual world when gathered together at the point where the physical body is present. For example, when Christ Jesus performs an act of healing, it is the Sun-force that heals, but the Sun must be in the right position in the heavens. Thus: `At evening, when the Sun did set they brought unto Him all that were diseased. . .' and so on. It was important to indicate that this healing force can flow down only when the physical Sun has set and is working in a purely spiritual way. Again when Christ Jesus needs special power in order to do His works, He must draw it from the spiritual Sun, not from the physically visible Sun. `And in the morning, rising up a great while before day, He went out . . .' The path of the Sun and the power of the Sun are expressly indicated, furthermore that it is the Sun-force that is working, that Jesus is simply the external sign and that this path taken by the Sun-force could also become visible to the naked eye. Wherever St. Mark's Gospel speaks of the Christ, what is meant is the Sun-force which, in that epoch of Earth-evolution, worked with special strength upon the land called Palestine. Moreover the Sun-force, gathered into a focus, was moving from place to place, and the body of Jesus was the outward sign making the movement of the Sun-force visible to physical sight. The paths of Jesus in Palestine were the paths of the Sun-force that had come down to the Earth. If you trace the paths of Jesus to form a kind of chart you will have before you the indication of a cosmic happening - the Sun-force had penetrated into the land of Palestine. It is a macrocosmic process - that is the essential point. This is made especially evident by the writer of St. Mark's Gospel, who was well aware that a body which was the bearer of a principle such as the Christ-Principle must be entirely subservient to it. The Gospel therefore directs attention to the world which lies behind the material world and influences the life of man. Through Christ Jesus it was again made clear how the forces of this spiritual world work into the Earth."

Later in Lecture XII Steiner remarks: "Everything Christ Jesus did was connected with macrocosmic events. Think of how often in St. Mark's Gospel it is said that Christ performed His acts of healing after the Sun had set or before it had risen. Thus we are told: In the evening, when the Sun had set, they brought to Him all manner of sick and possessed. Why were the sick and possessed brought to Him at just that time? Because the Sun had set and its forces were no longer working physically in Jesus, but spiritually; what He was to do was not connected with the physical forces of the Sun. The physical Sun had set, but the spiritual Sun-forces worked through His heart and body. And when He wanted to unfold His greatest and most powerful forces He had necessarily to exert them at a time when the physical Sun was not visible in the heavens. So also when we read: `Before the Sun had risen' - the words have a definite meaning. Every word in St. Mark's Gospel indicates great cosmic connections between processes in the universe and every step taken and every deed performed by Christ in the body of Jesus of Nazareth here on Earth. If you were to draw a map of the paths He trod and the deeds He performed and were then to study the corresponding processes in the heavens, the picture would be the same: processes in the heavens would seem to have been projected down to the Earth."

"The Gospel of St. Mark gives expression to the wonderful harmony between the great Cosmos and what was to come to pass once on our Earth through the deeds of Christ Jesus and the Mystery of Golgotha. We cannot understand this Gospel unless we can decipher the writing of the stars and that requires insight into the secrets of the language of the heavens. When the Gospel says that the Sun had set, this does not indicate merely that the Sun was no longer shining but also that the spiritual Beings of the Sun-Hierarchy had moved into a world of stronger spiritual powers because they must now

152

work through the Earth, through the physical substance of the Earth. All this was felt by men when they were told of what came to pass through Christ Jesus after the Sun had set. A whole world of meaning lay in the words."

XI

The Gospel of John

Steiner's 1908 lecture cycle in Hamburg, "The Gospel of St. John," adds even more to this study of the nature and mission of the Christ in relation to the evolution of humanity. The following words at the conclusion of Lecture II are inspiring: "And the meaning of life upon Earth is this: That men should overcome this darkness of the soul, in order that they may recognize the Light of the Logos."

To what is the Christ and the Cosmic Principle of Christ leading humanity and what is the goal of earthly and human evolution? In Lecture III Steiner gives us the answer by saying: "Just as wisdom was evolved upon the Moon, in order that it might now be found in all things, so in like manner is love evolving. Love came into existence first in its lowest, its most sensuous form, during the Lemurian period, but during the course of life upon the Earth, it will become ever more and more spiritualized, until at last, when the Earth has reached the end of its evolution, the whole of existence will have become pervaded with love, as today it is pervaded with wisdom, and this will be accomplished through the activity of human Beings if they but fulfill their task.

The Earth will then pass over to a future planetary condition which is called Jupiter. The Beings who will wonder about upon Jupiter, just as human Beings move about upon the Earth, will find love exhaling from all creatures, the love which they themselves, as human Beings, will have placed there during their life upon the Earth. They will find love in everything just as we today find wisdom everywhere. Then human Beings will develop love out of their own inner selves in the same way that they are now little by little evolving wisdom. The great cosmic love that here upon the Earth is beginning its existence will then permeate all things."

Steiner speaks of, "the whole of existence will have become pervaded with love." At another time Steiner also stated that through pain (and suffering) we gain wisdom. With that thought in mind the following is from his, "Esoteric Science": "Wisdom is the prerequisite for Love; Love is the result of Wisdom that has been reborn in the I."

Based on the above, the term Love needs to be examined and understood in the sense that pain and suffering are the seeds to the forces of Love that imbue the earth with soul impulses that are creating the future New Jerusalem. Over the millennia humanity has endured pain and suffering on a scope of which we can not begin to plumb its depths. By understanding pain and suffering as soul forces that convert to World Love within the earth's etheric/astral sphere, it is reasonable to assert that humanity has long been in the process of creating the New Jerusalem. This gives us a greater insight into the purpose and meaning of pain and suffering. Looking about the world on a daily basis the pain and suffering that humanity endures through every moment is inconceivable for any one human to truly behold. Yet, it is this pain and suffering that is fashioning the New Jerusalem.

Steiner continues in Lecture III: "The human Being, in fact, always follows along groping his way behind the cosmic wisdom. As a principle, all that men will discover in the course of the Earth's evolution is already present in nature. But what the human Being will really give to the Earth is love, a love which will evolve from the most sensuous to the most spiritualized form of love. This is the mission of the Earth-evolution. The Earth is the cosmos of Love. Let us ask: - What then is essential for love? What is essential in order that one person love another? It is this - that he be in possession of his full self-consciousness, that he be wholly independent. No one can love another in the full sense of the word if this love be not a free gift of one person to another."

"Human Beings exist in order that they may take into themselves the warm love of the Divine, develop it and return it again to the Divine. But they can only do this by becoming self-conscious Ego-Beings. Only then will they be able to render back this love."

John the Baptist was the one who led the way for this new understanding of the Christ Impulse which would allow for all humans to achieve an awareness of ourselves as self-conscious Ego-Beings. Steiner remarks in Lecture IV: "This separate Ego had to feel itself solitary and the forerunner of the Christ was compelled to say: I AM an Ego that has broken away, that feels itself alone, and just because I have learned to feel solitary, I feel like a prophet to whom the Ego gives real spiritual nourishment in solitude. Therefore, the herald had to designate himself as one calling in solitude, which means the individual Ego isolated from the group-soul calling for what can give it spiritual sustenance. 'I AM the voice of one calling in solitude.' Thus we hear again the profound truth: - Each human individual Ego is one wholly dependent upon itself; I AM the voice of the Ego that is freed, seeking a foundation upon which it, as an independent Ego, can rest. - Now we understand the passage, 'I AM the voice of one calling in solitude.'"

Steiner then speaks of the Initiates and their path to conscious Egohood: "They raised their souls to the spiritual worlds and they always bore the name, 'Children of God,' because they possessed knowledge of the Logos, of the Light, and of Life and could always bear witness of These. There were certain ones who already knew of the spiritual worlds through the ancient

155

Mysteries. What was present there in these Initiates? It was the eternal human living within them in full consciousness. In the mighty words, `I and the Father are One,' they felt, in fact, I and the great Primal Cause are One! And the most profound thing of which they were conscious, their individual Ego, they received not from father and mother but through their Initiation into the spiritual world. Not from the blood nor from the flesh did they receive it, nor from the will of father and mother, but `from God,' which means from the spiritual world."

Steiner then returns to John the Baptist and remarks on the Pleroma, the Fullness of Christ: "John the Baptist called himself - literally interpreted - the forerunner, the precursor, the one who goes before as herald of the Ego. He designated himself as one who knew that this Ego must become an independent entity in each individual soul, but he also had to bear witness of Him who was to come, in order that this be brought about. He said very clearly, `That which is to come is the `I AM,' which is eternal, which can say of Itself, `Before Abraham was, was the I AM.' John could say, `The I (the Ego) which is spoken of here existed before me. Although I am Its forerunner, yet It is at the same time my Forerunner. I bear witness of what was previously present in every human Being. After me will come One Who was before me.'

At this point in the Gospel very significant words are spoken: - `For of His Fullness have we all received grace upon grace.' There are men who call themselves Christians, who pass over this word, `Fullness,' thinking that nothing very special is meant by it. `Pleroma' in Greek means `Fullness.' We find this word also in the Gospel of St. John: `For from the Pleroma have we all received grace upon grace.' I have said that if we wish really to understand this Gospel, every word must be weighed in the balance. What is then, Pleroma, Fullness? He alone can understand it who knows that in the ancient Mysteries, Pleroma or Fullness was referred to as something very definite. For at that time it was already being taught that when those spiritual Beings manifested themselves who during the Moon period evolved to the stage of divinity namely, the Elohim, one of them separated from the others. One remained behind upon the Moon, and thence reflected, the power of Love until humanity was sufficiently matured to be able to receive the direct Light of the other six Elohim. Therefore they distinguished between Jahve, the individual God, the reflector, and the Fullness of the Godhead, `Pleroma,' consisting of the other six Elohim. Since the full consciousness of the Sun Logos meant to them the Christ, they called Him the `Fullness of the Gods' when they wished to refer to Him. This profound truth was concealed in the words: `For out of the Pleroma, we have received grace upon grace.'"

This Fullness of what lives within the Elohim is part of what Christ brought to the Earth. He brought the powers of the spiritual Sun to the Earth such that the Earth and Sun become forces of attraction to one another.

Thereby, the Earth becomes transfigured from within and gradually becomes Sun-like in itself. This is its eventual destiny in that the Earth unites with the Sun.

Steiner also adds, in Lecture IV, these key points: "The man who voluntarily places himself within the cosmic activities is an individual; he is not ruled by law. In the Christ Principle lies the victory over law. `For the law was given to Moses, but Grace through Christ.' According to the Christian acceptation of the word, the soul's capacity for doing right out of the inner self was called Grace. Grace and an inner recognition of truth came into being through Christ. You see how profoundly this thought fits into the whole of human evolution."

". . . the Christ is not only the guide of those who are united with the group-soul, but . . . He enters into each individual human Being and endows the individual Ego itself with His Impulse. The blood-tie indeed remains, but the spiritual aspect of love is added to it, and to this love which passes over from one individual, independent Ego to another, He gives His Impulse."

In Lecture V Steiner begins with examining the raising of Lazarus once more. In the Gospel of Mark we read that a, ". . . certain young man was following Him." (Mark 14: 51). We have also seen that the fleeing youth is a reference to the Cosmic Principle, the Cosmic Aura of the Christ Being; or what could be referred to as the Cosmic Christ. This is the youth which separates from the Christ at the time of His arrest. This is the youth, the cosmic element that flees from Christ at the same time that the Apostles had fled from Christ save Peter who then later denied knowing the Christ. The cosmic, zodiacal bond between Christ and the Twelve Apostles was then severed. As Steiner had mentioned, this bond was to remain connected between Him and the Apostles throughout the entire Mystery of Golgotha. It was not and therefore that bond was then exclusively taken up at this most critical time by John the Baptist who had interpenetrated the consciousness soul of Lazarus. Therefore, we should understand that this phrase, 'a certain young man', also has other extensive references to it. It directs our attention to the `young' Lazarus, who, with Peter, stayed with the Christ at the time of the arrest and trial. In addition, this "certain young man" also alludes to the spiritual presence of John the Baptist within the consciousness soul of Lazarus. John the Baptist was already becoming united with the youth Principle of Christ at the time of the feeding of the five thousand when he then became the group-soul of the Twelve Apostles. This bond between John the Baptist and the Cosmic Principle of Christ was now reaching its culmination during the Arrest and Trial, the Crucifixion, Death and finally the Resurrection of the Christ Being.

In Lecture V Steiner draws us back to the raising of Lazarus and directs our awareness to the construction of the Gospel of John: "In a consideration of the Gospel of St. John, we should never lose sight of that most important point which was brought out in the lecture yesterday namely, that in the original writer of the Gospel we have to do with the `Beloved Disciple,' initiated by Christ-Jesus Himself. One might naturally ask if, aside from occult knowledge, there exists, perhaps, some external proof of this statement by means of which the writer of this Gospel has intimated that he came to a higher order of knowledge about the Christ through the `raising,' through the Initiation which is represented in the so-called miracle of the raising of Lazarus. If you will read the Gospel of St. John carefully, you will observe, that nowhere previous to that chapter which treats of the raising of Lazarus is there any mention of the `Disciple whom the Lord loved.' In other words, the real author of the Gospel wishes to say: What precedes this chapter does not yet have its origin in the knowledge which I have received through Initiation, therefore in the beginning you must disregard me. Only later does he mention the `Disciple whom the Lord loved'. Thus the Gospel falls into two important parts, the first part in which the Disciple whom the Lord loved is not yet mentioned because he had not yet been initiated, and that part which comes after the raising of Lazarus in which this Disciple is mentioned."

Steiner also addresses the fact that in earlier human history the Christ Impulse could not be directly internalized within the human soul throughout the course of human evolution prior to the Advent of Christ on earth. It was reflected within us by means of the Eloha spirit named Jahve or Jehovah: "What the Christ brought spiritually through His powerful spiritual impulse had to be prepared gradually through other impulses. What Jahve did was to implant the group-soul Ego in the astral body and by gradually maturing it, prepare it for the reception of the fully independent I AM. But men could only comprehend this I AM when their physical body also became a fit instrument for sheltering It. You can easily imagine that the astral body might be ever so capable of receiving an Ego, but if the physical body is not a fit instrument for truly comprehending the I AM with a waking consciousness then it is impossible to receive it. The physical body must also always be a suitable instrument for what is imprinted upon it here upon the Earth. Therefore, when the astral body had been matured, the physical body had to be prepared to become an instrument of the I AM, and this is what occurred in human evolution. We can follow the process through which the physical body was prepared to become the bearer of the self-conscious, Ego-endowed human Being."

Here, we return to what Steiner had been saying in regard to the Phantom/Form of the human physical body. It was absolutely essential to redeem the human physical body and eventually restore it to its rightful condition so that it no longer acts as a tomb to the human Ego. If we read the account in the Gospel of Matthew of the women who approached the tomb on Easter morning we can extend its message about the Risen Christ to the resurrection of our own Ego. The women, in a sense, can be understood as representatives of human soul forces. Mary Magdalene can be thought of as the redeemed astral body. The redeemed astral body meets with its Angel-endowed Manas/Spirit Self that pronounces to it that the Lord/Ego has risen from the tomb of materiality. The stone of the dense, mineral-bound physical body has been removed which allows for a greater consciousness of one's own Ego. The physical body becomes a body that is translucent and diaphanous. The Ego has now Risen with greater force within the soul; it is no longer fettered in materiality. This one scene in the Gospel is a projection of the entire future course of human and earthly evolution. The passage from Matthew reads as follows: "Now late in the night of the Sabbath, as the first day of the week began to dawn, Mary Magdalene and the other Mary came to see the sepulcher. And behold, there was a great earthquake; for an Angel of the Lord came down from heaven, and drawing near rolled back the stone, and sat upon it. His countenance was like lightning, and his raiment like snow. And for fear of him the guards were terrified, and became like dead men. But the Angel spoke and said to the women, `Do not be afraid; for I know that you seek Jesus, who was crucified. He is not here, for He has Risen even as He said. Come see the place where the Lord was laid." (Matthew 28: 1-6).

Who is this Angel that is spoken of in the Gospel of Matthew? It would seem that it is the same Angel of Announcement that we find in the Gospel of Luke who announces the birth of Jesus of Nazareth to the shepherds. It would also seem that it is the Angel/Messenger referred to from the words of Isaiah in the opening of the Gospel of Mark. This is the Angel who is sent before the people to, ". . . make ready the way of the Lord/Ego . . .". It is in the opening of the Gospel of Mark that it is revealed to us that this Angel and John the Baptist are united with one another. As with the shepherds in the fields, once more this Angel, standing before the tomb in Matthew's Gospel, is the first to announce to humans a great Truth and this Truth is that of the Resurrection of the Christ. In like fashion to when he announced the incarnation of the Christ, the Logos, in Jesus of Nazareth at the time of the Jordan Baptism, John the Baptist, as the young man in the tomb, was the first human spirit to announce to other humans a great Truth which is the Truth of the Resurrection of the Christ. Therefore, it seems reasonable to surmise that this Angel is Vidar; the same Angel who administered to Christ Jesus in the Garden of Gethsemane.

Previously, it was mentioned that John the Baptist acted as a prophet of the Old Testament and that in his baptisms he was able direct one's vision to one's past and to the wisdom that flowed from the past ages. However, the Bible then crosses over from the Old Testament to the New Testament when Christ is Baptized in the Jordan and people are now directed to the future for their spirit awareness. Steiner addresses this in the following: "At the time the Earth was in a fluidic condition, the human Being was contained within the watery element, but he could only walk about upon the Earth after it had already deposited solid portions. Therefore, people felt the hardening of the physical body and could say: the human Being was born out of the Earth when it was still in its fluidic state, but at that time he was still wholly united with the Godhead. All that brought him into matter defiled him. Those who are to remember this ancient connection with the Divine were baptized with water. This was its symbol: Let yourself become conscious of your ancient union with the Godhead, conscious that you have become defiled, that you have descended to your present condition. The Baptist also baptized in this way in order to bring mankind into a closer union with the Godhead. And this is what all baptism signified in ancient times. It is a radical expression, but one which brings to our consciousness what is meant. Christ Jesus had to baptize with something different. He had to direct men, not to the past, but to the future through the development of a spirituality in their inner Being. Through the 'Holy', the undimmed and undefiled Spirit, the human spirit could be united with the Godhead. Baptism by water was a baptism of remembrance, that of the Holy Spirit is one of prophesy pointing to the future."

In Lecture VI Steiner continues the same theme: "As long as he was fluidic and airy in form, he remained above with the gods. He was not able to develop his Ego, for he had not yet released himself from the divine consciousness. Because he descended into physical matter, his astral consciousness became ever more darkened. If we wish to characterize the significance of this evolutionary process, we may say that formerly, when the human Being was still living with the gods, his physical and ether bodies were fluidic and gaseous in form, and were only gradually, simultaneously with the solidification of the earth, condensed to their present material form. That is the descent, but just as he has made this descent, so will he also ascend again. After he has had the experiences that are to be had in solid substance, he will again mount into those regions where his physical body will be fluidic and gaseous. He must bear within him the consciousness that if he wishes to unite himself again consciously with the gods, his true existence will be in those regions from which he has sprung. He has become condensed out of water and air and he will again become diffused into them. He can only spiritually anticipate this condition today by gaining within his inner nature a consciousness of the future state of his physical body. Only by becoming conscious of it today, however, will he gain the power to do so. When we have acquired this consciousness, our earthly goal will have been reached, our earthly mission attained. What does that mean? It means that human Beings were at one time born, not of flesh and earth, but of air and water and that they must later be truly re-born in the Spirit, of air and water."

Further in this lecture: "It may be asked, to what is this independent individual human Being indebted for its very existence, this inner Being that

160

seeks its strength outside the physical and ether bodies? It is indebted to the physical and ether bodies which were gradually formed in the course of evolution. They gave birth to that which dipped down into the physical senses and looked out into the physical world during the day, but which at night sank down into a state of unconsciousness, because it had severed itself from that condition in which it previously existed. In occult language, the part remaining in bed is called the real earth-man. That was `man.' And that part in which the Ego remained day and night, that part born out of the physical and ether bodies was called the `child of man' or the `son of man.' The `son of man' is the Ego and astral body, born out of the physical and ether bodies in the course of earthly evolution. The technical expression for this is the `son of man.'

Then comes the question, for what purpose did Christ Jesus come to Earth; what was imparted to the Earth through His Impulse? The `son of man' who had severed himself from existence in the bosom of the Godhead and had broken away from his earlier connections, and in place of which developed a physical consciousness will come again to a consciousness of the spirit through the force of the Christ Who appeared upon the Earth. He will not only perceive in his physical environment with physical senses, but by means of the force of his own inner Being of which he is now unconscious, a consciousness of his divine existence will flash up within him. Through the force of the Christ Who came upon the Earth, the son of man will again be raised to his divine estate."

In Lecture VII Steiner once again broaches the theme of the six Elohim of the Sun and what it meant for the evolution of the Earth and humanity when the Christ Being united Himself with the Earth: "It has been previously stated that what is called the Logos is the sum total of the six Elohim who, united with the Sun, present the Earth with their spiritual gifts, while externally the physical sunlight is falling upon the Earth. Therefore the light of the Sun appears to us like the outer physical body of the spirit and soul of the Elohim or of the Logos. At the moment of the Event of Golgotha, that force, that impulse which formerly could only stream down upon the Earth as light began to unite with the Earth itself. And because the Logos began to unite with the Earth, the Earth's aura became changed.

We shall now consider the Event of Golgotha from still another point of view. We have already reviewed the evolution of the human Being and of the Earth from various standpoints. We know that our Earth, before it became the Earth, passed through the three embodiments of Saturn, Sun and Moon. Therefore the embodiment just preceding that of our Earth was that of the ancient Moon. When a planet has attained the goal of its evolution, something happens to it similar to what happens to a human Being who, in a certain incarnation, has attained his life's goal. The planet passes over into a different invisible existence, a state called a `Pralaya' and then after a time

161

it embodies itself anew. Thus between the previous embodiment of our Earth, the Moon evolution, and the Earth's present embodiment, there existed an intermediate state. Out of a sort of spiritual, self-animated, externally invisible existence, the Earth gleamed forth in its earliest state and out of this state developed those states which we described yesterday. At that time, in that early age when our Earth gleamed forth, it was still united with all that now belongs to our solar system. It was then so large, that it reached to the furthest planets of this solar system. All was unity, for only later individual planets became segregated. The present Earth up to a certain point of time was united with our present sun and moon. Thus we see there was a time when sun, moon and earth were a single body. It was as though you were to take the present moon and sun and stir them together with the earth and thus make one large cosmic body. This was our Earth once upon a time when your astral body and your Ego were floating about in a vapor-like form. Even earlier than this the sun, moon and earth were joined together. At that time the forces which are now in the sun - the spiritual and physical forces - were bound up with the earth. Then came a time when the sun separated from the earth; but not only did the physical sun with its physical light which can be seen with physical eyes depart, but with it all its spiritual and soul Beings at whose head stood the Elohim, the real Spirits of Light, the denizens of the sun. What was left, was a mixture of the present moon and earth. Then for a time the earth, though separated from the sun, was still united with the moon. It was not until the Lemurian period that the moon separated from the earth, when, as a result, there arose that relationship between these three bodies, sun, moon and earth, that exists today. This relationship had to occur. The Elohim had to act without. It was necessary for one of them to become Lord of the moon and from there reflect the powerful force of the other Elohim. We live at present upon our earth, as though dwelling upon an island in cosmic space which has separated from the sun and moon. But the time will come when our earth will once more unite with the sun and again form one body with it. Then human Beings will be so spiritualized that they will again be able to bear the stronger forces of the sun, able to receive them and unite them with themselves. They, together with the Elohim, will then occupy the same field of action.

You will ask, what is the force that will bring this about? Had the Event of Golgotha not occurred, the earth and the sun would never be able to reunite. For through the Event of Golgotha, which bound the force of the Elohim in the sun to the earth - in other words the force of the Logos - the impulse was given which will again eventually impel one Logos-force toward the other, and finally once more unite them - sun and earth - in one body. Since the Event of Golgotha, the earth, spiritually observed, is possessed of the force to draw the sun again into a unity with it. Therefore it can be said that through this great Event, the force of the Logos, which formerly radiated down upon the earth from without, was now taken up into its spiritual Being. The question may be asked, what existed previously within the body of the earth? It was that force which streamed down upon it from the sun. But since that time, what exists there within the earth? The Logos itself which through Golgotha has become the spirit of the earth.

As truly as your soul and spirit dwell within your physical body, do also the soul and spirit of the earth dwell within the body of the earth - that earthly body which consists of stones, plants and animals and upon which you tread. This soul and spirit, this earth spirit is the Christ. Christ is the Spirit of the earth. When the Christ spoke to His most trusted disciples on an occasion which can be numbered among the most intimate of such occasions, what did He say to them? With what mystery had He occasion to entrust them? He was able to say to them: 'It is as though you can gaze into your own soul from your physical body. Your soul is within. It is the same when you observe the whole earth-sphere. That spirit which for a time now stands here before you in the flesh is also the spirit of the earth and will always continue as such.' He had occasion to point to the earth as His real body and ask: 'When you behold the cornfield and then eat the bread that nourishes you, what in reality is this bread which you are eating? You are eating My Body. And when you drink of the plant sap, it is like the blood in your own body; it is the blood of the earth - My Blood!' - These were the very words that Christ-Jesus spoke to His most intimate disciples and we must take them very literally. Then when He called them together and expounded to them symbolically what we shall call the Christian Initiation, He uttered those extraordinary words which we find in the 18th.verse of the 13th. Chapter of the Gospel of St. John, where He announced that one among them would betray Him: 'He who eats My bread treads Me under foot.' These words must be taken literally. Men eat the bread of the earth and tread upon the earth with their feet. If the earth is the body of the Earth-Spirit, that is, of the Christ, then men tread with their feet the earth's body, the body whose bread they eat. An immense deepening of the idea of the Last Supper as presented in the Gospel of St. John is granted us, when we learn about the Christ, the Earth-Spirit, and about the bread which is taken from the body of the earth. Christ points to the earth and says: 'This is My body!' Just as the muscular human flesh belongs to the human soul, so does bread belong to the body of the earth, that is to the body of the Christ. And the sap that flows through the plants, which pulsates through the vine stalk, is like the blood pulsating through the human body. Pointing to this, the Christ says: 'This is my blood!' That this truthful explanation of the Last Supper can cause some of the sanctity to be lost which has always been associated with it can only be imagined by someone possessing no understanding of it or who has neither desire nor capacity for such an understanding. But anyone who wishes to understand will acknowledge that this does not cause it to lose in holiness, but that through it the whole of the earth-planet becomes sanctified. What powerful feelings can be engendered in our souls, if we can behold in the Last Supper the greatest mystery of the earth, the connection between the Event of Golgotha and the entire evolution of the earth; if we can learn to feel that in the Last Supper the flowing of the blood from the wounds of the Savior had not only a human, but a cosmic significance, that is, it gave to the earth the force to carry forward its evolution."

In Lecture XII Steiner spoke of the fact that the Christ brought to Earth the Impulse which makes it possible to receive the Virgin Sophia and the Holy Spirit. He says this in the following manner in relation to Christian Initiation: "This cleansed, purified astral body, which bears within it at the moment of illumination none of the impure impressions of the physical world, but only the organs of perception of the spiritual world is called in esoteric Christianity the `pure, chaste, wise Virgin Sophia.' By means of all that he receives during catharsis, the pupil cleanses and purifies his astral body so that it is transformed into the Virgin Sophia. And when the Virgin Sophia encounters the Cosmic Ego, the Universal Ego which causes illumination, the pupil is surrounded by light, spiritual light. This second power that approaches the Virgin Sophia, is called in esoteric Christianity - is also so called today - the `Holy Spirit.' Therefore according to esoteric Christianity, it correct to say that through his processes of Initiation the Christian esotericist attains the purification and cleansing of his astral body; he makes his astral body into the Virgin Sophia and is illuminated from above - if you wish, you may call it overshadowed - by the `Holy Spirit,' by the Cosmic, Universal Ego. And the person thus illuminated, who, in other words, according to esoteric Christianity has received the `Holy Spirit' into himself, speaks forthwith in a different manner. How does he speak? When he speaks about Saturn, Sun and Moon, about the different members of the human Being, about the processes of cosmic evolution, he is not expressing his own opinion. His views do not at all come into consideration. When such a person speaks about Saturn, it is Saturn itself that is speaking through him. When he speaks about the Sun, the Spiritual Being of the Sun speaks through him. He is the instrument. His personal Ego has been eclipsed, which means that at such moments it has become impersonal and it is the Cosmic Universal Ego that is using his Ego as its instrument through which to speak. Therefore, in true esoteric teaching which proceeds from esoteric Christianity, one should not speak of views or opinions, for in the highest sense of the word this is incorrect; there are no such things. According to esoteric Christianity, whoever speaks with the right attitude of mind toward the world will say to himself, for instance: If I tell people that there were two horses outside, the important thing is not that one of them pleases me less than the other and that I think one is a worthless horse. The important point is that I describe the horses to the others and give the facts. In like manner, what has been observed in the spiritual worlds must be described irrespective of all personal opinions. In every spiritual-scientific system of teaching, only the series of facts must be related and this must have nothing to do with the opinions of the one who relates them.

Thus we have acquired two concepts in their spiritual significance. We have learned to know the nature of the Virgin Sophia, which is the purified astral body, and the nature of the `Holy Spirit,' the Cosmic Universal Ego, which is received by the Virgin Sophia and which can then speak out of this purified astral body. There is something else to be attained, a still higher stage, that is the ability to help someone else, the ability to give him the impulse to accomplish both of these. Men of our evolutionary epoch can receive the Virgin Sophia (the purified astral body) and the Holy Spirit (illumination) in the manner described, but only Christ Jesus could give to the Earth what was necessary to accomplish this. He has implanted in the spiritual part of the Earth those forces which make it possible for that to happen at all which has been described in the Christian Initiation."

Steiner continues in Lecture XII: "Thus we see that we have to do with the full reality and truth of the Resurrection and that only those are fully able to understand it, who have first developed the inner power to perceive in the spirit world. This will make the last chapter of the Gospel of St. John comprehensible to you, in which again and again it is pointed out that the closest followers of Christ Jesus have reached the stage of the Virgin Sophia, because the Event of Golgotha had been consummated in their presence. But when they had to stand firm for the first time, had actually to behold a spiritual event, they were still blinded and had first to find their way. They did not know that He was the same One Who had earlier been among them. Here is something which we must grasp with the most subtle concepts; for the grossly materialistic person would say: `Then the Resurrection is undermined!' The miracle of the Resurrection is to be taken quite literally, for He said: `Lo, I remain with you always, even unto the end of the age, unto the end of the cosmic age.'"

Steiner then concludes this lecture cycle again stressing the need for understanding and knowing: "If we try to make into a feeling, into an experience, what we can learn from Spiritual Science about the Gospel of St. John, we shall then find that this Gospel is not a text book, but a force which can be active within our souls. If these short lectures have aroused in you the feeling that this Gospel contains not only what we have been discussing here, but that indirectly, through the medium of words, it contains the force which can develop the soul itself further, then what was really intended in these lectures has been rightly understood. Because in them, not only was something intended for the understanding, for the intellectual capacity of understanding, but that which takes its round-about path through this intellectual capacity of understanding should condense into feelings and inner experiences, and these feelings and experiences should be a result of the facts that have been presented here. If, in a certain sense, this has been rightly understood, we shall also comprehend what is meant when it is said that the Movement for Spiritual Science has the mission of raising Christianity into Wisdom, of rightly understanding Christianity, indirectly through spiritual wisdom. We shall understand that Christianity is only in the beginning of its activity, and its true mission will be fulfilled when it is understood in its true spiritual form. The more these lectures are understood in this way, the more have they been comprehended in the sense in which they were intended."

As has been discussed previously John had attained the Initiation of a Sun-Hero or the attainment of Initiation of the sixth degree by means of the Angel that worked through him. This is an Initiation into the Mysteries of the solar system and also into a particular zodiacal constellation. What was needed for the full understanding of the Resurrection was an Initiate of the seventh degree. An Initiate of this level was known in the Mysteries as a Father. Steiner, in his, "An Outline of Occult Science," lists the various levels of Initiation and says of the sixth degree that it is the union with the Macrocosm. However, this is not to say that he is speaking in terms of being Initiated into the whole of the macrocosm; that is, of gaining wisdom that is related to the whole of the macrocosm. In the sixth degree one begins to feel as if one is merging with the macrocosm but only stage by stage. An Initiate attained to the level of the seventh degree, the level of a Father, when the Initiate had attained an Initiation into all of the zodiacal constellations. Steiner described the seventh level as the, "Total experience of all previous experiences as a fundamental mood of the soul." This would include the cumulative wisdom of all the previous stages of Initiation as well as all that the Initiate had gained in the Initiations into all Twelve zodiacal constellations. This is why it could be said that the Apostles were all to be initiated separately into a single zodiacal constellation each to his own personal soul development and that each would be a Sun-Hero for a particular constellation. Each was to be an Initiate of the sixth degree. This would have given Christ the necessary configuration of the spiritual forces of all Twelve zodiacal constellations flowing through the Apostles as a whole. Each Apostle would be the seed of a new beginning and regeneration of the human form in relation to the specific constellation with which he was aligned and to its particular spiritual forces. These spiritual forces of the constellations were to flow through the Apostles and later through all of humanity in a new way; a new way such that they are now directly imbued with the Cosmic Principle of the Christ Being. Since the Advent of the Christ on Earth a new Impulse had now entered into that which flows into humanity from the zodiacal constellations and, conversely, that which flows from out of humanity now flows into spheres of the planets and constellations thereby eventually creating the genesis of the future Jupiter Planetary Condition.

It had become painfully obvious to Christ that the Apostles were not going to meet the demands of attaining the achievement of becoming Sun-Hero Initiates prior to the Crucifixion and Resurrection. Even His chosen three Apostles, Peter, James and John, were incapable of this achievement. Christ anticipated this and took the necessary precautions thereby initiating Lazarus into the sixth degree and John the Baptist into the seventh degree at Bethany six days before His death on the Cross. The Initiation of Lazarus and of John the Baptist gave Christ the critically needed human souls through which He could accomplish His Deed for all of humanity. That which spiritually flowed from the Cross and from the empty tomb flowed into both Lazarus at the foot of the Cross and into John the Baptist as the young man in the tomb on the morning of the Resurrection. Lazarus and John the Baptist became the first human souls which received these forces. The Mantle of the astral body of Christ was given over to Lazarus while the Cosmic youth forces were received by John the Baptist. This then made it possible for all other human Beings to receive these very same elements of Christ over time through incarnation after incarnation as every human soul begins to fully acknowledge and understand the Mystery of Golgotha.

It was shown earlier that Lazarus gave us a clear indication that he was an Initiate of the sixth degree; a Sun-Hero Initiate. However, it is not so clear that John the Baptist was an Initiate of the seventh degree. We have already seen from Steiner's lectures that John the Baptist was an Initiate of the sixth degree in that he was initiated into the constellation of Aquarius. It is suggested here that he was then being prepared to become an Initiate of the seventh degree when he became the group-soul of the Twelve Apostles at the time of the feeding of the five thousand after his beheading. He was gradually and sequentially being made ready for this achievement of becoming an Initiate of all of the Twelve zodiacal constellations as Christ moved about in relation to the movement of the Sun and its relation to the constellations. This gradual development and preparation then reached its culmination at Bethany in the raising of Lazarus and in the Initiation of both Lazarus and John the Baptist. We see the auspicious portent of all of this simply in the time of the year that John the Baptist was said to have been born. It is the same time of the year, the summer solstice, that we have come to recognize in Christian Esotericism as the time when the Spirit of the Earth, the Christ Being, resurrects and ascends from the Earth and expands His Being into the farthest regions of all of the zodiacal constellations. He then brings back to Earth, from the constellations, the spiritual forces which we are eventually to develop within ourselves. Humanity is to awaken to these forces and become fully conscious of that which spiritually flows from the zodiacal constellations and weaves through our souls. In the lecture cycle,

"The Four Seasons and the Archangels," in Lecture I Steiner states, ". . . at St. John's Tide we celebrate the outpouring of human souls into cosmic space." We will eventually become awakened to this macrocosmic spiritual breathing process and partake in it in full awareness. Due to the cosmic breathing processes of our souls that expand and contract throughout cosmic space in conjunction with the Christ over the course of the year, in time we will become aware of this expansion and contraction of our souls. This will afford us ever greater capacities to consciously internalize the light, life and wisdom impulses that emanate from the hierarchies. In the further course of human evolution we will become fully conscious of these powers and forces that do breathe through our souls as we are presently aware of the air that fills and empties from our lungs as we inhale and exhale.

XII

Baptism and Initiation

In Steiner's lecture cycle, "The Gospel of St. John and Its Relation to the Other Gospels," he opens the lecture cycle with comments regarding St. John's Day: "The day of the year bearing this name was a festival as far back as the time of ancient Persia. There, on a day corresponding to a June day of today, the so-called Festival of the Baptism by Water and Fire was celebrated. In ancient Rome the Festival of Vesta was held on a similar day in June, and that again was a festival of the baptism by fire. Going back to the time of pre-Christian culture in Europe and including the period before Christianity had become widely disseminated, we find a similar June festival coinciding with the time when the days are longest and the nights shortest, when the days start to become shorter again, and when the Sun once more begins to lose some of the power that provides for all earthly growth and flourishing. This June festival seemed to our European forefathers like a withdrawal, a gradual disappearance of the God Baldur who was thought of as associated with the Sun. Then in Christian times this June festival gradually became the Festival of St. John in memory of the Forerunner of Christ Jesus."

Again, it is suggested here that the birth of John the Baptist at this time of the year was not merely coincidental. His whole Being was tied to the forces of the macrocosm and that the Festival of St. John the Baptist echoes this truth. In Lecture VI from, "The Gospel of St. John and Its Relation to the Other Gospels," Steiner once again addresses the meaning and purpose of the baptisms given by John the Baptist: "What, then, had John the Baptist brought about by baptizing in this way? People had become more and more attached to the physical world as a means of mutual contact, and believed the physical element to be the true reality. But those who came to the Baptist experienced their own lives as spiritual. After being baptized, they knew that they were something over and above what their physical body made them. The human mind had gradually developed in the direction of the physical world; but John evoked in those he baptized the awareness of the existence of a spiritual world to which their higher selves belonged. You need only clothe John's utterance in other words and you have: `Transform your mind that is now directed toward the physical world.' And that is what they did - those who received the baptism in the right way. They knew, then, that spirit dwelt in them, that their Ego belonged to the spiritual world.

Man gained this conviction in the physical body. No special procedure had taken place, as in Initiation; what occurred was experienced in the physical body. In addition, the whole experience of the baptism by John acquired a special meaning as a result of the manner in which the whole doctrine of the time was received and merged with the soul - the doctrine that existed since Moses' proclamation. After baptism, a man not only was aware of his union with the spiritual world, he also recognized the particular spiritual world which was approaching the Earth. He knew that what now pervaded the Earth was identical with what had revealed itself to Moses as `ehjeh asher ehjeh' in the burning bush and in the fire on Sinai; and he knew that the word Jahve or Jehovah, or ehjeh asher ehjeh, or I AM the I AM, truly expressed the nature of this spiritual world. So through the baptism by John, man knew not only that he was one with the spiritual world, but that in this spiritual world there dwelt the I AM out of which the spirit in him was born. That was the preparation John imparted through his baptisms; that was the feeling, the sensation, he aroused in those whom he baptized. Their number, of course, was necessarily small, since few of them were mature enough to experience all this when submerged; but some discerned the approach of the Spirit later to be called the Christ."

"Now, the Baptist had indeed prepared something that was of great significance for mankind; he had prepared the way for man to remain within his personality and at the same time find there, after the submersion, exactly what once he had experienced as the `gods' at the time when he himself still lived in water, when the atmosphere was saturated with moisture and fog. That experience in the divine worlds was now repeated. In spite of possessing an Ego, man, as a human Being, could now be reunited with his fellow-men, could be led back to a love that was now spiritualized."

In Lecture VII Steiner gives us a detailed description of the difference the Advent of Christ on Earth means in terms of a new procedure of Initiation by 'fire and spirit': "The procedure of the old Initiation was as follows: The candidate first learned comprehensively all that today we are taught by Anthroposophy. That was the preparation for the old Initiation. Then, all this was directed to a certain culmination which was achieved by having him lie in a grave for three and a half days, as though dead. When his etheric body was withdrawn and, in his etheric body, he moved about in the spiritual world, he became a witness of this spiritual world. In order that in the sphere of his etheric forces he might behold the spiritual world, thus achieving Initiation, it was necessary at that time to withdraw the etheric body. Formerly these forces were not available in the normal state of waking consciousness: the neophyte had to be brought into an abnormal condition. Christ brought this force to the Earth for Initiation also; for today, it is possible for man to become clairvoyant without the withdrawal of the etheric body.

170

When a person attains the maturity to receive so strong an impulse from the Christ, even for a short time, as to affect the circulation of his blood - this Christ influence expressing itself in a special form of circulation, an influence penetrating even the physical principle - then he is in a position to be initiated within the physical body. The Christ Impulse has the power to bring this about. Anyone who can become so profoundly absorbed in what occurred as a result of the Event of Palestine and the Mystery of Golgotha as to live completely in it and see it objectively, see it so spiritually alive that it acts as a force communicating itself even to his circulation, such a man achieves through this experience the same result that was formerly brought about by the withdrawal of the etheric body.

You see then, that through the Christ Impulse something has come to Earth which enables the human Being to influence the force that causes his blood to pulsate through his body. What is here active is no abnormal event, no submersion in water, but solely the mighty influence of the Christ Individuality. No physical substance is involved in this baptism - nothing but a spiritual influence; and the ordinary, every-day consciousness undergoes no change. Through the spirit that streams forth as the Christ Impulse something flows into the body, something that can otherwise be induced only by way of psycho-physiological development through fire - an inner fire expressing itself in the circulation of the blood. John still baptized by submersion with the result that the etheric body withdrew and man could see into the spiritual world. But if a man opens his soul to the Christ Impulse, this Impulse acts in such a way that the experiences of the astral body flow over into the etheric body, and clairvoyance results. There you have the explanation of the phrase, 'to baptize with the spirit and with fire,' and those are the facts concerning the difference between the John baptism and the Christ baptism. The Christ Impulse made it possible for an order of new Initiates to come into being."

"When did a Christ Initiate of this kind first arise? In all evolution the old must be merged with the new, and thus even Christ had to lead the old Initiation into the new one gradually. He had to create a transition, so to speak; He had to take into account certain procedures of the old Initiation, but in such a way that everything deriving from the old gods should be suffused by the Christ Being. Christ undertook the Initiation of that one among His disciples who was then to communicate to the world the Gospel of the Christ in the most profound way. An Initiation of this sort lies concealed behind one of the narratives in the Gospel of St. John, behind the story of Lazarus (Chapter 11)."

In Lecture IX Steiner briefly speaks in regard to the Feeding of Five Thousand: "The fourth sign is the Feeding of the Five Thousand. Again, we must seek for the most significant passage and we must bear in mind that an event of this sort should not be viewed in the light of present-day consciousness. Had those who wrote about Christ at the time the John Gospel

171

was written believed what our materialistic age believes today, their narratives would have been very different, for quite other things would have struck them as important. In this case they were not particularly surprised even at the phenomenon of five thousand being fed from so small a supply; but what is most important and specially emphasized is the following passage: `And Jesus took the loaves; and when He had given thanks, he distributed them to the disciples, and the disciples to them that were set down; and likewise of the fishes as much as they would.' (John 6: 11).

Just what is it that Christ Jesus does here? In order to bring about what was to take place He makes use of the souls of His disciples, of those who had been with Him and had by degrees matured to the level of His stature. They are a part of the procedure. They surround Him; in their souls He can evoke a power of Charity. His force flows forth into that of the disciples. . . . Previously, He infused His force into the man who had lain sick for thirty-eight years. Here, His force acts upon the force of the disciples' souls. What is active here is the intensification of forces that proceeds from the soul of the Master to the souls of the disciples. The force has been expanded from the one soul to the souls of the others. It has become stronger."

Here again we are told of the bond that existed between Christ and the Apostles. This bond was to be maintained throughout the entire time that Christ lived in the body of Jesus of Nazareth. We have already seen that it was not sustained and gradually became weakened throughout the course of the incarnation of Christ as He became increasingly incarnated within the body of Jesus of Nazareth. In Lecture X Steiner speaks of the paramount significance of Christ gradually incarnating within the body of Jesus of Nazareth until He eventually had mastery over the human skeleton: "In the structure of man there is one element to which the power of a pre-Christian Initiation could not penetrate; the subtle physico-chemical processes in the skeleton. . . . Previous to the Baptism of Christ Jesus there never had been a human individuality in Earth evolution, either among Initiates or elsewhere, with the power over the chemico-physical processes in the skeleton. Through the entry of the Christ into the body of Jesus of Nazareth the Egohood of Christ acquired dominion even over the skeleton. And the result was that, as a unique event, there once lived upon Earth a body capable of employing its forces in such a way as to incorporate the form of the skeleton - that is, its spiritual form - in Earth evolution. Nothing of all that man passes through in his Earth development would endure were he not able to incorporate in Earth evolution, as a law, the noble form of his skeleton, were he unable gradually to master this law of the skeleton."

"The human entity, then, that was the sheath of Jesus of Nazareth came under the dominion of the Christ; and the will of the Christ, His sovereign will, had the power to penetrate the skeleton, so that it could be influenced, as it were, for the first time. The significance of this fact can be set forth as

172

follows: Man acquired his present form, that he has by virtue of his skeleton, on the Earth - not during a previous embodiment of our planet; but he would lose it again had it not been for the coming of that spiritual power we call the Christ. He would carry over into the future nothing in the way of harvest and fruits of his sojourn on Earth had not Christ established His dominion over the skeleton. It was therefore a stupendous force that penetrated to the very marrow of the threefold sheath of Jesus of Nazareth at the moment of the Baptism by John."

This whole process of redeeming the human Form, even down to the marrow of the skeleton, began in Earth evolution at the Baptism of the Christ in the Jordan. The Mantle of the spiritual world was bestowed upon Christ who began His incarnation into the body of Jesus of Nazareth at this time. Steiner brings to our attention that at this moment the following words were, ". . . resounding out of the universe."; "This is my Son, imbued with my Love, in Whom I manifest myself." These are the words of the Father in recognition that the Christ is the Regent of our planetary system during the Earth Condition of Consciousness. Also, these words echo that which the entire spiritual world had given to the Earth evolution. The Father and the spiritual world manifest themselves to humanity in the flesh through the Christ who became One with Jesus of Nazareth. "This is my Son," are the words that proclaim that Christ is the supreme Macrocosmic Ego/Son of our planetary cosmos that has come to Earth and that with Him is the Cosmic Principle of the All-Prevailing Cosmic Love that He brought to Earth.

Steiner then adds this: "The whole Earth takes part in every life process. If this is the case even in a physical life process, you will not find it incomprehensible that in an event such as the Baptism the whole spiritual world participated, and that much, very much, occurred in order that this might take place." An added note to the Baptism is the following profound statement from Steiner: "At the same moment when the Spirit of Christ descended into the body of Jesus of Nazareth and the transformation occurred as described, an influence was exerted upon the Mother of Jesus of Nazareth as well. It consisted in her regaining her virginity at this moment of the Baptism; that is, her inner organism reverted to the state existing before puberty. At the birth of the Christ, the Mother of Jesus of Nazareth became a virgin."

We have read from, "The Fifth Gospel," that at this moment the soul of the deceased mother of the Nathan Jesus of the Luke Gospel now became united with the soul of the mother of the Jesus who descended from the line of Solomon of the Matthew Gospel. And through this act the step-mother of Jesus of Nazareth began to be imbued with the forces of the Divine Sophia and that of the Spirit Self. In regard to the physical body of Christ Jesus we read once again from Steiner who quotes from the Gospel of John: "Jesus answered and said unto them, `Destroy this temple, and in three days I will raise it up.' Then said the Jews, ` Forty and six years was this temple in building, and wilt thou rear it up in three days? But He spoke of the temple of his body." (John 2: 19-21).

"This indicates that the sheath which had been offered Him in sacrifice now has the power to control and master the physical body completely. Now this body, become independent, can move about at will, no longer subject to the laws of the physical world: regardless of the usual laws of the world of space, it can bring about and direct events in the spiritual world. Again we ask, does this occur? Yes: it is indicated in the chapter following the one in which the purging of the Temple is related. `There was a man of the Pharisees, named Nicodemus, a ruler of the Jews: The same came to Jesus by night, and said unto Him . . .' (John 3: 1-2).

Why does it say here, `by night?' . . . `By night' means nothing else than that this meeting between Jesus and Nicodemus occurred in the astral world: in the spiritual world, not in the world that surrounds us in our ordinary day consciousness. This means that Christ could now converse with Nicodemus outside the physical body - by night, when the physical body is not present, when the astral body is outside the physical and etheric bodies. Thus the threefold sheath of Jesus of Nazareth was prepared by the Christ, Who dwelt in it, for the acts that were to follow, for what was to be infused into the souls of men. This implied a degree of sovereignty in the soul dwelling in Jesus of Nazareth that would enable it to act upon other bodies. . . . To be seen in the flesh without being physically present called for something more; and so powerful had the force become, even at that stage, in the body of Jesus of Nazareth that the Christ was seen not only by His disciples but by others as well."

Later in this same lecture: "Hence the momentous words spoken of Him Who hung on the cross: `Not a bone of Him shall be broken.' (John 19:36 quoting Psalms 34:20). Why? Because the form over which Christ must retain His dominion was not to be desecrated. Had they broken His bones, a base human force would have interfered with the power Christ had to exercise even over the bones of Jesus of Nazareth. None must touch that form, for it was written that this should remain wholly subject to Christ's dominion."

In Lecture XI Steiner concluded this lecture with the following: "Thus we see the profundity, not only of the Gospels, but of all the interrelationships in the Mysteries. Truly, the old legends are related to the prophesies and Gospels of more recent times as is presage to fulfillment. In the legends of Oedipus and of Judas we are clearly shown that once upon a time there was a divine, primordial wisdom. But this wisdom vanished: a new wisdom has to come. And this new wisdom will carry men forward to a point that would never have been attainable through the old wisdom. The Oedipus legend tells us what would have had to occur without the

174

intervention of the Christ Impulse; and the nature of the opponents to the Christ, the rigid clinging to the ancient wisdom, is made clear in the Judas legend. But the principle which even the old legends and myths had declared inadequate is brought to us in a new light through the new revelation, through the Gospel. The Gospel gives the answer to what the old legends expressed in images of the old wisdom. In legends we were told that nevermore can the old wisdom provide what humanity needs for the future; but the Gospel, the new wisdom, says: I bring tidings of what mankind needs, of what could never have come without the influence of the Christ Principle, without the Event of Golgotha."

In Lecture XII Steiner continues with the theme of the Oedipus legend and its relation to Judas: "We are, of course, still involved in this process of deterioration taking place in the human blood, in as far as it has its origin in an ancient epoch, it will follow its lingering course to the end of Earth evolution. Therefore an impulse was needed in humanity capable of countering this condition."

"What the old sage meant was this: Once upon a time men possessed wisdom; but even had it been preserved, the development of the Ego must inevitably have proceeded, and egotism would have grown so strong that blood would rage against blood. Blood is no longer fitted to lead men upwards when it is guided only by the ancient wisdom. And thus the clairvoyant Initiate who gave us the original picture of the Oedipus legend wished to set up a warning for mankind, saying: That is what would happen to you if nothing came to supersede the old oracle wisdom. And in the Judas legend there is preserved even more clearly an indication of what the old oracle wisdom would have led to. Judas' mother, too, was prophetically told that her son would kill his father and wed his mother, thereby conjuring up untold misery. Yet it all came to pass in spite of the foreknowledge. This means that the primeval, inherited wisdom is not capable of saving man from the abyss into which he must fall unless a new impulse reaches mankind."

Steiner in this lecture then proceeds with what could have been the possible dire future of humanity if Christ had not brought Himself and His Cosmic Element to Earth: "When the etheric body entered the physical, bringing along a supply of divine wisdom from the treasury of the Godhead, it still provided wisdom for its physical body. But the Luciferic and Ahrimanic spirits prevented all augmentation of this wisdom in the physical body - contrived that none should be added. When now the etheric body begins to emerge again it takes nothing with it from the physical body. The consequence is that if nothing else had intervened man would be heading for a future in which his etheric body, though belonging to him, would contain no vestige of wisdom or knowledge. And with the complete desiccation of the physical body the etheric body would be destitute as well, for nothing could be drawn from the dried up physical body. Therefore, if the physical

175

body is not to desiccate in that future period, the etheric body must be provided with strength, with the strength of wisdom. Before emerging from the physical body the etheric body should have been endowed with the power of wisdom. Within the physical body it must have received something it can take out with it. Then, when it emerges - provided it has acquired this wisdom - it can react on the physical body, giving it life and preventing its desiccation.

The future evolution of humanity can take one of two courses of which one is as follows: Man develops without Christ. In this case the etheric body could bring with it nothing from the physical body, because it had received nothing from it; it emerges empty. But conversely, the etheric body cannot animate the physical body, having nothing to give it; it cannot prevent the attrition, the withering, of the physical body. Man would gradually forfeit all the fruits of his physical life; they could furnish nothing out of his physical body, which he would therefore have to abandon. But the very purpose for which man descended to Earth was to acquire a physical body in addition to his other principles. The germ of the physical body originated in an earlier period, but without its actual formation man would never fulfill his mission on Earth. Now the influences of Lucifer and Ahriman have entered the picture; and if man acquires nothing in his physical body, if his etheric body withdraws again with nothing to take with it - having even used up the old store of wisdom - then the Earth's mission is doomed. The mission of the Earth would be lost to the Universe. Man would carry over nothing into the future but the empty etheric skull which had been abundantly filled when he originally brought it into Earth evolution."

In the above, Steiner remarks: ". . .if man acquires nothing in his physical body, if his etheric body withdraws again with nothing to take with it - having used up the old store of wisdom - then the Earth's mission is doomed."

The Christ Impulse, the Cosmic Principle that the Christ Being had brought with Him and all that is endowed in it passed into the aura of the Earth at the moment that the blood of Christ spilled from the Cross. That was the objective actuality of the sacrifice of Christ for the Earth itself. For each human this same Divine Principle, this Impulse had to pass over into a human Form from which it then acts as a seed for all other human Forms to follow. The human Form draws its life from the Christ Form. However, the forces of the Christ Form had to be originally imbued into at least one human Form for the inception of this Impulse into all other future human physical Forms. This was made possible through the new wisdom and understanding that was gained by John the Baptist throughout the Ministry of Christ Jesus on through to the Passion and culminating in the tomb at the time of the Resurrection. John the Baptist was the young man sitting in the tomb. He was endowed with the new Cosmic Principle which filled his Being making him

176

visible to the women at the tomb. It is possible to say that he may have been temporarily visible in that he, as was Christ who later appeared to Mary Magdalene, was now present in a condensed phantom/etheric body. Steiner, in his ninth lecture on the Gospel of Mark, had said that the fleeing youth, the Cosmic Principle of Christ, ". . . is a spiritual, supersensible Being, who becomes sense-perceptible only through special circumstances." This Being became visible to the senses on Easter morning as the `fleeing youth' manifested itself in its first inception into a human Phantom; the condensed phantom/etheric body of John the Baptist.

Returning to Lecture XII from, "The Gospel of St. John and Its Relation to the Other Gospels": "An impulse had thus to come to the Earth through which the exhausted treasure of ancient wisdom might be replenished, through which the etheric body might be endowed with new life, thus enabling the physical element - otherwise destined to corruption - to put on the incorruptible and to become permeated by an etheric body capable of rendering it immortal, of rescuing it from Earth evolution. And that is what Christ brought to mankind - this pervasion of the etheric body with life. The transformation of the human physical body that would otherwise be doomed to death, its preservation from corruption, its ability to put on the incorruptible - all this is connected with the Christ. Life was infused into the human etheric body by the Christ Impulse - new life, after the old had been spent. And looking into the future, man must tell himself: When my etheric body will ultimately have emerged from my physical body, I should have developed in such a way that it is wholly saturated by the Christ. The Christ must live in me. In the course of my Earth development I must by degrees completely permeate my etheric body with the Christ."

"But what outer form did all this have to take? What was it that entered the physical body through the Luciferic and Ahrimanic Beings? The tendency to decay, to dissolution - in short, the tendency to die. The germ of death had entered the physical body. Had not Christ come, this death germ would have developed its full power only at the end of Earth evolution, for then the etheric body would be for all time powerless to reanimate man; and at the completion of Earth evolution, that which had come into being as human physical body would fall into decay and the Earth's mission itself would end in death. Whenever we encounter death today we can discern in it a symbol of the universal death that would occur at the end of Earth evolution. Mankind's ancient heritage dwindles but slowly and gradually, and the possibility of being born again and again, of passing from incarnation to incarnation, is due to the life fund that man was originally provided with. As regards his purely external life in the successive incarnations, the possibility for life to exist would not be fully exhausted before the end of Earth evolution; but as time goes on the gradual extinction of the race would manifest itself. This would occur piece by piece, and the physical body would continually wither. Had the Christ Impulse not come, man would perish member by member as Earth evolution approached its termination. At present the Christ Impulse is but at the beginning of its development. Only by degrees will it make its way among men; and only future epochs will reveal - and continue to reveal to the very end of Earth evolution - the full significance of Christ for humanity."

In this same lecture Steiner concludes with the call to take up the new understanding that revitalizes the etheric body: "But we now have an Anthroposophy, and this Anthroposophy will increasingly make the Christ Impulse comprehensible for mankind, thereby imbuing the etheric body with ever more life - with such a wealth of it, in fact, that the etheric body will cause the melting of that desiccated portion of the brain which is responsible for the present trend of scientific thinking. This is an illustration of the manner in which the Christ Impulse, penetrating gradually into mankind, will reanimate the dying members of the body. The future of humanity would see the withering of more and more members. But the flowing in of the Christ Impulse will increase proportionately with the dwindling of each part; and by the end of Earth evolution all the parts that would otherwise have perished will be revivified by the Christ Impulse, which will have saturated the whole etheric body; the human etheric body will have become One with the Christ Impulse.

The first impetus for this gradual revitalization of mankind, for the resurrection of humanity, was given at a particular moment during a scene most beautifully described in the Gospel of St. John. Think of the Christ as coming into the world a wholly universal Being, and commencing His great work by means of an etheric body completely saturated with His Spirit - for the transformation brought about in the etheric body of Jesus of Nazareth enabled it to animate even the physical body. At the moment in which the etheric body of Jesus of Nazareth, in Whom the Christ now dwelt, became completely a life giver for the physical body, the etheric body of Christ is seen transfigured. And the writer of the John Gospel describes this moment: 'Father, glorify thy name. Then came there a voice from heaven, saying, "I have both glorified it, and will glorify it again." The people, therefore, that stood by, and heard it, said that it thundered.' What is said is that those who stood by heard thunder; but nowhere does it say that anyone who had not been duly prepared had heard it. 'Others said, an Angel spoke to Him. Jesus answered and said, "This voice came not because of me, but for your sakes."'

Why? That what had taken place might be understood by all who were near. And Christ clarifies the event: 'Now is the judgment of this world; now shall the prince of this world be cast out.' (John 12: 28-31).

In that moment Lucifer-Ahriman was cast out of the physical body of Christ! There stands the great example which in the future must be realized by all mankind: through the Christ Impulse the obstacles placed by Lucifer-

178

Ahriman must be cast out of the physical body. Man's earth body must be so vitalized by the Christ Impulse that the fruits of the Earth's mission may be carried over into the time that is to follow this Earth epoch."

In Lecture XIII Steiner elaborates further the theme of the blood's deterioration and adds to this that death presents itself as maya: "We have seen that, as a consequence of the Luciferic and Ahrimanic influences, human blood became ever less fitted to provide the faculty of seeing the outer world in its true light; a steady increase in illusion was bound up with the blood's deterioration, with the dissolution of blood as it had been in the age of consanguinity, with the blood's dispersion and destruction by miscegenation. No longer could man consult the old wisdom he had once possessed as a legacy, a wisdom that told him: It is an error to believe that the outer world is nothing but matter; for if you consult the remnants of the old wisdom you inherited, these will tell you that a spiritual world underlies the physical world.

But these remnants kept dwindling, with the result that man became ever more dependent upon the physical world in regard to his entire soul life and his knowledge. That is what transformed all of his physical impressions into delusions and deceptions. Had it not been for the intervention of the Christ influence, he would ultimately have lost his whole heritage of ancient wisdom by being gradually reduced to complete dependence upon the outer sense world and its impressions. He would have forgotten the existence of a spiritual world - that is what would inevitably have occurred. He would have become blind to the spiritual world. It is now our duty to consider in all its gravity a truth such as this: the danger of man falling into ever greater delusion and error concerning the outer world. It is not a simple matter to do this - to contemplate in all its implications and its seriousness such a fact as man's lapse into error regarding the outer impressions of the sense world. Try to understand what it means to recognize as maya, as delusion, all external impressions of the senses as they confront us in the physical sense world. We are asked to learn that phenomena and impressions, as they exist in the sense world and as they impress us, are false; and that we must learn to see their true form behind the external impressions they give. There is one event to which it is especially difficult, as a rule, to apply the truth, to say to oneself: The form in which it confronts me in the outer world is untrue, is illusion - maya. Can you think what event I have in mind? It is death. As a result of the sort of impressions we have described, our comprehension has come to grasp only external physical events; and for this reason death, when faced in the physical world, bears certain attributes that render it impossible to contemplate other than from the standpoint of the outer physical world. Death is a phenomenon concerning which mankind has inevitably become entangled in particularly erroneous and harmful views. The inference we

179

must draw from this is that the form in which death presents itself is but maya - a delusion."

"Spirit underlies our physical-sensible world. Then, were we to seek the primordial form of spirit from which springs all that is physical and of the senses, we would have to call it the basis of all Being. In Christian Esotericism this is the aspect of divinity known as the Father principle. It underlies everything that is creature. So what exactly is it that was veiled from man when all things became obscured by maya, or illusion? It was the divine Father principle. Instead of the mirage of the senses, man should see everywhere and in all things the divine Father principle, of which all things and he himself are a part. The Father principle, then, to which belong all things as well as man, does not appear in its true form. Because of the decline in human faculties, of which we have spoken, we see the Father principle veiled by delusion, by maya.

What do we find woven into this great delusion? Among all the phenomena we perceive, one stands out as essentially fundamental: death. Therefore we should tell ourselves that the outer objects confronting our senses are in reality the Father principle, are expressions of the divine-spiritual Father element. And since death is interwoven in the totality of the sense world, it is something that pertains to the divine-spiritual Father principle. Owing to the nature of man's development, the divine Father principle has become obscured for him by many a veil, and ultimately by the veil of death. What must man seek behind death as in all sense phenomena? The Father, the cosmic Father! Just as he must learn to think of every object as being in truth the Father, so he must come to feel that death, too, is the Father. And why does a false picture of the Father appear to us in the physical sense world? Why is it distorted to the point of the grotesque image appearing to us so deceptively as death? Because the Lucifer-Ahriman principle has been infused into every phase of our life. What was needed, therefore, to disabuse man of this false, deceptive view of death and to provide a true conception of it was enlightenment arrived at by means of the actual facts. Something had to occur whereby he could learn that what he had known about death, what he had felt about it - everything he had been impelled to do as a result of his conception of death - was untrue. An event had to take place which would show him the true aspect of death. Its false form had to be obliterated and its true one set forth. To substitute, through His deed, the true aspect of death for the false one, that was Christ's mission on Earth.

Owing to the interference of Lucifer-Ahriman in human evolution, death became the distorted image of the Father. Death was the consequence, the effect, of the influence of Lucifer-Ahriman. So what had to be done by Him Who would rid the world of this false face of death? Never could human life have been released from this distorted form of death had not its source been

180

removed - Lucifer-Ahriman. But that is something no earthly Being could have accomplished. An earthly Being can extinguish, within Earth development, anything brought about by earthly Beings themselves, but not the Luciferic-Ahrimanic influence. This could be driven out only by a Being that had not been on the Earth but out in cosmic space when Lucifer-Ahriman intervened, a Being that came to Earth at a time when Lucifer-Ahriman had already fully entered the human body. Now, this Being did come to Earth and removed Lucifer-Ahriman, as we have seen, at exactly the right moment - eliminated the cause of all that had brought death into the world. This deed called for a Being having nothing whatever to do with any causes of death among men. It had to be a Being in no way connected with any cause of human death - that is, with anything brought about by Lucifer and later by Ahriman, with any individual human deeds done under the Lucifer-Ahriman influence - in short, with anything whereby men became guilty, fell a prey to evil. For the death of a Being affected by any of these causes would have been justified. Only an undeserved death, undertaken by one without guilt - an utterly innocent death - could extinguish all guilty death.

An innocent Being, accordingly, had to suffer death, wed death, submit to death. By so doing He infused into human life those forces which will gradually create knowledge concerning the true aspect of death; that is, the realization that death as it appears in the sense world is not truth - that on the contrary, this death had to occur to provide for life in the spiritual world; that precisely this death forms, in fact, the basis of that life in the spirit. Thus the innocent death on Golgotha furnished the proof, which will gradually be comprehended by humanity, that death is the ever-living Father. And once we have achieved the right view of death, once we have learned from the Event of Golgotha that external dying is of no importance, that in the body of Jesus of Nazareth there dwelt the Christ with Whom we can unite; once we have realized what Christ achieved, even though we see the image of death hung on the Cross, in rendering death a mere external event, that His life in the etheric body was the same before death as it was after this death, and that therefore this death cannot touch life - once we have understood that here is a death incapable of extinguishing life but is, rather, itself life, then the Christ on the Cross becomes the external emblem of the truth that death is in reality the giver of life. The plant comes forth from the seed: death is not the destroyer of life, but its seed. It has been sown into our physical sense world in order that the latter may not fall away from life, but may be raised into life. The refutation of death had to be furnished on the Cross by a contradictory death, by a death that was innocent.

We must now enquire what, exactly, was brought about by this event. From the previous lectures we know that as the fourth principle of his Being man has an Ego, and that as this develops, the blood is its outer physical

181

instrument. Blood is the expression of the Ego, hence with its steady deterioration the Ego fell to an ever increasing extent into error, into maya, or illusion. Hence, also, man is indebted for the growing power of his Ego to the circumstance that he is provided with blood. But this Ego, in turn, he owes in its spiritual aspect to the fact of his having learned to distinguish himself from the spiritual world, of his having become an individuality. This capacity could not have been bestowed upon him otherwise than by temporarily cutting off his view of the spiritual world; and the agency that effected this was precisely death. Had man always known that death is the seed of life he would not have achieved independence for his Ego, for he would have remained linked with the spiritual world. As it was, however, death appeared, gave him the illusion of being separated from the spiritual world, and so trained his Ego to independence. This Ego principle, however, grew more and more independent: it exaggerated its independence, strained it past a certain point. And this condition could be counteracted only by the withdrawal of the force which had caused it. Hence the factor which would have induced exaggerated egotism, which would have fostered not merely the Ego principle, egoism, but egotism - this factor had to be driven out. And this was accomplished in such a way that in the future it can be more and more eradicated from the individual Egos as well; it was accomplished when death came on the Cross of Golgotha and the blood flowed from the wounds. In the blood flowing from Christ's wounds we have the factual symbol of the excessive egotism in the human Ego. Just as blood is the expression of the Ego, so the blood that flowed on Golgotha is the expression of excess in the human Ego. Had not the blood flowed on Golgotha, man would have become spiritually hardened in his egotism and would have been doomed to the fate we described yesterday. But the blood that flowed on Golgotha gave an impetus for the gradual disappearance of the force that makes an egotist of the Ego.

But every physical event has its spiritual counterpart, and as the blood flowed from the wounds on Golgotha there occurred a corresponding spiritual event. At this moment, it happened for the first time that rays streamed forth from the Earth into cosmic space, where formerly there had been none. We must visualize, then, as created at this moment, rays streaming from the Earth into cosmic space. Darker and darker had the Earth become with the passing of time - up to the Event on Golgotha. Now the blood flows on Golgotha - and the Earth begins to radiate light. If in pre-Christian time some clairvoyant Being had been able to observe the Earth from a distant cosmic body, it would have seen the Earth's aura gradually fading out, and at its darkest immediately preceding the Event of Golgotha. Then, however, it would have seen it shine forth in new colors. The Deed on Golgotha suffused the Earth with an astral light that will gradually become an etheric and then a physical light. Every Being in the world continues to evolve. What is today the Sun was first a planet. And just as the old Saturn became a Sun, so our Earth, now a planet, will gradually develop into a Sun. The first impetus in this direction was given when the blood flowed from the wounds of the Redeemer on Golgotha. The Earth began to shine - for the time being astrally, visible only to the seer. But in the future, the astral light will become physical light and the Earth will be a luminous body, a Sun body.

. . . no new cosmic body comes into being through the agglomeration of physical matter, but through the creation, by a spiritual Being, of a new spiritual center, a new sphere of activity. The formation of a cosmic body begins in spirit. Every physical cosmic body was first spirit. What our Earth will ultimately become consists at present of the astral aspect of its aura which began to ray forth from the Earth at the time we are here considering: that is the first nucleus of the future Sun-Earth. But what a man of that time would have perceived with his misleading senses is a phantom: that has no truth, it dissolves, it ceases to be; and the further the Earth moves toward its Sun state, the more will this maya be consumed and perish in the fire of the Sun. But through having been suffused at that time with a new force, through the newly created possibility for the Earth to become a Sun, it became possible as well for this same force to permeate man. . . . the radiating of the Christ force into the etheric human body. And thanks to the streaming in of this astral force it could start absorbing new vitality such as it will need in the distant future. So if you will visualize the period in which the Event of Golgotha occurred and then compare it with a later period - that is, if you compare a future condition of humanity with that which prevailed at the time of the Event of Golgotha - you will find that at the time the Christ Impulse intervened, the Earth of itself had nothing left to infuse into the etheric bodies of men. Some time later, however, the etheric bodies of those who had found a contact with the Christ Impulse were irradiated: men who understood the Christ absorbed the radiant force that has been in the Earth ever since - the Earth's new radiance. They have taken the light of Christ into the etheric bodies of men.

What takes place, now that there is always something of the Christ light in human etheric bodies? What occurs in that part of the etheric body in which the Christ light has been received? What happens to it after death? What is it, in fact, that gradually permeates the etheric body as a result of the Christ Impulse? It is something that the Christ Impulse has brought and implanted into the etheric body of man, and that did not exist there previously. Since that time, as an effect of the Christ light, the possibility exists in human etheric bodies for something new to appear, something that breathes life and is immortal, something that can never perish in death. While men on Earth are still misled by the illusory image of death, this new factor will nevertheless be rescued from death, will have no part in it. Ever since

183

that time, then, something exists in the human etheric body that is not subject to death, to the death forces of the Earth. And this something which does not participate in death and which men gradually attain through the influence of the Christ Impulse, now streams back again - out into cosmic space; and in proportion to its intensity in man it generates a certain force that flows out into cosmic space. And this force will in turn create a sphere around our Earth that is in the process of becoming a Sun: a sort of spiritual sphere is forming around the Earth, composed of the etheric bodies that have come alive. Just as the Christ light radiates from the Earth, there is also a kind of reflection of it that encircles the Earth. What is here reflected as the Christ light, appearing as a consequence of the Christ Event, this is what Christ called the Holy Spirit. Just as the Event of Golgotha provided the first impetus for the Earth to become a Sun, so it is true that, beginning with this Event, the Earth begins to be creative, surrounding itself with the spiritual ring which, in turn, will in the future develop into a sort of planet circling the Earth.

Thus a momentous process that commenced with the Event of Golgotha has since been unfolding in the cosmos. When the Cross was raised on Golgotha and the blood flowed from the wounds of Christ Jesus, a new cosmic center was created. We were present when that occurred; we were present as human Beings, whether in a physical body or outside this physical life between birth and death. That is the way new worlds come into being; and we must comprehend that while we behold the dying Christ, we stand in the presence of the genesis of a new Sun. Christ espouses death, which on Earth had become the characteristic expression of the Father Spirit. Christ goes to the Father and unites with His manifestation, death - and the image of death now becomes false, for death becomes the seed of a new Sun in the universe. If we feel this Event, if we can feel this unmasking of death and feel that the death on the Cross becomes the seed from which a new Sun will germinate, then we also experience powerfully how mankind on Earth must have felt and sensed it as the supreme transition in human evolution."

In the same lecture Steiner then relates all of this to that which Christ taught to Apostles: " The moment arrives when Christ Jesus is prepared to talk to His Apostles without proverbs, without parables. The Apostles want to hear the name, the significant name, for the sake of which He had come into the world. `Hitherto have ye asked nothing in my name: ask, and ye shall receive, that your joy may be full. These things have I have spoken unto you in parables: but the time cometh, when I shall no more speak unto you in parables, but shall show you plainly of the Father.' Try to feel the moment approaching in which He would speak to His disciples of the Father. `At that day ye shall ask in my name; and I say not unto you, that I will pray to the Father for you: For the Father Himself loveth you, because ye have loved me, and have believed that I came forth from God. I came out from the Father. . .'

184

He had, of course, come forth from the Father's true form, not from the deceptive image. `I came out from the Father, and am come into the world: again, I leave the world, and go to the Father.'

Now it dawns upon the disciples, whose understanding has matured, that the world as it surrounds them is the expression of the Father, and that what is most significant precisely where the outer world is most densely shrouded in maya, in illusion, is equally the expression of the Father: that Death is the name for the Father. That is what the disciples realize. Only, the passage must be read aright. His disciples said unto Him, 'Lo, now speakest thou plainly, and speakest no parable. Now are we sure that thou knowest all things and needest not that any man should ask thee: by this we believe that thou camest from God.'

Jesus answered them, 'Now ye believe. Behold, the hour cometh, yea, is now come, that ye shall be scattered, every man to his own, and shall leave me alone; and yet I am not alone, because the Father is with me. These things have I spoken unto you, that in me ye might have peace. In the world ye shall have tribulation: but be of good cheer; I have overcome the world.' (John 16: 24-33). Did the disciples know whither He was about to depart? Yes, from now on they knew He would go to meet death, to wed death. Now read again what He said to them after they had learned the meaning of the words: `I came forth from death' - that is, from death in its true form, the life-Father - `and am come into the world: again, I leave the world, and go to the Father.' And to this the disciples replied: `Now are we sure that thou knowest all things, and needest not that any man should ask thee: by this we believe that thou camest from God.'

Now the disciples knew that the true form of death is founded in the divine Father Spirit; that death as it is seen and felt by men is a deceptive phenomenon, an error. Thus Christ reveals to His disciples the name of death behind which is hidden the fount of sovereign life. Never would the new life-Sun have come into being had not death entered the world and let itself be overcome by Christ. Death, therefore, when contemplated in its true form, is the Father. Christ came into the world because a false reflection of this Father had arisen in death. Christ came to create the true form, a true after-image of the living Father-God. The Son is the after image, the descendent of the Father, and His mission was to reveal the true form of the Father. Verily, the Father sent His Son into the world that the true nature of the Father be made manifest: life eternal, veiled behind temporal death."

In Lecture XIV the above themes of the Father, Death and the Christ are continued: "As a result of Christ's having espoused death - Christ, image of the Father Spirit, Son of the Father Spirit - death becomes the well-spring of a new life - and . . . of a new sun. And now that man has achieved an Ego for all eternity, everything that formerly existed as his apprenticeship can henceforth vanish, and he can advance into the future with his rescued Ego principle which will more and more be fashioned after the Ego Principle of Christ."

". . .at that point of time which our Christian reckoning designates the new `Year 1,' there occurred something of the most profound significance for the entire Earth evolution and, in as far as cosmic evolution is connected with the Earth, for cosmic evolution as well. Indeed, with the Event of Golgotha a new center was created. Ever since then, the Christ Spirit has been united with the Earth. It had long been gradually approaching, but since that time it has been within the Earth. Now, men's task is to learn to grasp this fact: that since the Golgotha Event the Christ Spirit has been in the Earth and in everything the Earth brings forth. Human Beings must learn that failure to recognize the Christ Spirit in all things means seeing them from the aspect of death, whereas finding the Christ in them means understanding them from the vantage point of life."

". . .Paul became the Apostle of Christianity who proclaimed most emphatically the living - the spiritually living – Christ. What made it possible for the Christ to be seen in the Earth's aura? The fact that in Christ Jesus - as in a primal impetus given Earth evolution for the future - the etheric body was completely permeated by the Christ. The etheric body of Jesus of Nazareth could not be otherwise than wholly permeated by the Christ. Because this was so it exerted full mastery over the physical body, even to the extent of being able to restore the latter after its death; that is, it could appear in such a form as to contain again all that the physical body had embraced before death - but through the power of the etheric body. So when Christ was seen after His death, it was His etheric body that was seen. But for those who were able, as a result of the strength imparted to them through the events in question, not only to recognize a physical-sensible body, but to see in an etheric body a real body with all the marks of a physical body - for such as these Christ was risen in reality. And in truth, He was."

In concluding the study of this lecture cycle Steiner once again emphasizes the significant role of Lazarus who wrote the Gospel of John. We should be aware that John the Baptist resided in the consciousness soul of Lazarus; thereby, making the understanding of the forces of the Risen Phantom and the understanding of the power of the etheric body more comprehensible to Lazarus. Steiner also mentions the Twelve Apostles and their bond with Christ while alluding to their connection to the forces of the twelve zodiacal constellations.

"Here we should pause to realize that such things could be written only by that one of Christ's pupils and disciples whom He himself had initiated: Lazarus-John. Hence it was this pupil alone who fully understood the power attained to by a Being Who, beginning with the Baptism, had gradually gained in His etheric body mastery over the physical body, to the extent of endowing the latter with ever new life. And for the same reason, this writer

186

of the John Gospel knew that it was possible to transform what appeared to be water - through its being received into the human organs - into wine. He understood how the power of the etheric body could be effective in such a way that a few fishes and loaves sufficed to satisfy the hunger of many. That is what the author of the John Gospel told us, if only we take the Gospel seriously. Does he say anywhere that the few loaves and fishes were eaten in the ordinary physical way? No, you will not find that in the Gospel. He says clearly and distinctly, as you will see by taking every word literally, that Christ broke the bread; but also, that He offered up thanks to heaven: `And Jesus took the loaves; and when he had given thanks, he distributed to the disciples, and the disciples to them that were set down; and likewise of the fishes as much as they would.' (John 6: 11).

The meaning of these words as they appear in the original text, which is poorly reproduced in translation, is about as follows: The disciples passed on the loaves and the fishes, letting each do with them what he would. But none desired anything whatever save to feel, at this moment, what emanated as a force from the mighty etheric body of Christ Jesus. No one desired anything else. And by what means was their hunger stilled? In the 23rd verse it says: `Howbeit there came other boats from Tiberias nigh unto the place where they did eat bread, after that the Lord had given thanks.' (6:23). It was through the agency of prayer that the people had eaten the bread. They had eaten the bread without the physical act having taken place. Hence Christ Jesus could later throw light on what had occurred by saying, `I AM the Bread of Life.' (6:35). What, then, had the people eaten? They had partaken of the power of Christ's body. And what could remain? Only the power of Christ's body; and the effect of this was so strong that afterwards one could gather something up.

According to occult teaching, every body consists of twelve members. The one uppermost is called the Ram; the adjacent one, the Bull, the one with the hands, the Twins; the chest is called the Crab; everything in the region of the heart is the Lion; below it - the trunk - is the Virgin; the hips, the Scales; below this, the Scorpion; and still farther down: the thigh, the Archer; the knee, the Goat; the lower leg, the Water-carrier; and the feet, the Fishes. The human body, then, is divided into twelve members - and with good reason. Now, if the fragments were to be gathered up after the power of Christ's body had been used to satisfy hunger, they would have to be gathered in twelve measures. `Therefore they gathered them together, and filled twelve baskets with the fragments of the five barley loaves, which remained over and above unto them that had eaten.' (6: 13).

They had not eaten the barley loaves. They had partaken of the power emanating from Christ. They had been satisfied by the power that radiated from Christ through His thanksgiving when He appealed to the spheres from which He had descended. That is the sense in which we must understand the

187

influence of the spiritual world on the physical world; and thus we can also understand the relation of the single incidents to the basic event, the evolution of our Earth into a Sun. They all take their place as mighty force-revealing events in the Earth's process of becoming a Sun. But it now becomes comprehensible that what communicated itself to the Earth at that time as a mighty Impulse can reach human Beings only by slow degrees, that it can be infused into humanity but slowly and gradually."

XIII

The Gospel of Matthew

In Steiner's lecture cycle on the Gospel of Matthew he begins by discussing the different aspects and vantage points that each of the Gospels gives to the reader. In Lecture I he addresses this in the following: "Study of the Gospels, even of their external form, makes us aware of a certain difference in the modes of expression, and this feeling will be intensified when we recall what was said in my lectures on the Gospels of St. John and St. Luke. In trying to fathom the mighty communications given in the Gospel of St. John, we are almost overwhelmed by their sublimity and spiritual grandeur; we feel that this Gospel reveals the very highest goal to which human wisdom can aspire and human cognition gradually attain. Man seems to be standing below, lifting the eyes of his soul to the heights of cosmic existence and saying to himself: However insignificant I may be, the Gospel of St. John enables me to divine that some element with which I myself am akin descends into my soul and imbues me with the feeling of infinitude. - Thus the spiritual magnitude of the cosmic life to which man is related is experienced by the soul when contemplating the Gospel of St. John.

In studying St. Luke's Gospel we found that the manner of its presentation was different. In contemplating the Gospel of St. John it is paramountly the spiritual greatness - even though divined but dimly - that pervades the soul like a magic breath, whereas in the Gospel of St. Luke the influence is more inward, causing in the soul an intensification of all that the powers of cosmic love and sacrifice can effect in the world when we are able to share in them. So, while St. John describes the Being of Christ Jesus in His spiritual stature, St. Luke shows us His immeasurable capacity for sacrifice. St. Luke gives us an inkling of what this power of sacrificing love has brought about in the evolution of the world and of mankind - this love, which, in the same way as other forces, pulsates and weaves throughout the universe. We see, therefore, that while it is mainly the element of feeling that is uppermost when we steep ourselves in the Gospel of St. Luke, it is the element of understanding - informing us, to some extent, of the very foundations of knowledge and of its goals - that is aroused by the Gospel of St. John. That Gospel speaks more to our faculty of cognition, our understanding, the Gospel of St. Luke more to our hearts. The Gospels themselves produce these feelings in us; but it was also my endeavor to let the keynotes sound through the lectures that were given on the two Gospels in the light of Spiritual Science. Those who heard only words in the lectures on the Gospel of St. John or in those on the Gospel of St. Luke, certainly did not hear everything. There was a fundamental difference in the manner and style of speaking in the two lecture-courses. And everything must again be different when we come to study the Gospel of St. Matthew.

The Gospel of St. Luke makes us feel as if all the human love that ever existed in the evolution of mankind poured into the Being who lived as Christ Jesus at the beginning of our era. Considered merely in its external aspect, the Gospel of St. Matthew appears at first to present a picture of greater variety than do the other two Gospels, even than do all the other three. For when the time comes to study the Gospel of St. Mark we shall find that in a certain respect it too presents one particular aspect. The Gospel of St. John reveals to us the magnitude of the wisdom of Christ Jesus; the Gospel of St. Luke, the power of His love. When we study the Gospel of St. Mark, the picture will primarily be one of might, of the creative Powers permeating the universe in all their glory. In that Gospel there is something overwhelming in the intensity with which the cosmic forces come to expression: when we really begin to understand the content of the Gospel of St. Mark, it is as though these forces were surging towards us from all directions of space. While the Gospel of St. Luke brings inner warmth into the soul and the Gospel of St. John fills it with hope, the Gospel of St. Mark makes us aware of the overwhelming power and splendor of the cosmic forces - so overwhelming that the soul feels well-nigh shattered.

The Gospel of St. Matthew is different. All three elements are present here: the warmth of feeling and love, the knowledge full of hope and promise, the majesty of the universe. These elements are present in the Gospel of St. Matthew in a modified form and for this reason seem to be more humanly akin to us than in the other Gospels. Whereas the wisdom, the love and the splendor depicted in the other three Gospels might overwhelm us almost to the point of collapse, we feel able to stand erect before the picture presented in the Gospel of St. Matthew, even to approach and stand on a level with it. Everything is more humanly related to us; we never feel shattered, although it too contains elements which in the other Gospels tend to have this effect. It is the most human of the four records and describes Christ Jesus as a man, in such a way that in all His deeds He is near us in a human sense. In a certain respect the Gospel of St. Matthew is like a commentary on the other Gospels. It clarifies to some extent what otherwise is often beyond the reach of human understanding and once we realize this, great illumination is shed upon the nature of the other three Gospels.

In the Gospel of St. John we are shown how with his wisdom and knowledge man can set out towards the goal that is attainable; this is made plain at the very beginning of the Gospel, where Christ Jesus is referred to as the Creative Logos. The highest spiritual conception our minds and hearts can attain is presented in the very first sentences of this Gospel. It is different in the Gospel of St. Matthew. This Gospel begins by giving the lineage of the man Jesus of Nazareth from a definite point in history and within a particular people. It shows us how the qualities that were concentrated in Jesus of Nazareth had been acquired through heredity from Abraham and his descendants; how throughout three times fourteen generations a people had allowed the best it had to impart to flow into the blood, in order that preparation might be made for the flowering, in one single Individuality, of the highest powers possible to man.

The Gospel of St. John points to the infinity of the Logos, the Gospel of St. Luke leads back to the very beginning of mankind's evolution. The Gospel of St. Matthew shows us a man, Jesus of Nazareth, born from a people whose qualities had been transmitted by heredity from Abraham, the father of the tribal stock, through three times fourteen generations. It can only very briefly be indicated here that anyone who desires really to understand the Gospel of St. Mark must have some knowledge of the cosmic forces streaming through the evolution of our world. For the picture of Christ Jesus presented in that Gospel shows us that the Cosmos itself - an essence of the cosmic forces in the infinitude of space - is operating in and through a human agency. St. Mark sets out to describe the deeds of Christ as extracts of cosmic activities, how in Christ Jesus, the God-Man on the Earth, we have before us a quintessence of the boundless power of the Sun. Thus St. Mark describes to us the manner in which the forces of the heavens and the stars operate through human powers.

In a certain way the Gospel of St. Matthew too is concerned with stellar activity, for at the very beginning it is clearly indicated that cosmic happenings are connected with the evolution of humanity, inasmuch as the three Magi are guided to the birthplace of Jesus by a star. But this Gospel does not describe cosmic workings as does the Gospel of St. Mark; it does not require us to raise our eyes to these heights. It shows us three men, three Magi, and the effect the Cosmos has upon them. We can contemplate these three men and become aware of what they are feeling. Thus if it is a matter of being able to experience cosmic realities, the Gospel of St. Matthew directs our gaze, not to infinitudes of space, but to man himself, to the effect, the reflection, of cosmic activities in human hearts."

In Steiner's lecture cycle on the Gospel of St. Matthew he divulges the mysteries that were involved in the birth of Zarathustra; the incarnation of the Jesus-child from the Solomon lineage . In Lecture IV Steiner ties the birth of Zarathustra with the cosmic forces that were in his blood-line: "Thus there is actual evidence of order prevailing in the generations enumerated in the Gospel of St. Matthew. This evangelist has shown how the blood of the body that was to receive the Zarathustra-Individuality was prepared in a very special way to be instrumental in bringing about the manifestation of Christ on the Earth. What had been achieved through the forty-two generations from Abraham to Joseph was that blood, blended in accordance with the laws of the stars and of the holy Mysteries, had finally been produced. In the composition of this blood - which was needed by the Zarathustra-Individuality for the fulfillment of his great mission - there was inner order and harmony, reflecting one of the most beautiful and significant principles manifest in the heavenly constellations. The blood available for Zarathustra was therefore an image of the Cosmos, having been prepared through generations in accordance with cosmic law. The basis of the record we now possess in a modified form in the Gospel of St. Matthew is this profound mystery of the evolution of a people as the image of cosmic evolution.

Those who were the first to know something of the sublime Christ-Mystery felt that the very blood of Jesus of Nazareth of whom the Gospel of St. Matthew tells was a reflected image of the Cosmos, of the Spirit holding sway in the Cosmos. And they expressed this secret by saying: The Spirit of the whole Cosmos lived in the blood wherein was to dwell the Ego who then became Jesus of Nazareth. - This physical body must therefore have been an imprint of the ruling Spirit of the Cosmos. Hence it was said originally that the power underlying the composition of the blood in the body of Zarathustra when incarnated as Jesus of Nazareth, was the Spirit of our whole Cosmos, the Spirit which, in the primal beginning, after the Sun had separated from the Earth, brooded over and permeated with warmth what had emerged into manifestation in the course of the evolution of worlds."

In Lecture V Steiner explains the need for two Individualities to prepare the body of Jesus of Nazareth for the incarnation of the Christ Being: "Hence the thoughts of those among whom the Gospel of St. Matthew originated were somewhat to the following effect. - The physical body used by Zarathustra must be of such maturity that after the 42 generations it is already at the point of spiritualization, therefore of deification. It is in existence at the beginning of the 43rd generation, but instead of passing into the further stages this body allows itself to be permeated by another Being - by the Spirit of Zarathustra who incarnated on the Earth as Jesus of Nazareth. - Thus through the fulfillment of the mystery of numbers the most fitting body and the most fitting blood had been provided for the Zarathustra-soul in Jesus of Nazareth. - Such is the preparation of whatever relates to the physical and etheric body in human evolution. But now there are in man - hence also in him who was to be the bearer of the Christ Being - not only physical body and etheric body but astral body and Ego as well. Therefore the astral body and Ego too, not only the physical and etheric bodies, had to be adequately prepared. For an event of such stupendous importance this could not be accomplished in one personality, and two were necessary. The physical body and the etheric body were prepared in the personality with whom the Gospel of St. Matthew is primarily concerned; the astral body and the Ego-principle were prepared in the personality of whom the Gospel of St. Luke tells and whom we know as the Nathan Jesus. During the early years this was a different personality. Whereas Jesus of St. Matthew's Gospel received the suitable physical and etheric bodies, Jesus of St. Luke's Gospel was to receive the suitable astral body and Ego-principle."

Steiner then enumerates the various stages of Initiation and relates this to the genealogies of the Matthew Gospel and the Luke Gospel: "When a man who possesses the clairvoyant faculties here described goes to sleep, his Being flows out into conditions expressed in the secret of the number 12 times 7. But at the last of these stages he is already in the super-sensible; for when he has completed the 11 times 7 stages he has reached the boundary of the conditions to which the numerical secrets apply. Just as the 7 times 7 stages have already led into the Spiritual, so too have the 12 times 7. To reach the Spiritual along this path a man must have passed through 11 times 7 stages in the astral body and Ego. This is indicated in the stellar script itself, 7 being the number of the planets and 12 that of the constellations of the Zodiac which the soul must traverse in cosmic space. As the seven planets group themselves within the twelve zodiacal constellations and pass in front of them, when a man is ascending in soul into the Cosmos he must pass through 7 times 12, or rather 7 times 11 stages to reach the Spiritual."

It may be noteworthy to read into this that which we are exposed to in the Gospel of St. John. This theme is veiled in the Gospel of St. John in such a way that the Twelve Apostles are brought into Initiation by the Christ gradually such that the Twelve Apostles, directly or indirectly, are witnesses to the Seven Signs performed by the Christ.

Continuing with Lecture V: "You can, if you like, picture the 12 constellations of the Zodiac as the spiritual periphery, with man himself in the center. If he is to reach the Spiritual, he cannot begin by spreading as it were from the center, but he must expand in spirals, gyrating in 7 spirals and passing all the 12 constellations in each complete circuit - therefore 7 times 12 stages. Man expands in spirals gradually into the Cosmos - all this is of course only a figurative description - and if, circling in this way, he were to have passed through the 12 constellations for the seventh time, he would have reached the Divine-Spiritual. Then, instead of looking into the Cosmos from the center, he looks inwards from the spiritual periphery, from the twelve stations, and from these vantage-points he can behold the external world and all that is in it. There must be twelve such vantage-points; one alone does not suffice. Thus a man who aspired to reach the Divine-Spiritual must sublimate astral body and Ego through 11 times 7 stages; when 12 times 7 stages had been scaled, he was within the Spiritual. Astral body and Ego had in this way to pass through 12 times 7, or rather 11 times 7 stages to reach the Divine. But if the Divine is to descend and a human Ego be made fit to be its vehicle, the descent must equally be through 11 times 7 stages.

Therefore in setting out to describe these spiritual forces whereby astral body and Ego were rendered fit to be bearers of the Christ, it was natural that the Gospel of St. Luke should indicate how the Divine-Spiritual Power descended through 11 times 7 stages. And this the Gospel does. Because the Gospel of St. Luke is describing that other Personality for whom astral body and Ego-bearer were prepared, it does not - as the Gospel of St. Matthew - describe 6 times 7 generations, but a sequence of 11 times 7 stages through which the Power indwelling the Individuality of the Jesus of whom this Gospel is speaking, came down from God Himself. This is expressly stated. Count the stages enumerated in St. Luke's Gospel as those through which the Divine Power descends, and you will find that there are 77. Because the Gospel of St. Matthew is describing the secret of what is taking effect during the descent of the Divine Power working formatively in the physical body and etheric body, the ruling number is 7 times 7. And in the Gospel of St. Luke the number 11 times 7 must necessarily appear, because this Gospel is describing the descent of the Divine Power by which the astral body and Ego are transformed. From this we can realize what deep foundations underlie these presentations and how in very truth the secrets of Initiation, the stages in the descent of the Divine-Spiritual into a human individuality and in the expansion into the Cosmos are indicated in the Gospels of St. Matthew and St. Luke."

In Lecture VI this same theme is continued: "It will now be easier for you to realize that the 77 names enumerated in St. Luke's Gospel extend over very long periods, actually reaching back to the time when the Being we may denote as the divine-spiritual entity in man was incarnated for the first time in a human physical body. The other aspect presented in the Gospel is this. - One who in passing through the 77 stages in the Great Mysteries had succeeded in purifying his soul from everything absorbed by humanity in Earth-existence, attained the state that is possible today only when a man is free of his physical body and can live entirely in the astral body and Ego. He is able, then, to pour his Being over the whole surrounding Cosmos from which the Earth itself arose. Such was the aim of the Initiation in these Mysteries. A man had then reached the level of the Divine-Spiritual Power which drew into the astral body and Ego-bearer of the Nathan Jesus. The Nathan Jesus was to exemplify that which man receives, not from earthly but from heavenly conditions of existence. Hence the Gospel of St. Luke describes the Divine-Spiritual Power by which the astral body and Ego of the Nathan Jesus had been permeated. The Gospel of St. Matthew describes the Divine-Spiritual Power through which the inner organ for the Jahve-consciousness had been brought into existence in Abraham; and this same

Power was working in the physical body and etheric body through 42 generations, constituting a line of heredity."

In Lecture VII Steiner extends these points further: "It is true that man can adapt himself to the Cosmos, but it is also true that the Cosmos does not adapt itself to man. Suppose someone full of preconceptions expands into the Cosmos in one direction only and insists upon adhering to this particular viewpoint; what happens is that conditions in the Cosmos have changed meanwhile and he is therefore left behind. Suppose - to use imagery deriving from the stars - he goes out in the direction of Aries and believes his viewpoint to be of that constellation. But the Cosmos, having moved onwards, is actually presenting to him what lies in the constellation of Pisces, and then - symbolically expressed - he sees what is coming from Pisces as an experience arising in Aries. Confusion is the result, and he finds himself in a labyrinth. The essential thing to remember is that man needs twelve standpoints, twelve viewpoints, to be able to find his bearings in the labyrinth of the Macrocosm."

Steiner then spoke of the purpose of the Christ Event: "The Christ Event itself took place for this very purpose: It was the starting-point from which it became possible for man to penetrate in complete independence into the physical and etheric bodies, as well as to pass outwards into the Macrocosm, into the Great World. It was, however, necessary that both the descent and the ascent (or expansion) should be accomplished in freedom once, in the fullest possible sense, by a Being as sublime as Christ Jesus. The fundamental significance of the Christ Event is that Christ, the all-embracing Being, accomplished in advance what it would become possible for a sufficiently large number of people to achieve in the course of Earth-evolution. - What was it that actually came to pass as a result of the Christ Event?

It was necessary on the one side that the Christ Himself should descend into a physical body and an etheric body. And because in one human Being these bodies had become so sanctified that it was possible for the Christ so to descend, once and once only, the Impulse was given in the evolution of mankind whereby every human Being who seeks for it is able to experience in freedom and independence the descent into his physical and etheric bodies. This had never before been accomplished, had never before taken place. For in the ancient Mysteries something quite different was brought about through the instrumentality of the Hierophant and his helpers. In the Mysteries a candidate for Initiation could descend into the secrets of the physical and etheric bodies and rise to those of the Macrocosm only when he was not living consciously in his physical body; he had to be entirely free from the body. When he returned from this body-free state he could remember his experiences in the spiritual worlds, but he could not bring them to physical experience. It was a matter of remembrance only. This state of things was radically changed through the Christ Event. Before Christ's coming, no Ego had ever consciously penetrated through the whole of the inner nature of man, right into the physical and etheric bodies. This had now come to pass for the first time through the Christ Event.

The other Impulse was also given, in that a Being of a rank infinitely more exalted than that of man, was nevertheless united with human nature and, so united, poured His Being into the Macrocosm through the power of His own Ego, without external aid. Christ alone could make it possible for man gradually to acquire the power to penetrate into the Macrocosm in freedom. These are the two basic facts presented to us in the two Gospels of St. Matthew and St. Luke."

In Lecture IX Steiner says the following which is tantamount to a Foundation Stone for all of his lectures concerning the Christ and the evolution of humanity: "The all-essential point is that Christ Jesus inaugurated an evolutionary process based upon the human Ego, upon the retention of full Ego-consciousness. The Initiation of the Ego - that was what He inaugurated. We can say that the Ego, the `I', is the kernel of man's whole Being, that all human nature today centers in the Ego, and that what was brought through the Christ Event to the Ego, and hence into the world, can also lay hold of all the other members of man's Being. But this, naturally, will have to take place in a very particular way and in keeping with the evolution of humanity."

In Lecture X Steiner elaborates this theme even further and then ties it to the Gospel accounts of the feeding of the four thousand and the feeding of the five thousand: "What Christ Jesus brought about can therefore be described as follows. - Through the force of attraction exercised by the physical and etheric bodies that had been specially prepared for Him, He drew down, through His very nature, the power of the Sun, of the Moon, of the Stars, of the whole Cosmos connected with our Earth. And the deeds He performed became channels for the health-bestowing, strength-giving life otherwise streaming from the Cosmos through man when he is outside his physical and etheric bodies during sleep. The forces with which Christ Jesus worked were forces which streamed down from the Cosmos through the power of attraction exercised by His body and streamed forth again from this body to His disciples. Receptive as they were, the disciples now rightly began to feel: Verily Christ Jesus is a Being through whom the forces of the Cosmos are brought to us as spiritual nourishment; they pour upon us. But the disciples themselves lived in two states of consciousness, for they were not yet men who had reached the highest stage of development; it was through Christ that the attainment of a higher stage was made possible for them. The two states of their consciousness may be compared with those of waking life and sleep. The magical power of Christ was able to work upon the disciples in both states of consciousness, not only by day, when He was actually near them, but also during sleep when they had left their physical and etheric bodies. Whereas in the ordinary way man's Being expands into the worlds of stars unknowingly, Christ's power was now with the disciples and they actually beheld these worlds; they knew too: Christ's power gives us nourishment from the worlds of stars.

But these two states of consciousness in which the disciples lived had still another effect. In every human Being - in a disciple of Christ Jesus too - we must pay attention both to what he is as a man in the immediate present and to the potentialities within him for future incarnations. In each and all of you lie the rudiments of what will present itself to the world in a quite different form when it appears again in a new incarnation during a future epoch of civilization. And if through these potential faculties that are already within you, you were to become clairvoyant, vision of the immediate future would arise as a first manifestation of super-sensible sight. Among the first clairvoyant experiences - provided they were genuine and pure - would be those concerning happenings of the immediate future. - This was the case in the disciples. In their normal waking consciousness Christ's power streamed into them and they could say: In our waking hours Christ's power takes effect in us in a way befitting our normal day-consciousness. - But what happened to them while they were sleeping? Because they were disciples of Jesus and the Christ-power had worked upon them, they always became clairvoyant at certain times during sleep. They did not, however, see what was taking place in the present but what would come to pass in the future. They plunged as it were into the ocean of astral vision and foresaw what was to happen to man in future time.

Thus the disciples lived in these two states of consciousness. Of the one they could say: In our waking state Christ brings us from the great Universe the forces of the cosmic worlds, communicating them to us as spiritual nourishment. Because He is an embodiment of the Sun's power, He brings down to us everything revealed by Zoroastrianism when understood in the light of Christianity. He is the intermediary for the powers which the Sun can send forth from the seven day-constellations of the Zodiac. From thence streams the nourishment for the day-consciousness. Of the night-consciousness the disciples could say: In this condition we become aware of how, through the power of Christ, the Sun that is invisible during the night while passing through the other five constellations, sends the heavenly food into our souls.

With their Imaginative clairvoyance the disciples could feel: In our waking state we are united with the power of Christ, with the power of the Sun. This power transmits to us what is meet and right for men of the present (i.e. the fourth) epoch of civilization. And in the state of sleep the power of Christ conveys the strengthening forces of the nocturnal Sun from the five night-constellations. But this applies to the epoch that is to follow our own -

197

to the fifth epoch of civilization. - That is what the disciples experienced. In what way could it be expressed? . . .

In ancient terminology, human Beings `en masse' were referred to as a `thousand' and when it was desired to particularize, a specific number was added. For example, men of the fourth epoch of civilization were the `fourth thousand' and those whose mode of life was already that of the fifth epoch were the `fifth thousand.' These were simply `termini technici'. Hence the disciples could say: During the waking state we are aware of what Christ's power transmits to us from the Sun-forces radiating from the seven day-constellations; we receive the nourishment that is destined for men of the fourth epoch, the `fourth thousand'. And in our clairvoyant state during sleep we are made aware, through the forces radiating from the five night-constellations, of what applies to the immediate future, to the `fifth thousand'. - Food that is destined for men of the fourth epoch, that is to say for the `four thousand', comes down from Heaven through the seven day-constellations, the seven `heavenly loaves'; and men of the fifth epoch - the `five thousand' - are fed through the five night-constellations, the five `heavenly loaves'. The point of division between the day-constellations and the night-constellations is indicated by specific mention of the constellation of Pisces, the Fishes.

A secret is touched upon here. Indication is given of something deeply significant, namely the magical intercourse of Christ with His disciples. Christ makes it clear to them that He is not speaking of the old leaven of the Pharisees but is bringing down heavenly food to them from the Sun-forces of the Cosmos. On one occasion He has at His disposal only the seven loaves of the seven day-constellations, and on another the five loaves of the five night-constellations. And between the day-constellations and the night-constellations stands the constellation of Pisces, the Fishes, indicating the division. Indeed in one place, for the sake of even greater clarification, mention is made of two fishes. These profundities in the Gospel of St. Matthew, lead back to the proclamation made by Zarathustra, who first pointed to the Sun-Spirit and was also one of the first missionaries to explain to those who were receptive, the mystery of the down-streaming, magical power of the Sun."

Further in Lecture X Steiner then proceeds to speak about the levels of Initiation that the Apostles were able to achieve through Christ: "The power of Imaginative, astral vision streamed from Christ to His disciples. This too is quite clearly indicated. One might well say: He who has eyes to read, let him read! - as in earlier days, when it was not customary to write everything down, it was said: he who has ears to hear, let him hear! . . . He who has eyes to read, let him read the Gospels carefully. Is there any indication that this power of the Christ-Sun was revealed to the disciples in one way by day and in another by night? There is indeed. In an important place in St. Matthew's Gospel the following is said. -

In the fourth watch of the night - therefore between three and six o'clock in the morning - while the disciples were sleeping, they saw, walking on the sea, a figure whom they took at first to be a spirit - that is to say, the nocturnal Sun-power reflected through Christ. The actual hour is indicated because it was only at a particular time that the disciples could be made aware that this power from the Cosmos could stream to them through the mediation of Christ. Constant references to the position of the Sun and its relation to the constellations, to the heavenly loaves, indicate that through the presence of Christ Jesus in Palestine, through this one personality and individuality, a means existed whereby the powers and forces of the Sun could penetrate into our Earth. It is upon this cosmic nature of Christ, this penetration of cosmic forces into the Earth through Christ that emphasis is everywhere laid. Christ Jesus was to initiate in a particular way those of His disciples who were specially fit for it, so that they would be able not only to see the spiritual worlds with Imaginative vision, as it were in astral pictures, but actually to hear what was taking place in those realms - this, as we know, indicates ascent into Devachan.

Hence, having been transported into higher worlds, these disciples would now be able to find in those worlds the personality known to them on the physical plane as Christ Jesus. They were to become clairvoyant in regions higher than the astral plane. This was not possible for all the disciples; it was possible only for those who were the most receptive to the power that could stream from Christ: these disciples were Peter, James and John. The Gospel of St. Matthew therefore relates how Christ led the three disciples to surroundings where he could guide them beyond the astral plane into the world of Devachan, where they could behold the spiritual Archetypes, first that of Christ Jesus Himself and - in order that they might be aware of the conditions under which He was working - also of two Beings who were connected with Him: Elias and Moses. Elias was the ancient prophet who, reincarnated as John the Baptist, was also the forerunner of Christ Jesus. The scene takes place after the beheading of John, when he was already in the spiritual worlds. The disciples also beheld Moses, another spiritual forerunner of Christ. Such an experience was only possible when the three chosen disciples were transported to the level of spiritual vision higher than that of astral vision. And the fact that they rose into Devachan is clearly indicated in St. Matthew's Gospel, for it is said that they not only beheld Christ filled with the power of the Sun but extra words are added: `And His face did shine as the Sun.' It is also said that the three figures - Christ, Elias , Moses - were talking together. An ascent has therefore taken place into the realm of Devachan; the disciples hear the three talking together. (Matthew 17: 1-13). Everything, therefore, is faithfully described and tallies with the characteristics of the spiritual world revealed to spiritual-scientific investigation. There is never any contradiction between the findings of this investigation and true accounts of the deeds of Christ. It was He Himself who led the disciples into the astral world and then into Devachan, the realm of spirit.

Christ Jesus is graphically depicted in the Gospel of St. Matthew as the vehicle, the bearer, of the Sun-power once proclaimed by Zarathustra. It is faithfully related in this Gospel that the Spirit of the Sun - Ahura Mazdao or Ormuzd - of whom Zarathustra could only declare that He lived in the Sun, had lived on the Earth through the instrumentality of Jesus of Nazareth and had united Himself with the Earth in so real a way that through a single life in a physical body, etheric body, and astral body, He became an Impulse in Earth-evolution and as time goes on will become even more deeply united with it. Expressed in other words, this means: Egohood was once present in a Personality on the Earth in such full measure that if men receive Christ into themselves in the sense indicated by St. Paul, they will themselves acquire in the course of successive incarnations the forces and power of this Egohood. As they pass from incarnation to incarnation during the rest of earthly evolution, men who imbue their souls with the power of that Personality who once lived on the Earth, will rise to greater and greater heights. At that time, chosen ones were able with their physical eyes to behold Christ in the body of Jesus of Nazareth. Once in the course of the Earth's evolution, and for the sake of mankind, Christ, who formerly could only be revealed to men's vision as the Spirit of the Sun, descended and united Himself with the forces of the Earth.

Man is the Being in whom the power of the Sun was to be present in its fullness - the power of the Sun that was once to descend and work in a human physical body. This was the inauguration of the epoch during which the forces outpoured from the Sun will flow in ever greater measure into men as they live on from incarnation to incarnation, and - as far as the earthly body permits - gradually permeate themselves with the Christ power. Obviously, this is not possible in the case of every physical body, just as it was only that very special body, prepared through the two Jesus figures in the complicated way described and then brought by Zarathustra to a very lofty stage of development - it was in that body only that the Christ could live in His fullness – once! Men who so resolve will permeate themselves with the Christ-power, first inwardly, then outwardly. Thus humanity in the future will not only understand the nature of the Christ but will be filled with His Power. In the Rosicrucian Mystery Play ("The Portal of Initiation") many of you have been shown what form this increasing experience of Christ will take in the evolution of humanity on the Earth. The seeress Theodora is to be regarded as a personality who has developed the power of seeing into the future, of perceiving the near approach of a period when a few human Beings to begin with, and then greater and greater numbers, will be able, not only through spiritual training but through the stage of earthly evolution reached by humanity in general, actually to see the figure of Christ - but now in the etheric, not in the physical world. In a more distant future Christ will be seen in a form again different. Once and once only He was to be seen in physical form by men living on the physical plane. But the Christ Impulse would not have taken effect had it not worked in a way that would ensure its own further development."

The conclusion of Lecture XI is noteworthy in light of the theme of this work: "This aspect too must give us deeper insight into the structure of St. Matthew's Gospel. We shall then feel profound reverence for a Gospel from which, as from no other, we can learn unmistakably how the disciples of Christ Jesus were the first to receive teaching that was directed to the Ego itself. We picture Christ's disciples standing around Him and perceive how the forces of the Cosmos are working through the human body He bore. We picture Him guiding His disciples in a way that enables them to acquire the knowledge accessible to all who are approaching Initiation. We hear of human situations formed around Him. This is what makes St. Matthew's Gospel seem so near to us in a human sense. Through this Gospel we learn to know the man Jesus of Nazareth, the bearer of the Christ; we learn to know what Christ accomplished through His descent into the nature of Man. Even happenings in the heavenly worlds are presented in terms of human situations and relationships in the Gospel of St. Matthew."

In lecture XII Steiner discusses the point that when a new step in human evolution is to take place a spiritual Being must first unite itself with a human soul. Though, in these following remarks from this lecture, Steiner is primarily speaking of the Christ Being uniting with Jesus of Nazareth. The same principle, however, may be applied to the Angel that united with John the Baptist which I surmise to be the Angel, Vidar. In conjunction with the Angel that unites with John the Baptist, this leap in human evolution is completed further by means of the union between Christ and John the Baptist. The Cosmic Element of Christ united with the entelechy of John the Baptist so that he became the first human to stand as the seed for all other humans in that the human physical Form now has the potential to recreate itself into the likeness of the Resurrected Form of the Christ.

Steiner refers to Scene 3 in his Mystery play, "The Portal of Initiation," as Benedictus is speaking: "A great step forward in world history can only be achieved if Divine Beings unite with man's condition. Only then can spirit eyes unfold which should develop in the human souls, when first a power of heaven has placed the seed within one human Being. . . . I had to join a deed of heaven unto a human destiny." [Translation by Adam Bittleston].

Steiner makes reference to it in the following way as a springboard for his thoughts on Avatar Beings: "A passage in the Rosicrucian Mystery Play points to the fact that when something of crucial importance is to take place in the evolution of humanity, a divine Being must as it were unite with and permeate a human soul. This is a necessity of evolution. To understand this in relation to the spiritual evolution of our planet, we will remind ourselves that in very early times of its existence the Earth was still united with the Sun. In a remotely distant past the Sun separated from the Earth. Anthroposophists know that this was not merely a separation of Earth-substance and Sun-substance in the material sense, but a separation of divine-spiritual Beings who were connected with the Sun or with the other planets. After the separation of the Sun from the Earth, certain spiritual Beings remained united with the Earth, whereas others remained united with the Sun; these latter were Beings who, because their development had progressed beyond the stage attainable in earthly conditions, could not complete their further evolution on the Earth. Thus certain spiritual Beings remained even more closely connected with the Earth, whereas other Beings sent their influences and forces from the Sun into earthly existence. After the separation of the Sun there are, as it were, two arenas - the Earth with its Beings and the Sun with its Beings. The spiritual Beings who can be helpers of man from a higher sphere are those who transferred their arena of activity from the Earth to the Sun. And from thence - from the Sun-sphere - come the Beings who from time to time unite with earthly humanity in order to lead the evolution of the Earth and of Man to further stages.

In the myths of many peoples there are constant references to `Sun Heroes' - Beings who work from spiritual spheres into the evolution of humanity. A man who is permeated by a Sun Being is of far greater significance than his exterior appearance at first reveals. The exterior appearance is an illusion, is maya, and the real Being is behind the maya - only to be divined by one who is able to look into the very depths of a nature such as this. In the Mysteries there was, and there still is, knowledge of this twofold aspect of the evolutionary course of humanity. Distinction has always been made between divine Spirits who come down from the spiritual realm and men who strive upwards from the Earth towards Initiation into the secrets of spiritual reality. What, then, is the nature of the Being we call Christ?

. . . `Christ, the Son of the Living God' is a Being who descends. If we were to use a term current in oriental philosophy, we should call Him an `Avatar' - a descending God. But it is only from a definite point that we can speak of Him as a descending Being. As such He is described by all the four Evangelists, Matthew, Mark, Luke and John. At the moment of the Baptism by John this Being came down from the realm of Sun-existence to the Earth and united with a human Being. We must realize that according to the views of the four Evangelists, this Sun Being is the greatest Avatar of all, the greatest of all other Sun Beings who have ever descended. Hence it is to be expected that a specially prepared nature in humanity must grow towards His level. All four Evangelists tell of the Sun Being, of the `Son of the living

God', who comes to man to help his evolution forward, but only the writers of the Gospels of St. Matthew and St. Luke tell of the man who developed to the stage where he could receive this Sun Being into himself. From these Gospels we learn that for thirty years the man in question prepared for the great moment when he could become the vehicle for the Sun Being. And because the Being we call Christ is so universal, so all-embracing, the preparation of the bodily sheaths able to receive Him could not be a simple process. Very specially prepared physical and etheric sheaths were needed to receive the descending Sun Being."

Continuing further in Lecture XII: "From epoch to epoch the tradition was preserved in the Mysteries that the coming of the Sun Word, the Sun Logos, had been prophesied to mankind and this was always the hope and the great consolation of those who longed for a nobler and better life. And the less exalted Sun-spirits who linked themselves with the Earth and were actually messengers of the Sun Word - they too were able to give more and more definite teachings about the Spirit of the Sun, the Sun Word, the Sun Aura. This was the one side of the Mystery-tradition as it lived on through the epochs. The other side was that it behooved men to know both in theory and by dint of effort that they could grow nearer to the Being who was to descend to the Earth. But in pre-Christian times it was not possible to believe that any weak individual man could without further ado approach the greatest of the Sun Beings, the Leader of the Sun Spirits, the Christ. It was not possible for an individual to achieve this through any form of Initiation. Hence the Gospel of Matthew describes how all the vital elements in the blood of the Hebrew people were assembled in order to make it possible for such a human Being to come into existence. And on the other side, the Gospel of Luke shows how the best and highest qualities attainable by earthly man were `filtered' through the seventy-seven successive stages in order to produce the body capable of receiving the greatest Being who was ever to descend to the Earth."

In the same lecture Steiner again elaborates on the differences in the Gospels as the Advent of Christ and the Mystery of Golgotha are understood from different aspects by the separate writers of the Gospels: "Because the acquisition of such knowledge entailed much arduous effort, pupils in the Mysteries were divided into classes. It is not to be wondered at that in certain sections of the Mysteries teaching was given as to how a man prepares himself to grow to the level where contact with the divine Being is possible, whereas in other classes the teaching concerned the actual descent of the Logos, the Sun Word, the essence of the Light in the Aura of the Sun Being. In the case of Christ, the descent was infinitely complex and it could be no surprise if more than four men had been needed to understand such a momentous event. But there were four who made efforts to do so. Two of them, the writers of the Gospels of Matthew and Luke, were at pains to

203

portray the nature of the personality who grew towards the descending Sun Being. Matthew concerned himself particularly with the physical body and the etheric body, Luke with the astral body and Ego-bearer. Mark, on the other hand, described the Sun Aura, the spiritual Light that pervades cosmic space and streamed into the figure of Christ Jesus. Hence his Gospel begins immediately with the Baptism, when the Light of Worlds descended. The Gospel of John describes the soul of the Sun Spirit, the Logos, the Sun Word, the inner aspect. The Gospel of John is therefore the most deeply inward of the four.

The facts were apportioned and the complex Being of Christ Jesus described from four sides. All four Evangelists tell of the Christ in Jesus of Nazareth. But each of these four writers of the Gospels is impelled to adhere to his starting-point, from whence came the clairvoyant insight enabling him to give some description of this complex Being. - And now we will repeat what has been said in order to impress it more firmly upon our minds. Matthew directs his gaze to the birth of the Solomon Jesus and follows the gradual preparation of the physical body and etheric body, perceiving how these sheaths are discarded by Zarathustra and how the qualities and faculties he had acquired in the physical body and etheric body of the Solomon Jesus are carried over by him into the Jesus of the Luke Gospel. The writer of the Matthew Gospel must then extend his gaze to what had not concerned him at the beginning. But his attention is directed first and foremost to the features that had formed his starting-point: the destinies of the faculties that passed over from the Solomon Jesus into the Nathan Jesus. His gaze is directed less to the pristine purity of the astral body and Ego-bearing principle in the Luke Jesus and more to what had passed over from the Jesus with whom he is chiefly concerned. And when the writer of the Matthew Gospel is speaking of the Sun Being who has descended, again he is more mindful of the faculties possessed by Jesus of Nazareth because the physical body and etheric body had been developed by the Solomon Jesus. These faculties and qualities were naturally still perceptible in Christ, and the writer of the Matthew Gospel describes with particular exactitude this aspect of Christ Jesus which was of primary importance to him and upon which his attention had been focused at the outset.

The writer of the Gospel of Mark directs his attention from the beginning to the Sun Spirit descending from heaven. His gaze is focused, not upon any Being of an earthly nature but upon the Sun Spirit who lived and worked in the physical body. The physical figure on the Earth is only the means whereby the indwelling Sun Spirit can be portrayed. Hence Mark draws special attention to how the forces and powers of the Sun Spirit take effect. Therefore although in the Gospels of Matthew and Mark a great deal seems to be identical, their standpoints are different. Matthew deals more especially with the aspect of the sheaths and draws particular attention to the

204

later manifestations of qualities and faculties that were already potentially present in early life; and he writes in a way that reveals the effects produced by these qualities. The writer of the Mark Gospel, on the other hand, uses the physical figure of Jesus merely as a means of showing what can be wrought on Earth by the Sun Spirit. This is everywhere apparent. If you want to understand the Gospels in detail, you must bear in mind that the attention of each Evangelist turns ever and again to the aspect with which he was primarily concerned. The writer of the Luke Gospel, as would be expected, has particularly in mind the astral body and Ego-bearing principle, that is to say, not what the Being experiences as an outer, physical personality, but in the astral body as the bearer of feelings and sentient perceptions. The astral body is also the bearer of creative faculties, of compassion, of mercy. Bearing as He did the astral body of the Nathan Jesus, Christ Jesus was the very embodiment of these qualities. Thus the eyes of Luke are directed from the beginning to all the manifestations of compassion, to whatever Christ Jesus is able to accomplish because He bears the astral body of the Nathan Jesus.

And the gaze of the writer of the John Gospel is focused upon the very highest Power that can work on the Earth, upon the inmost Being and nature of the Sun Spirit, brought down through the instrumentality of Jesus. John is not concerned primarily with the physical body; his eyes are turned to the Highest, to the Sun Logos, and the physical Jesus is for him simply a means for perceiving how the Sun Logos works and acts in humanity. His gaze too is fixed upon those things with which he was concerned at the beginning. The physical body and the etheric body are sheaths out of which we pass during sleep. Both these members of human nature contain forces outpoured by divine-spiritual Beings who for millions upon millions of years have been working at the building of this temple - the temple of the physical body. We have lived in this temple since the Lemurian epoch, causing its steady deterioration. But it came to us originally as a product of the Saturn, Sun and Moon periods of evolution. Divine Beings were living and weaving in it. We can say of our physical body that it is a temple built by the Gods who have fashioned it out of solid matter to be our dwelling place. The etheric body contains the finer substances of man's constitution but owing to the Luciferic and Ahrimanic influences they are imperceptible to him. Elements belonging to the Sun are also present in the etheric body; into it resounds the Music of the Spheres, that which is perceptible behind the physical as a manifestation of the Gods. Hence we can say: Beings of exalted rank live in the etheric body, Beings who are akin to the Sun Gods. - The physical body and the etheric body, therefore, are to be regarded as the most perfect members of human nature. When, during sleep, we have passed out of them, when they have fallen away from us, they are pervaded and worked through by divine Beings.

As he had done from the beginning, the writer of the Matthew Gospel was bound to give his chief attention to the physical body in the case of Christ Jesus too. But the first physical body was no longer in existence, having been abandoned, as we have heard, in the twelfth year of life. The divine element, the forces and powers, had passed (together with the Zarathustra-Individuality) from that body into the other physical body - the physical body of the Nathan Jesus. The perfection of this physical body of the Being now to be known as Jesus of Nazareth was due to the fact that it was filled with the forces and powers that had passed into it from the body of the Solomon Jesus. Let us now picture the writer of the Matthew Gospel turning his gaze to the dying Jesus on the Cross. His gaze had always been directed to the aspect most important to him, to what he had taken as his starting-point. At the Crucifixion the spiritual forsakes the physical body and therewith also the divine forces that had been taken over into it. The writer of the Matthew Gospel directs his gaze to the separation of the inner nature of Christ Jesus from this divine element in His physical constitution. The words that always rang out in the ancient Mysteries when the spiritual nature of a man emerged from the physical body in order to have vision in the spiritual world, were these: `My God, my God, how thou hast glorified me!' - The writer of the Matthew Gospel, with his attention fixed on the physical body, changes these words to: `My God, my God why hast thou forsaken me!' Thou hast gone from me, hast abandoned me (Matthew 27: 46). - The chief attention of the writer of the Matthew Gospel has been fixed upon this aspect."

Previously it was shown from Steiner's lectures that the Christ Being did not become completely united with the body of Jesus of Nazareth until the final moments on the Cross. This is confirmed by Steiner in his lecture cycle, "On the Fifth Gospel." Other lectures may seem to say that the Christ Being separated from the body of Jesus of Nazareth prior to the Death on the Cross such as lecture IX in his lecture cycle on the Gospel of St. Mark as well as the passage immediately above from Lecture XII on the Gospel of St. Matthew. Steiner uses the term, 'inner nature of Christ', to which it should be remembered that the 'inner nature' of the Christ Spirit, the Christ Ego, did stay fully incarnated within the body of Jesus of Nazareth on through to the very last moments on the Cross. The physical body became separated from the divine element. The cosmic forces that were in His physical constitution, that is, the Cosmic Principle, the Sun and Zodiacal Aura of the Christ that once enveloped and permeated the body of Jesus of Nazareth takes leave of the body. Steiner says here that, "the spiritual forsakes the physical." It is the spiritual aura, the fleeing youth, that now becomes ever more separated from the body of Jesus of Nazareth while the Christ Being was united within this physical body all the way through to the point of physical death. The Christ Being remained fully united with this death process to the very end. The descent into the human Form was only completed when the Christ Being became fully incarnated into the marrow of the human skeleton of Jesus of Nazareth. This was not fully consummated until the very final moments up to the time of His Death on the Cross.

Continuing the above discourse from Steiner: "The writer of the Mark Gospel describes the coming of the outer forces and powers of the Sun Aura, how the Sun Aura, the body of the Sun Being, unites with the etheric body. The etheric body was in the same situation as our etheric body is during sleep. As in our own case the outer forces pass out with us when we sleep, so did they at the physical death of Jesus. Hence the same words are found in the Gospel of Mark." (Mark 15: 34).

In the above, Steiner is speaking of the forces of the Cosmic Principle, the Aura of the Christ Being that passes out of the body of Jesus of Nazareth when He said, "My God, my God why hast thou forsaken me!", and not of the Macrocosmic Ego of the Christ Being. Steiner continues: "The writer of the Luke Gospel also directs his attention at the Death of Christ Jesus to what was his concern at the beginning: the astral body and Ego-bearing principle. Hence the words he uses are different. His chief attention is directed to the astral body in which at this moment compassion and mercy and love reach their greatest intensity. Hence the words: `Father, forgive them; for they know not what they do' (Luke 23: 34). These are words of love that could issue only from the astral body to which the writer of the Luke Gospel has been pointing from the beginning. And it is upon these qualities of humility and resignation to God's Will which have here reached their greatest intensity and issue from the astral body, that Luke directs his gaze at the end. Hence the words in this Gospel: `Father, into thy hands I commend my Spirit.' (Luke 23: 46).

The John Gospel describes what must be fulfilled by man in Earth-existence: the ordering of existence according to the Sun Word. Hence his gaze is directed mainly to the ordering of life as proclaimed from the Cross on Golgotha. He describes how in this hour Christ institutes a brotherhood of a higher kind than that based on blood-kinship. Brotherhood in its earlier forms arose from ties of blood. Mary was the mother of the child through blood-relationship. But soul united with soul in love - that is what was instituted through Christ Jesus. To the disciple whom He loved He gives, not the one who was the mother by blood, but He gives him the one who is his true mother in the spirit. And so the words resound from the Cross with their new meaning: `Behold thy son!' - `Behold thy mother.' (John 19: 26-27). The principle inherit in the life-ether by which the ordering of life is determined and community of a new kind established - that is what streamed into the Earth through Christ's Deed.

There is one supreme reality, the reality of Christ Himself behind everything the Evangelists describe. But each of them writes from the viewpoint he adopted at the beginning. Each had necessarily to direct his seership to what his particular preparation enabled him to understand; and the rest passed him by. We shall now admit that it is not because this momentous event is described from four different sides that it seems full of contradictions; on the contrary, we realize that we can in some measure come to understand it only through being able to gather the four sides into a whole. Why it is that Peter's avowal stands in the Matthew Gospel only and not in the others then seems entirely natural. Mark describes Christ as the Sun Power, as the Universal, Cosmic Power working into the Earth - but in a new way. He is therefore speaking of the direct effects wrought by the Sun Aura. And the Luke Gospel describes the inmost nature of Christ Jesus, especially, therefore, the astral body, the factor of individuality, how man lives in and for himself; for in the astral body man lives entirely within himself; it is there that he functions in his own essential nature. The urge to cultivate a communal life where a man enters into relationship with other men does not lie primarily in the astral body, but in the etheric body. Hence there is no opportunity or inducement for Luke to write about the founding of any community. And certainly there is none in the case of the writer of the John Gospel who is concerned first and foremost with the Ego-nature. On the other hand there is every inducement for the writer of the Matthew Gospel who is telling of Christ Jesus as Man, to describe happenings that are possible because God was once present in a human Being. What God as Man among men can establish in the way of relationships between human Beings, in the way of communities - this would necessarily be described by the Evangelist who tells of Christ Jesus in His essentially human aspect. The attention of this Evangelist has from the beginning been focused upon how Christ works as Man through the faculties derived from the physical body and the etheric body. If we have insight into these things it will seem quite natural that the words which have given rise to so much controversy occur only in the Matthew Gospel: `Thou art Peter, and upon this rock I will build my church', i.e. my community."

Concluding the lecture cycle on the Gospel of St. Matthew: "It is made absolutely clear that Christ was once present in a human physical body, that this event was not an event only, but an active cause, an Impulse. The Sun Word, the Sun Aura, once spoken of by Zarathustra as a reality outside and beyond the Earth, became through the Christ-Jesus-life a power that is and will remain united with the Earth. Something different from anything that had been present before that life was now united with the Earth."

"Spiritual Science should enable us to understand that since that time the Sun Aura has been united with the Earth Aura and that this can be seen by one whose eyes of spirit are opened; furthermore that this Sun Aura in the Earth Aura which became visible to Paul, can also be `heard' when the inner ears are open and the Sun Word becomes audible, as it did to Lazarus - the one initiated by Christ Jesus Himself. Spiritual Science exists in order to prepare us to know this in all reality. Spiritual Science is an interpreter of what has come to pass in the spiritual evolution of the world and for this reason will strive to give effect to what Christ Jesus Himself wished to establish, according to the Matthew Gospel."

"What is it that strikes us particularly about the Matthew Gospel, where from the very beginning the manhood of Christ Jesus is brought into prominence? Great though the distance assuredly is between an ordinary man on Earth and the one who was able to receive the Christ Being into himself, nevertheless the Matthew Gospel shows us - when we accept it with all humility - the dignity of man and what he may become. For although our own nature may be far, far removed from that of Jesus of Nazareth, we may yet say to ourselves that the human nature we bear is able to receive into itself the Son of God, the Son of the living God. Herein lies the promise that the Son of God will henceforth remain united with spiritual Earth-existence and that when Earth-existence has reached its goal all men will be filled with the substance and Being of Christ in so far as they themselves have inwardly desired this. We need humility to harbor such an ideal. For if we harbor it without humility it gives rise to arrogance, to pride; we think only about what we can be as men reminding ourselves all too seldom of how little we have hitherto achieved. This Ideal must be approached with humility. Then it appears so great, so mighty, so majestic, so impressive in its brilliance, that in itself it is an exhortation to humility. And when we are aware of the truth of this Ideal, no matter how meager our forces may be they will bear us to ever higher stages along the path to our divine goal."

XIV

The Gospel of Luke

Continuing this study of the Christ and His relationship with the Apostles, John the Baptist and Lazarus the following is from Lecture 1 of Steiner's cycle on the Gospel of St. Luke: "If with this in mind we turn our attention to the four Gospels, we may say that the Gospel of St. John is written from the vantage-point of one who in the fullest sense was an Initiate, cognizant at the stage of Intuition of the Mysteries of the supersensible world, and who therefore describes the Christ Event as revealed by the vision of Intuition. But if close attention is paid to the distinctive characteristics of St. John's Gospel it will have to be admitted that the features standing out most clearly are presented from the standpoint of Inspiration and Intuition, while everything originating from the pictures of Imagination is shadowy and lacks definition. Thus if we disregard what was still revealed to him through Imagination, we may call the writer of St. John's Gospel the messenger of everything relating to the Christ Event that is vouchsafed to one endowed with the power of apprehending the inner Word at the stage of Intuition. Hence he describes the Mysteries of Christ's Kingdom as receiving their character through the inner Word, or Logos. Knowledge through Inspiration and Intuition is the source of the Gospel of St. John.

It is different in the case of the other three Gospels, and not one of their writers expressed his message as clearly as did the writer of the Gospel of St. Luke. In a short but remarkable preface it is said, in effect, that many others had previously attempted to collect and set forth the stories in circulation concerning the events in Palestine; but that for the sake of accuracy and order the writer of this Gospel is now undertaking to present the things which . . . and now come significant words . . . could be understood by those who from the beginning were `eye-witnesses and servants (ministers) of the Word' - that is the usual rendering. The aim of the writer of this Gospel is therefore to communicate what eye-witnesses - it would be better to say `seers' - and servants of the Word had to say. In the sense of St. Luke's Gospel, `seers' are men who through Imaginative Cognition can penetrate into the world of pictures and there behold the Christ Event; people specially trained to perceive these Imaginations are seers with accurate and clear vision at the same time as being `servants of the Word' - a significant phrase - and the writer of St. Luke's Gospel uses their communications as a foundation. He does not say `possessors' of the word, because such persons would have reached the stage of Inspiration in the fullest sense; he says `servants' of the Word - people who could count less upon Inspirations than upon Imaginations in their own knowledge but for whom communications from the world of Inspiration were nevertheless available. The results of Inspirational Cognition were communicated to them and they could proclaim what their inspired teachers had made known to them. They were `servants', not `possessors' of the Word.

Thus the Gospel of St. Luke is founded upon the communications of seers, themselves knowers of the world of Imagination; they are those who, having learnt to express their visions of that world through means made possible by their inspired teachers, had themselves become `servants of the Word'."

Communication with and perception into the spiritual worlds had declined over the ages. This too was something which Christ was to restore to humanity. In Lecture II we read: "The cognitive faculty of mankind has developed gradually. Attention has repeatedly been drawn to the fact that in the Atlantean epoch a large proportion of humanity was clairvoyant and able to gaze into the spiritual worlds, and that certain remnants of this old clairvoyance were still present in post-Atlantean times. After the Atlantean epoch, in the periods of the civilizations of ancient India, Persia, Egypt and Chaldea - even as late as the Greco-Latin age - there were numbers of human Beings, many more than modern man would ever imagine, who possessed the heritage of this old clairvoyance; the astral plane was open to them and they could see into the hidden depths of existence. Perception of man's etheric body was quite usual in the Greco-Latin age; numbers of people were able to see the human head surrounded by an etheric cloud that has gradually become entirely concealed within the head. But humanity was to advance to a form of knowledge acquired through the outer senses and through the spiritual faculties connected with the senses. Man was gradually to emerge altogether from the spiritual world and to engage in pure sense-observation, in intellectual, logical thinking. By degrees he was to make his way to non-clairvoyant cognition, because he must pass through this stage in order to regain clairvoyant knowledge in the future. But such knowledge will then be united with the fruits of cognition based upon the senses and the intellect."

In Steiner's lecture cycle on the Gospel of St. Luke significant focus is placed upon the birth of the Nathan Jesus. The presence of the Buddha, however, is paramount in the birth of the Nathan Jesus. From Lecture II: "It was necessary for us today to look back to what happened six hundred years before our era because we shall neither understand the path of Christianity nor what is indicated about that path, above all by the writer of the Gospel of St. Luke, unless we follow evolution backwards from the events in Palestine to the Sermon at Benares. Since Buddha attained that rank there was no need for him to return to the Earth; since then he has been a spiritual Being, living

211

in the spiritual world and participating in everything that has transpired on Earth. When the greatest of all happenings on the Earth was about to come to pass, there appeared to the shepherds in the fields a Being from spiritual heights who made the proclamation recorded in the Gospel of St. Luke. Then, together with the Angel, there suddenly appeared a `heavenly host'. The `heavenly host' was the picture of the glorified Buddha, seen by the shepherds in vision; he was the Bodhisattva of ancient times, the Being in his spiritual form who for thousands and thousands of years had brought to men the message of compassion and love. Now, after his last incarnation on the Earth, he soared in spiritual heights and appeared to the shepherds together with the Angel who had announced to them the Event of Palestine.

These are the findings of spiritual investigation. It was the Bodhisattva of old who now, in the glory of Buddhahood, appeared to the shepherds. From the Akashic Chronicle we learn that in Palestine, in the `City of David', a child was born to parents descended from the priestly line of the House of David. This child - I say it with emphasis - born of parents of whom the father at any rate was descended from the priestly line of the House of David, was to be shone upon from the very day of birth by the power radiating from Buddha in the spiritual world. We look with the shepherds into the manger where `Jesus of Nazareth', as he is usually called, was born, and see the radiance above the little child; we know that in this picture is expressed the power of the Bodhisattva who became Buddha - the power that had formerly streamed to men and, working now upon humanity from the spiritual world, accomplished its greatest deed by shedding its luster upon the child born at Bethlehem.

When the Individuality whose power now rayed down from spiritual heights upon the child of parents belonging to David's line was born in India long ago - when the Buddha to be was born as Bodhisattva - the whole momentous significance of the events described today was revealed to a sage living at that time, and what he beheld in the spiritual world caused that sage - Asita was his name - to go to the royal palace to look for the little Bodhisattva-child. When he saw the babe he foretold his mighty mission as Buddha, predicting, to the father's dismay, that the child would not rule over his kingdom, but would become a Buddha. Then Asita began to weep, and when asked whether misfortune threatened the child, he answered: `No, I am weeping because I am so old that I shall not live to see the day when this Savior, the Bodhisattva, will walk the Earth as Buddha!' Asita did not live to see the Bodhisattva become Buddha and there was good reason for his grief at that time. But the same Asita who had seen the Bodhisattva as a babe in the palace of King Suddhodana, was born again as the personality who, in the Gospel of St. Luke, is referred to as Simeon in the scene of the presentation in the temple. We are told that Simeon was inspired by the Spirit to go into the temple where the child was brought to him (Luke 2: 25-32). Simeon was the same Being who, as Asita, had wept because in that incarnation he would not be able to see the Bodhisattva attaining Buddhahood. But it was granted to him to witness the further stage in the development of this Individuality, and having 'the Holy Spirit upon him' he was able to perceive, at the presentation in the temple, the radiance of the glorified Bodhisattva above the head of the Jesus-child of the House of David. Then he could say to himself: 'Now you need no longer grieve, for what you did not live to see at that earlier time, you now behold: the glory of the Savior shining above this babe. Lord, now let thy servant die in peace!' "

In Lecture III Steiner then takes up the discussion of the Nirmanakaya of Buddha and its relation to the astral body of the Nathan Jesus: "Of a Being such as the Bodhisattva who became Buddha, we said - and this is the teaching of all who know: When a Being passes through this stage he has had his last incarnation on the Earth, for his whole nature is contained within a human body. Such a Being never again incarnates in this sense. Hence when the Buddha became aware of the significance of his present existence, he could say: 'This is my last incarnation; I shall not again incarnate on the Earth!' - It would, however, be erroneous to think that such a Being then withdraws altogether from Earth-existence. True, he does not enter directly into a physical body but he assumes another body - of an astral or etheric nature - and so continues to send his influences into the world. The way in which such a Being who has passed through the last incarnation belonging to his own destiny continues to work in the world, may be understood by thinking of the following facts.

An ordinary human Being, consisting of physical body, etheric body, astral body and Ego, can be permeated by such a Being. It is possible for a Being of this rank, who no longer descends into a physical body but still has an astral body, to be membered into the astral body of another human Being. This man may well become a personality of importance, for the forces of a Being who has already passed through his last incarnation on the Earth are now working in him. Thus an astral Being unites with the astral nature of some individual on the Earth. Such a union may take place in a most complicated way. When the Buddha appeared to the shepherds in the picture of the 'heavenly host', he was not in a physical body but in an astral body. He had assumed a body in which he could still send his influences to the Earth. Thus in the case of a Being who has become a Buddha, we distinguish three bodies:

1. The body he has before he attains Buddhahood, when he is still working from above as a Bodhisattva; it is a body that does not contain in itself all the powers at his command; he still lives in spiritual heights and is linked with his earlier mission as was the Bodhisattva before his mission became the Buddha's mission. As

213

long as such a Being is living in a body of this nature, his body is called a `Dharmakaya'.

2. The body which such a Being builds as his own and through which he brings to expression, in the physical body, everything he has within him. This body is called the `body of perfection', `Sambhogakaya'.

3. The body which such a Being assumes after he has passed through the stage of perfection and can work from above in the way described. This body is called a `Nirmanakaya'.

We can therefore say that the `Nirmanakaya' of Buddha appeared to the shepherds in the picture of the angelic host. Buddha appeared in the radiance of his Nirmanakaya and revealed himself in this way to the shepherds. But he was to find further ways of working into the events in Palestine at this crucial point of time. To understand this we must briefly recall what is known to us from other lectures about the nature of man. Spiritual Science speaks of several `births'. At what is called `physical birth' the human Being strips off, as it were, the maternal physical sheath; at the seventh year he strips off the etheric sheath which envelops him until the change of teeth just as the maternal physical sheath enveloped him until physical birth. At puberty - about the fourteenth or fifteenth year in the modern epoch - the human Being strips off the astral sheath that is around him until then. It is not until the seventh year that the human etheric body is born outwardly as a free body; the astral body is born at puberty, when the outer astral sheath is cast off.

Let us now consider what it is that is described at puberty. In Palestine and the neighboring regions this point of time occurs normally at about the twelfth year - rather earlier than in lands farther to the West. In the ordinary way this protective astral sheath is cast off and given over to the outer astral world. In the case of the child who descended from the priestly line of the House of David, however, something different happened. At the age of twelve the astral sheath was cast off but did not dissolve in the universal astral world. Just as it was, as the protective astral sheath of the young boy, with all the vitalizing forces that had streamed into it between the change of teeth and puberty, it now united with the Nirmanakaya of Buddha. The spiritual body that had once appeared to the shepherds as the radiant angelic host united with the astral sheath released from the twelve-year-old Jesus, united with all the forces through which the freshness of youth is maintained during the period between the second dentition and puberty. The Nirmanakaya which shone upon the Nathan Jesus-child from birth onwards united with the astral sheath detached from this child at puberty; it became one with this sheath and was thereby rejuvenated. Through this rejuvenation, what the Buddha had formerly given to the world could be manifest again in the Jesus-child. Hence the boy was able to speak with all the simplicity of childhood about the lofty teachings of compassion and love to which we

214

have referred today. When Jesus was found in the temple he was speaking in a way that astonished those around him, because he was enveloped by the Nirmanakaya of Buddha, refreshed as from a fountain of youth by the boy's astral sheath.

These are the facts which can become known to the spiritual investigator and which the writer of the Gospel of St. Luke has indicated in the remarkable scene when a sudden change came over the twelve-year-old Jesus in the temple. We must grasp what it was that had happened and then we shall understand why the boy no longer spoke as he had formerly been wont to speak. It so happened that at this very time, King Kanisha of Tibet summoned a synod in India and proclaimed ancient Buddhism to be the orthodox religion. But in the meantime Buddha himself had advanced! He had absorbed the forces of the protective astral sheath of the Jesus-child and was thereby able to speak in a new way to the hearts and souls of men. The Gospel of St. Luke contains Buddhism in a new form, as though springing from a fountain of youth; hence it expresses the religion of compassion and love in a form comprehensible to the simplest souls."

In Lecture IV the mystery of the birth of the Nathan Jesus is examined further as well as its relation to the Individuality of Zarathustra: "We can well imagine that this Individuality (Zarathustra) rose to higher and higher stages during his subsequent incarnations, becoming more and more mature, more and more capable of the greatest sacrifices on behalf of humanity. Those of you who have heard other lectures of mine will know that Zarathustra gave up his astral body to Hermes, the leader of the Egyptian civilization, and his etheric body to Moses, the leader of the Hebrews. Such deeds can be accomplished only by a soul of very advanced development. Zarathustra was then reborn in Chaldea six hundred years before our era (at the time of Buddha in India) and worked there as the great teacher `Nazarathos' or `Zaratas', who was also the teacher of Pythagoras. All this was within the power of the former leader and inaugurator of the ancient Persian civilization. Since the days of ancient Persia he had become more and more mature, but when Buddhism needed rejuvenation this task was not within his powers, as you will understand from the foregoing. It was not possible for him to provide youthful forces, developed under childlike conditions until puberty, which could then be given over to the Nirmanakaya of Buddha. Precisely because he had reached such a high stage of development it would not have been possible for Zarathustra to develop as a child at the beginning of our era in such a way that the required results would have been forthcoming. Were we to review all the Individualities whose powers were unfolded at that time, we should find no single one capable of furnishing, in his twelfth year, such forces as were needed for the rejuvenation of Buddhism. Zarathustra was a great and unique Individuality, an altogether exceptional case. Yet not even Zarathustra himself could have ensouled the body of Jesus up to the time of puberty in such a way as to enable the discarded astral sheath to unite with the Nirmanakaya of Buddha."

In Lecture V Steiner then speaks of the quickening of the Ego of the unborn John the Baptist when Mary and Elizabeth meet: "It will seem strange to you that a soul without a really developed Ego could be guided from the great Mother-Lodge to a certain place. But the same Ego that was withheld from the Jesus of the Gospel of St. Luke was bestowed upon the body of John the Baptist; thus the soul-Being in Jesus of the Gospel of St. Luke and the Ego-Being in John the Baptist were inwardly related from the beginning. Now when the human embryo develops in the body of the mother, the Ego unites with the other members of the human organism in the third week, but does not come into operation until the last months before birth and then only gradually. Not until then does the Ego become active as an inner force; in a normal case, when an Ego quickens an embryo, we have to do with an Ego that has come from earlier incarnations. In the case of John, however, the Ego in question was inwardly related to the soul-Being of the Nathan Jesus. Hence according to the Gospel of St. Luke, the mother of Jesus went to the mother of John the Baptist when the latter was in the sixth month of her pregnancy, and the embryo that in other cases is quickened by its own Ego was here quickened through the medium of the other embryo. The child in the body of Elizabeth begins to move when the mother bearing the Nathan Jesus-child approaches; and it is the Ego through which the child in the other mother (Elizabeth) is quickened. (Luke 1: 39-44). Such was the deep connection between the Being who was to bring about the fusion of the two spiritual streams and the other who was to announce His coming!"

Earlier it was mentioned that John the Baptist was comparable to a Boddhisattva in that he was not fully incarnated in his body. The same could be said for his incarnation as Elijah. From Lecture VI on the Gospel of St. Luke: "The fact that some men lived with part of their Being in the spiritual world was known to all religions and cognate modes of thought. It was known that there were Beings destined to work on the Earth, for whom human embodiment was too restricted to contain the whole Individuality. In the religious thought of Western Asia this kind of union of a higher Individuality with a physical body was called `being filled with the Holy Spirit'. This is quite a definite, technical expression. In the language of those religions it would have been said of a Being such as a Bodhisattva while incarnated on Earth that he was `filled with the Holy Spirit' - meaning that the forces and powers possessed by such a Being were not fully contained within his human organism and that something spiritual must work from outside. Thus it might with truth be said that the Buddha, in his previous incarnations, was `filled with the Holy Spirit'.

Having grasped this we shall be able to understand what is said at the beginning of the Gospel of St. Luke. We know that in the etheric body of the

Jesus-child of the Nathan line of the House of David there was present the hitherto untouched part of the etheric body that had been withdrawn from humanity at the time of the `Fall into sin'. The etheric substance withheld from Adam had been preserved and was sent down into this child. This was necessary in order that a Being so young and entirely untouched by any experiences of earthly evolution might be in existence and assimilate all that he was destined to assimilate. Would an ordinary human Being who had passed through incarnations since the Lemurian Age have been able to receive the overshadowing power of Buddha's Nirmanakaya? No indeed! A human body of great perfection had to be made available, one that could only be produced through part of the etheric substance of Adam - untouched by all earthly influences - being united with the etheric body of this Jesus-child. This etheric substance was imbued with the forces that had worked upon Earth evolution before the Fall and now, in the Jesus-child, their power was immeasurably enhanced. This made it possible for the mysterious influence referred to in the lecture yesterday to be exercised by the mother of the Nathan Jesus upon the mother of the Baptist - that is to say upon John himself before he was born."

"Thus it was the Nirmanakaya of Buddha which now stirred the Ego-force of John into activity, having the same effect as spiritual forces that had formerly worked upon Elijah. At certain times the Being known as Elijah had been rapt in states of ecstasy; then the God spoke, filling his Ego with a force which could be communicated to the outer world. Now again a spiritual force was present - the Nirmanakaya of Buddha hovering above the head of the Nathan Jesus; this force worked upon Elizabeth when John was to be born, stimulated within her the embryo of John in the sixth month of pregnancy, and wakened the Ego. But being nearer to the Earth this force now worked as more than an inspiration; it had an actual formative effect upon the Ego of John. Under the influence of the visit of her who is there called `Mary', the Ego of John the Baptist awoke into activity. The Nirmanakaya of Buddha was here working upon the Ego of the former Elijah - now the Ego of John the Baptist - wakening it and penetrating right into the physical substance.

What may we now expect?

Even as the words of power once spoken by Elijah in the ninth century before our era were in truth `God's words', and the actions performed by his hands `God's actions', it was now to be the same in the case of John the Baptist, inasmuch as what had been present in Elijah had come to life again. The Nirmanakaya of Buddha worked as an inspiration into the Ego of John the Baptist. That which manifested itself to the shepherds and hovered above the head of the Nathan Jesus extended its powers into John the Baptist, whose preaching was primarily the re-awakened preaching of Buddha. This fact is in the highest degree noteworthy and cannot fail to make a deep impression upon us when we recall the sermon at Benares wherein Buddha spoke of the suffering in life and the release from it through the Eightfold Path. He often expanded a sermon by saying in effect: `Hitherto you have had the teaching of the Brahmans; they ascribe their origin to Brahma himself and claim to be superior to other men because of this noble descent. These Brahmans claim that a man's worth is determined by his descent, but I say to you: 'Man's worth is determined by what he makes of himself, not by what is in him by virtue of his descent. Judged by the great wisdom of the world, man's worth lies in whatever he makes of himself as an Individual!' Buddha aroused the wrath of the Brahmans because he emphasized the individual quality in men, saying: `Verily it is of no avail to call yourselves Brahmans; what matters is that each one of you, through his own personal qualities and efforts should make of himself a purified Individual.' Although not word for word, such was the gist of many of Buddha's sermons. And he would often expand this teaching by showing how, when a man understands the world of suffering, he can feel compassion, can become a comforter and a helper, how he shares the lot of others because he knows that he is feeling the same suffering and the same pain.

The Buddha, now in his Nirmanakaya, shed his radiance upon the Nathan Jesus-child and continued his preaching inasmuch as he let the words resound from the mouth of John the Baptist. These words were spoken under the inspiration of the Buddha and it is like a continuation of his former preaching when, for example, John says: `You who set so much store by your descent from those who in the service of the spiritual powers are called Children of the Serpent, and plead the Wisdom of the Serpent, who led you to this? You believe that you bring forth fruits of repentance when you merely say: We have Abraham for our father' . . . (now, however, John continues that actual preaching of Buddha) . . . `Say not that you have Abraham for your father, but be good men, whatever your place in the world. A good man can be raised up from the stones upon which your feet tread. Verily, God is able of these stones to raise up children unto Abraham' . . . And then again he says: `He that hath two coats, let him give to him that hath none!' Men came to him and asked: `Master, what shall we do?' - exactly as the monks once came to Buddha. All these sayings seem to be like utterances of Buddha himself, or a continuation of them. (Luke 3: 7-12)."

"To refuse to hear Buddha's utterances from the mouth of John the Baptist is like someone who had seen the seed of a rose-tree and later on, when the tree has grown and bears flowers, refuses to believe that the tree grew from the seed, insisting that it is something different! The truth is that what was once alive in the seed now blossoms in the rose-tree. And the living essence of the Sermon at Benares blossomed in the preaching of John the Baptist by the Jordan."

In Lecture VII Steiner speaks of the time in the Temple when the Zarathustra Ego incarnates into the body of the Nathan Jesus: "It must be borne in mind that up to the twelfth year the physical body was that of the Nathan Jesus, but that after the twelfth year the Ego of Zarathustra was living in that body. What does this mean? It means that from the twelfth year onwards, this mature Ego was working upon the sentient (astral) body, the sentient soul and the mind-soul of the Nathan Jesus, elaborating these members in a way possible only to an Ego of great maturity - an Ego that had undergone the destinies of the Zarathustra-Individuality through many incarnations. We therefore meet with the wonderful fact that the Ego of Zarathustra passed into the body of the Nathan Jesus in the twelfth year of life and elaborated the faculties of the soul to the highest degree of excellence. Thus there developed a sentient body able to gaze into the Cosmos and experience something of the spiritual nature of Ahura Mazdao; there developed a sentient soul able to harbor the knowledge and wisdom based on the teaching concerning Ahura Mazdao; and there developed a mind-soul able to apprehend, to formulate in intelligible concepts and words, that which men had hitherto been able to acquire only through spiritual currents flowing into them from outside.

The Nathan Jesus, having within him the Zarathustra-Ego, lived on until his thirtieth year was approaching. The event that had occurred when he was twelve, when his inmost nature was filled with a new Egohood, now took place again - but this time on an infinitely more sublime, more universal scale. Towards the thirtieth year the Zarathustra-Ego had accomplished its work in the soul of the Nathan Jesus; the faculties of this soul had been developed to the highest possible degree and the mission of the Zarathustra-Ego was thus fulfilled. Having instilled into the soul all the faculties he had acquired through his own previous incarnations, Zarathustra could declare: `My task is now accomplished!' - and a moment came when his Ego left the body of the Nathan Jesus. The Zarathustra-Ego had lived in the body of the Solomon Jesus until the twelfth year. No further development in earthly existence would thereafter have been possible for this boy. Because the Zarathustra-Ego had gone out of him, his development came to a standstill at the point reached at that time, although exceptional maturity had been attained owing to the presence of such a highly advanced Ego. Anyone observing the Solomon Jesus-child would have found him prematurely advanced to a conspicuous degree; but from the moment the Zarathustra-Ego left him he came to a standstill and could make no further progress. And when - comparatively soon - the mother of the Nathan Jesus died and the spiritual part of her Being was translated into the spiritual world, she took with her what was of eternal value and formative power in the Solomon-Jesus child. This child also died - at about the same time as the mother of the Nathan Jesus."

"Having indwelt the body of the Nathan Jesus from the twelfth to the thirtieth year, the Zarathustra-Ego was henceforth outside that body and

219

another Being descended into it. This happened, as all the Gospels relate, at the Baptism by John in the Jordan, when an Ego of untold sublimity entered into the Nathan Jesus in place of the Zarathustra-Ego. In the lectures on the Gospel of St. John, attention was drawn to the fact that `baptism' in those olden days was something very different from the mere symbol which it became later on. It was also enacted differently by John the Baptist. The body of one who was baptized was completely submerged in the water. You know from preparatory lectures that a definite experience may be connected with such a happening. Even in everyday existence it may happen that when a man is in danger of drowning, or sustains a violent shock, a tableau of his life hitherto appears before him. This is because something that otherwise takes place only after death, occurs momentarily: the etheric body is lifted out of the physical body and is freed from its power. This happened to most of those who were baptized by John, and in a very special way to the Nathan Jesus. His etheric body was drawn out - and during that moment the sublime Being we call the Christ descended into his body.

Thus from the time of the Baptism, the Nathan Jesus was filled with the Christ Being as is indicated in the words contained in the earlier Gospel records: `This is my well-beloved Son; this day I have begotten Him!' - meaning: the Son of Heaven, the Christ, is now begotten - begotten of the all-pervading Godhead and received into the body and whole constitution of the Nathan Jesus who had been prepared to receive the seed from heavenly heights. `This is my well-beloved Son; this day I have begotten Him!' - These were the words contained in the earlier manuscripts and this is how they ought still to stand in the Gospels. (Luke 3: 22).

Who is this Being who united at that time with the etheric body of the Nathan Jesus? The Christ Being cannot be understood if we think of Earth evolution alone. The Christ is the Leader of those spiritual Beings who left with the Sun when it separated from the Earth and established for themselves this higher sphere of action in order to work upon the Earth from the outside. If we think back to the pre-Christian period of Earth evolution, from the time of the separation of the Sun until the appearance of Christ, we must say: When men looked up to the Sun with mature faculties they would have recognized the truth of what Zarathustra taught, namely that the light and warmth streaming from the Sun are but the physical vestment of the spiritual Beings behind the Sun's light; for behind the physical phenomena are hidden the spiritual rays of power which stream from the Sun to the Earth. The Leader of all the Beings who send their beneficent influences from the Sun to the Earth is He who was later called Christ. In pre-Christian times, therefore, this Being was not to be sought on Earth but on the Sun. And Zarathustra rightly called Him `Ahura Mazdao', saying in effect: `On the Earth we do not find the Light-Spirit; but when we look up to the Sun we behold the spiritual Being - Ahura Mazdao - who has His habitation there. The light that streams to us is the body of the Sun-Spirit, Ahura Mazdao, even as the human physical body is the body of the human spirit. But in the course of great happenings in the Cosmos this sublime Being drew ever nearer to the Earth-sphere; His approach could be perceived more and more distinctly by clairvoyance, and was unmistakable when in the flame of lightning on Mount Sinai the revelations came to Moses, the great forerunner of Christ Jesus."

"What Being did Moses behold in the burning bush and in the fire on Mount Sinai? He beheld the Christ ! But just as the sunlight is not seen directly but reflected from the Moon, so did Moses see the Christ in reflection. And as we call the sunlight, `moonlight', when we see it reflected from the Moon, Christ was called at that time, Jahve, or Jehovah. Jahve or Jehovah is the reflection of the Christ before He Himself appeared on Earth. Christ announced Himself thus indirectly to a humanity as yet unable to behold Him in His immediate reality, just as the sunlight manifests itself through the rays of the Moon in the otherwise dark night of full Moon. Jahve or Jehovah is the Christ - but seen as reflected light, not directly."

It was through Jehovah, the leading Eloha who acted as the unitary consciousness of the other six Sun Elohim, that the Impulse of Christ had formerly worked. The light of Christ was thereby reflected in the Being of Jehovah in the elliptical, spiritual sphere of the Moon. Jehovah acted as the countenance of the Christ Being until the time when the Christ Being, the Sun-Logos, incarnated into Jesus of Nazareth at the time of the Baptism in the Jordan by John the Baptist. Steiner then had this to say concerning the Gautama Buddha, first as a Bodhisattva, and later as the Buddha and also of Christ's relation to the Lodge of the Twelve Bodhisattvas: "At that time the Bodhisattva too had nearly reached his thirtieth year but he could not then have made it possible for Christ to be received in the fullest sense into a human body. He had first to become sufficiently mature, and this stage was attained through his Buddha-existence. And when, later on, he appeared in the Nirmanakaya, his task was to make the body of the Nathan Jesus - in which he was not himself embodied - fit to receive Vishva Karman, the Christ."

"A survey of the whole of Earth evolution would reveal that there are twelve such Bodhisattvas. They belong to that great community of Spirits which from time to time sends one of the Bodhisattvas to the Earth as a special emissary, as one of the great Teachers. A Lodge of Twelve Bodhisattvas is to be regarded as the Lodge directing all Earth evolution. The concept of `Teacher' familiar to us at lower stages of existence can be applied, in essentials, to these Twelve Bodhisattvas. They are Teachers, the great Inspirers of one portion or another of what mankind has to acquire.

Whence do these Bodhisattvas receive what they have to proclaim from epoch to epoch? - If you were able to look into the great Spirit-Lodge of the Twelve Bodhisattvas you would find that in the midst of the Twelve there is

221

a Thirteenth - one who cannot be called a `Teacher' in the same sense as the Bodhisattvas, but of whom we must say: He is that Being from whom wisdom itself streams as very substance. It is therefore quite correct to speak of the Twelve Bodhisattvas in the great Spirit-Lodge grouped around One who is their Center; they are wrapt in contemplation of the sublime Being from whom there streams what they have then to inculcate into Earth evolution in fulfillment of their missions. Thus there streams from the Thirteenth what the others have to teach. They are the `Teachers', the `Inspirers'; the Thirteenth is Himself the Being of whom the others teach, whom they proclaim from epoch to epoch. This Thirteenth is He whom the ancient Rishis called Vishva Karman, whom Zarathustra called Ahura Mazdao, whom we call the Christ. He is the Leader and Guide of the Great Lodge of the Bodhisattvas. Hence the content of the proclamation made through the whole choir of the Bodhisattvas is the teaching concerning Christ, once called Vishva Karman. The Bodhisattva who became Buddha five to six centuries before our era was endowed with the powers of Vishva Karman. The Nathan Jesus who received the Christ into himself was not merely `endowed' but `anointed' - that is to say, permeated through and through by Vishva Karman, by Christ."

"The Baptism by John in the Jordan marked the point of time in the evolution of humanity when this heavenly `Thirteenth' - as spiritual substance itself - appeared on the Earth. This was the Being of whom all others - Bodhisattvas and Buddhas - had had to teach, and for whose descent into a human body such stupendous preparations had been necessary. That is the mystery of the Baptism in the Jordan. The Being is He who is described in the Gospels: Vishva Karman, Ahura Mazdao, or the Christ as He was called later on when in the body of the Nathan Jesus. As Christ, this Being was to tread the Earth in human form for three years, a man among men, within that purified terrestrial Being who up to his thirtieth year had undergone all the experiences of which we have heard in these lectures. The Being formerly hidden in the light and warmth-giving rays of the Sun streaming down from the Cosmos, the Being, that is, who had gone with the Sun when it separated from the Earth, now descended into the Nathan Jesus."

Previously it had been mentioned in this work that the human Phantom, the human physical body, is composed of will forces and that these will forces can be found in the `fire/warmth' element of the etheric body. This echoes back to our physical bodies of the Saturn Period when our physical bodies were composed of the `warmth' element of the etheric. Within these bodies flowed the `Will' forces of the spiritual Beings referred to as the Thrones.

In Lecture VII of the cycle on the Luke Gospel, Steiner remarks: "As physical man is constituted today, everything that is of the nature of soul expresses itself in his physical and etheric constitution, but is also connected with certain etheric substances. What we call `will' expresses itself etherically in what we call `fire'. Anyone who is at all sensitive to certain sentient experiences will be aware that there is justification for saying that the `will', which expresses itself physically in the blood, lives in the fire-element of the etheric; physically, the `will' expresses itself in the blood, that is to say in the movement of the blood."

In relation to the Tree of Life that is being restored to humanity, 'thought' is in the Tone or Sound-Ether while 'meaning' is in the Life-Ether.

"In the Lemurian epoch, after the onset of the Luciferic influence, of these four forms of ether only the two lower (light-ether and fire-ether) were left at the free, arbitrary disposal of man; the two higher kinds of ether were withdrawn from him. That is the inner meaning of the passage where it is said that when, as a result of the Luciferic influence, men had become able to distinguish between good and evil (pictorially expressed as eating of the `Tree of Knowledge'), the ` Tree of Life' was kept out of their reach. That is to say, the power freely and arbitrarily to penetrate the thought-ether and the sense-ether (`meaning'-ether) was withdrawn from them.

The conditions of man's development were therefore necessarily as follows. His will was given into his power to assert as his `personal' expression; the same applies to his feelings. Both feeling and will are at man's personal disposal. Hence the individual character of the world of feeling and the world of will. This individual character, however, ceases immediately (when) we pass from feeling to thinking - yes, even to the expression of thoughts, to the words on the physical plane. Whereas each man's feeling and will are personal, we immediately come into something universal when we rise into the realm of words and the realm of thoughts. No one individual can form thoughts that are his alone. If thoughts were as individual as feelings we should never understand one another. Thus thought and `meaning' were withheld from the power of arbitrary human will and preserved for the time being in the world of the Gods, in order not to be given to man until a later time. Everywhere on the Earth, therefore, we can find individual men with individual feelings and individual impulses of will; but thinking is uniform everywhere and language is uniform among the several peoples. Where there is a common language, there reigns a common Folk-Deity. This sphere is withheld from the arbitrary power of man, remaining for the time being a field into which the Gods work."

"What is Vishva Karman? What is Ahura Mazdao? What is Christ in His true form? The Divine, Creative Word ! Hence in Zarathustra's teaching the momentous communication is made that he was initiated in order not only to apprehend in the light the Being he called Ahura Mazdao, but also the Divine, Creative Word, . . . - which was to descend to the Earth and for the first time did descend into an individual etheric body at the Baptism by John. The Divine-Spiritual Word which had been preserved since the Lemurian epoch came forth from the ethereal heights at the Baptism by John and entered into the etheric body of the Nathan Jesus. And when the Baptism was completed, what was it that had happened? The Word had become Flesh!"

The sound and life etheric forces were preserved since the Lemurian Age and now could be returned to the human Being to which conscious and free control of them becomes a gradual evolvement. Moreover, through humanity, these etheric forces enter the Earth as a transforming power for the Earth and humanity.

In Lecture VIII Steiner then speaks of the timing of the Incarnation of Christ: "The mastery wielded by the soul-and-spirit over the physical gradually fell away from humanity until well into the fourth civilization-epoch when there were still enough human Beings living in whom the effect of the spiritual upon the physical could be perceived. It was then that Christ came to the Earth. Had He come later, none of the things that were then revealed could have been revealed. Such a stupendous manifestation had necessarily to appear in the world at exactly the right time.

What does the coming of Christ into the world signify?

It signifies that when a man rightly understands Christ he learns to exercise his self-consciousness to the fullest extent and his Ego eventually gains complete mastery over everything that is within him. That is what the coming of Christ signifies. The self-conscious Ego will re-conquer everything that mankind has lost in the course of the ages. But just as the teaching of the Eightfold Path had to be established for the first time by Buddha, so too the supremacy of the Ego-Principle over all the bodily processes had to be visibly established before the expiration of the old era. If the entry of the Christ-Principle into the world had taken place in our present epoch, it would not have been possible for the mighty influences of healing to be exercised upon the environment as they were at that earlier time. Conditions were necessary when there were still in existence human Beings whose etheric bodies were sufficiently detached to enable drastic effects to be wrought upon them merely by words or by touch - effects of which today there can be only faint echoes. Men began to develop the Ego in order to be able to understand the Christ, and through this understanding to re-acquire what they had lost. Through the last surviving examples of humanity belonging to the old era, it was to be shown with what power the Ego worked upon those who were living at that time, for the Ego was present here in its fullness in one human Being, in Christ Jesus, as will be the case in the rest of mankind at the end of the Earth Period. The Gospel of St. Luke records this in order to show that with Christ there came into the world an Ego which penetrated the human physical, etheric and astral bodies so completely that health-bringing influences could be brought to bear upon the whole physical organism. This had to be demonstrated as a proof that when mankind in the future, after thousands of years, has acquired in full measure the power that can proceed from the Christ-Ego, it will be possible for influences such as streamed into humanity from Christ while He was on Earth, to stream from the Egos of men. This truth had to be revealed but it was only through the humanity of that time that it could have been revealed."

"Thus we are shown quite clearly how the Christ-Ego worked upon all the other members of man's Being. That is the essential point. The writer of the Gospel of St. Luke, who gives special prominence in these parts of the Gospel to descriptions of the healings, wished to show how the healing influences proceeding from the Ego indicate the attainment of a lofty level in the evolutionary process; and he shows how Christ worked upon the astral body, the etheric body and the physical body of man. St. Luke has set before us this great Ideal of evolution: 'Look towards your future ! Your Ego, in the present stage of its development, is still weak; as yet it has little mastery. But it will gradually become master of the astral body, the etheric body and the physical body, and will transform them. Before you is set the great Ideal of Christ who reveals to mankind what this mastery can mean!'

It is upon truths such as these that the Gospels are founded - truths which could be recorded only by those who did not rely upon outer documents but upon the testimony of men who were 'seers' and 'servants of the word'. Conviction of what lies behind the Gospels can be acquired only by degrees. But men will gradually grasp with such intensity and strength the nature of the truths upon which the scriptures are founded that this understanding will have an effect upon all the members of the human organism."

In Lecture IX Steiner addresses the 'living power' of Love that Christ brought to the Earth: "We have heard that Buddha brought to mankind the great teaching of compassion and love. Here is one of the instances where what is said in occultism must be taken exactly as it stands, for otherwise it might be objected that at one time Christ is said to have brought Love to the Earth, and at another that Buddha brought the teaching of love. But is that the same? On one occasion I said that Buddha brought the teaching of love to the Earth and on another occasion that Christ brought Love itself as a living power to the Earth. That is the great difference."

"This living power of Love must stream into mankind in the intervening time in order that the Maitreya Buddha may find not only human Beings who understand what Love is, but those who have within them the power of Love. It was for this purpose that Christ descended to the Earth. He descended for three years only, never having been embodied on the Earth before, as you will have gathered from everything that has been said. The presence of Christ on the Earth for three years - from the Baptism by John until the Mystery of Golgotha - meant that Love will flow in ever-increasing measure into the human heart, into the human soul - in other words, into the human Ego; so that at the end of Earth evolution the Ego will be filled with the power of

Christ. Just as the teaching of compassion and love had first to be kindled to life through the Bodhisattva, the substance of Love had to be brought down from heavenly heights to the Earth by the Being who allows it gradually to become the possession of the human Ego itself. We may not say that Love was not previously in existence. What was not present before the coming of Christ was the Love that could be the direct possession of the human Ego; it was Love that was inspired that Christ enabled to stream down from cosmic Heights; it streamed into men unconsciously, just as previously the Bodhisattva had enabled the teaching of the Eightfold Path to stream into them unconsciously. Buddha's relation to the Eightfold Path was analogous to the status of the Christ-Being before it was possible for Him to descend in order to take human form. The taking of human form signified progress for Christ. That is the all-important point.

Buddha's successor - now a Bodhisattva - is well known to those versed in Spiritual Science and the time will come when these facts - including the name of the Bodhisattva who will then become the Maitreya Buddha - will be spoken of explicitly. For the present, however, when so many factors unknown to the external world have been presented, indications must suffice. When this Bodhisattva appears on Earth and becomes the Maitreya Buddha, he will find on Earth the seed of Christ, embodied in those human Beings who say: `Not only is my head filled with the wisdom of the Eightfold Path; I have not only the teaching, the wisdom of love, but my heart is filled with the living substance of Love which overflows and streams into the world.' And then, together with such human Beings, the Maitreya Buddha will be able to carry out his further mission in the world's evolution.

All these truths are interrelated and only by realizing this are we able to understand the profundities of the Gospel of St. Luke. This Gospel does not speak to us of a `teaching', but of Him who flowed as very substance into the Beings of the Earth and into the constitution of man. This is a truth expressed in occultism by saying: The Bodhisattvas who become Buddhas can, through wisdom, redeem earthly man in respect of his spirit, but they can never redeem the whole man. For the whole man can be redeemed only when the warm power of Love - not wisdom alone - flows through his whole Being. The redemption of souls through the outpouring of Love which He brought to the Earth - that was the mission of Christ. To bring the wisdom of love was the mission of the Bodhisattvas and of the Buddha; to bring to mankind the power of Love was the mission of Christ. This distinction must be made."

Steiner also speaks of Wisdom as a living power: "But there is a difference between wisdom in the form of thought and Wisdom as a living power; there is a difference between knowing what the Ego must become and allowing the living power to flow into our very Being so that it may stream forth again from the Ego into all the world as it streamed from Christ, working upon the astral, etheric and physical bodies of those around Him.

The Impulse given by the great Buddha enabled humanity to have knowledge of the teaching of compassion and love. What Christ brought is first and foremost a living power, not a teaching. He sacrificed his very Self, He descended in order to flow not merely into the astral bodies of men but into the Ego, so that the Ego itself should have the power to ray out Love as substantiality. Christ brought to the Earth the substantiality, the living essence of Love, not merely the wisdom-filled content of Love. That is the all-important point."

In Lecture X Steiner then comments on what it meant for the human Ego when Christ became One with the Earth and united His Being with the destiny of humanity: "Christ indicates clearly enough (according to the Gospel of St. Luke too) that an entirely new factor had now entered into the evolution of humanity, namely, Ego-consciousness. He shows - it is only a matter of being able to read the meaning - that in earlier times the spiritual world did not flow into the self-conscious Ego, for men received this spiritual stream through the physical, etheric and astral bodies; a certain degree of unconsciousness was always present when, as in previous epochs, divine-spiritual forces flowed into men. In the stream in which Christ Jesus was actually working, men had had formerly to receive the Law of Sinai, which could be addressed only to the astral body. The Law was imparted to man in such a way that it did indeed work in him, but not directly through the forces of his Ego. These forces could not operate until the time of Christ Jesus because it was not until then that man became conscious of the Ego in the real sense. This is indicated by Christ in the Gospel of St. Luke when He says that men must first be made ready to receive an entirely new Principle into their souls. He indicates this when speaking of His forerunner, John the Baptist. (Luke 7: 18-35)."

Steiner then turns to the Apostles: "Christ wished to show that because of the new element now present in the world there can also be men who even before they die are able to behold the Kingdom of Heaven. The disciples did not at first understand what this meant. Christ wanted to convey to them that they were to be the ones who would come to know the mysteries of the Kingdoms of Heaven before natural death or the death experienced in the old form of Initiation. The wonderful passage in the Gospel of St. Luke where Christ is speaking of a higher revelation, is as follows: `But I tell you of a truth, there be some standing here, which shall not taste of death, till they see the Kingdom of God.' (Luke 9: 27). The disciples did not understand that it was they themselves who, being closely around Him, were chosen to experience the tremendous power of the Christ-Principle which would enable them to penetrate directly into the spiritual world. The spiritual world was to become visible to them without the sign of Solomon, and without the sign of Jonah. Did this actually happen?

Immediately after these words in the Gospel comes the scene of the Transfiguration, when three disciples -Peter, James and John - are led up into the spiritual world. The figures of Moses and Elijah appear before them in that world and, simultaneously, Christ Jesus in Glory. (Luke 9: 28-36). The disciples gaze for a brief moment into the spiritual world - a testimony that insight into that world is possible without the faculties designated by the sign of Solomon and the sign of Jonah. But it is evident that they are still novices, for they fall asleep immediately after being torn out of their physical and etheric bodies by the stupendous power of what was happening. Christ finds them asleep. This account was meant to indicate the third way of entering the spiritual world, apart from the ways denoted by the signs of Solomon and of Jonah. Anyone capable in those days of interpreting the signs of the times would have known that the Ego itself must develop, that it must now be directly inspired, that the Divine Powers must work directly into the Ego.

It was also to be made evident that the men of that time, even the best among them, were not capable of taking the Christ-Principle into themselves. The event of the Transfiguration was to be a beginning but it was also to be shown that the disciples were not able, at the time, to receive the Christ-Principle in the fullest sense. Hence their powers fail them immediately afterwards, when they want to apply the Christ-power to heal one who is possessed by an evil spirit but are unable to do so. Christ indicates that they are still only at the beginning, by saying: I shall have to stay a long time with you before your forces are able also to stream into other men. (See Luke 9: 41). Thereupon He heals the one whom the disciples could not heal. But then He says, again hinting at the mystery behind these happenings, that the time has come when 'the Son of Man shall be delivered into the hands of men'. This means: the time has come when the Ego, which is to be developed by men themselves in the course of their Earth mission, is gradually to stream into them, to be given over to them. This Ego is to be recognized in its highest form in Christ. 'Let these sayings sink down into your ears; for the Son of Man shall be delivered into the hands of men. But they understood not this saying; it was hid from them, that they perceived it not.' (Luke 9: 44-45).

How many have understood this saying? Greater and greater numbers will, however, eventually understand that the Ego, the 'Son of Man', was to be given over to men at that time. And the explanation that was possible in those days, was added by Christ Jesus. He spoke to the following effect: As he stands before us, man is a product of the old forces that were active before the Luciferic Beings had laid hold of human nature; but the Luciferic forces drew man down to a lower level. The results of all these processes have passed into the faculties possessed by him today. Everything that comes from the seed, as well as all human consciousness, is permeated by the influence that dragged man to a lower sphere."

"Only the part of man that is `childlike' still retains a last remnant of the nature that was his before he succumbed to the influence of the Luciferic Beings. Hence there is a `childlike' part and also a `grown' part in man. It is the latter part of his Being that is permeated by the Luciferic forces but its influence asserts itself from the very earliest embryonic stage onwards. The Luciferic forces also permeate the child, so that in ordinary life what was already implanted in the human Being before the Luciferic influence, cannot make itself manifest. The Christ-power must reawaken this, must unite with the best forces of the child-nature in man. The Christ-power may not link itself with the faculties that man has corrupted, with what derives merely from the intellect; the link must be with that which has remained from the child-nature of primeval times. [note: that is, it must link with what we find in the earliest stages of consciousness in infancy, to which it is then brought to full development while in adulthood thereby being conjoined with one's Ego-consciousness. Steiner had referred to this as the merging of the `Son of God' consciousness of infancy with the `Son of Man' consciousness of adulthood.]. That is what must be reinvigorated and must thereafter fructify the other part (of man's nature).

`But there arose a reasoning among them, which of them should be the greatest,' that is, which of them was most fitted to receive the Christ-Principle into his own Being. `But Jesus, perceiving the thought of their heart, took a child, [note: the Christ-Principle], and set it by them and said unto them: Whoever shall receive this child in my Name, [note: `Name' denotes the `I AM' of Christ],' - that is, whosoever is united in Christ's Name with what has remained from the times before the onset of the Luciferic influence - `receiveth Me; and whosoever shall receive Me receiveth Him that sent Me' (Luke 9: 46-48) - that is, He who sent this (childlike) part of the human Being to the Earth. Emphasis is there laid upon the great significance of what has remained `childlike' in man and should be fostered and nurtured in human nature."

Steiner then addresses the Event of Golgotha: "Those who were to understand must now do so through the powerful influence of the Ego - not through what they had learnt but through what had poured into them from the spiritual Christ-Being Himself. Hence the chosen ones were not men who according to the old doctrines were properly prepared but men who, in spite of having passed through many incarnations, proved to be simple human Beings, able to understand through the power of Faith what had streamed into them. A `sign' was to be placed before them as well, a sign now to be enacted before the eyes of all mankind. The `mystical death' that had been a ceremonial act in the Mystery Temples for hundreds and thousands of years was now to be presented on the great arena of world-history. Everything that had taken place in the secrecy of the Temples of Initiation was brought into the open as a single Event on Golgotha. A process hitherto witnessed only by the Initiates during the three-and-a-half days of an old Initiation was now enacted before mankind in concrete reality. Hence those to whom the facts were known could only describe the Event of Golgotha as being what in very truth it was: the old Initiation transformed into historical fact and enacted on the arena of world-history.

That is what took place on Golgotha! In former times the three-and-a-half days spent in deathlike sleep had brought to the few Initiates who witnessed it the conviction that the spiritual will at all times be victorious over the bodily nature and that man's soul and spirit belong to a spiritual world. This was now to be a reality enacted before the eyes of the world. An Initiation transferred to the outer plane of world-history - such was the Event of Golgotha. Hence this Initiation was not consummated only for those who witnessed the actual Event, but for all of mankind. What issued from the death on the Cross streamed into the whole of humanity. A stream of spiritual life flowed into mankind from the drops of blood which fell from the wounds of Christ Jesus on Golgotha. For what had been imparted by other Teachers as 'wisdom' was now to pass into humanity as inner strength, inner power. That is the essential difference between the Event of Golgotha and the teachings given by the other Founders of religion.

Deeper understanding than exists today is necessary before there can be any true conception of what came to pass on Golgotha. When Earth evolution began, the human Ego was connected physically with the blood. The blood is the outer expression of the human Ego. Men would have made the Ego stronger and stronger, and if Christ had not appeared they would have been entirely engrossed in the development of egoism. They were protected from this by the Event of Golgotha. What was it that had to flow? The blood that is the surplus substantiality of the Ego! The process that began on the Mount of Olives when the drops of sweat fell from the Redeemer like drops of blood, was carried further when the blood flowed from the wounds of Christ Jesus on Golgotha. The blood flowing from the Cross was the sign of the surplus egoism in man's nature which had to be sacrificed. The spiritual significance of the sacrifice on Golgotha requires deep and penetrating study. The result of what happened there would not be apparent to a chemist - that is to say to one with the power of intellectual perception only. If the blood that flowed on Golgotha had been chemically analyzed it would have been found to contain the same substances as the blood of other human Beings; but occult investigation would discover it to have been quite different blood. Through the surplus blood in humanity men would have been engulfed in egoism if infinite Love had not enabled this blood to flow. As occult investigation finds, infinite Love is intermingled with the blood that flowed on Golgotha. The writer of the Gospel of St. Luke adhered to his purpose, which was to describe how, through Christ, there came into the world the infinite Love that would gradually drive out egoism. Each of the Evangelists describes what it was his particular function to describe.

. . . the writer of the Gospel of St. Luke perceives the out-streaming Love which forgives the most terrible of all wrongs the physical world could inflict. Words expressing this Ideal of Love, words of forgiveness even when

230

the most terrible of wrongs has been committed, resound from the Cross on Golgotha: `Father, forgive them, for they know not what they do!' (Luke 23: 34). Out of His infinite Love, He who on the Cross on Golgotha accomplishes the Deed of untold significance, implores forgiveness for those who have crucified Him."

"There is still something else, belonging to the same realm of the soul's life, upon which the writer of this Gospel wishes to lay emphasis. When a man's whole Being is pervaded with the Love that streamed from the Cross on Golgotha he can turn his eyes to the future and say: Evolution on the Earth must make it possible for the spirit living within me gradually to transform the whole of physical existence. We shall in time give back again to the Father-Principle which existed before the onset of the Luciferic influence, the spirit we have received; we shall let our whole Being be permeated by the Christ-Principle and our hands will bring to expression what is living in our souls as a faithful picture of that Principle. Our hands were not created by ourselves but by the Father-Principle, and the Christ-Principle will stream through them. As men pass through incarnation after incarnation, the spiritual power flowing from the Mystery of Golgotha will stream into what they achieve in their bodies - which are the creations of the Father-Principle - so that the outer world will eventually be imbued with the Christ-Principle. Men will be filled with the confidence that resounded from the Cross on Golgotha and leads to the highest Hope for the future, leads to the Ideal that can be expressed by saying: I let Faith germinate within me, I let Love germinate within me and I know that when they grow strong enough they will pervade all external life. I know too that they will pervade everything within me that is the creation of the Father-Principle. Thus Hope for humanity's future will be added to Faith and Love, and men will understand that in regard to the future they must acquire firm confidence, saying: If only I have Faith, if only I have Love I may entertain the Hope that what has come into me from Christ Jesus will gradually finds its way into the outer world. And then the words resounding from the Cross as a sublime Ideal will be understood: `Father, into Thy hands I commend My Spirit!' (Luke 23: 46)."

"The revelations pour down from the spiritual worlds upon the Earth and are reflected from human hearts as Love and Peace to the extent to which men unfold the power, the `good will', which the Christ-Principle enables to flow from the center of man's Being, from his Ego. The proclamation rings out clearly and with the glow of warmth when we truly understand the meaning of these words in the Gospel of St. Luke: The revelation of the spiritual worlds from the Heights and its answering reflection from the hearts of men brings peace to all whose purpose upon the evolving Earth is to unfold good will." (See Luke 2: 10-14).

In examining the Apostles and their relationship to Christ we have come to see that Christ was continuously attempting to bring them to a more spiritualized consciousness that would be capable of following Him through

231

His Death and Resurrection. If we were to understand the Last Supper as an attempt by Christ to initiate the Apostles into the mysteries of the spoken word we get an insight into some of the expressions that were used in the Gospels in their narration of the Last Supper and at the time of the arrest. A key in this understanding is the symbolic meaning of the `sword'.

Steiner unveils its meaning in the following: "For this reason the divine power of the word in the mouths of human Beings is everywhere signified by the sword. Everywhere, we find the sword employed as a symbol of the humanization of divine power." [Reading the Pictures of the Apocalypse; May 13, 1909] The sword signifies the spoken word of one who has attained a degree of Initiation and is able to use the spoken word to heal another. Steiner, in his lectures on the Gospel of Mark, speaks of this very phenomenon in that the ancient shamans were able to speak into the etheric body of another individual which would then act as a healing force for the sickened individual. Often it is difficult to establish when the Bible is narrating an account that is purely physical or when it is speaking of an occurrence that is supersensible. We know from Steiner that the fleeing youth is an account of a supersensible occurrence. It is the description of the loosening of the cosmic aura of Christ from the Christ Himself. The account of Christ walking on water is an Imagination initiation conducted by Christ for the Apostles. Also, the feeding of the five thousand describes an initiation of the Apostles and their union with John the Baptist as their group-soul Being. In light of these examples, the narration of Peter severing Malchus' right ear is a narration of an act that is coupled with esoteric undertones. It is an account of a mystery; in this case, the mystery of the power of the spiritualized spoken word.

At the conclusion of the Last Supper we read from Luke's Gospel: "And they said, `Lord behold, here are two swords. And He said to them, `Enough'."

The mentioning of the two swords prior to the agony in the garden in Luke 22: 38 is placed immediately after the mentioning of Christ's foretelling of Peter's vocal denial of the Christ. And it was Peter who had cut off the right ear of Malchus, the servant of the high priest. In this account, it was Peter's abuse of the healing word that pierces the soul of Malchus. In John's Gospel the account of Peter and Malchus is then immediately followed by Peter's spoken denial of knowing Christ. John's Gospel even reminds us of this incident immediately prior to Peter's third denial (John 19: 26-27). The sword of the spoken word is vital to any act of initiation. The Last Supper was a preparatory stage for Christ's own macrocosmic initiation as He was about to become the 'bread and the wine' of the earth. The entire scene then moves into the final stage of the Apostles' incomprehension of the Event of Golgotha thereby completely severing the bond between them and the Christ. Directly following Christ's agony in the garden Judas arrived with a cohort and attendants of the chief priests and Pharisees

(John 18: 3). In Luke's Gospel we can see how the spiritualized word, the sword, is not taken up properly by the Apostles.

"But when they who were about Him saw what would follow, they said to Him, 'Lord, shall we strike with the sword?' And one of them struck the servant of the high priest and cut off his right ear. But Jesus answered and said, 'Bear with them thus far. And He touched his ear and healed him.'" (Luke 22: 49-51). The Apostles asked Christ Jesus, "Lord, shall we strike with the sword . . . ," to which Peter's subsequent reaction against Malchus is followed by Christ saying to the Apostles, "Bear with them thus far," which is akin to His words on the Cross, "Father, forgive them for they know not what they do." It was when Peter struck Malchus that it became final that the Apostles were not going to be capable of following Christ through His Death and Resurrection in a spiritually conscious manner as would had been necessary to consummate the internalization of the Christ Principle within the souls of the Apostles. The severing of the ear of Malchus represented the Apostles' definitive point of severance from the cosmic aura of Christ.

Emil Bock wrote the following in his book, "The Three Years": "Last of all, the Gospel tells of the healing of Malchus in Gethsemane, whose ear has been struck off by Peter in a sudden impulse of resistance to destiny. Apart from the fact that the Gospel brings two imaginative pictures into strong contrast, the destructive power of Peter's sword, and the reconstructing, healing power of Jesus, there is no question here of a healing work performed by Jesus for the benefit of an individual. The Being of Christ is now directed solely and utterly towards the final consequences of His own resolve. A victory has already been won in Gethsemane, but only the Death on the Cross can set the seal upon it. The disciples cannot reach the height of His resolve. They want to hold back by their own will the events that must now take place. The wound inflicted by Peter is healed; this, in miniature, is a sign that the fight waged by Christ has for its goal nothing   less   than   the   healing   of   all   mankind."

XV

The Voice of Mary

In the Gospel of Luke there appears to be much that has to do with the aspects of speech in the first two chapters of the Luke Gospel. This presents a possible window into a very profound mystery pertaining to the voice of Mary. In Lecture IX from the 1908 Gospel of St. John cycle, Steiner poses the question : "Who was the Father (of Jesus)?" He applies this question specifically not only to the Gospel of John but especially to the Gospel of Luke. Steiner addresses Gabriel's Annunciation to Mary in which Gabriel proclaims: ". . . the Holy Spirit shall come upon thee, and the power of the Most High shall overshadow thee; therefore also, the Holy One which shall be born of thee shall be called the `Son of God'." (Luke 1: 35). Again, quoting Steiner from this lecture, he comments: "Even in the Gospel of St. Luke it is pointed out that the, `Father of Jesus is the Holy Spirit'. This must be taken literally . . ."

A similar theme is presented to us in the Matthew Gospel having to do with Joseph. The following is from Steiner's lecture, "Whitsun: the Festival of the Free Individuality," (Hamburg, Whitsunday, 1910) which will assist in explaining Joseph's consternation over the pregnancy of Mary with regard to the Holy Spirit: "The Spirit, also rightly named the Holy Spirit - for so He is - sent his forces down to the Earth in the first descent to the Earth of Christ Jesus. He next manifested himself when Jesus was Baptized by John the Baptist. Now, once again, this same Spirit, in another form, in the form of many single, shining fiery tongues, descended upon each single individual of the first Christian believers.

We are told about this Holy Spirit at the Whitsun Festival in a quite special way, but we must get clear in our minds the meaning of the words `Holy Spirit', as they are used in the Gospels. In olden times the Spirit was spoken of in many connections, but in one connection particularly. Through the new knowledge which Spiritual Science gives us, we are enabled to say that when a man passes through birth into his existence between birth and death, the body in which the individuality is incarnated is determined in two ways. Our bodily nature has actually a double function to fulfill: it makes us a human Being, but it also makes us members of this or that people, this or that race or family. In the ancient times which preceded Christianity, little as yet was experienced of what can be called world-wide humanity, of that feeling of human fellowship which in ever greater measure has lived in human hearts only since Christianity was proclaimed, and which says to us: Thou art fellow-man with all the human Beings of the Earth! On the other hand, that feeling was all the stronger which makes each man a member of a particular people or tribe. This indeed is expressed in the age-long religion of the Hindus in their belief that only one who is such through his blood, can be a real Hindu. In many directions - despite exceptions to the principle - this was also firmly held by the old Hebrew people before the coming of Christ. According to their view, a man belonged to his people only because his parents, themselves belonging to it and so blood-related, had placed him into it. But they were also always familiar with another feeling, which was more or less felt by all peoples in olden times, namely, that one was a member of one's family, a member of one's folk, and nothing more. The further we go back into antiquity the more intense this feeling is, the more the human Being feels himself as a member of his folk, and not in any way as a single individual. Gradually, however, there awoke the feeling of oneself as a single human Being, a single human individuality with individual human qualities. Thus these two principles were felt to be present in the outer nature of man: membership of a people, and awareness of oneself as a single personality.

Now the forces inherent in these two principles were ascribed in a different way to the two parents. The principle by virtue of which one belonged more to one's folk, by virtue of which one was related to the general race-community, was ascribed through heredity to the mother. When men felt according to this idea, they said of the mother: `In her the Spirit of the folk holds sway. She was filled with the Spirit of the folk and has passed on to the child the qualities common to her people.' But of the father it was said that he was the bearer and transmitter of the principle which gave rather the individual, personal characteristics of the human Being. Thus it could be said when a man came into the world through birth - and this was also the view of the old Hebrew people in pre-Christian times - that he was an individual personality through the forces of his father. The mother, however, through that which was special in her whole nature, was felt to be filled with the Spirit which held sway in the folk, and this she had handed on to the child. Thus it was said of the mother, that the Spirit of the folk dwelt in her, and it was in this connection that the Spirit was spoken of who sent his forces down out of spiritual realms into humanity - that he let his forces stream down into the physical world, into humanity, by way of the mother.

Through the Christ Impulse, however, a new conception had come - a conception which said that this Spirit of which men had previously spoken, this Spirit of the folk, was to be replaced by one which, though certainly related to it, worked at a far higher level, a Spirit which is related to the whole of mankind, as the earlier Spirit had been related to a particular people. This Spirit was to be given to man and to fill him with the power to say: `I feel I belong no longer only to a part of humanity, but to the whole of it; I am a member of the whole of mankind, and will become a member of it ever more and more!' This force, which poured a universal human quality over the whole of mankind, was attributed to the `Holy Spirit'. Thus, the Spirit which was expressed in the force which flowed from the folk into the mother was raised from `Spirit' to `Holy Spirit'.

The One who was to bring mankind the power to develop this universal human nature ever more and more in earthly life, could dwell - as the first Being of this nature - only in a body bequeathed through the power of the Holy Spirit. This the Mother of Jesus received in the Annunciation. In the Gospel of St. Matthew we have the consternation of Joseph, of whom it is said that he was a 'righteous' man. This word was used in the old sense, and meant that he was one who could only believe that any child of his would be born out of the Spirit of his people. Now he has discovered that the Mother of his child is filled, is penetrated through and through (for this is the right meaning of the original word in our language), by the power of a Spirit that was not merely a folk-Spirit, but the Spirit of universal humanity! And he did not feel that he could live with a woman who might one day bear him children, when there dwelt in her the Spirit of humanity as a whole and not the Spirit he held to in his righteousness. Accordingly he wished as it says, to put her away privily. It was only when he also had received a communication out of the spiritual world, that he received the strength to decide to have a son by that woman who was penetrated and filled with the power of this Holy Spirit.

Thus we have seen that this Spirit was creatively at work, first of all in letting its forces stream into human evolution in relation to the birth of Jesus of Nazareth, and again in the mighty act of the Baptism in the Jordan. Thus we now understand what the power of the Holy spirit is: it is the power which will raise each man ever more and more above all that differentiates and separates him from others, and makes him a member of the whole of humanity on the Earth, a power which works as a bond of soul between each and every soul, no matter in what bodies they may be."

The above excerpt explains Joseph's consternation in regard to his allegiance to the folk-Spirit of his people. He has great difficulty in accepting the truth that his child will not be exclusively united with this folk-Spirit but will be One with the Universal Spirit which is the Holy Spirit. The above excerpt from Steiner demystifies the doctrine of any miraculous conception that is found in traditional Christian orthodoxy. However, in doing so, the following verse needs to be reconciled: "When Mary his Mother had been betrothed to Joseph, before they came together, she was found to be with child by the Holy Spirit." (Matthew 1:18). The 'miraculous conception' doctrine would advocate that she became pregnant not by Joseph but miraculously by the power of the Holy Spirit. In this doctrine it is traditionally understood that Jesus was not conceived by means of any sexual

236

union between Mary and Joseph. When reading the verse as it stands, ". . . she was found to be with child by the Holy Spirit," one could certainly interpret it this way. This would be in accord with conventional doctrine when utilizing the preposition, 'by' in this particular verse of the Gospel. According to what Steiner gave us, the concise translation of this passage would be: ". . . she was found to be with child 'of' the Holy Spirit."

This revelation from Steiner overturns a major doctrine in Christianity theology. The verse is reconstructed to read, "of the Holy Spirit," instead of, "by the Holy Spirit." The Matthew Gospel is conveying to us that before Mary physically conceived the embryo for the Zarathustra-Jesus, of which the name 'Zarathustra' means - radiant star - as is narrated in the Gospel, he was already permeating the soul of Mary and that this Jesus-child was 'of' the Holy Spirit. In, "Theosophy of the Rosicrucian" - Lecture VII, Steiner states the following: "True knowledge, however, deepens mother-love, for it reveals that this love is present before birth, even before conception, as a force which guided the child to the mother. The child loves the mother even before birth and mother-love is the reciprocal force." The Zarathustra-Jesus was of the Universal Spirit and not of the folk-Spirt. Thereby, " . . . she was found to be with child of the Holy Spirit."

This question of a virginal miraculous conception is not completely resolved unless the following verse is answered as well: "And he did not know her till she brought forth her firstborn son. And he called his name Jesus." (Matthew 1:25). We may interpret this literally in that Mary and Joseph did not have any direct copulatory relationship with one another until after the birth of the Zarathustra-Jesus. Afterwards, Mary and Joseph allegedly continued to have children which is supposedly communicated to us in Matthew 13:55 and Mark 6:3. Many scholars and theologians argue that this was not so and that Joseph was previously a widower who had children from a former marriage. The gnostic Gospel of James narrates this same premise. Others assert that the words, 'brothers and sisters,' are expressive terminologies denoting spiritual solidarity and are not to be taken literally as meaning they were the siblings of Jesus. And lastly, the term, "firstborn", may also be interpreted to mean 'an only son' which indicates his obligations and rights under Mosaic Law. Steiner however, in his Matthew cycle, asserts that Mary and Joseph did have subsequent children of their own after the Zarathustra-Jesus.

Steiner makes it clear that Joseph is the physical father of the Zarathustra-Jesus in Lecture IV of his Matthew Gospel cycle: "If we feel the sanctity of such a Mystery we shall realize that in this way of presenting it there is something infinitely higher than any of the exoteric interpretations of the Virgin Birth. Consideration of just two points in the Bible will enable us to avoid trivial interpretations of this 'immaculate conception'. The one point is this: Why should the writer of St. Matthew's Gospel have enumerated the whole sequence of generations from Abraham to Joseph if he had wished to indicate that the birth of Jesus of Nazareth had no connection with this line of descent? He is at pains to show how the blood was led down the generations from Abraham to Joseph; how, then, could he possibly have intended to indicate that the blood of Jesus of Nazareth had nothing to do with this blood? And the other point of which account must be taken is that in the Hebrew language the gender of 'Ruach-Elohim', rendered 'Holy Spirit' in the Bible, is feminine." Since Steiner conveys that the Holy Spirit, the Ruach-Elohim, is understood to be of a spiritually feminine principle and that the child-to-be in the Matthew Gospel is of the Holy Spirit, this then adds another factor in perceiving the spiritual conception of the Zarathustra-Jesus within the soul of Mary as a holy virginal conception prior to the physical conception.

In his book, "The Book with Fourteen Seals," Welburn addresses the ancient understanding of a virginal immaculate conception pertaining to the prophets of the past. He writes the following: "Unlike 'enlightened' modern man, the ancient initiate was not tempted to suppose that he was actually a 'product' of the sexual process on earth, though he did enter into it through birth. In this sense, then, his mother is a 'virgin', and he can even be said to beget himself upon her. What we must further grasp is that this is not a denial of his earthly father and mother. It is the hidden side of birth, of incarnation, today almost completely forgotten, but in the myths the central reality."

Concurring with the above, it may be said, that once an Initiate or any child begins to draw near the mother-to-be and interpenetrates her soul, this is the beginning of the higher virginal conception. This was the perspective of the ancient Initiates. From their viewpoint this was the rightful meaning of an immaculate conception from a higher spiritual reality. The actual physical conception was not considered to be the true conception. Welburn goes on to write the following in regard to, "the esoteric knowledge of the mission of Zarathustra": "It showed that, in the case of spiritually awakened man, birth was not a matter of physical union and of continuity on the biological level; it was the irruption of new life from the spiritual world, the reincarnating spirit of the prophet. . . . He is born spiritually, that is to say, he understands himself as a Being originating from the world of Light, able to live on earth through the harmony of cosmic powers, fire and water."

In Emil Bock's, "The Early Childhood of Jesus," he draws attention to Mary and Joseph of the Matthew Gospel and the likelihood of their passage through a temple ritual. He wrote: "How it happened that Mary, hardly having left the protective environs of the Temple, felt herself becoming a mother; this is something that is shrouded in secrets. Perhaps these secrets are related to those that early on were woven around the implementation of the temple marriage between Joseph and Mary. Those who brought the parents together based on their eugenic insights and goals may have resorted

238

back to ancient times of humanity's evolution when, in certain cultic circles, any solemnization of marriage was brought about by the priests, and the conception of the first-born was withheld from the parents' earthly consciousness by means of a modified form of temple sleep."

Bock adds more to this theme with the following which is also applicable to Mary and Joseph of the Luke Gospel: "Far into historical times when men and women had assumed a corporeal form quite similar to the one we bear today, the protective role of sleep continued on. The innocence of the primal paradisal condition was preserved in conception and birth. Human reproduction occurred more through angels than through human Beings themselves. It signified a completely new stage of evolution when human Beings began to awaken to an awareness of the difference of the sexes and the process of procreation. The great protector, sleep, which had long since been replaced at the end of life by its somber brother, death, was replaced at the beginning of a new human life by the provocative forces of sensual desire. The legacy of innocence from paradisal primal times was being depleted. The mystery of birth increasingly passed from the hands of gods into the self-discretionary power of men. In this third stage, however, which began as early as several millennia before the turn of time, there still existed segments of humanity and single personalities here and there in whom the laws of the second state simply continued on quite naturally. Moreover, there were institutions that, through the guiding influence of certain individuals, were to preserve and cultivate at least something of the unawareness and innocence of the ancient form of procreation. In a number of temple traditions of the ancient world, the intention was to have the priests continue in the role that, previously, the angels played during the coming together of the two genders. Human communities existed where marriage was guarded against becoming a personal affair of husband and wife too early on. The attempt was made to preserve procreation as a holy mystery, meaning as an affair of the temple and religious community. Not only were the marriages solemnized and blessed in these instances by the priests in the temples; in addition, the mystery of conception remained under the guidance of the temple. This was either a rule applying to all the people or it was practiced at least in certain important cases. Instead of the divine Beings, the priests now caused a deep sleep, a variation of the temple sleep leading to Initiation, to fall upon the man and the woman in order to protect and preserve the mystery. Even extending into relatively late ages, at least the firstborn child, considered in the ancient world to be of particular importance, probably came into this world in many a place under such religious protection, in that the parents, following their wedding ceremony which had been solemnized by the priests, were kept in the domain and under the guidance of the temple for a period of time."

239

In continuation, Matthew 1:25 alludes to ancient temple rituals of insemination in which the semen from the male is extracted and transported to the female while both remain separated from one another. The conception of the Zarathustra-Jesus may have been enacted through a Temple ritual involving insemination from Joseph to Mary and conducted by the Temple priests. At the same time this was perhaps an Initiation as well; a Temple Sleep for both Mary and Joseph. The consternation of Joseph was resolved by the angel who appeared to him in a dream. However, this was not a dream as we commonly understand it. Rather, the dream narrative in the Matthew Gospel (1: 20-23) is a veiled narrative for what was commonly referred to as a Temple Sleep; an Initiation. The angel is not named in the Gospel but it is reasonable to presume that it was the Archangel Gabriel whose spoken word pervaded the soul of Joseph during this temple ritual. In Steiner's, "Karmic Relationships Vol III," August 3, 1924 (GA 237) he states the following: " . . . I have described how the rulership of Gabriel is connected with the forces that go through the line of physical inheritance - forces related to physical reproduction." In conjunction with the presence of the Temple priests Gabriel was active in the proceedings of the Initiations of both Mary and Joseph. He was also active in the processes of ritualistic insemination inducing Joseph, who was in a sleep-like condition, to produce the needed semen for the insemination of Mary who was also in a sleep-like condition. This procedure may have been planned from the earliest days of Mary's life. Prior to the time that Joseph "betrothed" Mary, she had spent most of her life as a Temple virgin. In his book, "The Early Childhood of Jesus," Emil Bock recounts how at the age of three Mary was "entrusted to the priesthood for instruction" in the Temple. Bock goes on to say that, "The Temple childhood of Mary was the recapitulation of a whole world of religious developments of humanity."

Throughout the processes of the conception and fetal development of Zarathustra we can assume that he was deeply involved in it all. Steiner says the following in Lecture V from the cycle, "Theosophy of the Rosicrucian," in which he speaks of high Initiates: "The higher the stage to which he attained, the earlier does he begin to work upon his own physical body in order to make it more suitable for the mission he has to fulfil on the earth. The later he takes command of the physical germ, the less control he will have over the physical body. The most highly developed Individualities, those who are the guides and leaders of the spiritual life of the earth, take command already at the time of conception. Nothing takes place without their collaboration; they direct their physical body right up to the time of their death and begin to prepare the new body directly the first impetus for this is given."

Turning from the Matthew Gospel to the Luke Gospel, the question of the conception of the Nathan-Jesus in the Luke Gospel also presents difficulties. In response to the Archangel Gabriel's annunciation that she will

240

conceive a son in her womb, Mary poses the following question: "How shall this happen, since I do not know man." (Luke 1:34). Here again this verse may seem to be an indication that Mary is not going to induce a pregnancy by means of procreation with a man but that she will miraculously conceive the Jesus child by means of the Holy Spirit. However, this was not so. The entire narration of Gabriel's appearance to Mary in the Luke Gospel alludes to the fact that the Nathan Jesus was already beginning to permeate her soul. Admittedly, the verse does indicate that she has yet to physically conceive of any child and though she is married to Joseph she remains a virgin. This does not, however, dismiss the truth that she and Joseph do conceive a child together by means of insemination and that this was likely done under the auspices of a Temple ritual as described above. Throughout the entire pregnancy Christ filled the etheric and astral bodies of Mary with His Holy Spirit. As Steiner indicated, the Holy Spirit in this event is to be understood as the activity of the Macrocosmic Ego of the Christ: "The One who was to bring mankind the power to develop this universal human nature ever more and more in earthly life, could dwell - as the first Being of this nature - only in a body bequeathed through the power of the Holy Spirit." This sentence from Steiner references the eventual birth of the Nathan Jesus. This is corroborated in the Luke Gospel when Gabriel says to Mary, ". . . the Holy Spirit shall come upon thee and the power of the Most High shall overshadow thee; and therefore the Holy One to be born shall be called the Son of God."

It is announced to Mary by the Archangel Gabriel that her soul is already being impregnated by the Nathan-soul who is also filled with the Universal Holy Spirit, and is now beginning to pervade her soul prior to any physical conception. Gabriel is providing the answer to her question, "How shall this happen, since I do not know man," because he is speaking of the spiritual conception of the Nathan soul within Mary's soul prior to her physically conceiving the body of the Nathan Jesus within her womb. It should be noted again that Steiner does point out that it would be futile to document the genealogies if such an occurrence as a miraculous conception did occur. It is reasonable to presume that Mary of the Luke Gospel also became pregnant by means of temple rites of insemination. Also, it could be concluded that within the whole context of the pregnancy of the Luke Mary the temple act of insemination was the point of departure from the normal course of human pregnancy and its subsequent gestation. That is, during the entire time of her pregnancy she carried in her voice etheric forces that were capable of forming and fashioning an embryo and its subsequent form as a fetus in a manner that had never been achieved before. According to Rudolf Steiner the Nathan Jesus-child, the Zarathustra Jesus-child and John the Baptist were filled with the Universal Holy Spirit. In Steiner's 1908 Gospel of St. John cycle he conveys to us in Lecture XII an indication of the nature

241

of this Universal Holy Spirit: "By means of all that he receives during catharsis, the pupil cleanses and purifies his astral body so that it is transformed into the Virgin Sophia. And when the Virgin Sophia encounters the Cosmic Ego, the Universal Ego which causes illumination, the pupil is surrounded by light, spiritual light. This second power that approaches the Virgin Sophia, is called in esoteric Christianity - is also so called today - the Holy Spirit. Therefore according to esoteric Christianity, it is correct to say that through his processes of Initiation the Christian esotericist attains the purification and cleansing of his astral body; he makes his astral body into the Virgin Sophia and is illuminated from above - if you wish, you may call it overshadowed - by the Holy Spirit, by the Cosmic, Universal Ego."

In regard to that which was presented earlier pertaining to the nature of the Holy Spirit in the chapter, "The Evolution of Christ," and that which is presented in the above quote it becomes incumbent to understand that the term 'Holy Spirit' has multiple designations. We have already observed in the aforementioned chapter that the term 'Father' also has various designations. In another lecture presented in Berlin on December 19, 1915 Steiner stated the following in regard to the Christ: "In the body of Jesus He prepared for Himself, in the way we know, in a twofold way, what was to serve Him as a body on the earth. . . . The Christmas festival shows how Christ prepared the human body for Himself during childhood."

Though the above excerpt is specifically addressing the preparation of the body of the Jesus infant of the Luke Gospel it is reasonable to add that when examining the two nativities of both the Luke and Matthew Gospels we are presented with the activity of the Holy Spirit, or what may be understood to be the spiritual fecundation processes of the Cosmic, Universal Ego of the Christ, within the gestation processes of both Jesus infants. This activity of the Christ Ego manifested itself in the births of both Jesus infants. In a sense, this may explain the difficult and perplexing passages in both Gospels which seemingly contradict that which Steiner related to us in regard to the incarnation of Christ. In the anthroposophical christologies we are told that the Christ incarnated into the bodily sheaths of Jesus of Nazareth at the time of the Baptism in the Jordan. However, the Luke and Matthew Gospels present us with the following passages: "And Jacob begot Joseph, the husband of Mary, and of her was born Jesus who is called Christ." (Matthew 1:16). Also, in Matthew's Gospel there is the following exchange between Herod and the Magi: "And gathering together all the chief priests and Scribes of the people, he inquired of them where the Christ was to be born. And they said to him, 'In Bethlehem of Judea' . . ." (Matthew 2: 4-5).

And in the Luke Gospel there is the following: " . . . for today in the town of David a Savior has been born to you who is Christ the Lord." (Luke 2:11). It has been the agelong orthodoxy of Christianity that there was only one Jesus infant and that the Christ was born as an infant in Bethlehem who was named Jesus. In reading the above verses at face value the preliminary indication would certainly seem to suggest that the Christ incarnated in a human form as an infant in Bethlehem. However, if we apply to these verses what Steiner had said pertaining to the Holy Spirit it becomes possible to explain the above Gospel verses from an anthroposophical perspective by asserting the premise that within both Jesus infants there dwelled a residual element of the Universal Holy Spirit; a residual element of the activity of the Cosmic Ego of the Christ which pervaded the bodies and souls of both infants. It then becomes a literal and yet esoteric truth that the Christ was born in Bethlehem; a truth that augured the eventual bodily incarnation of the Christ. Nonetheless, it should be comprehended that the residual essences of the spiritual fecundation processes of the Universal Ego of Christ, which is understood to be the Holy Spirit, were manifested in the births of both Jesus infants. It is similar to the lingering scent of an Easter lily after the actual lily is removed from its vessel.

In the Luke Gospel, the activity of the Christ's Cosmic, Universal Ego is the Holy Spirit that spiritually inseminates the Virgin Sophia, the purified astral body, of Mary which then gives her voice the capacity to shape and mold the initial embryo and subsequent fetus of the body of Jesus of Nazareth. Regarding the Luke Gospel, Steiner, in his own lectures, makes it clear that Jesus of Nazareth was conceived physically and that it was not a miraculous conception. The physical conception of the Nathan-Jesus was most likely also induced by means of a temple ritual of insemination free of passion to which Steiner asserts that Joseph was the father of the Nathan-Jesus. This resolves the aforementioned contradiction as Joseph was the physical father of Jesus and the Holy Spirit was the spiritual Father of Jesus. This resolution is clearly presented to us when we read what Steiner had said pertaining to the Holy Spirit as the Universal Spirit which also fills the soul of the Nathan Jesus-child.

As a brief side note, drawing from Steiner's remarks in regard to the Holy Spirit, we are able to acquire a better understanding of John the Baptist's exclamation that the Christ, ". . . will baptize you with the Holy Spirit," (Luke 3:16) in that the Christ has come to engage each human Ego from within to assist us in transmuting our astral bodies into Manas. Other points of interest are two brief but very significant passages in the Gospel of Luke which are prominent in this study. These passages make significant references to the voice of Mary. In the first two chapters of the Luke Gospel great emphasis is placed upon some form of vocal expression. The Luke Gospel's focus on the different voices and their powerful significance throughout the first two chapters is a prominent component of these early chapters; such as, the impact of Mary's greeting to Elizabeth, Gabriel's Annunciations, the angel 'announcing' to the shepherds, and even the loss of Zachary's voice. When we examine Mary's role in the Luke Gospel, however, there are two passages that are exceptionally notable and compel one's attention.

They are the following: Luke 1: 41-42: "And it came to pass, when Elizabeth heard the greeting of Mary, that the babe in her womb leapt. And Elizabeth was filled with the Holy Spirit, and cried out with a loud voice . . ." And when Elizabeth speaks to Mary: Luke 1: 44: "For behold, the moment that the sound of thy greeting came to my ear the babe in my womb leapt for joy." From the Luke cycle Steiner makes it clear that Mary's visit to Elizabeth ignited the Ego of John the Baptist within the fetus. In Lecture V Steiner had said, ". . . and the embryo that in other cases is quickened by its own Ego was here quickened through the medium of the 'other' embryo." In Lecture VI from the same cycle we read, "A human body of great perfection had to be made available, one that could only be produced through part of the etheric substance of Adam - untouched by all earthly influences - being united with the etheric body of this Jesus-child. This etheric substance was imbued with the forces that had worked upon Earth evolution before the Fall and now, in the Jesus-child, their power was immeasurably enhanced. This made it possible for the mysterious influence referred to in the lecture yesterday to be exercised by the mother of the Nathan Jesus upon the mother of the Baptist --- that is to say upon John himself before he was born."

It was both the presence of Mary and the Nathan soul within the womb of Mary that quickened the Ego of John within the womb of Elizabeth. When Mary first greeted Elizabeth the Ego of John the Baptist was simultaneously invigorated by the spirit essence of the Nirmanakaya of Buddha that was streaming into the soul of the Nathan Jesus-child at that time. Moreover, we also know from Anthroposophy that the human voice in the future will be an organ for bringing new life into being. As the Nathan soul carried the pure etheric forces of the Tree of Life within him so too did Mary harbor within her the 'pure' etheric substance of the sound and life ethers. This pure, 'virginal', etheric substance may be referred to as the Eternal Feminine. It was this virginal, etheric, life-forming substance which flowed through Mary. We are told by Steiner that human speech does create unseen forms in the etheric realm. Likewise, throughout the entire pregnancy, the virginal Eternal Feminine forces that flowed from Mary's voice became predominately active in fashioning the perfected human body that would later hold the Christ Being; the Logos/World-Word.

It may be proposed that the Christ-imbued astral body of Mary was interactive with the Manas element of the former angel of Buddha who was identified earlier in this work as Vidar. In Lecture I from, "The Theosophy of the Rosicrucian," Steiner states the following in regard to the long history of the evolution of the human physical form thereby framing how the effects of astral pictures in the souls of human Beings subsequently shaped the human physical body: "Just as a seal is pressed into liquid sealing wax, so did the

244

astral picture impress itself into the etheric body and this in turn molded the forms of the physical body. . . . The whole physical body of man in its plastic forms is nothing else than a product of the pictures of the astral body and the forces of the etheric body." All that streamed into the astral body of Mary from the Christ Ego as the Universal Holy Spirit in conjunction with that which flowed from the Manas element of Vidar united with the etheric forces that emanated from the spiritualized larynx of Mary. In accompaniment with these processes, the Nirmanakaya forces of Buddha were also permeating the astral body of the unborn Jesus at that time which then impacted the etheric body of Jesus. Together, these pre-fallen etheric forces in turn molded the physical body of Jesus of Nazareth. As a matter of intrigue, the history of the body of the Nathan Jesus is similar to the history and future of the Earth itself. The Earth existed for a lengthy period of time before Christ assumed it as His own physical body. The body of Jesus also lived most of its years before it too assumed the Christ within it. During the time of Jesus of Nazareth the normal length of life expectancy was less than what it is today. It may be postulated that at 30 years of age he would have been at his mid-life point or even somewhat beyond it. The same was true of the earth when Christ incarnated into the earth. At the time of the advent of the Christ the earth was to some degree beyond its mid-life point. In the Event of Golgotha the mineral body of Jesus died on the cross and dissolved to ashes while in the tomb. The ashes were then consumed by the earth by means of a fissure that opened in the tomb during the time of the body's interment. The mineral body of Christ Jesus was displaced after its death by the redeemed Phantom/physical body of the Christ at the time of the Resurrection. Further on, Christ later manifested within the higher sheaths of Jesus of Nazareth while ascending to higher spiritual spheres of the earth. This is the equivalent predestined course of events which the earth will assume in its eventual physical death and ascension. Subsequently, the earth proceeds in its ascension to higher conditions of form by means of the interactive relationship between the earthbound Christ and a Christ-imbued humanity while our cosmos, as a whole, transitions over time into its future Jupiter condition; the New Jerusalem as it is expressed in the Book of Revelation.

The active forces of the Christ Ego as the Holy Spirit endowed the astral body of Mary with the nascent prototypic stages of achieving the capacity to bring life into being through the faculty of her 'spiritualized' voice. While in the womb of Mary, the body of Jesus was being worked upon and fashioned in a unique way by the generating life forces of her 'spiritualized larynx' which in turn bestowed this body with all that was essential in becoming the eventual vehicle for the incarnation of the Logos; the Christ. The potential creative power of the human voice may have been alluded to in Steiner's, "From Jesus to Christ," when he mentions that the Nathan Jesus-child could speak in a language that only Mary could understand. From Lecture VIII:

"Now the body of this Nathan Jesus-child - or, better, his threefold bodily organization - physical body, etheric body, astral body - was formed in a quite special manner. In fact, this body was such that the child showed capacities exactly contrary to those of the Solomon Jesus-child. Whereas the latter was remarkable because of his great gifts in relation to things one can learn externally, it might almost be said that in this respect the Nathan Jesus-child was untalented. You will understand that saying this implies not the slightest deprecation. The Nathan Jesus-child was not in a position to familiarize himself with the products of human culture on Earth. By contrast, the remarkable fact is that he could speak as soon as he was born. A faculty which belongs more to the physical body was thus present in him from his birth. But - according to a good tradition which can be occultly confirmed - the language he spoke could be understood by his Mother only."

Both Mary and the Nathan Jesus-child carried within them pure etheric forces and that throughout the entire gestation period the voice of Mary impacted these etheric forces that brought about the creation and development of the physical body of the Nathan Jesus-child. In a sense, both souls were in communication with one another during the pregnancy in that their etheric forces intermingled greatly with one another. It was previously mentioned that Vidar, the former Angel of Gautama Buddha, worked as an active force in the formation of the physical body of the Nathan Jesus-child who then, as the Angel who appeared to Christ during His Agony, later revived the physical body of Christ Jesus in the Garden of Gethsemane. From the same lecture (VIII) Steiner then said the following in regard to the Nathan Jesus: "It is the disuniting spirits of the Luciferic and Ahrimanic world who have made many languages out of the primal language. The primal language is lost, and can be spoken today by nobody with an Ego which in the course of Earth-evolution has passed from incarnation to incarnation. This Jesus-child, who had not gone through human incarnations, acquired from the starting-point of human evolution the faculty of speaking, not this or that language, but a language of which we can rightly say that it was not comprehensible to those around him. But, because of the inner qualities of heart that lived in it, it was understood by his Mother's heart."

Sergei Prokofieff also addresses this phenomenon in his book, "Eternal Individuality": "This new organ of reproduction, called here the Holy Grail, will, however, as we have seen, be made up of the activity of two transformed organs: the heart and the larynx. Rudolf Steiner speaks about this as follows: `There are within man organs of two different kinds, those which are on the way to becoming imperfect and will gradually fall away and those which are still in the process of formation. All lower organs, the sexual organs, will fall away. The heart and the larynx, on the other hand, are organs which will be perfected and find their full development only in the future. [November 5, 1907; GA 98]. In another lecture he speaks about this with full

246

clarity: `Above all there will be a transformation of the larynx and the heart. In the future, they will be the organs of reproduction.' [December 17, 1907; GA 98]. The heart and the larynx are the new spiritual organs of reproduction whose interaction, in the far future, `will bring forth Beings similar to man.' [November 5, 1907; GA 98]. It is they that are engraved, as symbols of the future evolution of a humanity which has overcome earthly birth and death, in the Imagination of the Sun chalice and the lance of love, the transformed heart and larynx."

In footnote 552 to this same work Prokofieff also adds this in regard to the larynx: "However, this future activity of the Maitreya Buddha amongst mankind is only the first stage in the process whereby the human word, through the gradual mastery of its spiritual power, becomes the micrologos. In our fifth post-Atlantean epoch, as has been said, the word is merely the bearer of abstract thoughts, an instrument of the conscious Ego. In the sixth epoch, with the streaming of the Spirit-Self into humanity, the power of the word will extend to the astral body. This will be a time when the Maitreya Buddha will, through the spiritual power of the word, be able to awaken new moral impulses in human souls. In the seventh cultural epoch, with the flowing of the Life-Spirit into mankind, it will become possible to have a direct influence upon the etheric body. Then will man, through the word, be able to influence, for example, the forces of growth and propagation in the plant world. And, finally, in the next epoch, after the War of All Against All, with the outpouring of the impulse of the Spirit-Man into humanity, the possibility will arise of directly influencing the physical body through the word, and, with it, also the physical processes of the surrounding world.

With this threefold evolutionary sequence will also go a corresponding gradual transformation of the human larynx, first in the astral sphere, then in the etheric and, finally - in the physical - into a new organ of reproduction. In other words, the arising in the epoch of the Spirit-Man of the possibility of working through the word into physical substances will also represent the beginning of the fulfillment of the ideal which Rudolf Steiner describes in the following words: `In the future the larynx will not only bring forth words, but will be the creative organ of procreation which will bring forth Beings similar to man' (lecture of 5 November 1907, GA 98)."

In Steiner's lecture cycle, "Occult Signs and Symbols," he states in Lecture IV: "At present the larynx is at the beginning of its development, but in times to come it will be transformed into a spiritualized organ of reproduction."

"As men in the future will be able to call people into being through their speaking, so it was that the forerunner of mankind, the gods, were gifted with an organ with which they expressed all things that are around us today."

However, in the same lecture he went on to say that when humans achieve this ability the planet, "will consist of fiery matter," and humans will

247

call forth humans of fiery form. The voice of Mary acting upon the body of Jesus has prefigured this future capacity of our Selves. The same voice that gives us the ability to address oneself as I AM will in the future bring forth life itself as the Logos, the Word, creates life now. From, "The Spiritual Hierarchies and Their Reflection in the Physical World": "The first stirring of the 'I AM' is expressed in speech, in sound. All sound-formation is connected in a particular way with the forces of procreation. . . . The breaking of the voice at puberty, for example, is connected in a definite way with the powers of propagation. There is a hidden relationship between them. Everything related to this sphere in man was summed up by ancient consciousness as the Bull nature of the human Being. This is how the designation of this particular zodiacal sign arose." (Lecture VIII April 17, 1909).

The phenomenon of the human voice and its future potentiality may have also been presented to us at the opening of the Luke Gospel in the narration of Zachariah's loss of speech. Though the Luke Gospel states that Elizabeth was barren, the actuality may have been that Zachariah was infertile. Zachariah and Elizabeth were childless at the time when Gabriel appeared to Zachariah. Gabriel proceeds to remove Zachariah's capacity to speak. In actuality, the loss of speech by Zachariah may have been induced by Gabriel upon Zachariah as a temporary abatement of Zachariah's forces of speech which were then transmuted into forces of procreation. This may have also been preordained in the pre-lives of Zachariah and Elizabeth who were elderly at the time of the birth of John the Baptist. Since Zachariah and Elizabeth were elderly, this provided a congruence of their souls with the 'old soul' element of John the Baptist. To acquire an understanding of the power that the human voice once had and will revive again in the future Steiner says the following from his Luke cycle, Lecture VIII: "In the days of the very ancient Indian civilization, for example, what is called `healing' was a very different matter from what it came to be later on . . . Because by working upon the soul a tremendously strong effect could at one time be produced upon the body, it was possible so to impress the soul of another by means of a word charged with the right impulse of Will that this soul transmitted the effect to the etheric body, and the latter in turn to the physical body. . . . But the time is approaching when such ways of working will again be effective."

In Lecture III from, "Building Stones for an Understanding of the Mystery of Golgotha," Steiner says this: ". . . man as he is today cannot possibly exist six thousand years hence, any more than it is possible for a man who is now twenty years old to be alive in two hundred years time. We can discover through occult investigation that in the sixth millennium women as they are constituted today will become sterile and that an entirely different reproductive process will exist by that time." From the same lecture cycle in Lecture IV Steiner then says: "And bear in mind also what I mentioned recently: that spiritual investigation shows that in the sixth and seventh millennium there will be a decline in fertility. Women will become increasingly sterile. The present method of reproduction will no longer be possible; it must be transposed to a higher plane. In order that the world may not fall into a state of decadence, when opinions as to what is good and evil will be treated medically, in order that good and evil, all personal determination of what is good and evil, should not be recorded merely as a matter to be decided by State regulation or human conventions in order that this should not arise at a time when the natural order that at present prevails in the human species will of necessity have ceased to maintain the race - for just as in women fertility ceases at a certain age, so too the present method of reproduction in the human species will cease at a certain stage of Earth evolution - in order to forestall this, the Christ Impulse was bestowed upon mankind."

In the lecture cycle, "Macrocosm and Microcosm," Steiner unfolds the connection of the Human to the heart and the Divine to the larynx. In Lecture XI he states: "And finally we ask: Is there something in man that points to the future? According to yesterday's lecture the human heart is a very ancient organ. In an entirely different form it was already in existence on the Old Moon and on the Earth has simply been transformed. On the Old Moon there was as yet no brain; but the heart was in existence and moreover had within it the basis for a future transformation. Just as a blossom bears within it the seed of the fruit, so the Old Moon-heart bore within it the Earth-heart. Are there organs in the human body which already today point prophetically to the future? There are indeed such organs. True, they are by no means fully developed today but they will reach greater perfection and after the decline of other organs will belong to man in a higher form when he becomes the future Jupiter-man. One such organ is the larynx. Today it is only on the way towards higher development. It reveals itself in a germinal state and will become something quite different in time to come. If we study the larynx in its relation to the lung, we can say that in a certain way it presupposes the lung, it evolves on the basis of the lung's existence. But we realize at the same time that man is still at an imperfect stage with respect to what he produces in his larynx. Where is the greatest human perfection to be found today? In that which gives man the possibility of calling himself an `I'. This is what sets him above the other Beings of the Earth. Man is an individuality centered in the Ego and it is this individuality who passes from one incarnation to another. We can look back into a life which preceded the present life on Earth, then further and further back into the past, and we can also look forward into the future. Man passes on into his following incarnations with whatever he has made his own in his Ego. If any one of you could look back into your earlier incarnations you would find yourself incarnated, for example, in the Greco-Latin epoch, in the Egypto-Chaldean epoch, in the ancient Persian epoch, in the ancient Indian epoch, and so on.

But the work accomplished by the human larynx is not in the same sense bound up with the Ego. What the larynx can do comes to expression in each incarnation in a different form of speech; man does not carry it with him from one incarnation to another. Speech is not something that is individualized today. In the course of incarnations a man may belong to different peoples and use different languages, different linguistic idioms. It is therefore clear that speech is not so intimately bound up with the Ego as thinking is. Speech is not bound up with our true individuality, with that which constitutes our real human worth. Speech is something we have in common with other human Beings; it comes to us from conditions outside. Nevertheless there is no denying that speech is something in which our inmost Self, the Spirit, expresses itself. The quality of feelings and the configuration of thoughts are carried into the sounds of the words; so that we possess in our larynx an organ through which, with our individuality, we are part and parcel of something wrought by the Spirit, but not of something we have ourselves wrought. If speech were not wrought by the Spirit, the Spirit of man could not express itself through that medium. If the larynx were unable to capture in song the tone imparted by the Spirit, the human soul could not express itself through the medium of song. The larynx is an organ which brings to expression spiritual activities, but not individualized spiritual activities. The larynx reveals itself to the spiritual investigator as an organ through which man is membered into a group-soul which he cannot yet bring to the stage of individualization; but the larynx is developing to the point where it will eventually be able to be a receptacle for man's individual activities. In the future, man will so transform his larynx that through it he will be able to give expression to his own individual reality. That is only a prophetic indication of a process which we must call the formation of a germinal organ which will be transformed in the future. If we pay heed to this we shall find it comprehensible that as individuals we have no power over what our larynx produces, that it is given to us by grace and that we must first grow into it with our individuality. Just as with our own Egohood we are rooted in ourselves, so with our larynx we are rooted in the Macrocosm as a whole. Out of the Macrocosm there still flows into us that which makes us human.

Through our heart we make ourselves men; through the larynx the Macrocosm makes us men. When in a new incarnation we grow into the Macrocosm, we grow into an organism of which the heart is the center, but this organism, this bodily constitution, is unceasingly maintained by the Macrocosm, the forces of the Macrocosm stream into it. Through the larynx there streams into us from the Macrocosm something that is a supreme manifestation of the spirit. There we are linked with the Macrocosm. We not only receive into ourselves influences from the Macrocosm but in a certain sense we also give them back, although we still have no individual control of them. We are born into a folk-language; we have as yet no individual control over what is innate in the folk-spirit. Hence a great truth is contained in what is said at the very beginning of the Bible: that man's earthly evolution waited until there could be created for him the crowning structure of his breathing apparatus - the larynx which is created by the Spirit, bestowed by God Himself. `God breathed into man's nostrils the breath of life and he became a living soul.' This is an indication of the point of time when there flowed into man that which is connected with the divine, with the Macrocosm. The Human is connected with the heart, the Divine with the larynx.

In that man not only breathes but can also transmute his breathing processes into song and speech produced by the larynx, he has in his breathing a faculty capable of the highest possible development. Hence there are good grounds for saying that man is always developing, that he will rise to higher and higher stages of spirituality. In Oriental philosophy the highest member that man, as Spirit-Man, will develop in the future is called `Atma' - a word derived from `Atmen' (breath). But man must himself participate in the development of this Spirit-Man from the present rudimentary beginnings. He must work at the development of speech and song in which, as a transformed breathing process, there are infinite possibilities."

In addition to examining the role of the voice of Mary and that of the human voice, other points of interest are the genealogies of the Luke and Matthew Gospels. Luke 1:35 in part reads, ". . . the Holy One which shall be born of thee shall be called the Son of God." The phrase 'Son of God', or more specifically the term 'Son', is often a reference to the Ego. If we look at Mary as a figure that is a personification or archetypal picture of the human soul, we have the image of the human soul giving birth to the 'Son of God' within the soul. That is, the soul gives birth to the Ego. The Ego then is born to which it gradually develops over time in a sequence of physical earthly incarnations. It is the human Ego to which Luke is more specifically referring when he gives us the genealogy of Jesus in his Gospel; i.e. "Jesus. . .- as was supposed - the Son of Joseph, the Son of Heli," etc.,. Luke's genealogy is purposely placed immediately after the Baptism in the Jordan when the Christ at that point in time had incarnated into the body of Jesus of Nazareth. Not only do the words of the Gospel give us insight into deeper mysteries but the construction of the Gospel reveals deeper truths also. In Luke's Gospel, the genealogy of Jesus of Nazareth is intentionally placed 'after' the incarnation of Christ within a human Form at the time of the Baptism in the Jordan by John the Baptist. And because it is purposefully placed after the incarnation of the Christ into a human Form it presages the direction which this incarnation by Christ into human flesh and soul will eventually lead us in our own future evolution. It is the Christ that advances our Ego, the 'Son' of our soul, in its on-going development. It is at this point where Luke wishes to show that when Christ entered a human Form He brought with Him the 'First

Principle' from which every human Ego can draw its life and begin its ascension. In the Luke Gospel we are given a genealogy that ascends back to Adam, then to God. There is a clear distinction between the genealogy of Luke's Gospel and that of Matthew's Gospel. In Luke's Gospel the physical genealogy and blood-line is not so much the point of emphasis since the body of the Nathan Jesus is more of a creation of the forces of Mary's spiritualized 'voice' once the physical conception had been consummated. In Matthew's Gospel, however, the word 'begot' is used throughout the entire genealogy. This is a more emphatic means of description in detailing the physical blood-line of the Zarathustra-Jesus than what Luke's Gospel uses.

In Matthew's Gospel, the actual physicality of a descending genealogy is emphasized in the ancestry of the blood-line by the use of the word `begot'. The blood-line is in a descending order which is significant because it alludes to the overall historical path of all human Egos descending ever deeper into matter. It is also a genealogy that places much importance on past human 'history'. The genealogy of Matthew's Gospel is the genealogy of Zarathustra. In Luke's Gospel we are given a genealogy that looks to the 'future' though conversely it returns us to Adam. It returns us to Adam in one sense in that it wishes to draw our attention to the time when we had a devachanic consciousness. However, what was lacking in our earliest stages of development was the capacity to stand within the spiritual realms with our own individuated 'I' consciousness. Our consciousness then was nothing more than the consciousness of higher spiritual Beings permeating our own souls. We had no true individuated 'I' consciousness at that time. Matthew's genealogy alludes to the Fall of humanity. Only by gradually descending further into matter did we then develop an individuated consciousness. We had moved further and further from the spiritual realms as we moved deeper within matter and consequently deeper within our own Selves. We were then ready to slowly receive and develop our own Ego. Conversely, the genealogy of Luke's Gospel alludes to the ascendency of human consciousness and, therefore, uses the term Son/Ego throughout until it returns to God. Luke places the genealogy after the Baptism in the Jordan because with the Christ now here on Earth, the human Ego, over future eons, ascends back to God; that is, it evolves and ascends consciously to higher realms. In conjunction with the ascension of humanity, the Earth as the Holy Grail is then spiritualized and ascends to the spiritual worlds. Luke, therefore, shows us that our consciousness ascends back to its former spiritually-endowed, devachanic capacity when he traces the genealogy back to Adam and then back to God. However, in contrast to our pre-fallen consciousness, we will have an individuated, awakened, Christ-filled, ascended Ego-consciousness which is to be attained in full freedom. We will have achieved the Ego-endowed, Adam-consciousness which reaches up to God and to the spiritual worlds.

In conclusion, Steiner weaves the revelations of the Holy Spirit as the Father of Jesus, the Baptism in the Jordan and the Sophia at the foot of the Cross into a single whole in the lecture, "The Mystery of Golgotha," (December 2, 1906): "John baptized Jesus in the Jordan. A dove descended from heaven and in that moment a spiritual fertilization occurred. The mother of Jesus, who is fertilized here - who is she? The Chela, Jesus of Nazareth takes his I-Being away in this moment and the highly developed Manas is fertilized and Buddhi enters. The highly developed Manas that receives Buddhi is wisdom, Sophia, the mother fertilized by Jesus' Father. The name Mary, like Maya, indicates in general the name of his mother. We read in the first chapter of Luke's Gospel, `An angel came to her and spoke, Hail, O favored one . . ., Behold, you will conceive . . . and bear a son . . . The Holy Spirit will come upon you and the power of the most high will overshadow you.' The Holy Spirit is the Father of Jesus, the dove that flies down fructifies Sophia, who is found in Jesus.

Therefore, the text should be read, `Standing by the Cross was Sophia, the mother of Jesus.' He says to this mother, "Woman behold that is your son." He himself passed Sophia - who has been in Him - to John. He made John into the son of Sophia and said, "That is your mother," indicating, 'Divine wisdom you must henceforth recognize as your mother and dedicate yourself to her alone.' What John then wrote was this divine wisdom Sophia, who is incarnated in John's Gospel itself. He himself received this wisdom from Jesus and was authorized by Christ to bring this wisdom to the earth."

XVI

The Cosmic Significance of the Mystery of Golgotha

In the lecture cycle, "Building Stones for an Understanding of the Mystery of Golgotha," Steiner clarifies the difference between the baptism by John the Baptist to what Christ brought to humanity. From Lecture III: "What was the significance of baptism with water? Externally, of course, John the Baptist baptized with the waters of the Jordan. We know that the candidates for baptism suffered total immersion. During the immersion they experienced a kind of loosening of the etheric body, which bestowed on them a temporary clairvoyance. This is the real significance of the baptism by John and of similar baptisms. But when John spoke of baptism with water he was referring not only to this form of baptism, but more especially to the passage in the Old Testament which says: `The Spirit of God moved upon the face of the waters.' What was the purpose of the baptism with water in the Jordan ? It was intended that through the loosening of their etheric bodies and the experiences they underwent the candidates for baptism should feel themselves transposed into the condition of consciousness of the time before the `Fall'. Everything that had occurred since the Fall was to be erased from their consciousness. They were to be restored to their pre-lapsarian state in order that they might experience the condition of man before the Fall. They were made aware that through the Fall man had entered upon a wrong path and that to continue on this path would be to court disaster. He had to return to his original state of innocence, to cleanse his soul of the evil which this aberration had brought."

"Compare this with a widespread movement of the time which reflected in various ways what was indicated in the Gospel of St. John. People declared that one must renounce the world and follow the life of the spirit. An echo of this desire to `withdraw from the world' is still to be found in Gnosis and monachism. Now why did this powerful impulse of the Baptist which was a comparatively recent development become so widespread? The answer is to be found in the words: `The Kingdom of Heaven is at hand.' At this point we must recall what was said in the last lecture about the soul - that since the Fall it had progressively deteriorated, was less and less fitted to perform its function as intermediary between the spirit and the body. This continuous decline could persist for a certain period of Earth evolution but ultimately had to be arrested. This moment will arrive when Divine evolution takes over Earth evolution. Men such as John the Baptist had a prophetic intimation of this moment. The time is now at hand, he felt, when souls can no longer be saved, when souls must perish without some special dispensation. He realized that either the souls of men would have to withdraw from life as it had been since the Fall, the cause of their corruption - and in that event Earth evolution would have been in vain - or something else must supervene. And this realization found expression in the following words: `He that cometh after me shall baptize you with the Holy Ghost.' John felt that only by withdrawing from the world could man be saved from the consequences of the Fall. Christ wished to save mankind in another way: he wished them to remain in he world and yet find salvation. He had no wish that mankind should return to the time before the Fall, but that they should experience the further stages of Earth evolution and yet participate in the Kingdom of Heaven."

Continuing in Lecture III Steiner unites the Ideal of the moral element of humanity to the future condition of Jupiter and how this is deeply related to the fleeing youth and the young man in the tomb in Mark's Gospel: ". . . according to Christian belief there lives in the Christ Being a power that lays hold of our moral conceptions and creates out of them a new world order: `Heaven and Earth may pass away, but my words shall not pass away.' This is the power that will carry over to Jupiter the moral element developed on the Earth. Now picture the Earth as an organism, like a plant, the moral law as the seed which is formed within the organism, and the Christ force as the Impulse which stimulates the seed to grow into the future Earth, into Jupiter. We then have a totally new conception of the Gospels from the standpoint of Spiritual Science.

But how can this be? How can that which belongs solely to the realm of thought according to the materialist, which is only an idea or theory towards which one feels a moral obligation - how can that be transformed into real force such as the one which burns in coal or which causes the bullet to fly through the air? How can such ideas which are so tenuous possess solid reality? To achieve this transformation a new Impulse is needed and these moral ideas must be imbued with the Impulse. What Impulse is this? You will recall that we said earlier that faith must not be merely a substitute for knowledge: it must be an active agent that effects something. It must make our moral ideas a reality, lift them to a new plane and create a new world out of them. It is important that our articles of faith are not simply a form of unverified knowledge, a blind faith, but that our faith has the power to transform the seed `morality' into a cosmic reality. It was the mission of the Mystery of Golgotha to imbue Earth evolution with this power. This power had to be implanted in the souls of the disciples. At the same time they were reminded of the loss suffered by those who possessed only the written records. It is the power of faith which is of paramount importance. And if we do not understand what we owe to Christ when one so often hears the words `faith' or `belief', then neither do we understand what entered Earth evolution at the time of the Mystery of Golgotha.

You will now realize that the Mystery of Golgotha has cosmic significance. That which belongs to the natural order is subject to the laws of nature. And just as at a certain stage of its evolution a plant bears seed, so too at a certain point of time the Mystery of Golgotha will bring a new Impulse in preparation for the new Jupiter evolution in which the future incarnation of man can participate. From our study of the unique nature of the Christ Being I have indicated the relation of this Being to the whole Cosmos and how, at a definite point in time, Earth evolution was imbued with a new vitalizing force, which is revealed from time to time with impressive effect, but only to those who can apprehend such manifestations intuitively. The author of the Mark Gospel, for example, was a case in point. When Christ was led away after the betrayal by Judas and the author of that Gospel had a clairvoyant vision of the scene, he saw, among the multitude that had forsaken Him, a `certain young man' clad only in a linen cloth. The linen cloth is torn from him, but he wrests himself free and flees from them naked. (Mark 14: 51). This was the same young man who, according to the Mark Gospel, was sitting clothed in a long white garment on the right of the sepulcher and announced: Christ is Risen. This is the account given in the Gospel of St. Mark as the result of Imaginative cognition. Here is portrayed the encounter between the former body of Christ-Jesus and the `seed' of a new world order as seen by Imaginative cognition.

. . . the human body, in virtue of its original constitution, was destined for immortality. Compare this with the fact that the animal is mortal by virtue of its organization, while this does not apply to man. He is mortal because of the corruption of his soul and this stain will be washed away by Christ. If you reflect upon this you will understand that the physical body must be transformed by the living force that streams into Earth evolution through the Mystery of Golgotha. When Earth evolution comes to an end the power which has been lost through the `Fall' and which brought death to the body will be restored through the power of Christ, and the body of man will be seen in its true physical form. If we recognize the trichotomy of body, soul and spirit, then the `resurrection of the body' takes on meaning also, otherwise it cannot be understood. The modern rationalist will no doubt regard this as a most reactionary idea, but he who derives his knowledge of reincarnation from the well-spring of truth is also aware of the real significance of the resurrection of the body at the end of time. And when Paul rightly said: `If Christ be not risen, then is our preaching vain, and your faith is also vain' (Corinthians I 15: 14), we know from the investigations of Spiritual Science that he bore witness to the truth. If this dictum of Paul be true, then it is equally true to say: if earthly evolution does not lead to the conservation of the corporeal form which man can perfect in the course of evolution, if the human form were to perish, if man could not rise again through the power of Christ, then the Mystery of Golgotha would have been in vain and vain also the faith that it inspired. This is the necessary complement of the words of Paul."

In Lecture IV Steiner makes the following intriguing comment about speech as a creative force as well as how our thoughts impact the Cosmos: "On the other hand, minds such as Goethe's will always insist that man's understanding must be enlarged, that man must become sensitively aware so that he will be able to think, feel and experience that up to the sixth and seventh millennium the spoken word will once again become a reality and will have the same creative power in the external world as the power of fecundation in the seeds of the plant kingdom today. The word which has become abstract today must regain the original creative power it once possessed 'in the beginning'. Those who, in the light of Spiritual Science, are reluctant to amplify the opening words of the Gospel of St. John, 'In the beginning was the Word, and the Word was with God and the Word was a God', by adding 'and the Word one day will live again', have not fully grasped the Christian message. For Christ Jesus has set forth His teaching in a form that conflicts with the external world. It is to Him that we owe the Impulse to regeneration. The world meanwhile has declined rapidly and the Christ Impulse must be increasingly reinforced before this decline can be arrested. To a certain extent we have gone some way towards reversing this doctrine since the Mystery of Golgotha, but for the most part without being consciously aware of it. Man must learn once again to participate consciously in cosmic events. He must begin to realize not merely: 'when I think, something takes place in my brain', but 'when I think, something takes place in the Cosmos!' And he must learn to think in such a way that just as he can entrust his thinking to the Cosmos, so too, he can once again unite his Being with the Cosmos."

In the lecture course, "How Can Mankind Find the Christ Again," Steiner brings to our attention in Lecture II the roles which Judaism, Hellenism and Romanism played in establishing Christianity in the world: "Something new had to enter world evolution. And so in the course of time the destruction of Solomon's temple and the rise, the birth, of Christianity exactly coincided. Solomon's Temple: a spatial symbolic image of the content of the cosmos; Christianity, comprehended as a time-phenomenon: a new image of the cosmos. Christianity is not something that appears as a spatial image, as in the case of Solomon's Temple; one only understands Christianity if one grasps it in images of time. One must see that Earth evolution proceeded as far as the Mystery of Golgotha; then the Mystery of Golgotha intervened; then, through the Christ pouring Himself into humanity,

257

evolution moves on in this way or that. Its deeper content is not to be equated in the remotest degree with anything appearing in spatial images, not even in the gigantic, magnificent spatial images of Solomon's Temple. Nevertheless, Solomon's Temple, as also the inner aspect of Pharisaic and Sadducean life, contained the soul of the world consciousness of that time. The soul of the world consciousness two thousand years ago was to be found in Old Testament Judaism. Into this soul was laid the seed of Christianity, a new seed that, while growing out of all that may be expressed in space, can only be expressed in time. The becoming following the existing: that is the inner relation of Christianity that was then born to the soul element of the world of that time, to Judaism that was embodied in Solomon's Temple, which later collapsed. Christianity was born into the soul of ancient Judaism.

As Christianity sought the soul in Judaism, so it sought the spirit in Hellenism. The Gospels themselves, as transmitted to the world . . . have in the main passed through the Greek spirit. The thoughts through which the world could think Christianity are the spiritual wisdom of Greece. The first apologia of the Church Fathers appeared in the Greek tongue. Just as Christianity was born into the soul that for the humanity of that time lived in Judaism, so it was born into the spirit provided by Hellenism. Romanism furnished the body. It was Romanism that at that time could provide an external organization for concepts of empire. Judaism soul, Hellenism spirit, Romanism body - body of course, in the sense that the social structure of humanity is body. Romanism is in reality the forming of external inclinations and institutions; the thoughts concerning external institutions live within them. It is the corporeal element in historical existence, the corporeal element in historical development. Just as Christianity was born into the soul of Judaism and into the spirit of Hellenism, so it was born into the body of the Roman Empire."

In Lecture III from the same lecture cycle Steiner adds: "The state of our development since the Mystery of Golgotha is this, that starting from our thirtieth year we can really gain nothing from our own organism, from what is bestowed upon us by nature. If the Mystery of Golgotha had not taken place, we would be going about here on Earth after our 30th year saying to ourselves: Actually we live in the true sense only up to our thirty-second or thirty-third year at most. Up to that time our organism makes it possible for us to live; then we might just as well die. For from the course of nature, from the elemental occurrences of nature, we can gain nothing more for our soul development through the impulses of our organism. If the Mystery of Golgotha had not taken place, the Earth would be filled with human Beings lamenting thus: Of what use to me is life after my thirty-third year? Up to that time my organism can give me something. After that I might just as well be dead. I really go about here on Earth like a living corpse. If the Mystery of Golgotha had not taken place, many people would feel that they are going about on Earth like living corpses. But the Mystery of Golgotha, dear friends, has still to be made fruitful. We should not merely receive the Impulse of Golgotha unconsciously, as people now do: we should receive it consciously, in such a manner that through it we may remain youthful up to old age. And it can indeed keep us healthy and youthful if we receive it consciously in the right way. We shall then be conscious of its enlivening effect upon our life. This is important!

Thus you see that the Mystery of Golgotha can be regarded as something intensely alive during the course of our earthly life. I said earlier that people are most predisposed to brotherliness in the middle of life - around the thirty-third year, but they do not always develop it. You have the reason for this in what I just said. Those who fail to develop brotherliness, who lack something of brotherliness, simply are too little permeated by the Christ. Since the human Being begins to die, in a certain sense, in middle age from the forces of nature, he cannot properly develop the impulse, the instinct, of brotherliness - and still less the impulse toward freedom, which is taken up so little today - unless he brings to life within himself thoughts that come directly from the Christ Impulse. When we turn to the Christ Impulse, it enkindles brotherliness in us directly. To the degree to which a man feels the necessity for brotherliness, he is permeated by Christ.

One is also unable alone to develop the impulse for freedom to full strength during the remainder of one's earthly life. (In future periods of evolution this will be different.) Something entered our Earth evolution as human Being and flowed forth at the death of Christ Jesus to unite Itself with the earthly evolution of humanity. Therefore Christ is the One who also leads present-day mankind to freedom. We become free in Christ when we are able to grasp the fact that Christ could really not have become older, could not have lived longer, in a physical body than up to the age of thirty-three years. Suppose hypothetically that He had lived longer: then He would have lived on in a physical body into the years when according to our present Earth evolution this body is destined for death. Had He lived to be forty years old, He would have experienced the forces of death in His body. These He would not have wished to experience. He could only have wished to experience those forces that are still the freshening forces for a human Being. He was active up to His thirty-third year, to the middle of life; as the Christ He enkindled brotherliness. Then He caused the spirit to flow into human evolution: He gave over to the Holy Spirit what was henceforth to be within the power of man. Through this Holy Spirit, this health-giving Spirit, a human Being develops to freedom toward the end of his life. Thus is the Christ Impulse integrated into the concrete life of humanity.

This permeation of man's inner Being by the Christ Principle must be incorporated into human knowledge as a new Christmas thought. Mankind must know that we bring equality with us out of the spiritual world. It comes, one might say, from God the Father, and is given to us to bring to Earth. Then brotherliness reaches its proper culmination only through the help of the Son. And through the Christ united with the Spirit we can develop the impulse for freedom as we draw near to death."

The Tree of Life forces of the etheric are returned to humanity by Christ which will increasingly come under the control of human Beings. In the lecture cycle, "Christ and the Human Soul," Steiner addresses this and adds to it the disclosure of the regions from which Christ came to us. In Lecture IV he states: "When we call Spiritual Science to our aid, we distinguish four grades of substance - earth, water, air and warmth. We then enter the realm where we speak of warmth-ether, of light-ether. As far up as the light-ether we kill that which penetrates us; we slay it unceasingly in order that we may have our Earth-consciousness. But there is something we cannot kill by our Earth-existence. We know that above the light-ether there is the so-called chemical-ether, and then there comes the life-ether. These are the two kinds of ether that we cannot kill. But because of this, they have no special participation in us. If we were able to kill the chemical-ether, the waves of the Harmony of the Spheres would sound perpetually into our physical body, and we would perpetually destroy these waves with our physical life. And if we could also kill the life-ether, we would destroy and continuously kill within ourselves the cosmic life that streams down to the Earth. In earthly sound we are given a substitute, but it is not to be compared with what we would hear if the chemical-ether were audible to us as physical human Beings. For physical sound is a product of the air and is not the spiritual sound; it is only a substitute for the spiritual sound.

When the Luciferic temptation came, the progressive gods were obliged to place man in a sphere where, from the life-ether downwards, death lives in his physical body. But at that time the progressive gods said - and the words are there in the Bible - `Man has come to know the distinction between Good and Evil, but Life he is not to have. Of the Tree of Life he shall not eat.' In occultism, we can continue the sentence, `Of the Tree of Life man shall not eat.', by adding the words, `and the Spirit of Matter he shall not hear.' Of the Tree of Life man shall not eat and the Spirit of Matter he shall not hear! These are the regions which were closed to man. Only through a certain procedure in the old Mysteries were the tones of the Sphere-Music and the Cosmic Life, pulsating through the universe, revealed to those who were to be initiated when it was given them, outside the body, to see the Christ in advance. Hence it is that the old philosophers speak of the Music of the Spheres.

In drawing attention to this, we indicate at the same time those regions from which the Christ came to us at the time of the Baptism by John in the Jordan. Whence did Christ come? He came from those regions which had been closed to man as a result of the Luciferic temptation - from the region of the Music of the Spheres and from the region of Cosmic Life. These regions had to be forgotten by man because of the Luciferic temptation at the beginning of Earth-evolution. At the Baptism by John in the Jordan, Christ entered into a human body, and that which permeated this human body was the spiritual essence of the Harmony of the Spheres, the spiritual essence of the Cosmic Life - the element that still belonged to the human soul during the first phase of its time on Earth, but from which the human soul had to be shut out as a result of the Luciferic temptation. In this sense also man is related to spirit. With his soul he really belongs to the region of the Music of the Spheres and to the region of the Word, of the living Cosmic Ether. But he was cast out from those regions. They were to be restored to him in order that he might gradually be permeated again by the spiritual elements from which he had been exiled. So it is that from the standpoint of Spiritual Science the words of St. John's Gospel touch us so deeply: In the primal beginning, when man was not yet subject to temptation, was the Logos. Man belonged to the Logos . . . the Logos was with God, and man was with the Logos, with God. And through the Baptism by John in the Jordan the Logos entered into human evolution - He became Man."

"There is perpetually engendered in man something that is also spiritual - the life in him. This is forever passing out into the world. Man projects an aura around him, an aura of rays whereby he continually enriches the earthly-spiritual element of the Earth. This earthly-spiritual element of the Earth, however, contains all the qualities, moral or otherwise, that man has acquired and bears within himself, for he sends it all out into his earthly environment. This is absolutely true. Clairvoyant sight perceives how man sends out his moral, intellectual and aesthetic aura into the world, and how this aura continues to live as earthly spirit in the spirituality of the Earth. As a comet draws its tail through the Cosmos, so does man draw through the whole of earthly life the spiritual aura which he projects. This spiritual aura is held together, phantom-like, during a man's life, but at the same time it rays out into the world his moral and intellectual properties of soul.

When in our occult studies we go back to the times before the Mystery of Golgotha, we find that the men of those days simply radiated this phantom-like entity, which contained their moral qualities, into the external world, into the external spiritual aura of the Earth. But humanity developed in the course of the Earth's existence, and just at the epoch where the Mystery of Golgotha came to pass, a certain stage had been reached in the evolution of this phantom-like entity. In earlier times it was much more evanescent; by the time of the Mystery of Golgotha it had become denser, had more form; and into this phantom-like entity there was now mingled, as a fundamental characteristic, the death which man develops in himself by killing the ray of light that enters into his eye, and so on, as I have explained. These earth-spirit entities which radiate from man are like a stillborn child, because he imparts his death to them. If Christ had not come upon the Earth, then, during the sojourn of their souls in earthly bodies, human Beings could have continuously rayed out entities with the impress of death upon them. And with this impress of death there would have been bound up the moral qualities of man of which we spoke yesterday: objective guilt and objective sin. They would have lain within it.

Let us suppose that the Christ had not come. What would have happened in the evolution of the Earth? From the time in which the Mystery of Golgotha would otherwise have taken place, men would have spiritually created dense forms to which they had imparted death. And these dense forms would have become the very things that had to pass over to the Jupiter stage with the Earth. Man would have imparted death to the Earth. A dead Earth would have given birth to a dead Jupiter. It could not have been otherwise, because if the Mystery of Golgotha had not come about, man would not have been able to permeate the radiations he gives out with the essences of the Music of the Spheres and the Cosmic Life. These essences would not have been there; they would not have flowed into the human radiations; but Christ brought them back through the Mystery of Golgotha. And when there is a fulfillment of the words, 'Not I, but Christ in me,' when we bring about a relationship to Christ within ourselves, that which rays out from us and would otherwise be dead, is made living. Because we bear death within us, the living Christ has to permeate us, in order that He may give life to the spiritual Earth-Being that we leave behind us. Christ, the living Logos, permeates and gives life to the objective guilt and sin which detaches itself from us and is not carried further in our Karma, and because He gives it life, a living Earth will evolve into a living Jupiter. This is the outcome of the Mystery of Golgotha.

The soul, if it reflects, can receive Christ in the following way. It can realize that there was once a time when man was within the bosom of the divine Logos. But man had to succumb to the temptation of Lucifer. He took death into himself. Into him there passed the germ by which he would have brought a dead Earth to birth as a dead Jupiter. The endowment which, before the temptation, the human soul had been destined to receive for its Earth-existence was left behind. With Christ it entered again into man's Earth-existence. When man takes Christ into himself, so as to feel permeated with Christ, he is able to say to himself: 'The endowment which the gods had allocated to me before the Luciferic temptation, but which owing to the temptation by Lucifer had to remain behind in the Cosmos, enters into my soul with the Christ. The soul becomes whole again for the first time by taking the Christ into itself. Only then am I fully soul; only then am I again all that the gods intended me to be from the very beginning of the Earth.' 'Am I really a soul without Christ?' man asks himself, and he feels that it is through Christ that he first becomes the soul that the guiding divine Beings meant him to be. This is the wonderful feeling of `home' that souls can have with Christ; for out of the primal cosmic home of the soul of man the Christ descended, in order to give back to the soul of man that which had to be lost on Earth as a result of the temptation by Lucifer. The Christ leads the soul up again to its primordial home, the home allotted to it by the gods."

" . . . we understand how Christ takes upon Himself the guilt and sin of Earth humanity, in so far as these are objective guilt and sin. And if we have inwardly realized this `Not I, but Christ in me,' the Christ in us, then He takes over the objective remains of our incarnations, and they stand there vivified by Christ, irradiated by Christ and permeated by His life. Yes, the remains of our incarnations stand there, and what do they come to, taken as a whole? Because Christ unites them all - Christ who belongs to all mankind in the present and in the future - the remains of the single incarnations are all compressed together. Every human soul lives in successive incarnations. From each incarnation certain relics or remains are left, as we have described. Further incarnations will leave other remains, and so on, up to the end of the Earth period. If these relics are permeated by Christ, they are compressed together. Compress what is rarefied and you will get density. Spirit also becomes dense, and so our collective Earth-incarnations are united into a spiritual body. This body belongs to us; we need it because we evolve onwards to Jupiter, and it will be the starting-point of our embodiment on Jupiter. At the end of the Earth period we shall stand there with the soul - whatever the particular karma of the soul may be - we shall stand there before our earthly relics which have been gathered together by Christ, and we shall have to unite with them in order to pass over with them to Jupiter. We shall rise again in the body, in the earthly body that has condensed out of the separate incarnations. Truly, my dear friends, from a heart profoundly moved I utter these words: `In the body we shall rise again'!"

In a lecture given in London, April 24, 1922, "The Threefold Sun and the Risen Christ," Steiner made these remarks about Christ and the Cosmic Principle of Christ: "My dear friends, if the Christ had undergone only what took place from the time of the Baptism in the Jordan until the time of the Crucifixion and the Death on the Cross, then, having undergone all this, He would still not have been able to speak of the Mysteries of which He did speak to His Initiate disciples after His Resurrection. I must explain to you that, to the divine teachers who were able to descend to Earth, and to the initiated teachers in olden times, all Mysteries were open in the whole expanded world save only the Mysteries of the interior of the Earth. The Initiates knew that down there within the Earth spiritual Beings hold command, of quite another kind than the Gods Who before the Mystery of Golgotha used ever and again to descend to human Beings. The Greeks, for instance, were not unaware of the Spiritual Beings in the interior of the Earth; they called them in their mythology the Titans. But Christ was the first of the Upper Gods to learn to know the interior of the Earth. That is an important fact. The Christ, because He was buried in the Earth, brought knowledge to the Upper Gods of a region of which before They had no knowledge. And this secret, that the Gods too undergo evolution - this secret Christ communicated to His Initiate pupils after His Resurrection. This secret Paul also learned through the natural Initiation that he experienced outside Damascus. What stunned and shook Paul to the depths of his Being was the knowledge that the Power that had formerly been sought in the Sun had now become united with the powers of Earth.

For what was the reason why Paul, when he was still Saul, persecuted the followers of Christ? The reason was, he had learned in the old Chaldean Initiation that the Christ lives outside the Earth in the Cosmos, and that those who declare that Christ lives in the Earth are in error. But when Paul received enlightenment on his way to Damascus, at that moment he knew that it was he himself who had been mistaken, in that he was ready to believe only what had hitherto been true. For now he saw that what had been true, had become changed; the Being Who dwelt formerly only in the Sun had now descended to Earth and continued to live in the forces of the Earth. Thus was the Mystery of Golgotha, for the understanding of those who first made it known to men, not an event for Earth alone, but a cosmic event, an event for all the worlds. This was how it was understood in early Christian times. And the true Initiates described the event in the following way.

They were deeply initiated, the earliest Christian Initiates; and they knew that the Christ, Whom we think of today as the Being Who passed through the Mystery of Golgotha at the beginning of our era, - they knew that the Christ, Who came hither from the Sun, had also descended to the Sun from yet more distant heights. It was in the Sun that Zarathustra beheld Him. Then His power went over into the rays of the Sun. The Initiates of Egypt beheld Him in the rays of the Sun. And then His power lived in the environment of the Earth. It was there that the Initiates of Greece beheld Him. And now in the present time - so said the earliest Christian Initiates - it is given to man to behold Christ as One Who walked on Earth in an earthly body, and Who is seen by us in His true form when we behold Him as the Risen One - the Christ Who is in the Earth, and has seen the Mystery of the Earth and can now bring it about that this Mystery shall gradually flow into the evolution of mankind."

In a series of lectures titled, "Cosmosophy," in Lecture II Steiner makes the contrast between the Father God and the Christ: ". . . outer matter is thrown back into nothingness, into chaos, so that the spirit may become newly creative. If one looks at this new creativity, one realizes that the Father God works in matter, bringing it to its completion. Matter confronts us in the outer world in the greatest variety of ways, so that it is visible to us. Within our inner Being, however, this matter is thrown back into its nothingness and then permeated with pure spiritual Being, with our moral ideals or anti-moral ideas. There new life springs up. The world must appear to us in its double aspect. We see first the Father God, creating what is outwardly visible; we see how what is outwardly visible comes to an end in man's inner Being, where it is thrown back into chaos. We must feel intensely how this world, the world of the Father God, comes to its end; only then will we be able to reach an inner understanding of the Mystery of Golgotha. It will become clear to us through this how the very thing that comes to an end, the creation of the Father God, is endowed with life once more by God the Son; a new beginning is made.

Everywhere in the Western world it can be seen how since the fifteenth century there has been a tendency to study and investigate only the perishing, the corpse-like part of nature, which is all that is accessible to the intellect. All so-called education or culture has been formed under the influence of a science that concerns itself only with what is dead. This kind of culture is directly opposed to real Christianity. Real Christianity must have a feeling for what is living but must also be able to separate this feeling of what is reviving from what is passing away. Hence the most important idea that must be connected with the Mystery of Golgotha is the idea of the Risen Christ, the Christ Who has vanquished death. What matters is to comprehend that the most important idea is that of Christ Who passes through death and rises again. Christianity is not merely a religion of salvation; the Oriental religions were also that. Christianity is a religion of Resurrection, a religion that awakens again to life what would otherwise be nothing but matter crumbling away into nothingness.

Out in the cosmos we have the crumbling away of matter in the moon, and in the sun we have a perpetual coming into being, forever new and fresh. Seen spiritually, seen through spiritual vision - when we get beyond ordinary sense perception and reach the point where Imagination is active - we can see in the moon a continuous process: it is continuously splintering and scattering itself abroad. There, where the moon is situated, its matter splinters and disperses like dust into the world. The matter of the moon is perpetually being gathered from its environment and then splintered and scattered. If one looks at the moon in the consciousness of Imagination, one sees a continuous convergence of matter in the place where the moon is; it gathers there, and then it splinters and is scattered like dust into the world. The moon is actually seen like this: first a circle, then a smaller, narrower circle, becoming ever narrower until the circle becomes the moon itself. Then it dissolves, splinters; it is strewn out over the entire world. In the moon, matter cannot tolerate a center. Matter concentrates toward the center of the moon but cannot tolerate it; it stops short there and disperses like cosmic dust. It is only to ordinary, sensory vision that the moon appears peaceful. It is not peaceful. It is continuously gathering matter together and scattering it.

265

When we come to the sun, we find it is all quite different. Already in Imagination we are able to see how matter does not splinter in this way at all; true, it does approach the center, but then it begins to receive life in the rays of the sun that stream out from the center. It does not splinter and disperse; it becomes living and spreads out life from the center in every direction. Together with this life it develops astrality. In the moon there is no astrality; there the astrality is destroyed. In the sun, astrality unites itself with all that streams forth. The sun is in truth something that is permeated with inner life, where the center is not only tolerated but has a fructifying activity. In the contrast between sun and moon we thus see a cosmic manifestation of two opposing processes: in the moon matter is thrown back into chaos, while in the sun it is perpetually unfolding, springing and welling up with renewed life. When we dive down into our inner Being, we look into our inner chaos, into our own moon nature. That is the inner moon. Matter is destroyed there, as in the outer world it is destroyed only where the moon is. Then, however, the radiance of the sun penetrates our senses; the sun's radiance enters our inner moon nature. The matter inwardly dissolving there into dust is renewed by the sun's radiance. Here, in the inner Being of man, matter is continuously falling under the moon influence, and just as continuously man absorbs through his senses the radiance of the sun. Such is the relationship in which we stand to the cosmos, and so one must have the capacity to perceive these two opposite activities in the cosmos: the moon nature directed toward splintering and scattering, and the quickening, life-giving radiance of the sun.

Through both these experiences one comes to behold, in what is splintering and crumbling to dust, the world of the Father God, which had to be there until such time as the world changed into the world of God the Son, which basically has its physical source in what is sun-like in the world. What is of the moon nature and the sun nature relate to one another as Father God to Son God. During the early Christian centuries these things were seen instinctively. Now they must be known again with full presence of mind if the human Being wishes to be able to say of himself in all honesty: I am a Christian."

So often Steiner had shown that human Beings are created out of the forces of the Macrocosm. In Lecture VI of the lecture cycle, "Macrocosm and Microcosm," there is the following example: "One who has attained Initiation recognizes that if only the Elementary World (Astral World) and the World of Spirit (lower Devachan) existed, man's organ of intelligence could never have come into being. The World of Spirit is indeed a lofty world but the forces which have formed the physical organ of thinking must have streamed into man from a yet higher world in order that intelligence might manifest outwardly, in the physical world. Spiritual Science has not without reason figuratively expressed this frontier of the world we have described as the world of the Hierarchies, by the word `Zodiac.' Man would be at the level of the animal if only the two worlds that have been described were in existence. In order that man could become a Being able to walk upright, to think by means of the brain and to develop intelligence, an instreaming of even higher forces was necessary, forces from a world above the World of Spirit. Here we come to a world designated by a word that is totally misused today because of the prevailing materialism. But in a past by no means very distant the word still conveyed its original meaning. The faculty man unfolds here in the physical world when he thinks, was called `Intelligence' in the spiritual science of that earlier period. It is from a world lying beyond both the World of Spirit and the Elementary World that forces stream down through these two worlds to build our brain. Spiritual Science has also called it the World of Reason (Upper Devachan). It is the world in which there are spiritual Beings who are able to send down their power into the physical world in order that a shadow-image of the Spiritual may be produced in the physical world in man's intellectual activity. Before the age of materialism no one would have used the word `reason' for thinking; thinking would have been called intellect, intelligence. `Reason' would have been spoken of when those who were Initiates had risen into a world even higher than the World of Spirit and had direct perception there. In the German language `reason' is connected with perception, with what is directly apprehended, perceived as coming from a world still higher than the one denoted as the World of Spirit. A faint image of this world exists in the shadowy human intellect. The architects and builders of our organs of intellect must be sought in the World of Reason.

It is only possible to describe a still higher world by developing a spiritual faculty transcending the physical intellect. There is a higher form of consciousness, namely, clairvoyant consciousness. If we ask: how is the organ evolved which enables us to have clairvoyant consciousness? - the answer is that there must be worlds from which emanate the forces necessary for the development of this clairvoyant consciousness. Like everything else, it must be formed from a higher world. The first kind of clairvoyant consciousness to develop is a picture-consciousness, Imaginative Consciousness. This Imaginative Consciousness remains mere fantasy only for as long as the organ for it is not formed by forces from a world lying beyond even the World of Reason. As soon as we admit the existence of clairvoyant consciousness we must also admit the existence of a world from which emanate the forces enabling the organ for it to develop. This is the World of Archetypal Images. Whatever can arise as true Imagination is a reflection of the World of Archetypal Images."

Also, in the same lecture cycle he adds this in Lecture VIII: "Our nerves are ordered according to the laws of the planetary world outside, for the planetary world is the outer expression of spiritual realities and spiritual worlds. If it is the case that the World of Spirit works at the forming of our nervous system, it follows that underlying our nervous system there must be a certain law and order corresponding to that of the solar system. Our nervous system must be an inner solar system, for it is organized from the Heaven World. We will now ask ourselves whether this nervous system really functions as if it were a mirror-image of the solar system out in the distance of the Macrocosm. As you know, our measurement of time is governed by the relation of the planets to the Sun and again in the yearly cycle by the passage of the Sun through the twelve constellations of the Zodiac. That is an arrangement of time based upon the law contained in the number twelve as a number which expresses the movements taking place in the solar system. There are also twelve months in the year, and in the longest months there are thirty-one days. That again is based upon the mutual relations of the heavenly bodies and is connected with our time-system. There is a certain irregularity for which there is a good reason, but we cannot go into it now.

Let us try to picture this remarkable time-system in the universe and ask ourselves how these cosmic processes would be reflected in our nervous system. If the forces underlying the Macrocosm are also the forces which have formed our nervous system, we shall certainly find a reflection of them in ourselves; and in fact we have twelve cerebral nerves and thirty-one pairs of spinal nerves. The cosmic laws are actually reflected in these spinal and cerebral nerves. The existence of a certain irregularity is explained by the fact that man is destined to be a Being who is independent of what is going on outside him. Just as the Sun's passage through the constellations of the Zodiac takes place in twelve months, and this is reflected in the twelve cerebral nerves, so the days of the month are regulated in accordance with the circuit of the Moon - twenty-eight days. How is the connection of the thirty-one days in the month with the human nervous system to be explained? We have three additional pairs of nerves. i.e. thirty-one in all, which makes us independent Beings; otherwise here too we should be governed by the number twenty-eight. Here you can glimpse a deep mystery, a wonderful connection between our nervous system and what is expressed in the great symbols of space - symbols which in themselves are mirrorings of spiritual Beings and activities."

And finally from Lecture IX in the cycle, "Macrocosm and Microcosm": "We have described how it is possible to look back upon the Ego from outside. On passing the Guardian of the Threshold the Ego is objectively before us. But we may look at this Ego once, twice, three times, four times, and each time obtain different pictures. According to conditions prevailing in the physical world we might say to ourselves: Now I have seen what I am in the higher world. And the second time: Now I have found myself again and am something different. And the third time again we find something different. -When through the training described we enter the Imaginative world and see a picture of our Ego, it is essential to know that twelve different pictures of the Ego can be seen. There are twelve different pictures of every single Ego, and only after contemplating it from twelve different standpoints have we a complete picture. This view of the Ego from outside corresponds exactly to what is reflected in the relationship of the twelve constellations of the Zodiac to the Sun. Just as the Sun passes through the twelve constellations and has in each a different power, just as it illumines our Earth through the course of the year and even of the day, from twelve different stations, so the human Ego is illumined from twelve different stations in the higher world."

In the lecture cycle, "Man and the World of Stars," there is the following example of humanity's relation to the Macrocosm. In Lecture I Steiner gave the following: "Here on Earth, we learn to speak. This again belongs to our inherent nature, but within the spiritual world between death and a new birth we cannot speak; the physical organs needed for speech are not there. In the spiritual world between death and a new birth, we have, however, the following experience. - We feel ourselves in rhythmically alternating conditions; at one moment we have contracted, as it were, into our own Being; our higher consciousness also contracts. Between death and a new birth there are times when we shut ourselves within ourselves, just as we do while we are asleep on Earth. But then we open ourselves again. Just as on the physical Earth we direct our eyes and other senses out towards the Universe, so in that other world we direct our spiritual organs of perception outwards to the Beings of the Hierarchies. We let our Being stream out, as it were, into the far spaces, and then draw it together again.

It is a spiritual breathing process, but its course is such that if we were to describe in earthly words, in pictures derived from earthly life, what man says to himself there in the spiritual world, we should have to speak somewhat as follows: I, as a human Being in the spiritual world, have this or that to do. I know this through the powers of perception I have in the spiritual world between death and a new birth. I feel myself to be this human Being, this individuality. As I breathe out on Earth, so do I pour myself out in soul into the Universe and become one with the Cosmos. As I breathe in on the Earth, so do I receive back into myself what I experienced while my Being was poured out into the Cosmos. - This is constantly taking place between death and a new birth. Let us think of a man feeling himself enclosed within his own Being and then as though expanded into the Cosmos. At one moment he is concentrated in himself and then has expanded into the Universe. When he draws into himself again it is just as when we breathe in the air from the physical spaces of the Universe. Now when we have poured our Being over the Cosmos and draw it in again, it begins - I cannot express it otherwise - it begins to tell us what it was that we embraced when our Being was outspread as it were, in the cosmic expanse. When we draw our Being together again it begins to tell us what it is in reality, and we then say, between death and a new birth: The Logos in whom we first immersed ourselves - the Logos is speaking within us. Here on the Earth we have the feeling that in our physical speech we shape the words when we exhale. Between death and a new birth we become aware that the words which are outspread in the Universe and reveal its essential nature, enter into us when our Being is inbreathed and manifest themselves within us as the Cosmic Word. Here on Earth we speak as we breathe out; in the spiritual world we speak as we breathe in. And as we unite with our own Being what the Logos - the Cosmic Word - says to us, the Cosmic Thoughts light up within our Being. Here on Earth we make efforts through our nervous system to harbor earthly thoughts. In the spiritual world we draw into ourselves the Cosmic Thoughts out of the Cosmic Speech of the Logos when our Being has been spread over the Universe. Now try to form a vivid conception of the following. Suppose that you say to yourself between death and a new birth: I have this or that to do . . . all that you have experienced hitherto makes you aware that you have this or that task to perform. Then, with the intention of performing it, you spread your Being into the Universe; but the process of expansion is actually one of orientation.

. . . Between death and a new birth you also have intentions - in connection, of course, with what has to be achieved in that other world. Then you expand your Being; this is done with the intention of acquiring orientation - it may be that you are drawn to an Angel or perhaps to a Being of Will, or to some other Being. Such a Being unites with your own expanded Being. You breathe in; this Being communicates to you its participation in the Logos and the Cosmic Thoughts connected with this Being light up within you. When the spirit-seed of man comes down to the Earth . . . he is not organized for thinking or speaking in the earthly sense, nor for walking in the earthly sense, when gravity is involved; but he is organized for movement and for orientation among the Beings of the Higher Hierarchies. He is not organized for speaking but for enabling the Logos to resound within him. He is not organized for the shadowy thoughts of earthly life, but for the thoughts that become radiant in him, within the Cosmos. Walking, speaking and thinking here on the Earth have their correspondences in the spiritual world: in the orientation among the Hierarchies, in the resounding of the Cosmic Word, and in the inner lighting up of the Cosmic Thoughts."

XVII

The Revelation of the Cosmic Christ

Steiner had remarked that in the course of evolution, a Sun and its solar system eventually become a Zodiac. The same would hold true for our own Sun and solar system. It could very well be possible that this expansion of our Sun and solar system as a whole then spiritualizes and in the far and distant future splits away from our Milky Way galaxy to which our solar system eventually becomes the spiritual, non-physical core and center of a new galaxy.

In the lecture cycle, "The Spiritual Hierarchies and Their Reflection in the Physical World," Steiner touches on this similar theme in Lecture V: "The course of evolution for a system that has its starting point in a Sun proceeds in such a way that, at first, the Sun is too weak and thus has to throw off its planets so that it can develop itself to a higher stage. The Sun then grows in strength, reabsorbs its planets, and becomes a Vulcan. Then the whole is dissolved and the Vulcan globe is emptied. Here we have something similar to the round of the Thrones, Cherubim and Seraphim. The Sun will dissolve into the cosmos, sacrifice itself, send forth its Being into the Universe, and thus becomes a choir of Beings like the Seraphim, Cherubim and Thrones who advance to new creative tasks in the Universe.

Why were the Thrones able to give forth their substance, which was needed by Saturn? Because the Thrones had prepared themselves in an earlier system through seven conditions such as those through which our solar system is now passing. Before a system of Thrones, Cherubim and Seraphim comes about, it must first have been a solar system. This means that a Sun must have reached the stage when it could unite itself again with its planets; then it can become peripheral. The Sun itself becomes a Zodiac. What we have come to know as the exalted Beings in the Zodiac are the remnants that have passed over to us from a previous solar system. What previously evolved within a solar system can now work creatively into cosmic space and bring a new solar system to birth out of its own forces. Seraphim, Cherubim and Thrones represent for us the highest hierarchy among divine Beings because they have already accomplished their development as a solar system and have risen to an exalted rank of cosmic sacrificial service.

As a result, these Beings have come into the closest vicinity of the most exalted divinity of which we can speak, the Trinity, the threefold divine power.

We must, therefore, picture the Godhead as beyond the Seraphim. We find this threefold divinity among most peoples as Brahma, Siva and Vishnu, as the Father, the Son and the Holy Ghost. The creative source of a new cosmic system also resides within this lofty Trinity. Looking back, we may say that before anything of ancient Saturn came into existence the plan for it had to ripen within the divine Trinity, but the divine Trinity needs Beings to execute its plans and these Beings must first prepare themselves for the task. The Seraphim, Cherubim and Thrones are the Beings who are, so to speak, closest to the Godhead. In Western Christian Esotericism they are appropriately described as `enjoying the unveiled countenance of the Godhead'."

In Lecture VI from the same cycle we are given this key point: "As far as the spiritual influences are concerned, the Earth and not the Sun stands at the center of the cosmic system. It was maintained by the men of all periods who placed emphasis on spiritual development that certainly the Sun is a nobler heavenly body; Beings superior to man have developed there, but in evolution everything depends on man as he dwells on Earth. Furthermore, the Sun separated off so that man's development might proceed in the right way."

In Lecture X there are these concluding thoughts from this lecture cycle: "We have thus endeavored to fathom the significance of man by considering the meaning of our cosmos. Today, we have to some extent at least raised the spiritual question of the significance of man and we have attempted to provide an answer according to the teachings of the Mysteries by considering man as a center and to solve the riddle out of the periphery. In doing so, our knowledge enters the sphere of reality. Now this is the essential point, that true spiritual scientific knowledge provides a real and concrete insight, which means that by means of Spiritual Science we are given a picture of the cosmos and of the Spiritual Hierarchies. We are at the center of our surrounding world. Everything around us loses its significance because we have to admit that the outer sense perceptible world cannot solve the riddles that beset us. Everything appears to be concentrated at a point. But the solution of the riddle of the cosmos comes to meet us in its full reality from the periphery; so is it in the case of matter, which is a reflection and symbol of the spirit. It gathers itself together, disappears at the center and reappears from the periphery. That is the true state of affairs. Our knowledge becomes real when we are able to behold this as the structure and process of the cosmos as a whole. It is no longer a form of speculation, a weaving of fanciful theory, for our knowledge is then born out of the cosmos. We should develop a certain feeling so that wisdom must become an Ideal for us that is born out of the periphery of the cosmos capable of filling us with the strongest power - a strength to fulfill our destiny and to achieve the great Cosmic Ideal, and through this to realize the Ideal of mankind that awaits us in the immediate future."

Much of Steiner's work was oriented towards the preparation for the appearance of Christ in etheric. Also, he spoke of how so many did not recognize the Christ when He incarnated in the flesh 2,000 years ago. He made the same observation today in regard to the presence of the Etheric Christ. He says the following in the lecture, "The Event of the Appearance of Christ in the Etheric World." (January 25, 1910; Karlsruhe; GA 118): "Indeed, it is true, not everyone realized that something of the utmost importance had taken place, an event which, striking into the unearthly darkness as divine light, was capable of carrying human Beings over Kali Yuga! The possibility for further evolution was given to humanity through the fact that there were certain souls who comprehended that moment in time, who knew what it meant that Christ had walked upon the Earth. If you were to imagine yourselves for a moment in that period, you could then easily say, 'Yes, it was quite possible to live at that time and yet know nothing of the appearance of Christ Jesus on the physical plane! It was possible to dwell on Earth without taking this most significant event into one's consciousness.' Might it not then also be possible today that something of infinite importance is taking place and that human Beings are not taking it into their consciousness? Could it not be that something tremendously important is taking place in the world, taking place right now, of which our own contemporaries have no presentiment? This is indeed so. Something highly important is taking place that is perceptible, however, only to spiritual vision. There is much talk about periods of transition. We are indeed living in one, and it is a momentous one. What is important is that we are living just at the time when the Dark Age has run its course and a new epoch is just beginning, in which human Beings will slowly and gradually develop new faculties and in which human souls will gradually undergo a change."

Looking ahead to the future Steiner reveals the following in his lecture, "The Etherization of the Blood." (October 1, 1911; Basel; GA130). "Just as in the region of the human heart the blood is continually being transformed into etheric substance, so a similar process takes place in the Macrocosm. We understand this when we turn our eyes to the Mystery of Golgotha, to the moment when the blood flowed from the wounds of Jesus Christ. This blood must not be regarded simply as chemical substance, but by reason of all that has been described as the nature of Jesus of Nazareth, it must be recognized as something altogether unique. When it flowed from His wounds and into the Earth, a substance was imparted to our Earth which, in uniting with it, constituted an Event of the greatest possible significance for all future ages of the Earth, and it could take place only once. What happened with this blood in the ages that followed? Nothing different from what otherwise takes place in the heart of man. In the course of earthly evolution, this blood passed through a process of 'etherization'. Just as our blood streams upward from the heart as ether, so, since the Mystery of Golgotha, the etherized blood of Christ Jesus has lived in the ether of the Earth. The etheric body of the Earth is permeated by what the blood that flowed on Golgotha became.

This is important. If what has thus come to pass through Christ Jesus had not taken place, man's condition on the Earth could only have been as previously described. Since the Mystery of Golgotha, however, there has existed the continuous possibility for the activity of the etheric blood of Christ to flow together with the streamings from below upward, from heart to head.

Because the etherized blood of Jesus of Nazareth is present in the etheric body of the Earth, it accompanies the etherized human blood streaming upward from the heart to the brain, so that not only do these streams that I described earlier meet in man, but the human bloodstream unites with the bloodstream of Christ Jesus. A union of these two streams can come about, however, only if man is able to unfold true understanding of what is contained in the Christ Impulse. Otherwise, there can be no union.; the two streams then mutually repel each other, thrust each other away. In every age of earthly evolution, we must acquire understanding in the form suitable for that epoch. At the time when Christ Jesus lived on Earth, preceding events could be rightly understood by those who came to His forerunner, John, and were baptized by him according to the rite described in the Gospels. They experienced baptism in order that their sin, that is to say, the karma of their previous lives, karma that had come to an end, might be changed, and in order that they might realize that the most powerful Impulse in earthly evolution was about to descend into a physical body. The evolution of humanity progresses, however, and in our present age it is important that man should learn to understand that the knowledge contained in Spiritual Science must be received and gradually be able so to fire the streams flowing from heart to brain that Anthroposophy can be understood. If this comes to pass, individuals will be able to comprehend the event that has its beginning in the twentieth century: the appearance of the Etheric Christ in contradistinction to the physical Christ of Palestine.

We have now reached the moment in time when the Etheric Christ enters into the life of the Earth and will become visible, at first to a small number of people, through a natural clairvoyance. Then in the course of the next 3,000 years, He will become visible to greater and greater numbers of people. This will inevitably come to pass; it is an event of nature. That it will come to pass is as true as were the achievements of electricity in the nineteenth century. A certain number of individuals will see the Etheric Christ and will themselves experience the event that took place at Damascus. This will depend, however, upon such human Beings learning to observe the moment when Christ draws near to them. In only a few decades from now it will happen, particularly to those who are young in years - already preparation is being made for this - that some person here or there has certain experiences. If only he has truly sharpened his vision through engaging himself with Anthroposophy, he may become aware that suddenly someone has come near to help him, to make him alert to this or that. The truth is that

Christ has come to him, although he believes that what he sees is a physical man. He will come to realize, however, that this is a supersensible Being, because it immediately vanishes. Many a human Being will have this experience when sitting silently in his room, heavy-hearted and oppressed, not knowing which way to turn. The door will open, and the Etheric Christ will appear and speak words of consolation to him. The Christ will become a living comforter to men. However strange it may as yet seem, it is true nevertheless that many a time when people, even in considerable numbers, are sitting together not knowing what to do and waiting, they will see the Etheric Christ. He Himself will be there, will confer with them, will cast His word into such gatherings. We are now approaching these times, and the positive, constructive element now described will take hold of the evolution of humanity.

No word shall be said here against the great advances made by culture in our day; these achievements are essential for the welfare and the freedom of human Beings. Whatever can be gained in the way of outer progress, however, in mastering the forces of nature, is something small and insignificant compared with the blessing bestowed upon the person who experiences the awakening in his soul through Christ, Who will now take hold of human culture and its concerns. What thereby awakens in human Beings will be unifying, positive forces. Christ brings constructive forces into human civilization." "We make all culture of the outer world with the products of fragmentation. In the course of the coming years you will understand even better how much in our culture is the product of destruction.

Light is destroying itself within our post-Atlantean earthly processes. Until the time of Atlantis the earthly process was a progressive process, but since then it has been a process of decay. What is light? Light decays, and the decaying light is electricity. What we know as electricity is light that is destroying itself within matter. The chemical force that undergoes a transformation within earthly evolution is magnetism. Yet a third force will become active, and if electricity seems to work wonders today, this third force will affect civilization in a still more miraculous way. The more of this force we employ, the faster the Earth will tend to become a corpse and its spiritual part prepare for the Jupiter embodiment. Forces have to be applied to destroy the Earth in order that man can become free of the Earth and that the Earth's body can fall away. As long as the Earth was involved in a progressive process, this was not done, since only the decaying Earth can use the great achievements of electricity. Strange as this sounds, it must gradually become known. We must understand the process of evolution to evaluate our culture in the right way. We shall learn thereby that it is necessary for the Earth to be destroyed; otherwise, the spirit will not become free. We shall also learn to value what is positive, namely, the penetration of spiritual forces into our existence on Earth.

We thus realize what a tremendous advance was signified by the fact that Christ necessarily lived for three years on the Earth in a specially prepared human body in order that He might be visible to physical eyes. Through what came to pass during those three years, human Beings have become ripe to behold the Christ Who will move among them in an etheric body, Who will enter into earthly life as truly and effectively as did the physical Christ in Palestine. If human Beings observe such happenings with undimmed senses they will know that there is an etheric body that will move about within the physical world, but they will know that this is the only etheric body able to work in the physical world as a human physical body works. It will differ from a physical body in this respect only, that it can be in two, three, even in a hundred, a thousand places at the same time. This is possible only for an etheric, not for a physical form. What will be accomplished in humanity through this further advance is that the two poles I have mentioned, the intellectual and the moral, will more and more become one; they will merge into unity. This will come about because in the course of the next millennia human Beings will learn increasingly to observe the Etheric Christ in the world; more and more they will be permeated in waking life, too, by the direct working of the good from the spiritual world. Whereas now the Will sleeps by day, and man is only able to influence it indirectly through thought, in the course of the next millennia, through what from our time onward is working in us under the aegis of Christ, it will come about that the deeds of human Beings in waking condition, too, can be directly productive of good."

From the collection of lectures titled, "The Festivals and Their Meanings," there are several references from the collection that are helpful in our understanding of the Christ Principle and its relation to the evolution of the Earth. The following is from the lecture, "The Revelation of the Cosmic Christ." (December 26, 1921; Basel): "When people of today speak of Christ, they still associate with His name certain memories of the Holy Story, but they have no clearly defined feeling of the difference in the nature of the Son God on the one hand and of the Father God on the other. But at the time when the Mystery of Golgotha was fulfilled in the realm of earthly existence, this feeling was still quite living. Over in Asia, in a place of no great importance to Rome at the time, the Christ had appeared in Jesus of Nazareth. According to the early Christians, Christ was that Divine Nature Who had ensouled a human Being in a way that had never before occurred on the Earth, nor would occur thereafter. And so this one Event of Golgotha, this one ensouling of a human Being by a Divine Nature, by the Christ, imparts meaning and purpose to the whole of earthly evolution. All previous evolution is to be thought of as preparatory to this Event of Golgotha, and all subsequent evolution as the fulfillment, the consequence of the Mystery of Golgotha.

The scene of this Event lay over beyond in Asia, and on the throne of Rome sat Augustus Caesar. People of today no longer realize that Caesar

Augustus on the throne of Rome was regarded as a Divine Incarnation. The Roman Caesars were actually regarded as Gods in human form. And so we have two different conceptions of a God. The one God upon the throne of Rome and the other on Golgotha - the place of a skull. There could be no greater contrast! Think of the figure of Caesar Augustus, who, according to his subjects and according to Roman decree, was a God incarnate in a man. He was thought to be a Divine Being who had descended to the Earth; the Divine forces had united with the birth-forces, with the blood; the Divine power, having come down into earthly existence, was pulsing in and through the blood. Such was the universal conception, although it took different forms, of the dwelling of the Godhead on Earth. The people thought of the Godhead as bound up with the forces of the blood. They said: Ex Deo Nascimur. - Out of God we are born. And even on lower levels of existence they felt themselves related to what lived, as the crown of humanity, in a personality like Caesar Augustus.

All that was thus honored and revered was a Divine Father Principle. For it was a Principle living in the blood that is part of a human Being when he is born into the world. But in the Mystery of Golgotha the Divine Christ Being had united Himself with the man Jesus of Nazareth - united Himself not, in this case, with the blood, but with the highest forces of the human soul. A God had here united with a human Being, in such a way that mankind was saved from falling victim to the earthly forces of matter. The Father God lives in the blood. The Son lives in the soul and spirit of man. The Father God leads man into material life: Ex Deo Nascimur. - Out of God we are born. But God the Son leads man again out of material existence. The Father God leads man out of the supersensible into the material. God the Son leads man out of the material into the supersensible. In Christo Morimur. - In Christ we die.

Two distinctly different feelings were there. The feeling and perception of God the Son was added to the feeling associated with God the Father. Certain impulses underlying the process of evolution caused the loss of the faculty to differentiate between the Father God and God the Son. And to this day these impulses have remained in mankind in general and in Christianity too. Men who were possessed of the ancient, primordial wisdom knew from their own inner experiences that they had come down from Divine-Spiritual worlds into physical and material life. Pre-existence was a certain and universally accepted fact. Men looked back through birth and through conception, up into the Divine-Spiritual worlds, whence the soul descends at birth into physical existence. In our language we have only the word `Immortality'. We have no expression for the other side of Eternity, because our language does not include the word `Unborn-ness'. But if the conception of Eternity is to be complete, the word `Unborn-ness' must be there as well as the word `Immortality'. Indeed all that the word `Unborn-ness' can mean to

277

us is of greater significance than what is implied by the word `Immortality'. It is true that the human Being passes through the gate of death into a life in the spiritual world, but it is no less true that an exceedingly egotistical conception of this life in the spiritual world is presented to man today. Human Beings live here on the Earth. They long for Immortality, for they do not want to sink into nothingness at death."

"In olden times men knew that they had lived in Divine-Spiritual worlds, had descended through birth into material existence. They felt that the forces around them in a purely spiritual environment were united with the blood, were living on in the blood. And from this insight there arose the conception: Out of God we are born. The God Who lives in the blood, the God whom the man of flesh represents here on Earth - he is the Father God. The other pole of life - namely, death - demands a different impulse of the life of soul. There must be something in the human Being that is not exhausted with death. The conception corresponding to this is of that God Who leads over the earthly and physical to the supersensible and superphysical. It is the God connected with the Mystery of Golgotha. The Divine Father Principle has always been associated, and rightly so, with the transition from the supersensible to the material, and through the Divine Son the transition is brought about from the sensible and material to the supersensible. And that is why the Resurrection thought is essentially bound up with the Mystery of Golgotha. The words of St. Paul that Christ is what He is for humanity because He is the Risen One - these words are an integral part of Christianity.

In the course of the centuries, understanding of the Risen One, of the Conqueror of Death, has gradually been lost and modern theology concerns itself wholly with the man Jesus of Nazareth. But Jesus of Nazareth, the man, cannot be placed at the same level as the Father Principle. Jesus of Nazareth might be regarded as the messenger of the Father but he could not, according to the arguments of early Christianity, be placed beside the Father God. Co-equal and co-existent are the Divine Father and the Divine Son: the Father Who brings about the transition from the supersensible to the material - `Out of God we are born' - and the Son Who brings about the transition from the material to the supersensible - `In Christ we die.'

And transcending both birth and death there is a third Principle proceeding from and co-equal both with the Divine Father and the Divine Son - namely, the Spirit - the Holy Spirit. Within the Being of man, therefore, we are to see the transition from the supersensible to the material and from the material to the supersensible. And the principle which knows neither birth nor death is the Spirit into which and through which we are awakened: `Through the Holy Spirit we shall be re-awakened.' For many centuries Christmas was a festival of remembrance. How much of the substance of this festival has been lost is proved by the fact that all that is left of the Being

Christ Jesus is the man Jesus of Nazareth. But for us today Christmas must become a call and a summons to something new. A new reality must be born. Christianity needs an Impulse of renewal, for inasmuch as Christianity no longer understands the Christ Being in Jesus of Nazareth, it has lost its meaning and purpose. The meaning and essence of Christianity must be found again. Humanity must learn again to realize that the Mystery of Golgotha can be comprehended only in the light of supersensible knowledge.

Another factor, too, contributes to this lack of understanding of the Mystery of Golgotha. We can look with love to the Babe in the manger, but we have no wisdom-filled understanding of the union of the Christ Being with the man Jesus of Nazareth. Nor can we look up into the heavenly heights with the same intensity of feeling which was there in men who lived at the time of the Mystery of Golgotha. In those days men looked up to the starry worlds and saw in the courses and constellations of the stars something like a countenance of the Divine soul and spirit of the cosmos. And in the Christ Being they could see the spiritual Principle of the universe visibly manifested in the glories of the starry worlds. But for modern man the starry worlds and all the worlds of cosmic space have become little more than a product of calculation - a cosmic mechanism. The world has become empty of the Gods. Out of this world which is void of the Gods, the world that is investigated today by astronomy and physics, the Christ Being could never have descended. In the light of the primeval wisdom possessed by humanity, this world was altogether different. It was the body of the Divine World-Soul and of the Divine World-Spirit. And out of this spiritual cosmos the Christ came down to Earth and united Himself with a human Being in Jesus of Nazareth. The truth is expressed in history itself in a profound way. All over the Earth before the Mystery of Golgotha there were Mysteries, holy sanctuaries that were schools of learning and at the same time schools for the cultivation of the religious life. In these Mysteries, indications were given of what must come to pass in the future. It was revealed in the Mysteries that man bears within his Being a power that is the conqueror of death, and this victory over death was an actual experience of the Initiates in the Mysteries. In deep and profound experience the candidate for Initiation knew with sure conviction: Thou has awakened within thyself the power that conquers death. The Initiate experienced in a picture the process that would operate fully in times still to come, in accordance with the great plan of world-history. In the Mysteries of all peoples, this sacred truth was proclaimed: Man can be victorious over death. But it was also indicated that what could be presented in the Mysteries in pictures only would one day become an actual and single event in world-history. The Mystery of Golgotha was proclaimed in advance by the Pagan Mysteries of antiquity; it was the fulfillment of what had everywhere been heralded in the sanctuaries and holy places of the Mysteries."

279

From the lecture, "The Birth of Christ Within Us." (December 27, 1914; Berlin): "Every human Being on the Earth is related individually to the Christ. Folk-history, as it may be called, is woven by the affairs of the several peoples, for it is concerned with human affairs in general, within the orbit of general human destiny. But what Christ Jesus has brought into the world penetrates deeply and inwardly into the experiences of every human heart, every human soul - belonging to no matter what part of earthly evolution - in so far as it feels itself truly Man. We must realize that this `feeling of oneself as man' arose for the first time from what came into human evolution through the Mystery of Golgotha."

And from the lecture, "Spirit Triumphant." (March 27, 1921; Dornach): "Christ descended to humanity in order to unite the souls of men with this cosmic Spirit. And He alone proclaims the Gospel of the Christ truly, who affirms that what the Sun reveals to the physical senses is the outer expression of the Spirit of our universe, of its resurrecting Spirit. There must be a living realization of the connection of this Spirit of the universe with the Sun, and of how the time of the Easter festival has been determined by the relationship prevailing between the Sun and the Moon in spring. A link must be made with that cosmic reality in accordance with which the Easter festival was established in Earth-evolution. We must come to realize that it was the ever-watchful Guardian-Spirits of the cosmos who, through the great cosmic timepiece in which the Sun and the Moon are the hands in respect of earthly existence, have pointed explicitly to the time in the evolution of the world and of humanity at which the Festival of the Resurrection is to be celebrated. With spiritual insight we must learn to perceive the course of the Sun and Moon as the two hands of the cosmic time piece, just as for the affairs of physical existence we learn to understand the movements of the hands on a clock. The physical and earthly must be linked to the super-physical and the super-earthly.

The Easter thought can be interpreted only in the light of super-earthly realities, for the Mystery of Golgotha, in its aspect as the Resurrection Mystery, must be distinguished from ordinary human happenings. Human affairs take their course on the Earth in an altogether different way. The Earth received the cosmic forces and, in the course of its evolution, the human powers of Will penetrate the metabolic processes of man's Being. But since the Mystery of Golgotha took place, a new influx of Will streamed into earthly happenings. There took place on Earth a cosmic event, for which the Earth is merely the stage. Thereby man was again united with the cosmos. That is what must be understood, for only so can the Easter thought be grasped in all its magnitude. Therefore it is not the picture of the Crucifix alone that must stand before us, however grandly and sublimely portrayed by art. `He Whom ye seek is not here' - is the thought that must arise. Above the Cross there must appear to you the One Who is here now, Who by the spirit calls you to a spirit-awakening. This is the true Easter thought that must find its way into the evolution of mankind; it is to this that the human heart and mind must be lifted. Our age demands of us that we shall not only deepen our understanding of what has been created, but that we shall become creators of the new. And even if it be the Cross itself, in all the beauty with which artists have endowed it, we may not rest content with that picture; we must hear the words of the Angels who, when we seek in death and suffering, exclaim to us: 'He Whom ye seek is no longer here.' We have to seek the One Who is here, by turning at Eastertime to the Spirit of Whom the only true picture is that of the Resurrection. Then we shall be able, in the right way, to pass from the Good Friday mood of suffering to the spiritual mood of Easter Day. In this Easter mood we shall also be able to find the strength with which our Will must be imbued if the forces of decline are to be countered by those which lead humanity upwards. We need the forces that can bring about this ascent. And the moment we truly understand the Easter thought of Resurrection, this Easter thought - bringing warmth and illumination - will kindle within us the forces needed for the future evolution of mankind."

From the lecture, "The Teachings of the Risen Christ." (April 13, 1912; the Hague): "External tradition had lost well-nigh everything that was known in those days about the Risen Christ, the Christ Who had passed through the Mystery of Golgotha and then, in a spirit-body, like the early teachers of primeval humanity, had taught certain chosen disciples after His Resurrection. In the story, for example, of Christ meeting the disciples who had gone out to seek Him there are indications in the New Testament - but scanty indications even there - of the significance of the teachings given by the Risen Christ to His disciples. And Paul himself regards his experience at Damascus as a teaching which, given by the Risen Christ, made the man Saul into Paul. In those early times there was full realization that Christ Jesus, the Risen One, had secrets of a very special kind to impart to men. The fact that later on they were unable to receive these communications was due entirely to their own human evolution. For it was necessary that man should begin to unfold those forces of soul which, later, were to operate in the exercise of human freedom and of the human intellect. Evidence of this is clear from the fifteenth century onwards, but its beginnings can be traced to the fourth century.

The question naturally arises: What was the content and substance of the teachings which could be given by the Risen Christ to His chosen disciples? He had appeared to them in the same manner in which the divine Teachers had appeared to primeval humanity. But now, if I may so express it, He was able to tell them out of divine wisdom what He had experienced and other divine Beings had not. From His own divine vantage-point He was able to explain to them the mystery of birth and death. He was able to convey to them the knowledge that in the future there would arise in the men of Earth

281

a day-consciousness, unable to have direct perception of the immortal element in human life, a consciousness that is extinguished in sleep, so that in sleep too the immortal element is invisible even to the eyes of the soul. But He was also able to make them aware that it is possible for the Mystery of Golgotha to be drawn into the field of man's understanding. He was able to make clear to them what I will try to express in the following words. They can only be feeble, stammering words because human language has no others to offer, but I will try to express it in these halting words: - `The human body,' He taught, `has gradually become so dense, the death-forces in it so powerful, that, although man will now be able to develop his intellect and his own inner freedom, he can do this only in a life that definitely experiences death, a life into which death makes a marked incision, a life from which vision of the immortal soul is obliterated during waking consciousness. But,' so Christ taught His initiated disciples, - `you can receive into your souls a certain wisdom. It is the wisdom which through the Mystery of Golgotha, my own Being has made possible for you, something with which you yourselves can be filled if only you can attain the insight that Christ came down from the spheres beyond the Earth to the men of Earth; if only you can come to realize that here on the Earth there is something which cannot be perceived by earthly means, but only by means higher than those of the Earth; if you can behold the Mystery of Golgotha as a Divine Event set into earthly life; if you can apprehend that a God has passed through the Mystery of Golgotha. Through everything else that comes to fulfillment on Earth you can acquire earthly wisdom, but in order to understand the significance of death to humanity it would avail you nothing. Earthly wisdom would suffice you only if you, like the men of earlier times, could feel no intense interest in death. But since you must needs be concerned with death, you must strengthen your perceptive faculty by drawing into it a force stronger than all earthly forces of perception, a force so strong that you can realize that in the Mystery of Golgotha there came to pass something to which all earthly laws of nature are inapplicable. If you include in your beliefs only the laws of earthly nature, you will, it is true, be able to observe death, but you will never discover its significance for human life. But if you can attain the insight that the Earth has now for the first time received its true meaning and purpose, that at this middle point of Earth-evolution a Divine Event has taken place in the Mystery of Golgotha, an Event beyond the comprehension of earthly means of perception, then you are preparing a special power of wisdom.'

This power of wisdom is the same as the power of faith; it is a special power of Spirit-Wisdom, a power of faith born of wisdom. Strength of soul is expressed when a man says: `I believe! I know through faith what I can never know by earthly means.' A man is lacking, even were he to possess all the science known on Earth, if his wisdom is able to embrace only what can be grasped by earthly means. To perceive the reality of the super-earthly within the earthly, a far greater inner activity must be unfolded. Contemplation of the Mystery of Golgotha gives a stimulus to unfold such inner activity. And in ever new variations, this teaching that a God had lived through a human destiny and had thereby united Himself with the destiny of the Earth - an experience hitherto unknown to the gods in their own realm - was proclaimed over and over again by the Risen Christ to His disciples. And it worked with stupendous power."

"Paul knew that if the Mystery of Golgotha had not taken place, if Christ had not risen, the soul would be involved in the destiny of the body, that is to say in the dispersion of the elements of the body into the elements of the Earth. Had Christ not risen, had He not united Himself with earthly forces, the human soul would unite with the body between birth and death in such a way that the soul would be united, too, with all the molecules which become part of the Earth through cremation or decomposition. It would have come about that at the end of Earth-evolution, human souls would go the way of earthly matter. But in that Christ had passed through the Mystery of Golgotha, He wrests this fate away from the human soul. The Earth will go her way in the universe, but just as the human soul can emerge from the single human body, so will all human souls be able to free themselves from the Earth and go forward to a new cosmic existence. Christ is thus intimately united with earth-existence. But the union can be understood only if the mystery is approached in the way indicated. To one or another the thought may occur: `What, then, of those who cannot believe in Christ?' Here let me give you reassurance. Christ died for all men, for those, too, who today cannot unite with Him. The Mystery of Golgotha is an objective fact, unaffected by human knowledge. Human knowledge, however, strengthens the inner forces of the soul. All the means, therefore, at the disposal of human knowledge, human feelings, and human Will, must be applied, in order that in the further course of Earth-evolution the presence of Christ in this Earth-evolution shall be an experienced reality, through direct knowledge."

From, "Spiritual Bells of Easter II." (April 11, 1909; Cologne): "In the eleventh, twelfth, thirteenth and fourteenth centuries replicas of the astral body of Jesus of Nazareth were woven into other human Beings when their karma so permitted and they were sufficiently mature. Francis of Assisi, Elizabeth of Thuringen, for example, and others too, bore within them a replica of the astral body of Jesus of Nazareth. Without this knowledge, the lives of Francis of Assisi and Elizabeth of Thuringen are unintelligible to us. Everything that seems so strange today in the life of Francis of Assisi is because the `I' was the human `I' of that individuality; but the humility, the devoutness and the fervor we so admire in him are due to the fact that a replica of the astral body of Jesus of Nazareth was woven into his own astral body. And it was so in the case of many other personalities living at that time. When we know this, they become examples for us. How can

283

anyone who really studies the matter understand the life of Elizabeth of Thuringen if he does not know that a replica of the astral body of Jesus of Nazareth was woven into her? And very many were called in this way by the onworking Christ Power to bear this mighty Impulse forward to posterity.

But there was something else, too, which was preserved for still later times, namely innumerable replicas of the `I' of Jesus of Nazareth. True, his original higher `I' had departed from the three sheaths when the Christ drew into them; but a replica, exalted yet further as a result of the Christ-indwelling, remained present, and this replica of the `I' of Jesus of Nazareth was multiplied many times. This replica of the `I' of Jesus of Nazareth is present to this day in the spiritual world. Moreover it can be found, together with the glory of the Christ Power and Christ Impulse it bears within it, by men who are sufficiently mature. Now the outer, physical expression for the `I' is the blood. This is a great mystery; but there have always been men who knew of it and were aware that replicas of the `I' of Jesus of Nazareth are present in the spiritual world. There have always been men whose task it was, through the centuries since the Event of Golgotha, to ensure in secret that humanity gradually matures, so that there may be human Beings who are fit to receive the replicas of the `I' of Jesus Christ of Nazareth, just as there were persons who received replicas of his etheric body and astral body. To this end it was necessary to discover the secret of how, in the quietude of a profound mystery, this `I' might be preserved until the appropriate moment in the evolution of the Earth and of humanity. With this aim a Brotherhood of Initiates who preserved the secret was founded: the Brotherhood of the Holy Grail. They were the guardians of this secret. This Fellowship has always existed. It is said that its originator took the chalice used by Christ Jesus at the Last Supper and in it caught the blood flowing from the wounds of the Redeemer on the Cross. He gathered the blood, the expression of the `I' in this chalice - the Holy Grail. And the chalice with the blood of the Redeemer, with the secret of the replica of the `I' of Christ-Jesus, was preserved in a holy place, in the Brotherhood of those who through their attainments and their Initiation are the Brothers of the Holy Grail.

The time has come today when these secrets may be made known, when through a spiritual life the hearts of men can become mature enough to understand this great Mystery. If souls allow Spiritual Science to kindle understanding of such secrets they become fit to recognize in that Holy Chalice the Mystery of the Christ-`I', the Eternal `I' which every human `I' can become. This secret is a reality - only men must allow themselves to be summoned through Spiritual Science to understand this, in order that as they contemplate the Holy Grail, the Christ- `I' may be received into their Being. To this end they must understand and accept what has come to pass as fact, as reality.

But when men are better prepared to receive the Christ Ego, then it will pour in greater and greater fullness into their souls. They will evolve to the level where stood Christ Jesus, their great Example. Then for the first time they will learn to understand the sense in which Christ Jesus is the Great Example for humanity. And having understood this, men will begin to realize in the innermost core of their Being that the certainty of life's eternity springs from the corpse hanging on the wood of the Cross of Golgotha. Those who are inspired and permeated by the Christ-`I', the Christians of future time, will understand something else as well - something that hitherto has been known only to those who reached enlightenment. They will understand, not only the Christ Who passed through death, but the triumphant Christ of the Apocalypse, resurrected in the spiritual fire, the Christ Whose coming has already been predicted. The Easter festival can always be for us a symbol of the Risen One, a link reaching over from Christ on the Cross to the Christ triumphant, risen and glorified, to the One Who lifts all men with Him to the right hand of the Father. And so the Easter symbol points us to the vista of the whole future of the Earth, to the future of the evolution of humanity, and is for us a guarantee that men who are Christ-inspired will be transformed from Saul-men into Paul-men and will behold with increasing clarity a spiritual fire. For it is indeed true that as the Christ was revealed in advance to Moses and to those who were with him, in the material fire of the thorn-bush and of the lightning on Sinai, so He will be revealed to us in a spiritualized fire of the future. He is with us always, until the end of the world, and He will appear in the spiritual fire to those who have allowed their eyes to be enlightened through the Event of Golgotha. Men will behold Him in the spiritual fire. They beheld Him, to begin with, in a different form; they will behold Him for the first time in His true form, in a spiritual fire.

But because the Christ penetrated so deeply into Earth-existence - right into the physical bony structure - the power which built His sheaths out of the elements of the Earth so purified and hallowed this physical substance that it can never become what in their sorrow the Eastern sages feared: that the Enlightened One of the future, the Maitreya Buddha, would not find on the Earth men capable of understanding him because they had sunk so deeply into matter. Christ was led to Golgotha in order that He might lift matter again to spiritual heights, in order that the fire might not be extinguished in matter, but be spiritualized. The primal wisdom will again be intelligible to men when they themselves are spiritualized - the primal wisdom which, in the spiritual world, was the source of their Being. And so the Maitreya Buddha will find understanding on the Earth - which would not otherwise have been possible - when men have attained deeper insight. We understand far better what we learned in our youth, when tests in life have matured us, and we can look back upon it all at a later time. Mankind will understand the primal wisdom through being able to look back upon it in the Christ-light streaming from the Event of Golgotha."

From, "The Whitsun Mystery and its connection with the Ascension." (May 7, 1923; Dornach): "In the Schools of Initiation it was known, and can of course also be known today, that at about the time of the Mystery of Golgotha the human physical body had reached a degree of decline where the men who were then in incarnation or who were to be incarnated in the near future, that is, up to about the fourth century A.D., were faced with the danger of leaving an Earth that was growing more and more desolate and barren, and of finding no possibility in the future of descending from the world of spirit-and-soul and building a physical body out of materials provided by the physical Earth. This danger existed, and the inevitable consequence would have been the failure of man to fulfill his allotted earthly mission. The Ahrimanic and Luciferic powers working in combination had succeeded to the extent that at the time of the Mystery of Golgotha, earthly mankind was face to face with the possibility of dying out. Mankind was rescued from this fate through that which was achieved by the Mystery of Golgotha, whereby the human physical body itself was imbued again with the necessary forces of life and freshness. Men were thereby enabled to continue their further evolution on Earth, inasmuch as they could now come down from worlds of spirit-and-soul and find it possible to live in physical bodies. Such was the actual effect of the Mystery of Golgotha. I have often spoken of this, as for example in the lecture course given in Carlsruhe under the title, "From Jesus to Christ." The greatest hostility was aroused by these lectures because, out of a sense of esoteric duty, certain truths were presented which many people wish to keep concealed. Indeed it can be said that from a certain quarter the hostility to Anthroposophy started from these very lectures.

What I have described, however, is one aspect of the actual effect of the Mystery of Golgotha. This same fact can, of course, be expressed in many different ways. It was expressed differently in that lecture-course, but what I am now describing is the same fact, merely seen from another side. Through the Mystery of Golgotha, the forces promoting the growth and thriving of man's physical body were quickened anew, with the following result. - It was now made possible for man to receive, during his life of sleep, an Impulse he would not otherwise have received. The whole evolution of man on Earth takes its course, as we know, in the alternation of waking-life and sleep-life. In sleep, the physical body and ether body remain behind; from the time of falling asleep until that of waking, the Ego and the astral body make themselves independent of them. During this state of independence in sleep the influence of the Christ-Force takes effect in the Ego and the astral body in those men who through the requisite mood and content of their soul-life have made fitting preparation for this condition of

286

sleep. Penetration of these higher bodies by the Christ-Force, therefore, takes place mainly during the state of sleep. To turn now to the biblical Event of the Ascension, we must realize that at that time the disciples had become clairvoyant to a degree at which they were able to behold what is, in truth, a deep secret of earthly evolution. These secrets remain unnoticed by man's everyday consciousness, which is incapable of knowing whether at one point or another in the evolution of humanity something of supreme importance is taking place. There are many such happenings, but the everyday consciousness is unaware of them. The picture of the Ascension actually signifies that at this moment Christ's disciples were able to witness spiritually an event of untold significance, enacted `behind the scenes' as it were of earthly evolution.

What they witnessed revealed to them, as in a picture, the prospect of what would have come about for men had the Mystery of Golgotha not taken place. They beheld as a concrete spiritual happening what would have then befallen, namely, that the physical bodies of men would have so deteriorated that the whole future of humanity would have been endangered. For the consequence of this physical deterioration would have been that the human etheric body would have obeyed the forces of attraction which properly belong to it. The etheric body is being drawn all the time towards the Sun, not towards the Earth. Our constitution as human Beings is such that our physical body has earthly heaviness, gravity, but our etheric body, Sun-levity. Had the human physical body become what it must have become if the Mystery of Golgotha had not taken place, the etheric bodies of men would have followed their own urge towards the Sun and have left the physical body. The existence of mankind on Earth would inevitably have come to an end. Until the Mystery of Golgotha, Christ's dwelling-place was the Sun. Therefore in that the etheric body of man strives towards the Sun, it is striving towards the Christ. Now picture to yourselves the scene on the day of the Ascension. In spiritual vision the disciples see Christ Himself rising heavenwards. A vision is conjured before them of how the power, the Impulse of Christ unites itself with the etheric nature of man, in its upward striving; of how at the time of the Mystery of Golgotha man was facing the danger of his etheric body being drawn out into the Sun like a cloud, but how, in its sunward streaming, it was held together by Christ. This picture must be understood, for in truth it is a warning. Christ is akin to those forces in man which naturally strive towards the Sun and away from the Earth, and will always do so. But Christ remains in union with the Earth. Thus the Christ Impulse holds man securely on the Earth.

In this picture of the Ascension, something more is manifest to the disciples. Suppose that the Mystery of Golgotha had not taken place and that numbers of men had become clairvoyant to the degree to which the disciples became clairvoyant at this moment. These men would have seen the etheric

287

bodies of certain human Beings departing from the Earth in the direction of the Sun, and they would have come to this conclusion: 'This is the path man's etheric body is taking. The etheric-earthly element in man is being drawn away into the Sun.' But now, by carrying to its fulfillment the Mystery of Golgotha, Christ has rescued for the Earth this sunward-striving etheric body. And thereby is manifest the fact that Christ remains united with mankind on the Earth. Thus something else became apparent here, namely that through the Mystery of Golgotha Christ brought to pass within Earth-evolution a cosmic event. Christ came down from the heights of spirit, linked Himself with humanity in the man Jesus of Nazareth, fulfilled the Mystery of Golgotha, united His evolution with that of the Earth. It was a cosmic Deed accomplished for the whole of humanity. Mark these words: The Deed on Golgotha was fulfilled for all mankind. The eye of clairvoyance can never fail to perceive how, since that Deed, the etheric forces in man, with their urge to escape from the Earth, are united with Christ in order that He may keep them in the Earth-evolution. This applies to the whole of mankind.

This leads us to another consideration. Suppose that only a handful of human Beings had been able to acquire knowledge of these facts that relate to the Mystery of Golgotha, and that a large section of mankind - as is actually the case - had not recognized its significance. If this had come about, the Earth would be peopled by a few true believers in Christ and by a large number who do not acknowledge the essential content and meaning of the Mystery of Golgotha. What, then, is to be said of the latter? How are these human Beings who do not acknowledge the Mystery of Golgotha related to it? Or, better put, how is the Deed of Christ on Golgotha related to these human Beings? The Deed of Christ on Golgotha is an objective fact; its cosmic significance does not depend upon what men believe about it. An objective fact has, in itself, reality of being. If an oven is hot, it does not become cold because a number of people believe that it is cold. - The Mystery of Golgotha rescues mankind from the decay of the physical body, no matter what men believe or do not believe about it. The Mystery of Golgotha was enacted for the sake of all men, including those who do not believe in it. - That is the cardinal fact to be remembered.

We realize, then, that the Deed on Golgotha was enacted in order that by this means mankind on Earth might be quickened to the degree necessary for its rejuvenation. That has come to pass. It has been made possible for men to find on the Earth bodies in which they can and will for long ages of future time - be able to incarnate. It is, however, fundamentally as Beings of spirit-and-soul that men will pass through existence in these now rejuvenated earthly bodies, and it is as Beings of spirit-and-soul that they will be able to appear on Earth again and again. Now the Christ Impulse, which must have significance for the spiritual nature of man as well as for his bodily nature, can impress itself upon a man's waking state, but it can make no impression on his sleeping state unless this Impulse has been received into his soul. The Mystery of Golgotha, therefore, would have produced its effect in the waking life of men who had no knowledge of it; but it would not, in such circumstances, have affected them in their life of sleep. The inevitable result would have been that while men would have gained the possibility of incarnating time and again on the Earth, nevertheless, if they had acquired no knowledge of the Mystery of Golgotha, the condition of their sleep would have been such that the connection of their spirit-and-soul nature with Christ would have been lost.

Here you see the difference in the relation to the Mystery of Golgotha of those men who have, so to speak, no desire to know anything about it. Christ performed His Deed for their bodies, in order that earthly life should be made possible for them, just as He performed it for utterly unbelieving, non-Christian peoples. But to take effect in man's spirit-and-soul nature, the Christ Impulse must also be able to penetrate into the human soul during the state of sleep. And this is only possible if a man consciously acknowledges the import of the Mystery of Golgotha. The spiritual effect of the Mystery of Golgotha, therefore, can proceed only from a true recognition of its content. Thus there are two things that mankind must realize: on the one hand that Christ holds back the ether-body in its perpetual urge towards the Sun; and on the other, that man's spirit-and-soul nature, his Ego and astral body, can receive the Christ Impulse only in the time between falling asleep and waking - and this is only possible when knowledge of this Impulse has been acquired in waking life.

To sum up: the urge of the etheric bodies of men to draw towards the Sun is perceived by the disciples in clairvoyant vision. But they also perceive how Christ unites Himself with this urge, restrains it, holds it fast. The mighty scene of the Ascension is that of the rescue of the physical-etheric nature of man by Christ. The disciples withdraw in deep contemplation. For in their awakened souls is the knowledge that through the Mystery of Golgotha complete provision was made for the physical-etheric nature of mankind as a whole. But what happens, they wonder, to the Being of spirit-and-soul? Whence does man acquire the power to receive the Christ Impulse into his nature of spirit-and-soul, into his Ego and astral body? The answer is found in the Whitsun festival. Through the Mystery of Golgotha the Christ Impulse has taken effect on the Earth as a reality which is within the comprehension of spiritual cognition alone. No materialistic knowledge, no materialistic science can understand the Mystery of Golgotha. Hence the soul must acquire the power of spiritual cognition, of spiritual perception, of spiritual feeling, in order to be able to understand how, on Golgotha, the Christ Impulse was united with the impulses of the Earth.

Christ Jesus fulfilled His Deed on Golgotha to the end that this union might take effect, fulfilled it in such a way that ten days after the event of the

Ascension He sent man the possibility of imbuing also his inner nature of spirit-and-soul, his Ego and astral body, with the Christ Impulse. The permeation of the human spirit-and-soul with the power to understand the Mystery of Golgotha is the sending of the Holy Spirit.. This is the picture of the Whitsun festival, the festival of Pentecost. Christ fulfilled His Deed for all mankind. But to each human individual, in order that he may be able to understand this Deed, Christ sent the Spirit, in order that the individual Being of spirit-and-soul may have access to the effects of the Deed that was accomplished for all men in common. Through the Spirit man must learn to experience the Christ Mystery inwardly, in spirit and in soul. Thus these two pictures stand side by side in the history of the evolution of humanity. That of the Ascension tells us: The Deed on Golgotha was fulfilled for the physical body and the etheric body in the universal human sense. That of Whitsun tells us: The single human Being must make this Deed bear fruit in himself by receiving the Holy Spirit. Thereby the Christ Impulse becomes individualized in each human Being.

And now something else can be added to the picture of the Ascension. Spiritual visions such as came to the disciples on the day of the Ascension always have bearing upon what man actually experiences in one or another state of consciousness. After death, as you know, the etheric body leaves the human Being. He lays aside the physical body at death, retains the etheric body for a few days, and then the etheric body dissolves, is actually united with the Sun. This dissolution after death betokens union with the Sun-nature streaming through the space in which the Earth, too, is included. Since the Mystery of Golgotha, man beholds, together with this departing etheric body, the Christ Who has rescued it for earthly existence through the ages of time to come. So that since the Mystery of Golgotha there stands before the soul of every human Being who passes through death the Ascension picture which the disciples were able to behold that day in a particular condition of their soul-life. But for one who makes the Whitsun Mystery, too, part of his Being, who allows the Holy Spirit to draw near to him - for such a one this picture after death becomes the source of the greatest consolation he can possibly experience: for now he beholds the Mystery of Golgotha in all its truth and reality. This picture of the Ascension tells him: You can with confidence entrust all your following incarnations to Earth-evolution, for through the Mystery of Golgotha Christ has become the Savior of Earth-evolution. - For one who does not penetrate with his Ego and astral body - that is to say, does not penetrate with knowledge and with feeling - to the essence of the Mystery of Golgotha, for him this picture is a reproach until such time as he too learns to understand it. After death, the picture is as it were an admonition: Endeavor to acquire for the next earthly life such forces as will enable you to understand the Mystery of Golgotha! - That this picture of the Ascension should, to begin with, be an admonition, is only natural; for in subsequent earthly lives men can endeavor to apply the forces they have been admonished to acquire, and gain understanding of the Mystery of Golgotha.

You can now perceive the difference between those who with their inmost forces of faith, knowledge and feeling put their trust in the Mystery of Golgotha, and those who do not. The Mystery of Golgotha was fulfilled for mankind as a whole, in respect of the physical body and etheric body only. The sending of the Holy Spirit, the Whitsun Mystery, signifies that the soul and spirit of man can partake of the fruits of the Deed on Golgotha only if he finds wings to bear him to actual understanding of the essence and meaning of that Deed. But because this essence and meaning can be fully grasped by spiritual knowledge alone, not by material knowledge, it follows that the truth of the Whitsun festival can be grasped only when men realize that the sending of the Holy Spirit is the challenge to humanity more and more to achieve Spirit-knowledge, through which alone the Mystery of Golgotha can be understood. That it must be understood - this is the challenge of the Whitsun Mystery. That it came to pass for all mankind - this is the revelation given in the Ascension. And so it can truly be said that Anthroposophy enables us to understand the relation of the Whitsun Mystery to the Ascension revelation. We can feel Anthroposophy to be like a herald bringing illumination to these festivals of Spring, and to its many facets we have added yet another, essentially belonging to it. This should convey to you the mood-of-soul in which the true feeling for the festivals of the Ascension and of Whitsun can arise. The pictures which such festivals bring before the soul are like living Beings: we can approach nearer and nearer to their reality, learn to know them more and more intimately. When once again the year is filled with spiritual understanding of the festival seasons, it will be imbued with cosmic reality, and within earthly existence men will experience cosmic existence.

Whitsun is pre-eminently a festival of flowers. If a man has a true feeling for this Festival he will go out among the buds and blossoms opening under the influence of the Sun, under the etheric and astral influences - and he will perceive in the flower-decked Earth the earthly image of what flows together in the picture of Christ's Ascension, and the descent of the tongues of fire upon the heads of the disciples which followed later. The heart of man as it opens may be symbolized by the flower opening itself to the Sun; and what pours down from the Sun, giving the flower the fertilizing power it needs, may be symbolized by the tongues of fire descending upon the heads of the disciples. Anthroposophy can work upon human hearts with the power that streams from an understanding of the festival times and from true contemplation of each festival season; it can help to evoke the mood-of-soul that conforms truly with these days of the Spring festivals."

291

XVIII

A New Genesis

As Steiner had so often stated, the future planetary condition of the Earth and its present solar system will become the next planetary condition of consciousness: the Jupiter Manvantara. The Book of Revelation speaks of the same future condition of the Earth and of humanity as the New Jerusalem. This work has attempted to accentuate the importance of the Twelve Apostles who were to be as seedlings for the new Christ-imbued Impulses emanating from the Twelve Zodiacal constellations which will continue to be integrated into the Earth's aura as well as into the souls and spirits of all humans. These impulses are impulses that live in all of us and they are crucial for the advancing stages of earthly and human evolution. These impulses are now imbued with the forces of the Christ Principle that has united itself, along with the Christ Being, with the evolution of the Earth and of humanity.

In the construction of the Book of Revelation, it passes from the stages of Seven Letters, Seven Seals, Seven Trumpets and Seven Bowls to that of references to the number twelve or multiples of twelve. This is congruent with the far distant future of the Earth when it passes from the planetary condition of consciousness of the Earth Manvantara to its future zodiacal condition of consciousness of the Jupiter Manvantara. This is alluded to in the 21st chapter of the Book of Revelation. Certainly some intriguing observations and insights can be drawn from this chapter. The following are passages from the Book of Revelation in regard to the New Jerusalem; the Jupiter Planetary Condition of Consciousness: "And it had a wall great and high with twelve gates, and at the gates twelve angels, and names written on them, which are the names of the twelve tribes of the children of Israel." (Rev. 21: 12). The New Jerusalem, the future Jupiter Planetary Condition of Consciousness, is to be created out of the Christ-imbued Ego and soul forces of all humanity which is referenced in this passage as, " . . . the names of the twelve tribes of the children of Israel." "And the wall of the city has twelve foundation stones, and on them Twelve Names of the Twelve Apostles of the Lamb." (Rev. 21: 14). It should be noted that the reference to the Twelve Names in the above passage is a reference to the I AM of each of the Twelve Apostles. "And the city stands four square. . ." (Rev. 21: 16). "And he measured its wall, of a hundred and forty-four cubits, man's measure, that is, angel's measure." (Rev. 21: 17). "And a great sign appeared in heaven: a woman clothed with the sun, and the moon was under her feet, and upon her head a crown of twelve stars." (Rev. 12: 1). "And I heard the number of those who were sealed, a hundred and forty-four thousand sealed out of every tribe of the children of Israel." (Rev. 7: 4).

The Book of Revelation moves from seven letters, seals, trumpets and bowls to the number twelve. The stages of seven are the stages of the condition of Time which then pass into that of Space. (See Emil Bock below). After the last Trumpet, which the Book of Revelation marks as the ending of the 7th. post-Atlantean epoch, the Earth unites with the sun and passes over into an astral condition of form which is a prefiguration of its future planetary condition: the Jupiter Manvantara. Returning to the above passages we see that the city has twelve foundation stones with the names of the Twelve Apostles. The new human soul forces that would begin to create the future conditions of the astral condition of form and eventually the Jupiter Period were to begin with the Apostles. They were to consciously internalize the Christ forces that lived in the Cosmic Aura of Christ. The Cosmic spiritual impulses that stream from the constellations toward Earth and humanity were to be integrated within each individual Apostle who in turn was related to a corresponding singular constellation. They were to be the seed forces of this new direction of Ascension as Abraham was once a seed force for all of humanity in the evolution of a new consciousness and a transformation of cognition. Buddha was also a seed force for all of humanity for the understanding of the impulse of love and compassion. Elijah was the seed force in humanity for the eventual development of the individualized human conscience. That which worked from the constellations was to be mediated through Christ and internalized by the Apostles. The twelve foundation stones, that is, the twelve zodiacal constellations were to begin to work into the human soul at a higher and more conscious level and that their newly, Christ-imbued spiritual forces were to begin to germinate within the spirits and souls of the Apostles. However, the Apostles were unable to succeed in their mission at the crucial point of time during the Passion of Christ; the Event of Golgotha. Therefore, from the time of the arrest of Christ Jesus to Pentecost, John the Baptist was the carrier of the Cosmic Aura, the carrier of the fleeing youth of Christ. Since John the Baptist was the group-soul and unitary consciousness of the Twelve Apostles he acted during this time as the composite surrogate soul of the Apostles. It seems reasonable to surmise that at Pentecost the bond of the Cosmic Aura of Christ with the Apostles was then restored. This is why we read in Rev. 21:14: "And the wall of the city has twelve foundation stones, and on them twelve Names of the Twelve Apostles of the Lamb."

The Book of Revelation also describes the city as a 'four square' construction; that is, it is constructed in the form of a cube. Steiner had remarked that the cube is a symbol of the Ego. The Ego is impressed upon by all twelve constellations as well as by the nine Hierarchies and the Holy

Trinity. The New Jerusalem, the future Jupiter planetary condition, is built and created from the Christ-imbued Ego forces of humanity. It is measured in, "144 cubits, man's measure, that is, angel's measure." Again we see the forces of the twelve zodiacal constellations in their higher measure (12x12) living in humanity during the Jupiter condition when humanity, during the Jupiter Manvantara, will have reached the level of consciousness which the present day Angel Hierarchy has attained. The Book of Revelation also speaks of a great wall with twelve gates. At the gates were Twelve Angels (Rev. 21: 12). This may be a reference to a new group of Twelve World Initiators who would be present among the twelve zodiacal constellations as were the Ones that initiated Christ during the Sun Period. [see Lecture X from, "Man in the Light of Occultism, Theosophy and Philosophy," June 12, 1912; GA137]. A symbolic picture of the future human Being is addressed in the depiction of the woman clothed with the sun carrying a child. This is a picture of the Spirit Self, the Manas of the human, and within it the Ego's sun-like forces. Though, in the Book of Revelation, this picture of the future human soul and Ego predates the New Jerusalem condition its prefiguration is given to us nonetheless. Her head, that is, her consciousness is surrounded by twelve stars or we may say the twelve zodiacal constellations, while under her feet are the forces of the moon that indicate the material forces of the Earth Period which are sublimated by her. Sergei Prokofieff has addressed this theme in his book, "The Heavenly Sophia and the Being Anthroposophia."

And lastly: "And I heard the number of those who were sealed, a hundred and forty-four thousand sealed out of every tribe of the children of Israel."(Rev. 7: 4). In this passage, humanity's ascension to its Jupiter consciousness is heralded. The one hundred and forty-four thousand are sealed. The spiritual streams of the constellations, of the Twelve World Initiators, and of the nine hierarchies and the Holy Trinity are sealed within the consciousness of humanity. Humanity's number is 144,000. A symbolic number for the eventual attainment of the Jupiter consciousness by humanity. The forces of Israel are also then sealed within the soul and Ego of each human Being. That is, the forces of Isis, the Divine Sophia; Ra, the forces of the sun Elohim; and El, 'of God', the Christ. In Steiner's, "Speech and Drama," course [September 5-23, 1924; GA 282] he speaks of the 'R' sound which is to be understood as a sound that rolls in waves and streams outwardly. The 'A' or `ah' sound is the sound of awe and reverence. When we picture the sound of `Ra' we have the sound, the Word-forces, of the sun Logoi that rolls out mightily and majestically from the sun towards the Earth and humanity and continues farther outwards to the constellations.

In Emil Bock's, "The Apocalypse of St. John," he makes the following observations in regard to the Heavenly Jerusalem: "The vision of the Heavenly Jerusalem shows Earth becoming sun. The golden crystals of the

294

spiritual sun-sphere pervade our planet. This is also the mystery of transubstantiation, the conversion of Bread and Wine. And this in turn is linked together by mysterious bonds with the Resurrection, whereby Christ wrested from the corruptible earthly body the transubstantiated spirit-body in which He revealed Himself to the disciples. The vision of the Heavenly Jerusalem shows the fulfillment of what was begun on the Hill of Golgotha. Novalis expresses this with poetic exactitude:

'. . . How He by Love alone was driven
To lie for us beneath the sod.
His body as the stone was given
To found the City of our God.'"

"With the Vision of the Heavenly Jerusalem, Seven, the number of Time, gives way to Twelve, the number of Space. When the number Twelve makes its appearance, we enter a spiritual temple which is a variation of the dome of stars, encircled by the twelve signs of the Zodiac. Anyone reading through the whole book of the Apocalypse with a feeling for numbers will share in the experience of Parsifal when he was in the precincts of the Grail: `Time here becomes Space.' Out of the ever-moving stream of Time we come to a cosmic Castle of the Grail. The dominion of the number Seven, governing everything that is in constant movement within the human Being, is left behind. The number Twelve reveals its mysteries, because the concentrated inwardness here becomes an outer world again. Building is taking place, and a World is being founded. Man becomes World. After the Seer has described the dimensions of the Heavenly Jerusalem - the wall with the twelve gates, guarded by twelve Angels, and on the gates the names of the twelve tribes of the Old Testament; on the foundations the names of the twelve Apostles of the New Testament, embellished with the twelve precious stones and the twelve pearls - the Angel with the golden reed takes the measurement and proclaims: `It is the measure of Man.' The spiritualizing of the New Creation is at the same time a humanizing of it.

As preparation for entry into the Heavenly Jerusalem, wherein Man becomes World, humanity had to be ranged on the holy mountain as the host of 144,000. At that moment the number Twelve already revealed its inherent law. Now the measure of the great Twelve, twelve times twelve, recurs. The wall which the Angel has measured is 144 furlongs in length. The number of the universal entirety of individual possibilities surmounts all individuality and community.

Now the architecture of the Apocalypse as a whole, itself a spiritual building, lies clearly before us. The vision of the Son of Man is the beginning of the path along which the writer of the Apocalypse leads us. The vision of the City is its goal. The revelation of the inmost cosmic secrets begins with Man and shows in the end how Man becomes World. But before he can become World he must become Humanity. When through the power of the

Higher Ego Man becomes Humanity, the great Twelve shines forth in the host of those who are gathered round the Lamb on the Holy Mountain. The Twelve becomes the governing law of existence when, under the sign of the Heavenly Jerusalem, Man who through Christ has regained the image of God intended for him, becomes the focus and raw material of a new cosmic Creation, the new Heaven and the new Earth. The Heavenly City is described as being of the same length, breadth and height. This description alone should be sufficient to refute the sentimental, easy-going ideas of Heaven held by those who picture it in terms of what gave them pleasure on Earth. A great crystal cube emerges as the figure of the Heavenly City. On Earth, rock salt, the most common form of salt, crystallizes in cubic form. Is the Heavenly Jerusalem also the fulfillment of the charge which Jesus gave to the disciples in the Sermon on the Mount, 'Ye are the salt of the Earth?' In the same context the Heavenly Jerusalem is referred to as from a distance: 'A city that is set on a hill cannot be hid.' The disciples who according to Christ's charge are to be the salt of the Earth are, in their spirituality, the building material of the Heavenly Jerusalem. In them, Man truly becomes World. Every further indication of the raw material of the Heavenly City confirms this. The foundations with the Names of the Twelve Apostles are adorned with twelve precious stones. The precious stone mentioned in the first place is Jasper, whose brilliance adorns the City in many forms. The City shone in 'the glory of God; her light was like unto a stone most precious, even like a jasper stone, clear as crystal.' 'And the building of the wall of it was of jasper.' In our world, when the Sun rises, the light of the stars is extinguished by the brighter light of the day-star. In the alternating day and night we see either the stars or the Sun. In the Eternal City, Stars and Sun shine at the same time - from within outwards. The glitter of the twelve precious stones is not extinguished by the sunshine of the gold crystals; it is concentrated and deepened: 'The City itself was pure gold, like a transparent crystal.' 'The streets of the City were pure gold, as it were transparent crystal.' The ground, the plane upon which everything moves, is gold crystal, through which one can see deep into the world below.

The crystalline gold of which especially the ground of the City is formed, is the further development of the 'sea of glass', in which the newly purified creation began to crystallize out from the ocean of evolution. The admixture of red which distinguished the new crystal sea from that of the first creation, because human warmth of soul and the power of love have flowed into the substance of the new world, has now been refined to pure gold which shines like a Sun. 'The City has no need of the Sun, neither of the Moon, to shine in it , for the glory of God Himself lightens it, and the Lamb is the light thereof.' In the Heavenly City day and night no longer alternate. The 'Marriage of the Lamb' is celebrated. Earth and Sun have again become One. The 'New Earth' is itself Sun. The Principle of the Lamb, the sacrificial love of Christ, has become the point of crystallization of the new world. Behind the sunlight that brightens our day, the love of the Gods of Creation is hidden. So the love of the God of Consummation, Who as Son of Man is also the center of all true humanity, will be the source of light for the new Age. The gold crystals are the sunshine of Christ-filled human hearts become World.

If the golden crystals show that the Sun is once more in the Christ-filled Earth, so the precious stones show that once more the differentiated wealth of the Stars is contained in it. Through the love of Man's heart, Earth becomes Sun; through the spiritual purity of his thinking, the Earth becomes star-like, radiant, a concentration of the whole starry firmament. The predominance of jasper as the first and noblest of the precious stones links the pictures of the beginning with those of the end. In the fourth chapter, between the Messages and the Seals, He who sits on the Throne, Father of the Worlds, is pictured as a jasper stone. He does not appear in human form, but as a center of rays, flashing and shining like a precious stone. The power of pure thinking passes over from the Being of God to Man. (There is a hint of this also in the story of the Holy Grail, for it is said that the Chalice of the Grail was cut out of jasper.) As Man becomes World he causes creation itself to assume the starry countenance of God. In the Eternal City, the enthroned One becomes the World, the Creator becomes Creation.

And what is the secret of the pearls, of which the twelve gates consist? The oyster forms the pearl by transforming a painful foreign body which has penetrated into its shell. This process of Nature can, and must, become one of the guiding principles of human spiritual life. The gates of the City of God can only be passed through under the sign of the pearl. Only pain and suffering conquered and transformed can enable men to share in the new Creation. Just as the gold shows the Sun in the new Earth and the precious stones cause the stars to shine forth in it, so the pearls are the transformed Moon incorporated in the Earth. When the Will of Man has attained to pure endurance through all the trials of destiny, then the New World will have its gates, through which he can enter who has reached maturity. We have seen that the Whore Babylon also has, in her own way, gold, precious stones and pearls at her disposal. The great lamentation over the fall of Babylon rings out: `Alas, alas, that great City that was clothed in fine linen and purple and scarlet, and decked with gold and precious stones and pearls! For in one hour so great riches is come to naught.' Here is appended outward magnificence which, in the Heavenly Jerusalem, is an integral part of a new Creation. The pearls with which the great Whore decks herself do not represent suffering fruitfully endured. The materialistic outlook is characterized by its inability to understand the value and purpose of pain, sickness and death. The Whore Babylon decks herself with the pearls springing from the suffering and tribulation of others. Her principle is power. But the outward assumption of riches only increases the dead weight which ultimately brings about the plunge into the abyss.

In Chapter 12, the Women in Heaven clothed with the Sun, Moon and Stars appeared as a picture of the Soul of the World and of Man. The picture of the Bride Jerusalem, with gold, pearls and precious stones, is a progressive metamorphosis of this. Now the human soul is no longer clothed with Sun, Moon and Stars alone; she has become World and carries Sun, Moon and Stars as constituent parts of her own Being. Now she has absorbed the Cosmos into herself, she herself has become Cosmos. The inner world becomes the outer World. The City of God is built through the incarnation of the inward Sun, the inward Moon and the inward Stars."

In a collection of lectures which were brought together and published under the title, "Reading the Pictures of the Apocalypse," Steiner gave many indications and insights that are supportive of the themes presented in this present work. Munich; May 8, 1907: "The Apocalypse is one of the greatest spiritual documents. There are hardly any great spiritual truths whose significance is not to be found there. The study of the Apocalypse is not without its connections to theosophical evolution."

In the same lecture Steiner also spoke of the evolution and transformation of the physical body: "What comes forth from the Earth, Sun and Moon sound together in our astral body. But what comes forth from the planets sounds in our etheric body. There is a sevenfold influence from the planets on the etheric body, as there is from the seven musical intervals: the unison interval, major second, major third, perfect fourth, perfect fifth, major sixth, major seventh - Saturn, Sun, Moon, Mars, Mercury, Jupiter, Venus. These seven planets resound into our etheric body. There are twelve influences from the signs of the zodiac that resound into our physical body. The seer experiences twelve fundamental tones on the Devachanic plane. They influence our physical body. Everything in the I, astral body, etheric body and in the physical body resounds in tones. One tone resounds in the I, three tones in the astral body, seven tones in the etheric body and twelve tones in the physical body. Altogether this results in harmony or disharmony. There is an expression in occultism: the twelve goes into the seven, which means that the physical body is constantly becoming more like the etheric body. If the physical body sounds right then we can hear the seven tones of the stars (planets) through the twelve tones (the Zodiacal constellations). `Become such that the twelve becomes the seven, that the seven stars appear' is said to the Ephesians, because with them the physical body is especially developed. They should turn to look at the seven stars. We know that the development of Christianity means a transition from the old forms of community based on blood ties to spiritual love, that the spiritual will take over from the flesh. Those who tell us that we should endeavor, above all, to insure that the sensual, the elemental gets its due - those people were called the Nicolaitans: They wanted to remain rooted in the material forces of the blood; hence, the warning concerning the Nicolaitans. They are the ones who will bring about the downfall. Opposing them are those who want to overcome material evolution, who want spiritual life. The letter closes with the symbol of the Tree of Life: `He who has an ear, let him hear what the Spirit says to the churches. To him who conquers I will give some of the hidden Manna . . . .` (Rev. 2: 17).

The second letter is directed to the community that is supposed to be most concerned with the cultivation of the etheric body. The etheric body must gradually be developed into Life Spirit. The human Being now goes through birth and death, but later this etheric body will become Life Spirit. Then it will have overcome death. In the Sermon on the Mount we read: `Blessed are those who pray for spirit, for they find through themselves the Kingdom of Heaven.' (compare Matthew 5: 3). Those who pray for spirit are blessed; that means that soul permeates their life. Just as the physical body is developed by the Ephesians, so, too, in the second community, is the etheric body developed into a body of soul. When they strive for this blessing they are called `beggars for spirit'; they pray for a blessing through the enlivening of the etheric body. This is indicated by the words: `Be faithful unto death and I will give you the crown of life.' With these words the development of the etheric body is clearly expressed."

Munich; May 15, 1907: "What does the writer of the Apocalypse think of the future? He speaks entirely in the following way: What you can see today on the astral plane is nothing other than the formation of the physical future of human Beings. Look at what is on the astral plane and you will experience the future of humankind. There is no future that does not result from the present. You know that the human Being is enveloped in an astral body that permeates the physical body. You know , too, that there are sense organs in the astral body that are entirely different from the sense organs in the physical body. We speak of the lotus blossoms or wheels. What the human Being can develop today in terms of such astral senses, the human physical body will have in the future as physical senses. The astral is on the way to becoming physical. How do human Beings form these organs of the future, which today are still astral? Through what we achieve today in terms of the true, the beautiful, and the good. Work and deeds of today form the foundation for organs in the future. There was a time when human Beings did not have eyes - they couldn't perceive light and color. Human Beings acquired eyes through their actions at that time. They had other organs previously - by turning to the light they developed eyes. Present deed is future destiny; the deeds of the past were such that eyes could be created, and from your deeds in the present day, your sense organs of the future will be created.

Human Beings who are active in terms of the true, the beautiful, and the good will have normal organs in the future. If they strive against the true, the beautiful, and the good then they will have crippled organs in the future. It is impossible to erase what we do in the present. A deed laid down in the present in order that it emerge in the future is termed `sealed' in Christian esotericism. In terms of Christian esotericism one says: Today you have eyes that were nonexistent in the past but you did this or that. Your eyes were `sealed', now they are `unsealed'. Your eyes are the `unsealing' of your past deeds. We have now the sealing of what will be unsealed on the physical plane in the future. For anyone who looks only at the physical plane, evolution is a book with seven seals. Anyone who looks at the astral plane can see all future organs already laid out. The organs reveal themselves as pictures. An esotericist would say: If you look to the middle point, which is characterized as the lamb, then the lamb will put the book into your hand; and the book is unsealed in such a way that what will have form in the future can only be expressed in pictures. Therefore, what can occur is expressed through pictures, piece by piece. In the first seal a future condition is portrayed pictorially by a horse, a further condition is revealed in the second seal through another horse and so forth. In order to discern the meaning we will consider one image, let us say, the third horse. This is the picture that appears when the third seal is broken. It is presented in the following way: `When he opened the third seal, I heard the third living creature say, `Come!' And I saw, and behold, a black horse, and its rider had a balance in its hand.' (Rev. 6: 5).

What does this mean? A future condition of the human Being is here portrayed, a condition that proceeds from the evolution of the third member of the human Being, the astral body, which has been worked on and purified by the `I'. An unpurified astral body is one that knows only itself, that finds everything that does not belong to it to be antipathetic. A purified astral body is one that receives everything coming to it weighed out with a just balance. If we rightly purify the astral body, an organ is created that can be expressed pictorially by a rider with a balance. An organ in the astral body arises for the human Being out of just deeds in the present. This is expressed here pictorially. We could explain the other pictures in the same way. Then we would see the inadequacy of the usual explanations that are given. When the fifth seal is opened we are told something very significant: `When he opened the fifth seal, I saw under the altar the souls of those who had been slain for the Word of God and for the witness they had borne. . . .' (Rev. 6: 9) What happens to a soul that develops itself up to the fifth step? It is strangled in its lower soul; the impurities that cling to it are done away with, and the soul thereby appears clothed in innocence: `And they were each given a white robe. . . .' (Rev. 6: 11). The soul is white; it has become innocent when it has developed to the fifth step."

We can make the comparison here from Mark's Gospel of the young man sitting in the tomb "clothed in a white robe" (Mark 16: 5) to that which Steiner had said of the future purified soul of the human Being as a `white

300

robe'. The phantom body of John the Baptist as the `young man in the tomb' is also enveloped in his purified astral body. The phantom body of John the Baptist in the tomb on Easter morning is "clothed in a white robe."

Kristiania: May 11, 1909: "We must understand the difference between the evolution of souls and the evolution of bodies. From epoch to epoch human souls find themselves again and again in different bodies. These souls will one day see the strife that will reign among the human souls who will be born in the last post-Atlantean Age. This experience will be a lesson for them and will help to free them from egotism. Then they will be able to grow into an era where they will have the fruits of selfhood but without its disadvantages. An Age will come with clairvoyant conditions similar to those prevailing in ancient Atlantis, but with this difference: human Beings will have a free consciousness of Self. We will then have learned, in these seven cultures of the post-Atlantean Age, what can be achieved in the physical world. This self-perception or consciousness of Self can only awaken in a physical body; but the human Being must again subjugate the physical body. After the War of All against All, we will have achieved a stage of evolution where we live in a bodily nature in such a way that we are no longer slaves of our physical bodies.

The impulse for this development comes from the Christ Principle. Christ even falls right in the middle between the Age of the Atlantean catastrophe and the War of All against All. On the one hand we can thank the descent into matter for our consciousness of Self within our physical bodily nature. On the other hand, we thank the Christ Event for our ability to ascend with the achievements of the physical world. We thank the Christ Principle for our ability to ascend to universal brotherly love, to the universal love of humanity, since we will again unite in groups with love for one another. If we look back to the time of the original group souls of Atlantis and then into the future we see these four group souls appearing again. The lamb will stand in the middle as a sign for the love that will unite people who will then be living in a bodily nature that is less dense. But this state must be prepared today through the setting aside of a small group that will carry brotherly love into the future. Therefore, a stream has arisen in our time that will lead to brotherly love through real spiritual knowledge. Humankind will not attain brotherly love through preaching but rather through knowledge. . . . if people are given wisdom, knowledge of evolution, in such a way that it becomes life in the soul, then humanity will arrive at love. The soul can attain this when it is warmed by wisdom. Then it can radiate love. For this reason the `Masters of Wisdom and Harmony of Feelings' have formed this stream for the raying forth of love into humanity and for the influx of wisdom into humanity. Humankind, rushing toward the War of All against All, will then find the fruit of the theosophical movement in an understanding of peace - while all around it, the nature of humankind will have everywhere led into strife those who have not heard the call of the `Masters of Wisdom and Harmony of Feelings' on the basis of the Christ Impulse in the fourth age."

Kristiania - May 14, 1909: "If a clairvoyant Being had been in a position to observe the Earth through millennia then, it would have appeared that the entire aura of the Earth suddenly changed color, radiated with different colors when the Redeemer died on Golgotha. Ahura Mazdao, who had been proclaimed by Zarathustra, became at that time the Elemental Spirit of the Earth. Christ expressed this when, at the Last Supper, he said: `This is my body' (Matthew 26: 26) and, for the grape juice, found the expression, `This my blood.' (Matthew 26: 26). If we really studied the Earth we would have to see members of the Spirit of Christ in everything that lives and grows, even in the smallest thing we look at. Human Beings of the future will not speak of atoms; they will scientifically understand the Earth as the expression of Christ. We are standing only at the beginning of this development. Christ must first be understood in the simplest way. In the future all science will find Christ, even though it finds today nothing but a dead corpse-like existence in the sensible world. The fifth epoch can feel, to begin with, only as a perspective, that this new science is approaching, that humanity will understand in a new way what Zarathustra meant when he spoke of Ahura Mazdao. The ancient wisdom of Zarathustra will appear again in a new form in the sixth age. Finally, the age of the holy Rishis will come again in a new form. There may be only a small band of people who understand Theosophy in our age; there may be only the smallest of groups present to hear the re-enlivened wisdom of Zarathustra in the sixth age; and, finally there may be only a fraction remaining for the seventh age. The further course of human evolution will be such that more and more people will gather together who will understand what Zarathustra proclaimed.

Then an age will come upon the Earth when the victors will be those who lead the War of All against All. But the souls who will have been preserved from the sixth age must found a new culture after the War of All against All. The seventh age will have neither people who glow with enthusiasm for the spiritual, nor those who glow with enthusiasm for sense existence; even for that these people will be too blasé. Very little of the Indian, the first culture, will be perceptible on the Earth in the seventh age. But these souls from the sixth age when carried up into the spiritual world, purified and `Christened', will walk as it were etherically, no longer touching the Earth, while humanity then will be able to master what the entire culture of Earth has to offer. The seventh age will be such that here below on the Earth, people living in increasingly dense and hardened bodies will make the greatest discoveries and inventions. In the seventh age, human Beings wholly entangled in matter will no longer have to fear much from Theosophy, for on Earth there will no longer be much to find of those transformed human

Beings who will have increasingly spiritualized themselves in the sixth age by absorbing Theosophy.

The people who have understood the call of the Master today will be carried over into a distant future. The key will be turned in the sixth cultural epoch. Those who have heard the call will be the founders of a new humanity. If only a few people are entangled with matter, the community of Laodicea will not last long. It lies within the free will of every human Being to belong to either the community of Philadelphia or the community of Laodicea."

Kristiania - May 16, 1909: "The `I' of Jesus of Nazareth left the three sheaths at the Baptism in the Jordan. Nevertheless, an image of this `I', like the imprint of a seal, remained in the three sheaths. The Christ Being took possession of these three bodies but he also took possession of something else, something that remained behind like an imprint of the `I' of Jesus. From the twelfth, thirteenth and fourteenth centuries on, something like a copy of Jesus' `I' was woven into those men who then began to speak of an `inner Christ'. Meister Eckhart and Johannes Tauler were speaking out of their inner experience of something like an imprint of the `I' of Jesus of Nazareth. Although there are still many people present today carrying something like a copy of the various bodies of Jesus of Nazareth, they no longer become leading personalities. More and more we see how in our fifth age there are people who must rely on themselves, on their own `I'. Such inspired people will become increasingly rare. Therefore, steps were taken to provide for the future so that a particular spiritual stream could arise in our time, a spiritual stream with the task of insuring that spiritual knowledge will still reach humanity. Those individuals who could see into the future had to provide for human Beings who are wholly dependent on their merely human `I'. We are told in a legend that the vessel used by Christ Jesus with His disciples at the Last Supper was preserved. This is the legend of the Holy Grail. We see in the story of Parzival an expression of a pupil's typical path of development in our fifth post-Atlantean Age. Parzival neglected to do one thing. He had been told the he should not ask questions. That is the important transition from the old age to the new. In ancient India, a devotion as passive as possible was necessary for the pupil; this was also true in Augustine's time and in the time of Francis of Assisi. All of these humble people let themselves be inspired by what lived in them, what had been woven into them. But now the `I' must carry the question in itself. Every soul today that passively receives what is given to it cannot go beyond itself. It can only observe what is going on in the physical world around it. Today the soul must ask questions, must lift itself above itself; it must grow out of itself. The soul today must ask questions as Parzival had to ask about the secrets of the Grail castle."

Kristiania - May 17, 1909: "There are forces again working outward in human Beings today. The more the `I' has mastery over the astral body, the

303

more the physical body can be molded and transformed. Today we have our karma within us like a life account, with a balance of everything we have prepared in our various incarnations. But because the human Being's physical nature expresses very little of the 'I', we carry our karma inwardly and unmediated. But later it will show itself on the human face. Humankind will evolve in the future so that its karma is carried in the countenance. No longer will the fact that a human Being is born into a specific race or in a specific climate be decisive for external appearances. There will be rather a class of good people and a class of evil people. Let us understand Paul correctly, who said: 'I live, but it is no longer I who live, but Christ in me.' (Galatians 2: 20). What is called 'receiving the Yahweh-Christ Being' will later show itself in human Beings externally. Today it is still possible to be a rogue and yet hide it; but in the future, human Beings will carry the mark of their inner life on their foreheads. Let us look at the human Being after the War of All against All. We can think of him or her as someone with radiant, good features and a noble benevolent expression. This will become the fate of those who have taken in spiritual impulses at the right time. All moral, intellectual, and spiritual forces will, in the future, confront us visibly in the external features of a human Being. What is taken in today will be sealed into souls. After the seventh age, after the War of All against All, they will be unsealed."

Kristiania - May 19, 1909: "In the Lemurian Age the Earth still existed entirely within the element of fire. Human Beings lived in fire before descending into a dense bodily nature - this will be repeated in a spiritual state. When the seventh trumpet sounds forth a kind of blessed state will come upon humanity. Then we come to a repetition of the time when the Sun was separated from the Earth. The human Being, together with the Earth, will have advanced to the time when the Sun again unites with the Earth. The Earth will pass over into what is called an astral state. Human Beings able to live in the astral world will raise up the finer part of the Earth and then be united with the Sun. The portion of the Earth that has remained course will be united with the Moon to form a new kind of Moon. The kind of conditions prevailing during the Hyperborean Age will enter in again, but at a higher stage of evolution. This is characterized by the woman clothed with the Sun and having the Moon at her feet. The beasts that rise up out of the sea or fall from heaven also belong to this whole stream of evolution that is pictured, as if captured in a moment of time. (Rev. 12:1 - 13:10)."

Kristiania - May 20, 1909: "Human Beings today are already creative on the Earth. They can force the lifeless forces of nature to serve them. They can build cathedrals, they can sculpt marble. Today they are masters of lifeless nature. Even though Raphael's paintings of the Madonna are falling to dust, even though the external physical world is passing away, what the human Being achieves in terms of art during the evolution of the Earth will one day resurrect in a different form. The crystals we see today were once forms worked out by human Beings during the old Moon embodiment of the Earth, in a way similar to how we create and form artistically today. What the spirits once achieved in infinite ages of time now grows out of the Earth; today it rises up. So, too, the matter of Raphael's Madonnas will also rise up. In the distant future, everything that human Beings now create will rise again with the brightness of crystals. The place that humanity has prepared and will find waiting is called the `New Jerusalem' by the writer of the Apocalypse. A new world will arise, inhabitable by human Beings who will have achieved the requisite state of maturity. In a new state, in the Jupiter existence, they will find the place where, out of love and out of human work, peace will reign."

In his Nuremberg lecture cycle of 1908, "The Apocalypse of St. John," Steiner gave further points of interests that are useful for this study.

Nuremberg - June 24, 1908: "And when the fifth seal is opened what is then brought to our notice? Those who in the preceding period have learned to understand the Event of Christ Jesus! These are clothed in white garments, they have been passed by, figuratively they have been slain, they are those who are preserved for the spiritualization of the world. Thus it is the union with the Christ-Principle which brings it about that men have these white garments and appear when the fifth seal is opened. Here we see a clear indication that the time when Christ appears is an important epoch for mankind; it is the epoch which brings it to pass that after the War of All against All the four Ages again appear when those who have remained behind are tormented by the materiality which has proceeded with evolution and to which they have chained themselves; they are tormented by all the evils and torments of coarsened, hardened materiality. Everything which is now described in the breaking of the seals represents nothing else than the descent into the abyss. While in the fifth period we are only briefly directed to those who are chosen, we are shown for the rest all those who remain in materiality, who go down into the abyss, who assume the forms which existed previously because they did not progress, because they have not acquired the power to transform these shapes."

Nuremberg - June 26, 1908: "We might say that the important stage of passing over into the Earth which has become spiritualized is wonderfully expressed in the Bible where it says that everything which man now accomplishes within himself in the physical body during the Earth Period is like a sowing whose fruit will appear when the Earth has become spiritual: And that which thou sowest is not the body that shall be, but bare grain, it may chance of wheat or of some other grain. But God giveth it a body as it hath pleased Him, and to every seed his own body . . . (That is, the body which is the expression of the soul, of the individuality). There are also celestial bodies and bodies terrestrial, but the glory of the celestial body is one, and the glory of the terrestrial body is another . . . (The earthly bodies will be dissolved, the celestial will appear as the luminous expression of what

305

the soul is). It is sown corruptible and will rise incorruptible . . . (The incorruptible body will then be resurrected). It is sown a natural body; it is raised a spiritual body. - (I Corinthians 15: 37). Paul calls the etheric or life body, spiritual body, after the physical has dissolved and the etheric passes into the astral Earth. Paul here sees beforehand the incorruptible spiritual body, as he calls it.

And now let us consider what it is that man will contribute as the expression of his own Christ-capacity. It is the same that hovered before Paul in spirit, and that he calls `the last Adam', while he calls the first man who entered into existence in a physically visible body `the first Adam'. At the end of the Lemurian epoch we already find various animals below, but man is not yet visible to external eyes; he is still etheric. He condenses, he absorbs mineral constituents and appears in his first form; the physical man gradually appears, just as water condenses into ice. Physical evolution then proceeds so far that what is earthly can dissolve and eventually disappears. Hence the man who has the etheric body appears as the `last Adam'. The `first Adam' has the capacity of seeing the Earth in the physical body through the physical senses; the `last Adam', who assumes a spiritual body, is an expression of the inner Christ-capacity. Hence Christ is also called by Paul the `last Adam'. This comprises the whole of human evolution; in spirit we see what man will become in the future, whereas before we saw how he descends to the Earth."

Earlier in this work it had been proposed that there was no certainty that the mission of Christ would succeed. It was imperative that a select group of individuals succeed in understanding both the Mystery of Golgotha and the nature of the Christ Being. Steiner mentioned that the Advent of Christ on Earth was not only opposed by Lucifer and Ahriman depicted by the Temptations in the Desert, but also by Sorat, the two-horned beast.

Nuremberg - June 30, 1908: "This seductive Being is of quite a different nature from man. It originates from other world periods; it has acquired the tendencies of other world periods and will feel deep satisfaction when it meets with Beings such as those evil ones who have refused to take up inwardly the good which can flow from the Earth. This Being has been unable to receive anything from the Earth; it has seen Earth evolution come but has said: I have not progressed with the Earth in such a way that I can gain anything from Earthly existence. - This Being could only have got something from the Earth by being able to gain the rulership at a certain moment, namely when the Christ-Principle descended to the Earth. If the Christ-Principle had been strangled in the germ, if Christ had been overcome by the adversary, it would have been possible for the whole Earth to succumb to the Sorat-principle. This, however, did not take place, and so this Being has to be content with the refuse of mankind who have not inclined towards the Christ-Principle, who have remained embedded in matter; they in the future will form his cohorts."

306

Later in the same lecture Steiner addresses the meaning of the `First and Second' deaths in relation to the Christ-Principle: ". . .it must be possible for man during his Earthly evolution to imprint ever and again at least in the etheric body, what he has taken into himself. It is necessary for this etheric body also to receive effects from what man develops in his astral body. Man cannot yet of himself work into this etheric body. Upon Jupiter, when he has transformed his astral body, he will be able to work into this etheric body also, but today he cannot do this; he still needs helpers, so to speak. Upon Jupiter he will be capable of beginning the real work on the etheric body. Upon Venus he will work on the physical body; this is the part most difficult to overcome. Today he still has to leave both the physical and etheric bodies every night and emerge from them. But in order that the etheric body may receive its effects, so that man shall gradually learn to work into it, he needs a helper. And the helper who makes this possible is none other than the Christ, while we designate the Being who helps man to work into the physical body as the Father. But man cannot work into his physical body before the helper has come who makes it possible to work into his etheric body: No man cometh to the Father, but by Me. - No one acquires the capacity of working into the physical body who has not gone through the Christ-Principle. Thus, when he has reached the goal of Earthly evolution, man will have the capacity - through being able to transform his astral body by his own power - to work down into the etheric body also. This he owes to the living presence of the Christ-Principle on the Earth. Had Christ not united Himself with the Earth as a living Being, had He not come into the aura of the Earth, then what is developed in the astral body would not be communicated to the etheric body. From this we see that one who shuts himself up by turning away from the Christ-Principle deprives himself of the possibility of working into his etheric body in the way that is necessary during Earthly evolution.

Thus we shall be able to characterize in another way the two kinds of man whom we find at the end of the Earth's evolution. We have those who have received the Christ-Principle and thus transformed their astral body, and who have gained the help of Christ to transform the etheric body also. And we have the others who did not come to the Christ-Principle; who also were unable to change anything in the etheric body, for they could not find the helper, Christ. Now let us look at this future of mankind. The Earth spiritualizes itself, that is, man must lose completely something which he now in his physical existence considers as belonging to him. We can form an idea of what will then happen to man if we consider the ordinary course of his life after death. He loses the physical body after death. It is to this physical body that he owes the desires and inclinations linked to ordinary life; and we have described what man experiences after death. Let us take a person who is fond of some particularly dainty food. During life he can enjoy this, but not after death. The desire, however, does not cease, for this is seated, not in the physical body but in the astral body, and as the physical instrument is absent it is impossible to gratify this desire. Such persons look down from kamaloka to the physical world which they have left; they see there all that could give them satisfaction, but they cannot enjoy it because they have no physical instrument for the purpose. Through this they experience a burning thirst. Thus it is with all desires that remain in man after death and are related to the physical world, because they can only be satisfied through physical instruments. This is the case every time after death; each time man sees his physical body fall away, and as something remains in him from this physical body it still urges him to the ordinary world of the physical plane, and until he has weaned himself from this in the spiritual world he lives in the fire of desires.

Now imagine the last earthly incarnation before the spiritualization of the Earth, the laying aside of the last physical body. Those who are now living on the Earth will have progressed so far through the Christ-Impulse that, in a certain way, it will not be very difficult for them to lay aside the very last physical body; they will, however, be obliged to leave something, for all that can give pleasure from the objects of this Earth will have disappeared once and for all from the spiritual Earth. Think of the last death possible in our Earth evolution, think of the laying aside of the last physical body. It is this last death of the incarnations which in the Apocalypse is called the `first death', and those who have received the Christ-Principle see this physical body as a sort of husk which falls away. The etheric body has now become important to them for, with the help of Christ, it has become so organized that it is for the time being adapted to the astral body and no longer desires and longs for what is below in the physical world. Only with all that has brought into the etheric body through the help of Christ do men continue to live on in the spiritualized Earth. They have created a harmony between their astral body and their etheric body. The Christ-Principle has created this harmony. On the other hand there are those who have not received the Christ-Principle. These do not possess this harmony. They too must lose the physical body, for there is no such thing at first in the spiritual Earth. Everything physical must first be dissolved. It remains as desires for the physical, as the unpurified spirituality, as the spiritual hardened in matter. An etheric body remains which the Christ has not helped to be adapted to the astral body, but which is suited to the physical body. They are the souls who will feel hot fires of desire for physical sensuality; in the etheric body they will feel unappeasable, burning desire by reason of what they have had in the physical life and which they must now do without. Thus, in the next period, after the physical has melted away, we have men who live in an etheric body which harmonizes with the astral body, and we have others whose etheric body lives in discord because they desire what has fallen away with the physical body.

Then in the course of further evolution there comes a condition where the spiritualizing of the Earth has proceeded so far that there can no longer be even an etheric body. Those whose etheric body completely harmonizes with the astral body lay aside this etheric body without pain, for they remain in their astral body which is filled with the Christ-Being. They feel the laying aside of the etheric body as a necessity in evolution, for they feel within them the capacity to build it up again for themselves because they have received Christ. Those, however, who in this etheric body desire what belongs to the past can also not retain this etheric body when all becomes astral. It will be taken from them, it will be torn out of them, and they now feel this as a second dying, as the 'second death'. This second death passes unnoticed over those who have made their etheric body harmonize with the astral body through the reception of the Christ-Principle. The second death has no power over them. But the others feel the second death when they have to pass over into the future astral form. The condition of mankind will then be such that those who have reached the goal of evolution will have entirely permeated their astral body with Christ. They will be ready to pass over to Jupiter. Upon our Earth they have made the plan of the Jupiter evolution. This is the plan which is called the New Jerusalem. They live in a 'new Heaven' and a 'new Earth', that is Jupiter. This new Jupiter will be accompanied by a satellite, composed of those who are excluded from the life in the spiritual, who have experienced the second death and are, therefore, unable to attain the Jupiter consciousness. Thus we have those men who have pressed forward to the Jupiter consciousness, who have attained Manas; and those Beings who have thrust away the forces which would have given them this consciousness. They are those who only upon Jupiter have attained to the Ego-consciousness of the Earth, who exist there, so to speak, as man now exists on the Earth with his four members. But such a man can develop himself only on the Earth, the Earth alone has the environment, the ground, the air, the clouds, the plants, the minerals which are necessary to man if he wishes to gain what may be gained within the four members. Jupiter will be quite differently formed, it will be a 'new Earth'; soil, air, water, and every Being will be different. It will be impossible for Beings who have only gained the Earth consciousness to live a normal life; they will be backward Beings. But now comes something that will once again comfort us. Even on this Jupiter there is still a last possibility, through the strong powers which the more advanced will have, to move those fallen Beings to turn back and even to convert a number. Only with the Venus incarnation will come the last decision, the unalterable decision. When we reflect upon all this, the thought we recently considered will be seen in a new light. It will no longer call forth anxiety and disquietude, but only the determination: I will do everything necessary to fulfill the Earth mission."

Concluding this lecture: "It is now necessary to point out for what purpose the Apocalypse was written. I should indeed have to say a great deal if I were to describe this in detail, but you can at least take away with you one hint, one which we find at a definite point in the Apocalypse. The writer of the Apocalypse says: A time will come when that high degree of consciousness will actually have developed, when man will see the Beings who direct the world, and Beings represented by the Lamb, by the appearance of the Son of Man with the flaming sword. - We are referred to this in tones which contain within them that assurance of which we have spoken. The writer of the Apocalypse, who is a great seer, knows that in ancient times men were gifted with a dim clairvoyance. We have described this and have seen how at that time men were the companions, so to speak, of Beings in the spiritual world, and themselves saw the spiritual world. But who lost this gift of seership? Who? We must now put this forward as an important question. We have seen that fundamentally it was lost by those men who were led to the physical plane, the physical life, when the second half of the Atlantean epoch began. Man looked upon the solid formation of our Earth, upon the clearly outlined objects of our Earth. The ancient clairvoyance disappeared; he became conscious of his Self, but the spiritual world was closed to him. The formations, which in ancient times filled the air like an ocean of mist, disappeared; the air became clear, the ground free. Man stepped out on to the free Earth. This took place comparatively late; it coincided with the attainment of the present intellect, the present self-consciousness of man. Now let us remember what we said about this Earth as well as about the great Event of Golgotha. If someone had observed the Earth at that time from a distance with clairvoyant vision at the moment when the blood flowed from the wounds of the Redeemer, he would have perceived that its whole astral aura changed. The Earth was then permeated by the Christ-force. Through this Event the earth will be able to reunite with the Sun. This power will grow. This is the power which preserves our etheric body from the `second death'. Christ becomes more and more the Earth-Spirit, and the true Christian understands the words: He who eats my Bread treads Me underfoot. - He considers the body of the Earth to be the body of Christ. The earth as a planetary body is the body of Christ; of course at present this is only at its beginning. Christ has still to become the Earth-Spirit; He will unite Himself fully with the Earth, and when the Earth later unites with the Sun, the great Earth-Spirit, Christ, will be the Sun-Spirit."

"If you go further along the path which in a certain way you have begun by turning your attention to the exposition of the Apocalypse of John, you will gradually penetrate into the depths of spiritual life. You will come into depths which cannot possibly be expressed today, because they could not be brought into consciousness, because no one has yet ears to hear. The ears must first be prepared to hear, by such explanations as have now been given. Then they will gradually be there, ears able to hear the Word which flows at such profound depths through the Apocalypse. If you have been able to receive a little of what could be imparted, you must be aware that only the most superficial things could be given, and of these only a few observations. May it give you the impulse to penetrate more and more deeply into what can only be surmised through these lectures. If I were to say only what can be said about the surface, I should have to lecture still for many, many weeks. These lectures could only be a stimulus for further study, and those who feel the impulse to penetrate more deeply into the Apocalypse will have received them in the right way."

Rudolf Steiner stated that the Cross on Calvary was the seed of a new Cosmos. From, "The Gospel of St. John and Its Relation to the other Gospels," Steiner says the following: "When the Cross was raised on Golgotha and the blood flowed from the wounds of Christ Jesus, a new cosmic center was created." [July 6, 1909; GA 112]. This new Cosmos is to be a Cosmos that completes the work of Love and Freedom that is being cultivated during the Earth Manvantara. As the Moon Period was the Cosmos of Wisdom in that wisdom was worked into that cosmic body throughout the entire Moon Period, Love is now being worked into the aura of the Earth as well as into this solar system. The human Ego is the seed force for this future cosmic body. It is only in complete freedom and in full-consciousness that Love can be expressed and given. When the Earth Manvantara, the present planetary condition of consciousness, is completed we will then advance to the following Jupiter Period as it is called in Christian esotericism when, ". . . all things will breathe out Love." All things will be permeated with Love. The conditions of life in the future Jupiter planetary condition will be quite different than what they are now. However, in all of our incarnations we have been slowly and gradually developing into independent Beings. Moreover, in time we will increasingly integrate more of the Christ Principle within our Egos. There, it is nurtured and will flower into the Pleroma, the Fullness of the Grace of Christ. In the ages to come we will seed the Earth with the living impulses of Love that fill our thoughts, feelings, actions and speech. Throughout our successive incarnations, the soul and spirit essence of Love that lives within and emanates from human Beings will increasingly unify with the Christ-imbued, etheric-astral sheath that now envelopes the Earth where the Etheric Christ now resides. This sunlike, etheric-astral sheath to which we participate in creating is the beginning stage of development for the future Jupiter planetary condition.

However, during the years of 1933 through 1945 this sunlike, Christ-imbued etheric-astral sheath was in danger of separating itself from the Earth and humanity. Jesaiah Ben-Aharon's spiritual research which is detailed in

311

his book, "The Spiritual Event of the Twentieth Century: An Imagination - The Occult Significance of the 12 Years 1933-1945 in the Light of Spiritual Science," is a corroboration of the rise of the Beast, Sorat, in 1933 as Steiner had foretold. Steiner had also alluded to the return of the Etheric Christ during this time period of 1933-1945. Jesaiah Ben-Aharon writes that this was the period in which the, " . . . apocalyptic Beast is set free from its captivity in the Earth and, on the other, the Etheric Christ begins to be perceived by the new, natural supersensible faculties." He then quotes Steiner in regard to these "new, natural supersensible qualities": "This condition of soul, this experiencing of soul, is called in esotericism the `Second Coming of Christ'." ["The Reappearance of Christ in the Etheric" - GA118].

"The deed of Golgotha suffused the earth with astral light which by degrees will become etheric and then physical." [July 6, 1909; GA112]. It was during the period of 1933-1945 that the etheric realm of the earth had reached its culmination of becoming sun-like. The earth's etheric body had now attained what the earth's astral body had attained when the blood of Christ flowed from the Cross on Golgotha. What transpired for the earth's astral body at the time of Christ's first Dispensation was now being repeated for the earth's etheric body at the time of the beginning of Christ's second Dispensation. In the same lecture Steiner adds the following which addresses the earth's future condition: "The first impetus towards becoming a Sun was given to our earth when the blood flowed from the wounds of the Redeemer on Golgotha. The earth then began to glow, first astrally and visible only to the seer; but in future ages the astral light will become physical light and the earth will be a luminous body: a Sun-body."

The years of 1933-1945 were also a time in which the lower Self of humanity began to separate from its Higher Self, the Christ. Humanity's lower Self at this time consisted of its own unresolved karmic world debt since the time of the incarnation of Christ on Earth. It also consisted of humanity's incomprehension of the Christ. From this, we can draw a parallel between the Apostles, during the time of Christ's physical incarnation, to that of humanity as a whole during His etheric manifestation. Though at times Christ had brought their consciousness to cross over into the spiritual realms, the continued incomprehension of the Apostles eventually resulted in severing the bond between them and their Higher Self, the Christ Being. The Apostles, then, could no longer hold the cosmic forces of the Aura of Christ within their souls. In like fashion during the period of 1933-1945 the new and youthful `Tree of Life' forces of the Aura of Christ were in jeopardy of separating from the Earth and humanity. On a larger, macrocosmic level the failing of humanity as a whole to comprehend and recognize the Etheric Christ resulted in similar circumstances during the time period of 1933-1945. Since the ending of the Age of Darkness, the Kali Yuga, which lasted 5000 years a "new age of light begun in 1899." Humanity's consciousness, as a single whole, began crossing the threshold into the spiritual world in a way that it hadn't achieved as a whole for 5000 years. However, humanity was unconscious of it and unprepared to apprehend the spiritual world. This was analogous to an illicit Initiation. Humanity was unable to consciously unite with the Etheric Christ at this most critical point in time. The tragic result was the same as that of the severance of the Apostles' bond with Christ. However, in this twelve year period it was on a worldwide scale. Humanity, as a whole, was not cognizant of the new manifestation and mission of the Etheric Christ during this historically critical time. Therefore, the sun-like Christ-imbued portion of the earth's etheric-astral sphere began to separate itself from the earth. The very element that is to ultimately create and evolve into the future Jupiter Planetary condition, the New Jerusalem, was losing its earthly connection. A bridge of consciousness and comprehension had to be forged between the soul element of humanity and the Etheric Christ in order for this sun-like, etheric-astral sphere to remain united with the earth and humanity. A group of souls who were capable of comprehending the Etheric Christ provided such a bridge. Jesaiah Ben-Aharon states that three stages were involved during this time period. They consisted of: 1) the separation of humanity's lower Self with its higher Self, the Christ; 2) a group of Michaelic souls who, because of their comprehension of the Christ and their awakened consciousness, acted with free will as surrogates for the whole of humanity; thereby, bridging the abyss between humanity and the Etheric Christ; 3) Christ descended into the depths of humanity's lower Self and united with the Being of humanity's lower Self in a Manichean sacrifice.

Jesaiah Ben-Aharon writes: "Since the Mystery of Golgotha the Sun power of Christ has been working in the heart of humanity and the Earth. In the heart of those human Beings who were truly given to Him, He created the living substance needed for the building stones of the human temple of His Kingdom of Heaven on the Earth. In the beginning of the second third of the twentieth century, it was made manifest what an advance was achieved in this work. Its Revelation shows clearly that, helped by the new Michael Impulse, the Christ could now gather its substance together and condense it to such an extent that a wholly Christ-permeated sphere of human activity and life could for the first time be made a planetary reality of the Earth. The revelation shows the founding of Christ's own new human land and kingdom, the true Shamballa, in which the life-giving source for all positive future earthly evolution is found."

This human Michaelic-bridge afforded the Etheric Christ the capacity to work through these human souls and bring to pass His Second earthly deed; His Manichean Sacrifice of dying to evil in order to overcome evil. In His First earthly sacrifice, during His physical incarnation, Christ experienced physical death and united with the forces of death and matter, thereby, overcoming these forces. This formulates the conditions for the eventual

313

transfiguration of the current mineral condition of form to that of the future astral condition of form. This time period, 1933-1945, was a recapitulation of Christ's Agony in the Garden, His Crucifixion, Death and Resurrection.

Jesaiah Ben-Aharon then writes: "Christ's Manichean demonstration of infinite love and sacrifice is the future archetype of all transformation and redemption of evil in our universe. That which He suffered and overcame through His becoming One with humanity's evil Being belongs to the things that cannot yet be grasped by earthly human cognition. Humanity must evolve morally much further before even a preliminary attempt to penetrate this Mystery will be possible. But when we observe the visible etheric results of Christ's unfathomable sacrifice, we are comforted by the realization that from now on His eternal Being germinates and grows for humanity in the core of all evil. The result of what we lost sight of in the sub-earthly depths below comes back to us from above. It appears in its pictorial reflection as light-radiating spirit holiness from the expanding circumference of the Earthly-Human Sun. That is, at the unseen moment of the merging of Christ with the primordial evil Being of humanity, the upper Kingdom of the Earthly-Human Sun, until now separated from its lower, demonized self, turned inside out and around and embraced its lost half of Self. It thus became one cosmic body, carrying in its center that which was formally outside itself. This part would have become ever more separated from it if the human-Michaelic sacrificial questioning and Christ's sacrificial answer had not been consummated. This deeply fissured Self will be borne consciously from the twentieth century onward as its inwardly burning wound of unresolved past cosmic evolution. The turning of Shamballa inside out and around had surrounded the whole of Earth with a glorious but inwardly humble holy illumination. This light is the youthful, new life radiation of the Earthly-Human Sun. The imaginative gaze observes how for the first time in the evolution of the Earth since its separation from the Old Sun, but now as an independent Being, it becomes an outwardly radiating, cosmic Earthly-Sun Being."

"The Earth could be born as a new Sun in the middle third of the century because its Higher Self, the Christ, was so deeply accepted by a representative group of free human Beings. These are the true pupils of Michael in the age of the consciousness soul, as we showed above. They could take upon themselves the karma of humanity out of free moral Intuition, Inspiration and Imagination. Christ's sacrifice was then the macrocosmic counterpart of their microcosmic-planetary Sun act of moral freedom in face of the evil Being of humanity. It was the first fully conscious co-operation between a free representative group of humanity, representing its upward aspiring earthly Self, which ascends to the etheric heights of the Earthly-Human Sun, and its all embracing, descending Higher Self, the Christ. He answered their sacrificial questioning with His mighty descent into humanity's seduced lowest Being. And this co-operation and mutual penetration between the higher and lower Selves of humanity and Earth is the occult cause and significance of the Sun birth of the Earth in the etheric universe. It consummated the greatest Event of the new Michael age at the dawn of the new cosmic age of light. Earth and humanity were born again as an evolving fixed star: a new Sun was born in the universe. The Earth and humanity as a whole passed through its first stage of conscious initiation and became a Christ-permeated, holy planet. The sacred work of transforming evil into the highest good had begun. This is the third stage which completes the century's Event: the Earth becomes a Sun through humanity's conscious and free collaboration with its Higher Self, the Christ. The Earth Being experienced its Earthly Sun Birth."

The eventual condition of the present Earth is that it and the other planets will ultimately reunite with the Sun. Christ brought to the Earth the forces of the six Elohim who reside within the spiritual sphere of the Sun. Due to these sun-like forces, which Christ brought to the Earth and are now within the sphere of the Earth, there is a 'force of attraction' that now impels the Earth to unite with the Sun. The Sun and the Earth are now induced to unite with one another since they both contain within themselves 'like forces'. On a microcosmic level the same can be said concerning the relationship of each human Being to Christ. Christ is the Divine, Macrocosmic Ego. Within each of us resides our own Ego. Here again, a 'force of attraction' is at work. Our microcosmic Ego is drawn to the Macrocosmic Ego of the Christ. Our Ego becomes increasingly conjoined with the Ego of the Christ Being. In a lecture from the previously cited collection, "Reading the Pictures of the Apocalypse," Steiner had said the following: "If we try to imagine the very highest Being, the One Who was as highly developed at the beginning as others will be at the end of evolution, then we have the image of Christ. He was the I that was as highly developed at the beginning as the human Being will be at the end." [May, 1 1907; Munich]. In like manner, on a macrocosmic level, our earth's etheric-astral sphere becomes increasingly spiritualized until it finally unites with the sun and thereby becomes the 'seed force' for a new sun and a new cosmos. According to Steiner, though Christ is recognized as the Sun-Spirit, he descended from spiritual realms beyond the sun and from beyond the constellations. He is a Being that stands above all of the Divine Hierarchies. What we see in the way of planetary and solar bodies, these planets and stars are the outer physical vestments behind which spiritual dimensional realities exist. As our own physical bodies are the outer external physical vestments of our souls and spirits so are the planets and stars external physical vestments for the spiritual Beings who reside behind them in variegated spiritual dimensions. Our physical sun is the physical vestment for the six Elohim and other Beings who reside within its spiritual sphere. The planets' elliptical spheres are the regions of other hierarchical Beings and the same can be said for the regions of the constellations.

Christ descended from spiritual dimensions beyond the constellations. In the Book of Job the Lord addresses Job saying: "Have you fitted a curb to the Pleiades, or loosened the bonds of Orion? Can you bring forth the Mazzaroth in their season, or guide the Bear with its train?" (Job 38: 31-32). In Ephesians 1:19-21 it reads: ". . . its measure is the working of His mighty power, which He (the Father) has wrought in Christ in raising Him from the dead, and setting Him at His right hand in heaven above every Principality and Power and Virtue and Dominion – in short, above every name that is named, not only in this world, but also in that which is to come." And in Colossians 1:15-17: "He is the image of the invisible God, the firstborn of every creature. For in Him were created all things in the heavens and on the Earth, things visible and things invisible, whether Thrones, or Dominions, or Principalities or Powers. All things have been created through and unto Him, and He is before all creatures, and in Him all things hold together."

When Christ descended to earth and began the process of creating a new cosmic body of Love and Freedom on earth, He began the process of uniting the entire solar system into one body which will eventually form a new sun that would mirror the past Hyperborean conditions. The earth is now becoming the seed for this eventual new condition of the sun. In the distant future this becomes a new cosmic body of constellations. What may be taking place in our cosmos is that not only are we becoming a seed force for a new sun but we may actually be at the beginning stages of becoming a seed force for an entirely new galaxy; a cosmic galaxy of Love and Freedom; a cosmic galaxy in which, ". . . all things will breathe out Love."

Nick Thomas once presented a photo in which he displayed a picture of the position of our sun in relation to other stars within a radius of 38 light years. The picture shows the distribution of all the stars and our sun in relation to each other within a 38 light-year radius from our sun. The results are very dramatic and breathtaking. We see that all of the other stars are clustered closely to each other but that the space around our own star, the sun, is significantly hollowed out and that our sun clearly stands alone among the other stars. After careful examination of the other stars, our star, our sun is the only one within this cluster of stars that has such a configuration.

Nick Thomas writes: "The picture shows the distribution of stars within a 38 light-year radius of the Sun (which is at the center). In order to show this in two dimensions each star was rotated onto the plane of the equator so as to keep its distance from the Sun and right-ascension correct. This gives a correct impression of distance distribution. The surprising and unexpected result was to see the large gap in the center. To check this out other locations were chosen to see if there was a gap there too, but not so! Finally a full statistical test was made by dividing the whole three dimensional volume into

316

small cubes and counting the number of stars in each, and sure enough that with the sun in it had the least. These results have been checked by a professional astronomer." [See Plate 1].

What we can derive from this picture is that the collective formation of our solar system could be providing the gestation and incubation of a newly forming galaxy in its seed form within the Milky Way galaxy which is the mother galaxy to our solar system. Our solar system may be the embryo of a new galaxy gestating within its mother galaxy. In time this new, embryonic galaxy will separate from the Milky Way as a newborn child separates from its own mother to which it will form its own galactic sphere. The new sun that we are now creating could possibly be the new spiritual center of this future galaxy. The spiritualized earth would be the seed force within this new sun and new galaxy. As Steiner had remarked, the Cross of the Crucifixion and the forces that were present on Calvary were the seed forces of a new cosmos.

Golgotha was the 'Turning Point in Time'. It provided the redirection for the course of human and earthly evolution. As mentioned earlier, the Gospels state that Christ was on the Cross between the two thieves while the sun became darkened. (Luke 23: 39-45). The Bible often records actual historical events yet, at the same time, it conveys through them profound, esoteric truths. Steiner had mentioned that what was incorporated within the two thieves on Golgotha were the Beings Lucifer and Ahriman. Again, it should be noted that the Bible makes a very subtle allusion to the presence of Sorat, the Sun Demon, in its reference to the 'darkened sun'. With this conveyance of the Adverse Trinity in the Luke Gospel it sheds a veiled light on the presence, at Golgotha, of the forces that oppose both Christ and the whole course of human and earthly evolution. The human soul in those times had a more unconfined interpenetrating bond with the physical body than what is common today. This was a significant factor for those who were baptized by John the Baptist. He was able to partially separate the soul from the body even further so that a baptism could become an Initiation to some level. Considering the conditions that the two thieves were enduring at that time they may have been losing their connection to their bodies and the separation from their bodies became ever greater as the Event of Golgotha reached its final moments. Lucifer and Ahriman were then able to interpenetrate the souls of the two thieves. They were then able to work through the two thieves which afforded Lucifer and Ahriman access to a deeper ingression into the physical plane. Their words to the Christ were probably not addressed at an audible level that would be sense-perceptible. Instead, they were words spoken at a spiritual-archetypal level. The repentant thief in the Gospel of Luke, as stated earlier, is the redemption of Lucifer while the other thief displays Christ's and humanity's ongoing struggle with Ahriman-Satan which will continue long after Golgotha. While even further

317

into the future is the struggle with the Asuras and the sun-demon, Sorat, which is conveyed in Luke's Gospel as the darkened sun.

When Christ spoke the words - It Is Finished - while upon the Cross, what He spoke of cosmically was that the Fall of humanity into matter, into Death, and all of the forces that brought humanity deeply into this condition were now to be reversed. Christ died upon the Cross of 'matter' and has united His Being with the earth itself. A new Impulse of spiritual Life was brought into the sphere of the earth that would now bring a reversal of direction to the course of human and earthly evolution. The two earthquakes that took place, one immediately after the death of Christ on the Cross and the other at the time of the Resurrection acted as signs from the earth itself. (Matthew 27: 51 & 28: 2). The original luciferic forces that precipitated the earth's downward course and had permeated the earth for ages were brought to a halt by Christ at the Crucifixion on Golgotha. When the primordial luciferic forces of the Fall came to a sudden cessation, this literally shook the physical earth at its foundations as the Christ began to enter into the sub-realms. The return of Christ from the sub-realms at the moment of the Resurrection also shook the earth at its foundations as this Event initiated the reversal of the downward course of the Fall. It was at this time that the new forces of the Resurrection and the eventual Ascension of the earth and humanity to the spiritual spheres were begun by Christ on Easter Sunday morning . As a result, a reversal in the direction of human and earthly evolution was now ushered in. Steiner, therefore, refers to the Mystery of Golgotha as the Turning Point in Time.

Christ's words - It Is Finished - marks this turning point. The Fall had reached its nadir and the Ascension was about to begin. When one reflects on these three words from Christ on Calvary and carefully considers the vast implications of their meaning, it is possible to say that these three words may have been the most powerful words ever spoken in all of human and earthly evolution. With these three words the new course of human and earthly evolution now begins to expand outwardly from within the Christ-imbued inner Selves of humanity and from the core center of the earth. Earlier it had been indicated that the Christ had become a Macrocosmic Being at the beginning of the Earth Manvantara. He was given regency over our solar system and the zodiacal constellations from the Father Being who had been its Regent from the time of the Saturn Period. From the lecture cycle, "Materialism and the Task of Anthroposophy," Steiner comments: "Now, these earthly things we see around us with our senses, the things that have come about on earth, neither originate from these nature spirits nor from the Father God Who actually expressed His creative Being only in the metamorphoses preceding the earth. What we see as earth does not originate from the Father God nor from the nature spirits. It comes from the Son, from the Logos, whom the Father God let spring forth from Himself so that the earth might be created by the Logos. And the Gospel of St. John, a mighty, significant monument was written in order to indicate: No, it is not as the people of old believed; the earth was not created by the Father God. The Father God made the Son come forth from Him; and the Son is the creator of the earth." [Lecture XVI; Dornach, June 3, 1921].

At the beginning of the Earth Manvantara Christ emerged from the Father Being as a Macrocosmic Being and was given regency over this solar system and the zodiacal constellations. However, this conveyance of regency was not fully completed until Christ once again returned to within the Being of the Father after the death on the Cross and then re-emerged from the Father. This 'Second' emergence of the Christ Being from the Father Being during the Earth Manvantara was consummated from within the core center of the earth. This was the Resurrection of Christ. The post-Crucifixion Initiation of the Christ Being within the Being of the Father gave Christ the capacity to transubstantiate the Father Principle which still resides within the element of matter and which comprises this solar system. It is the Father Principle within matter which the Christ will invert and raise to the next condition of form: the astral condition. The stage at which the Christ presented Himself to Mary Magdalene on Easter morning marked the initial point of His personal ascension process as well as the ascension process of our cosmos. Christ intimated these principles in His priestly prayer to the Father immediately prior to His arrest: "Father, the hour has come! Glorify thy Son, that thy Son may Glorify thee . . . ," (John 17: 1). Also, "And now do thou, Father, glorify me with thyself, with the glory that I had with thee before the world existed." (John 17: 5). In the final moments of the Crucifixion, when Christ said the following words, "Father, into thy hands I commend my Spirit." (Luke: 23: 46), Christ acknowledges His imminent union with the Father Being. These words were then followed by His death; His descent into the sub-realms; His macrocosmic Initiation within the Being of the Father; His emergence from the Father Being from within the core of the earth; and, the eventual coalescence of His Being with the realm of the Father element of the earth and with the cosmic space of our cosmos that extends outwardly from the core of the earth to the ends of our solar system and beyond which would include the zodiacal constellations.

The new 'Son' creation begins 'within' the soul and spirit of the human Being and thereby reverses the pre-Crucifixion creation of our cosmos. The human Self now becomes the foundation stone for a new cosmos. When Christ said to the Pharisees, "For behold, the kingdom of God is within you," (Luke 17: 21) He was addressing these words to the old Order of understanding. He specifically spoke these words to the Pharisees because their understanding was based on that which was to be gained only from the past prior to the Advent of the Christ on earth. The past wisdom was now to give way to the new wisdom. Contained in these words spoken to the

Pharisees is the admonition to understand that the kingdom of God, the Christ-imbued soul and spirit of the human Being, is now the center of the new creation. In this Gospel verse, we can see the boundless cosmic evolutionary implications that are often contained in the words of Christ. In a lecture given December 27, 1918 Steiner stated the following: "At the time that the Mystery of Golgotha took place, the human Being was hollowed out; he became hollow. And it is important that we learn to recognize the Mystery of Golgotha as an Impulse that has a reciprocal relation to this hollowed-out condition of man. If we speak truly, we must make it clear that the hollow space in man, which indeed could be found still earlier - let us say, in the Egypto-Chaldean royal Mysteries - had to be filled up in some way. In that ancient time it had been partly filled by the real Ego; but this now comes to a stop at birth - or at least, in early childhood; there is some evidence of its presence in the first years of childhood. This hollow space has been filled by the Christ Impulse."

The above statement from Steiner presents an intriguing question in regard to the following when he said: "And it is important that we learn to recognize the Mystery of Golgotha as an Impulse that has a reciprocal relation to this hollowed-out condition of man." This reciprocal relation could possibly be expressed by the following in that this cosmos was also hollowed-out when Christ, the Macrocosmic Ego and Higher Self of this cosmos, experienced Death on the Cross. After Christ's death on the Cross our planetary system and the zodiacal constellations reflected the condition of the human soul such that they too were hollowed-out and devoid of their Macrocosmic Ego. The Christ, during His Initiation by the Father, passed through a pralaya; a Cosmic Night of His Being. This cosmos, for whatever brief time, no longer had its Macrocosmic Ego within it. From this, we can draw a parallel to the hollowed-out soul condition of humanity, as stated by Steiner, to that of the hollowed-out condition of our cosmos. This Macrocosmic Initiation of the Christ Being by the Father, as stated previously, is a complete reversal to the pattern of a human Initiate's experience. While on the Cross, Christ's utterance of the words, "My God, my God, why have you forsaken Me," inaugurates the beginning of the Macrocosmic Initiation of the Christ. This is the reversal to the human Initiate's, "My God, my God, you have glorified me," which is expressed at the conclusion of the Initiation process. Christ then descended into lower realms whereas the human Initiate ascends into higher realms. The human Initiate subsequently reaches an illumination of consciousness whereas the Christ is momentarily extinguished from our cosmos while in His pralaya condition within the Being of the Father. This is the key point. The entirety of His descent to earth, His Baptism, His Crucifixion and Death on the Cross culminated in the Death of His Being within this cosmos. The protracted death process which actually began when He first took leave of the highest

320

spheres consummated in the momentary hollowing-out of His Macrocosmic Ego from this cosmos which was preceded by His words, ". . . Father, into thy hands I commend my Spirit." (Luke 23:46). At the completion of His descent into the sub-realms, the Christ Being was drawn into the Being of the Father where He resided, momentarily, in a pralaya or Cosmic Night condition. Thereby, this cosmos was momentarily without its Macrocosmic Ego; the Christ. Throughout Christ's time on earth, while incrementally incarnating deeper within the body of Jesus of Nazareth, He was increasingly losing his conscious connection with the spiritual world. Thereby, it becomes possible to assert that Christ completed His Death process to the fullest only when He ultimately passed into a momentary subjugation of His macrocosmic consciousness. That is, He lost all consciousness, all spiritual illumination during His pralaya; the Cosmic Night of His Being. This was the ultimate state of Christ's death and its eventual culmination into the Being of the Father. Again, this would complete the reversed pattern of His Initiation to that of the human Initiate's illumination. It also completed the actuation of fulfilling His experience of losing consciousness as humans would, in their sojourns after death, eventually lose consciousness. The Christ Being, a Being of the Highest Order, had now experienced the parallel to the human earthly experience; the momentary vanquishing of awakened consciousness.

Christ's momentary vanquishing of consciousness is intimated by Steiner from the following: "Human beings here in the physical world are born and they die; the characteristic of the divine, spiritual beings who belong to the higher hierarchies is that they are not born, neither do they die, but only undergo a transformation. Christ, Who until the time of the Mystery of Golgotha lived with the other divine, spiritual beings, resolved to know death, to descend to Earth, to become man, and within the nature of man to pass through death, thereafter to return to consciousness through the Resurrection. In the divine-spiritual world it was an event of the deepest significance that a God should experience death." [Dornach; March 24, 1922; "The Three Stages of Sleep"; GA:211; source: www.elib.com]

During the course of the progression of the Manvantaras a Cosmic Night precedes each new Manvantara. At the beginning of the Earth Manvantara the Christ Being stood as the First Cause. Christ came from beyond the constellations and descended to Earth. This course was now reversed. After His Cosmic Death and pralaya, Christ emerged from the Father from within the center of the earth. He reawakened and resurrected from His own post-Crucifixion pralaya from within the Father, thereby ending the transitory Cosmic Night of His Being. This inaugurated the genesis of a new cosmos from within the earth which then works outwardly and reverses the primordial condition of creation that worked from without. The emergence from His pralaya was the beginning stage of His Resurrection to which He again manifested His Being within the realm of the dead. This emergence from within is reflected in the human Being as well such that the Christ Impulse now works from within the human soul and creates a new human Being who, along with the Christ, creates a new cosmos. If we accept the account from the Gospel of Nicodemus which chronicles John the Baptist accompanying Christ's descent into the sub-realms coupled with the premise that he appeared as the young man sitting in the tomb, it then becomes possible to assert that John the Baptist, the Adam soul, was the first human soul to interact with the Risen Christ. As the young man in the tomb, it was John the Baptist who told the women that the Christ had Risen.(Mark16:5-7). As John the Baptist was the first human to recognize and interact with the Christ embodied in a physical/mineral body at the time of the Jordan Baptism, he was also the first human to recognize the Risen Christ, as well, on Easter morning.

Later, during Easter morning, when the Risen Christ appeared to Mary Magdalene He admonished her, saying, ". . . Do not cling to me [Greek: me mou haptou], for I have not yet ascended to my Father, but go to my brethren and say to them, 'I ascend to my Father and your Father, to my God and your God.'" (John 20:17). If the Greek words - me mou haptou - are properly translated as a prohibitive present imperative we can then surmise that Christ is entreating Mary Magdalene to discontinue from physically grasping and clinging to Him. In the earliest hours of Easter morning Christ had yet to become fully integrated within the resurrected phantom body of Jesus of Nazareth. This moment stood as a Second Baptism of the Christ Being in that these processes consisted of integrating His Ego within the newly redeemed phantom body of Jesus of Nazareth while simultaneously integrating His resurrected microcosmic phantom body with that of the macrocosmic phantom body of our cosmos. Christ had not yet ascended to the Father because His phantom body and the macrocosmic phantom body of our cosmos had not yet fully integrated with one another at that hour. These processes were not completed until after sunset of that day. Also, when Christ said that He had not yet ascended to the Father he was referring to two conditions which succeeded His post-Crucifixion pralaya state of Being. One condition was internal while the other condition was external. The internal expression of the term, Father, to which the Christ refers is the burgeoning attainment of the microcosmic Atma aspect of the former phantom body of Jesus of Nazareth which Christ had occupied since the time of the Baptism in the Jordan. On Easter morning, the phantom body that Christ had occupied during His ministry was still in the post-Resurrection process of being fully configured into its purest Atma condition. In Lecture XI of Steiner's 1910 Matthew cycle, he addresses the various terms of an Initiate's condition of Being. Steiner conveyed the following: "And one with whom Atma, or Spirit-Man, had made contact was called, 'Father' in the ancient Mysteries." In regard to the external condition, Christ also speaks of the Father as the

322

macrocosmic mineral element of our own particular cosmos which exists within its own macrocosmic phantom body. The Father, in this instance, is the metaphorical term used to describe the entire cosmic space that originates from the center of our earth and extends outwardly to the limits of the twelve zodiacal constellations. The integration of the microcosmic phantom body of Christ Jesus with that of the macrocosmic phantom body of our cosmos was the initial phase of the Ascension. Christ's recorded Ascension, at the end of the forty days, marked His post-pralaya integration into the phantom/physical and etheric realms of this cosmos while Pentecost marked His earliest stage of integration into the cosmic astral realm of our cosmos. In summation, Christ was expressing to Mary Magdalene that His internal and external conditions of Being had not been altogether consummated in those early hours on Easter morning. He expressed to Mary Magdalene that He had not yet ascended to the Father. That is, He had yet to fully attain the Atma condition of the phantom body of Jesus of Nazareth at that hour and, thereby, His phantom body had not yet wholly integrated itself with the macrocosmic phantom body of our cosmos. These processes were not finalized until the Macrocosmic Ego aspect of the Christ had completely integrated Itself within His microcosmic phantom body, while in unison, the phantom body of Christ Jesus became One with the macrocosmic phantom body of our cosmos. When these processes had been completed by sunset a human phantom body had now become One with the macrocosmic phantom body of our cosmos. When Christ had said earlier during His ministry that He and the Father are One He was expressing that His macrocosmic aspect was One with our cosmos. Now, however, through the Resurrected Christ a wholly redeemed microcosmic human phantom body, the phantom body which had previously belonged to Jesus of Nazareth now redeemed, had become One with our cosmos. A redeemed human phantom body and the Father had become One as well.

The entirety of John 20:17 in which Christ speaks to Mary Magdalene is not a reference to the Father Being. Rather, it is a direct reference to cosmic space. Moreover, this passage also alludes to the macrocosmic Ego principle of the Christ and to the Ego principle of the human Being. As Steiner had so often pointed out, the term 'Father' had several meanings; one of which meant cosmic space. It is also a term that refers to the Ego of the Christ and to the Ego of the human Being as well. In this particular instance, Christ was referring to the fact that not only was He integrating His Macrocosmic Being/Ego into the resurrected microcosmic phantom body of Jesus of Nazareth but that He was also integrating His newly initiated Macrocosmic Ego into the macrocosmic phantom body of our own cosmos; the 'physical' aspect of our cosmos. After His pralaya, Christ reintegrated His Macrocosmic Ego into this cosmos which is the realm of the Father element of matter. In addition, the macrocosmic Ego Impulse of the Christ is also a principle that now works into the Ego of each human Being. This explains His words, " . . . I ascend to my Father and your Father, to my God and your God." On Easter morning Christ began the process of resurrecting this cosmos from the center of the earth out to the zodiacal constellations and preparing this cosmic space for its next Manvantara: the Jupiter Manvantara; the New Jerusalem.

At the tomb, the phantom/physical body of the Christ had only initially begun the process of becoming one with the macrocosmic phantom/physical body of the earth and our cosmos while He spoke these words to Mary Magdalene. This process is referred to as the Ascension of Christ. As Emil Bock illustrates in his book, "The Three Years," that Mary Magdalene's vision of Christ at sunrise, after His Resurrection, is the initial stage of Christ's Ascension. It seems reasonable to presume that later in the evening of that very day, after sunset, when Christ appeared before His disciples and told them to see and to touch His wounds (Luke 24: 38-40), this marked the completion of the full configuration of the resurrected Phantom body of Christ. The Ascension then reaches its culmination after forty days to which the, "two men . . . in white garments," (Acts 1: 10) appear before the eleven remaining Apostles. These 'two men' are the Christ-imbued, replicated etheric and astral bodies of Jesus of Nazareth.

Prior to 1933, those who had experienced visions of the Resurrected Christ over the centuries were witnessing the appearance of Christ in His resurrected non-mineral, physical-phantom body within the earth's own redeemed non-mineral, physical-phantom realm as well as within the earth's etheric realm. However, during the years from 1933 to 1945 the New Dispensation of Christ had begun. This time period marked the beginning of the phenomenon which can be understood as the Second Coming of Christ. At present, Christ now appears in an etheric body within the earth's newly created etheric/astral sun realm. At future stages, Christ will appear in an astral form within lower Devachan. While further in the future He will appear in an Ego form within upper Devachan. Steiner had expressed the point that the external cosmic wisdom becomes internalized in the human Being and flows out again as human and cosmic Love which carries over to the Jupiter Period. Steiner writes: "Beginning with the Earth phase of evolution, the wisdom of the outer cosmos becomes inner wisdom in the human Being. Internalized in this way, it becomes the seed of love. Wisdom is the prerequisite for love; love is the result of wisdom that has been reborn in the I." [GA# 13].

Michael Debus in his afterward to Emil Bock's lectures, "Threefold Mary," writes the following:

"In the outer world of the senses, the Logos has totally expressed, exhausted itself; it has reached its end. But the process of creation may now continue within humanity. The Gospel of John recounts seven signs performed by Christ. They are the prototypes of a new week of Creation, the beginning of the Son's creation, issuing from the Father's completed creation. The first of these signs, performed at the wedding at Cana, marked the beginning of this creative period, but not only its outer beginning. The Greek word used here -'arche'- means more than "beginning," as indicated by the Latin translation 'principium'. So this first miracle is the principle of all seven signs. It is of principle importance that the mother of Jesus be present here. Key to Christ's creative act, that of turning water into wine, is his conversation with his mother. They continue on a higher level what was of such basic importance during the previous eighteen years. But now it is Mary Sophia in whose mirror Christ's creative power awakens; this is similar to the Old Testament's description of Yahweh's creation. New creation springs up through the interaction between the incarnated Logos and incarnated Sophia. The creation here begun is completed on Golgotha. The crucified Christ's last words are, 'It Is Accomplished' or 'The goal has been reached.'"

Within our blood are the spiritual forces of the Ego. The forces of the blood at the time of death etherize into the etheric realms. When Christ died on the Cross and spilled His blood, these Ego forces of Christ were lifted into the etheric-life realm of the Earth where they have remained. Normally for a human Being these blood forces etherize and return to the cosmic etheric forces of the sun. However, with Christ, His etherized blood has remained here on earth and has permeated the etheric-astral sheath of the earth. Since the Event of Golgotha, we now have an etheric-astral sphere around the planet of the earth that is the initial spiritual essence of a new earth, a new sun and possibly a seed for a new galaxy. The Bible specifies that Christ descended into Hell after the Crucifixion. This is primarily a reference to the realm of the dead where at that time in human history the dead retained very little awakened consciousness or sometimes no consciousness in their afterlife. This sleep-like consciousness of the dead in their afterlife is often mentioned in the Bible. Christ brings with Him to this realm a source of Light and Life to which the dead in their afterlife are able to respond correspondingly to the Christ-Logos Impulse that one has assimilated in one's earthly life in full consciousness and in full freedom. The dead are then able to ascend into the higher spheres in their afterlife with the ability to retain a greater level of awakened consciousness throughout their afterlife sojourn. Paul states in 1Corinthians 15: 50-55 that the dead shall rise first then we who are the living shall meet Him in the air. This is literally true in the sense that the microcosmic post-life pattern of ascending into the higher spheres for any one individual is exactly the same pattern, now speaking macrocosmically, which will take place over eons of time for the whole of humanity and the earth itself. The course of an individual's afterlife is the same course the earth and humanity will achieve in our ascension into the higher spiritual spheres throughout the remaining conditions of evolution to come. A Christ-filled human consciousness is vital for the ascension of humanity and of the cosmos. It is the Foundation Stone for the building of the heavenly city; the New Jerusalem; the Jupiter Manvantara.

Retaining consciousness as long as possible after death is essential in anyone's spiritual evolution. This is where we gather the harvest of our earthly life and it is here where we plant new seeds for our next life. A significant point in our afterlife is the period immediately after our death when we spend time reviewing our past life. This is referenced by Paul in Hebrews 9:27 when he says, ". . . it is appointed unto men to die once and after this comes the judgment." Our physical death, the death of the physical body, is the first death. After this we undergo a life review where all that we had done in our earthly life is imparted to us in reverse sequential order as we endure the impact of all that we had done to others from their perspective. The verse which reads, ". . . it is appointed unto men to die once . . . ," tells us in a veiled expression that a second type of death is not meant to be for humans. This second death would be the death, or better said, the loss of consciousness in one's afterlife. It also alludes to the proper course of human evolution. It indicates the future progression of the human condition from a physical/mineral condition of Being to an etheric condition and later to an astral condition of Being and so on. This retention of consciousness after death is what Christ made possible for our afterlives when He descended into the realm of the dead after the Crucifixion. Another point of significance is the question of the wording that Christ Jesus uses to describe His own Death and Resurrection. In John 2:19 He says, ". . . destroy this Temple and in three days I will raise it up." When Christ spoke of the destruction of the Temple which He would raise in three days it is clear that he was speaking in the language of the Mysteries. When the writers of the Gospels gave their accounts of Easter morning, none of them wrote that three days had passed. Rather, they used the expression, ". . . on the morning of the first day of the week." Only Christ referred to it as, 'three days'. All Initiations in the pre-Christ Mystery oracles, which raised the celebrant to a higher stage of development, are referred to as the three days of death. This would allow the celebrant to ascend into the spiritual worlds to which the celebrant would be initiated into the wisdom and truths of the spiritual worlds. Other examples of reference to Initiation in the Bible would be the raising of Lazarus from the dead and Jonah in the belly of the whale for three days. These are clear intimations to the ancient art of Initiation into the Mysteries.

The Initiation and the raising of the Temple to which Christ referred was an Initiation of His own Self. However, this Initiation was an Initiation of the Highest Cosmic Order. It was an Initiation of a Logos Being that stands above all other hierarchical Beings in our cosmos. This Initiation, the Event of Golgotha, may possibly have been the seed force to which Christ rises ever higher to become the future central Being, the First Principle, of a new galaxy and to which new spiritual, dimensional realities become the Life and Light behind this new galaxy. The Event of Golgotha may have been the beginning of the creation of a new galaxy of the distant future; the genesis of a galaxy, ". . . from which all things will breathe out Love." The foundation stone for this future cosmos of Love is the entirety of every Christ-imbued, human I AM; the truth of which is disclosed to us in the following verse that Christ spoke to His Apostles and which He who is the Light of the World speaks to all of us as well:

"This is My commandment, that you Love one another as I have Loved you." (John 15:12).

Plate 1

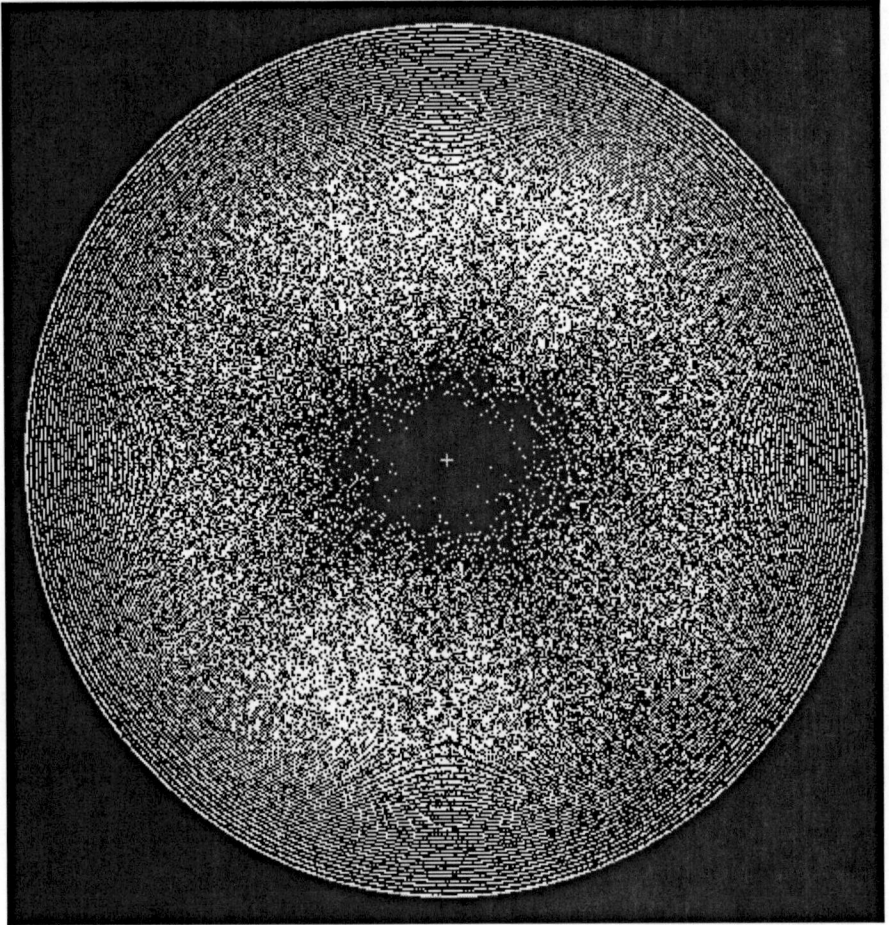

Bibliography

The Apocalypse of St. John: Rudolf Steiner; Rudolf Steiner Press, London 1977; Anthroposophic Press, Inc., New York.

The Apocalypse of St. John: Emil Bock; First published in English by the Christian Community Press, London in 1957. Floris Books, Edinburgh.

Background to the Gospel of St. Mark: Rudolf Steiner; Rudolf Steiner Press, London 1968. Anthroposophic Press Inc., New York.

The Beginnings of Christianity: Andrew Welburn; Floris Books, Edinburgh 1991.

The Bhagavad Gita and the Epistles of Paul: Rudolf Steiner; Anthroposophic Press, Inc., New York 1971.

The Book with Fourteen Seals: Andrew Welburn; Floris Books, Edinburgh 1991.

The Book of Revelation and the Work of the Priest: Rudolf Steiner; Rudolf Steiner Press, London 1998.

Building Stones for an Understanding of the Mystery of Golgotha: Rudolf Steiner; Rudolf Steiner Press, London 1972.

The Burning Bush: Edward R. Smith.; Anthroposophic Press Inc., New York 1997.

Caesars and Apostles - Hellenism, Rome, Judaism: Emil Bock; Floris Books, Edinburgh 1998.

The Childhood of Jesus - The Unknown Years: Emil Bock; Floris Books, Edinburgh 1997.

Christ and the Human Soul: Rudolf Steiner; Rudolf Steiner Press, London 1972.

Christ and the Son of Man: Wilhelm Kelber; Floris Books, Edinburgh 1997.

The Christian Mysteries/Early Lectures: translated by James H. Hindes; Anthroposophic Press, Inc., Great Barrington, Massachusetts 1998.

Christianity and Occult Mysteries of Antiquity: Rudolf Steiner; Rudolf Steiner Publications, Inc., Blauvelt, New York 1961.

The Christmas Thought and the Mystery of the Ego: Rudolf Steiner; Mercury Press, Spring Valley, New York 1986.

The Cosmic Christ: Hans-Werner Schroeder; Floris Books, Edinburgh 1997.

Cosmic Forces in Man: Rudolf Steiner; Anthroposophical Publishing Company, London 1948. Cosmosophy, Vol. I: Anthroposophic Press Inc., New York 1985.

David's Question: What is Man?: Edward R. Smith; Anthroposophic Press, Great Barrington, Massachusetts 2001.

The Deed of Christ and the Opposing Spiritual Powers: Lucifer, Ahriman, Asuras: Rudolf Steiner; Steiner Book Center, Inc., N. Vancouver, Canada 1976.

The Disciple Whom Jesus Loved: Edward R. Smith; Anthroposophic Press, Great Barrington, Massachusetts 2000.

Esoteric Christianity and the Mission of Christian Rosenkreutz: Rudolf Steiner; Rudolf Steiner Press, London 1984.

Eternal Individuality: Towards a Karmic Biography of Novalis: Sergei O. Prokofieff; Temple Lodge Publishing, London 1992.

The Festivals and Their Meaning: Christmas, Easter, Ascension and Pentecost, Michaelmas: Rudolf Steiner; Rudolf Steiner Press, London 1981.

The Fifth Gospel: Rudolf Steiner; Rudolf Steiner Press, London 2001.

The Four Seasons and the Archangels: Rudolf Steiner; Rudolf Steiner Press, London 1984.

From Jesus to Christ: Rudolf Steiner; Rudolf Steiner; Rudolf Steiner Press, London 1973.

The Gospel of St. John: Rudolf Steiner; Anthroposophic Press, Inc., New York 1962.

The Gospel of St. John and Its Relation to the Other Gospels: Rudolf Steiner; Anthroposophic Press, Inc., New York 1982.

The Gospel of St. Luke: Rudolf Steiner; Rudolf Steiner Press, London 1964.

The Gospel of St. Mark: Rudolf Steiner; Anthroposophic Press, Inc., New York 1986.

The Gospel of St. Matthew: Rudolf Steiner; Rudolf Steiner Press, London 1965.

The Heavenly Sophia and the Being Anthroposophia: Sergei O. Prokofieff; Temple Lodge Publishing, London 1996.

How Can Mankind Find the Christ Again?: Rudolf Steiner; Anthroposophic Press, Inc., New York 1984.

Isis Mary Sophia: Her Mission and Ours: Selected lectures and writings by Rudolf Steiner; Edited and introduced by Christopher Bamford; SteinerBooks, Great Barrington, Ma. 20. 03

Macrocosm and Microcosm: Rudolf Steiner; Rudolf Steiner Press, London 1968.

Man and the World of Stars: Rudolf Steiner; Anthroposophic Press, Inc., New York 1963.

Manifestations of Karma: Rudolf Steiner; Rudolf Steiner Press, London 1969.

Menschheitsentwicklung und Christus-Erkenntuis lecture: Rudolf Steiner; Basel, November 20, 1907 (GA 100).

The Mystery of John: The Cycle of the Year: Karl Koenig; Camphill Books 2000. Published by TWT Publications Ltd. on behalf of The Camphill Movement.

The Mystery of John the Baptist and John the Evangelist at the Turning Point of Time: Sergei O. Prokofieff; Temple Lodge Publishing, Forest Row, England 2005.

The Mystery of the Two Jesus Children and the Descent of the Spirit of the Sun: Bernard Nesfield-Cookson; Temple Lodge Publishing, Forest Row, England 2005.

The New Experience of the Supersensible: Jesaiah Ben-Aharon; Temple Lodge Publishing, London 1995.

The New Mysteries and the Wisdom of Christ: Virginia Sease & Manfred Schmidt-Brabant; Temple Lodge Publishing, Forest Row, England 2005.

New Testament Studies: Rudolf Frieling; Floris Books, Edinburgh 1994.

Occult Signs & Symbols: Rudolf Steiner; Anthroposophic Press, Inc., New York 1972.

An Outline of Occult Science: Rudolf Steiner; Anthroposophic Press, Inc., New York 1972.

Planetary Spheres and Their Influence on Man's Life on Earth and in Spiritual Worlds: Rudolf Steiner; Rudolf Steiner Press, London 1982.

The Portal of Initiation; translation by Adam Bittleston: Rudolf Steiner; Rudolf Steiner Publications, Inc. Englewood, New Jersey, U.S.A. 1961.

Reading the Pictures of the Apocalypse: Rudolf Steiner; Anthroposophic Press, Inc., New York 1993.

The Reappearance of Christ in the Etheric: Rudolf Steiner; Anthroposophic Press Inc., New York 1983.

Rosicrucian Esotericism: Rudolf Steiner; Anthroposophic Press Inc., New York, 1978.

Saint Joseph Edition of the Holy Bible: Catholic Book Publishing Company, New York 1963.

Seeking Spirit Vision: Dennis Klocek; Rudolf Steiner College Press, Fair Oaks, California 1998.

The Son of Man and the Cosmic Christ: Oskar Kurten; from Mitteilungen aus der anthroposophischen Arbeit in Deutschland. Easter 1971. Translated by Maria St. Goar.

Speech and Drama: Rudolf Steiner; Anthroposophic Publishing Company, New York 1959.

The Spiritual Event of the Twentieth Century: An Imagination: Jesaiah Ben-Aharon; Temple Lodge Publishing, London 1996.

The Spiritual Hierarchies and Their Reflection in the Physical World: Rudolf Steiner; Anthroposophic Press Inc., New York 1970.

Theosophy: Rudolf Steiner; Anthroposophic Press Inc., New York, 1971.

Theosophy in the Gospel of John: Rudolf Steiner's lecture on November 5, 1906; Munich (GA 94). From: Isis Mary Sophia: Her Mission and Ours: Selected lectures and writings by Rudolf Steiner; Edited and introduced by Christopher Bamford; SteinerBooks, Great Barrington, Ma. 20. 03

Theosophy of the Rosicrucian: Rudolf Steiner; Rudolf Steiner Press, London 1981.

The Three Years: Emil Bock; Floris Books, Edinburgh 1987.

Threefold Mary: Emil Bock, SteinerBooks, Great Barrington, Ma. 2003.

The Tree of Life and the Holy Grail: Sylvia Francke & Thomas Cawthorne; Temple Lodge, London 1996.

Turning Points in Spiritual History: Rudolf Steiner; Berlin: December 14, 1911: GA 60/61 Garber Communications, Blauvelt, New York 1987.

LaVergne, TN USA
30 January 2011
214557LV00001B/131/P